AF695090

FINANCING TRANSPORT CONNECTIVITY IN THE BIMSTEC REGION

DECEMBER 2023

BIMSTEC

ADB

6 ADB Avenue, Mandaluyong City, 1550 Metro Manila, Philippines
Tel +63 2 8632 4444; Fax +63 2 8636 2444
www.adb.org

ISBN 978-92-9270-350-9 (print); 978-92-9270-351-6 (electronic); 978-92-9270-352-3 (ebook)
Publication Stock No. TCS230387-2
DOI: http://dx.doi.org/10.22617/TCS230387-2

Notes:
In this publication, "€" refers to euros, "B" refers to Thai baht, "A$" refers to Australian dollars, "S$" refers to Singapore dollars, "$" refers to United States dollars, "₹" refers to Indian rupees, "NRs" refers to Nepalese rupees, and "SLRs" refers to Sri Lanka rupees.

ADB recognizes "America" as the United States; "Ceylon" as Sri Lanka; "China" as the People's Republic of China; "Hong Kong" as Hong Kong, China; and "Bangalore" as Bengaluru.

The main publication for the preparation of this report was undertaken in 2020 and 2021, while there were substantial limitations in travel among most BIMSTEC countries due to the pandemic. To curb this impact and complete this publication, virtual interactions with various stakeholders were conducted across BIMSTEC member states. Certain updates were made in 2022 and 2023 based on inputs from the BIMSTEC member states. While continuous efforts have been made to update the publication to incorporate the latest interventions and reforms in the financial framework, some sections may lack the most current status of transport infrastructure financing scenario in the region and among certain BIMSTEC members.

ADB has placed a hold on sovereign project disbursements and new contracts in Myanmar effective 1 February 2021.

Cover design by Edith Creus.

Printed on recycled paper

Contents

Tables, Figures, and Boxes

Tables

Figures

Boxes

Foreword

The Bay of Bengal Initiative for Multi-Sectoral Technical and Economic Cooperation (BIMSTEC) recognized the importance of transport connectivity as a cornerstone of regional integration right from the beginning when BIMSTEC was founded 25 years ago.

Convinced that connectivity is a vital component of integration, BIMSTEC in collaboration with Asian Development Bank (ADB) prepared a BIMSTEC Master Plan for Transport Connectivity. The Master Plan, after 3 years of consultation with the member states, was adopted during the 5th BIMSTEC Summit held on 30 March 2022.

The BIMSTEC Master Plan for Transport Connectivity presents a comprehensive 10-year (2018–2028) strategy and action plan for improving the subregion's transport linkages. Out of the 267 transport projects identified in the plan, 216 are in transport infrastructure. The aim of these 216 projects is not only to improve transport infrastructure in the BIMSTEC region but also to enhance regional trade. Based on the study by ADB, about 60% of the transport infrastructure projects are in the planning stage and will require securing financing. Also, to ensure the timely development of these projects, it is important to assess the financing landscape and construct an overarching financing framework, particularly for cross-border transport infrastructure projects.

In conjunction, ADB also completed the study "Financing Transport Connectivity in the BIMSTEC Region" that aims at developing a comprehensive financing framework for cross-border transport infrastructure projects. It evaluates the current state of transport infrastructure financing in the BIMSTEC region—analyzing strengths and weaknesses of existing financing options. It also provides practical and innovative recommendations to improve the financing framework further as well as meeting the financing needs for transport infrastructure development in the region.

With the aim to identify and recommend appropriate actions to address the financing gap in the BIMSTEC region, a Virtual Consultation Workshop on Financing Transport Connectivity in the BIMSTEC Region was conducted by ADB on 16 September 2021. The workshop presented the findings of the preliminary study on transport connectivity infrastructure financing and sought to stimulate linkages and interrelationships between various financing tools.

Finally, I would like to express my appreciation to ADB for its dedication and support in successfully conducting this study. I also thank Thailand, the lead country for the connectivity sector, and all the BIMSTEC member States for their cooperation and contributions to help prepare this report. I firmly believe that this report on Financing Transport Connectivity in the BIMSTEC Region will be a very useful guiding tool for all member States in their endeavors toward enhancing transport connectivity in the region.

Tenzin Lekphell
BIMSTEC Secretary General

Preface

Transport connectivity is one of the most critical requirements of any regional integration process. An efficient and extensive transport network will greatly help reap the benefits of a free trade area, promote trade and investment, and make progress in other areas of cooperation, such as tourism and cultural exchanges.

The Bay of Bengal Initiative for Multi-Sectoral Technical and Economic Cooperation (BIMSTEC) adopted the BIMSTEC Master Plan for Transport Connectivity 2018–2028 in March 2022 to enhance cross-border connectivity and trade in the region. Most of connectivity projects that have been included in the master plan are being undertaken as national initiatives by each BIMSTEC member state. To develop these projects, each country in the region is highly dependent on grants, aid, or external borrowing. Viable financing remains a big bottleneck. This is largely because of inadequate government funding sources, insufficient financing options, underdeveloped institutional structure and enablers for regional coordination, and a lack of private sector interest in the transport financing sector.

The Asian Development Bank (ADB), in *Financing Transport Connectivity in the BIMSTEC Region*, has developed a financing strategy for transport infrastructure in BIMSTEC countries. The study analyzes the current status of this financing in the region, including legal and regulatory frameworks, options, tools, practices, approaches, mechanisms, and financing gaps. It comprehensively examines the strengths and weakness of the financing options, and identifies the challenges and opportunities that can be used to make feasible and innovative recommendations to establish an overarching financing framework. The study also looks at how to meet the financing needs for the development of this financing based on an analysis of good international practices that can be applied here with some necessary adjustments.

The study delivers country-specific recommendations for each BIMSTEC country that takes account of its specific characteristics; recommendations are also offered for the region as a whole. The study also explores options for setting up a regional transport fund or a new development finance institution. Its recommendations are categorized by their readiness for adoption and implementation with a view to eventually developing a mature and sustainable domestic as well as regional capital market capable of financing transport infrastructure projects.

I would like to acknowledge the big effort made by the study team from ADB's Regional Cooperation and Integration Unit, South Asia Department. And I thank the private stakeholders and officials in the BIMSTEC Secretariat and member states who contributed greatly to this study through surveys, interviews, and sharing information. The process began just before the coronavirus disease (COVID-19) started to affect the transport and logistics industries, which created unprecedented challenges for researching and writing this study, all of which would not have been possible without the cooperation of these public and private sector stakeholders. Thanks also go to the relevant ADB resident missions, Climate Change and Sustainable Development Department, Office of Markets Development and Public–Private Partnership, and the Southeast Asia Department for providing comments to enhance the study. All contributions are gratefully acknowledged.

K. Yokoyama

Kenichi Yokoyama
Director General, South Asia Department
Asian Development Bank

Abbreviations

ADB	Asian Development Bank
AIIB	Asian Infrastructure Investment Bank
ASEAN	Association of Southeast Asian Nations
BDF	BIMSTEC Development Fund
BIFFL	Bangladesh Infrastructure Finance Fund Limited
BIMSTEC	Bay of Bengal Initiative for Multi-Sectoral Technical and Economic Cooperation
BOT	build–operate–transfer
DFI	development finance institution
EIB	European Investment Bank
EU	European Union
EUR	euro
FDI	foreign direct investment
FY	fiscal year
GDP	gross domestic product
GMS	Greater Mekong Subregion
IBRD	International Bank for Reconstruction and Development
IDCOL	Infrastructure Development Company Limited
IIFCL	India Infrastructure Finance Company Limited
InvIT	infrastructure investment trust
MDB	multilateral development bank
MCA	model concession agreement
NBFI	nonbank financial institution
NHAI	National Highways Authority of India
NPA	nonperforming asset
OECD	Organisation For Economic Co-operation and Development
PPP	public–private partnership
PPPAC	Public Private Partnership Approval Committee
RICBL	Royal Insurance Corporation of Bhutan Limited
SASEC	South Asia Subregional Economic Cooperation
SOE	state-owned enterprise
UK	United Kingdom
US	United States
VGF	viability gap funding

Executive Summary

The Bay of Bengal Initiative for Multi-Sectoral Technical and Economic Cooperation (BIMSTEC) has prepared a master plan—the BIMSTEC Master Plan for Transport Connectivity—comprising 267 transport projects. Of these, 216 are in transport infrastructure and 51 of them are in soft infrastructure, e.g., process automation, single-window custom clearance, and capacity building. The aim of the 216 projects is not only to improve transport infrastructure in the BIMSTEC region but also to enhance regional trade. About 60% of the transport infrastructure projects (134) are in the planning stage and will require financing to be secured. The estimated value of these projects is $89.9 billion at 2018 prices. Some of these projects have not been costed, however. To ensure the timely development of these projects, it is important to assess the financing landscape and construct an overarching financing framework, particularly for cross-border transport infrastructure projects.

To develop the framework, an as-is assessment of the financing landscape for national and regional transport infrastructure projects in the BIMSTEC region was conducted. This covers three categories of finance: public funding, commercial financing, and private sector participation. To further facilitate financing of these projects, regional institution structure and soft system bottlenecks were assessed.

Public funding. Government budgetary support and multilateral financing are the major funding sources for regional transport projects in the BIMSTEC region. For national projects, some countries have set up user-pay mechanisms—e.g., toll roads in India—to supplement public financing. Budgetary allocations for transportation infrastructure are, however, likely to be constrained by limited headroom for increasing government borrowing because of high ratios of debt-to-gross domestic product as well as fiscal deficits, unfavorable outlooks for sovereign debt by international credit rating agencies, and government spending focused on coronavirus disease (COVID-19) relief initiatives. Provisions exist for collecting direct user charges in railways, ports, airports, and inland waterways, among other sectors, in the BIMSTEC region. But for national roads, most BIMSTEC countries, especially Bangladesh, Nepal, and Sri Lanka, have few toll-based projects and the number is negligible for regional roads. This strongly suggests there is plenty of scope for project authorities in BIMSTEC countries to enhance revenue and monetize assets.

Commercial financing. Globally, bonds are major debt instruments for financing infrastructure. However, capital markets are nascent in most BIMSTEC countries, where the main financing route remains over-the-counter lending by domestic commercial banks and specialized nonbank financial institutions (NBFIs), among other institutions. The participation of institutional funds, such as pension and private equity funds, is limited. Among financial institutions, commercial banks are the most significant investors in infrastructure in BIMSTEC countries. Even so, their appetite to lend to the sector is constrained by asset–liability mismatches; limited project appraisal capabilities in Bangladesh, Bhutan, Myanmar, and Nepal; and high levels of nonperforming infrastructure assets. Bangladesh and India have set up specialized NBFIs for investing in infrastructure, but most of them concentrate on sectors perceived to be less risky than transport infrastructure, such as power. NBFIs in BIMSTEC countries also have limited experience in doing project appraisals in transport infrastructure sectors, and this affects their participation. Institutional funds typically do not take on construction-stage risk, but may become interested in operational infrastructure assets. Capital markets are a key route for the participation of institutional funds markets, but underdeveloped capital markets in most BIMSTEC countries limit this potential. Insurance and pension funds are more risk averse and mandated by regulations to invest in bonds with credit ratings above a certain threshold, which most private developers are not able to meet. Private equity funds typically look for exit opportunities in the short- to medium-term; this generally does not match the tenure of major transport projects. And experiences of delayed exits in transport infrastructure investments further dampen interest from this quarter. Foreign direct investment in BIMSTEC countries faces various challenges, including foreign exchange risks and associated hedging costs, and factors related to the business environment and policy. Mutual funds, export credit agencies, and external commercial borrowing, among other financing instruments, are not significant investors in infrastructure globally.

Private sector participation. BIMSTEC countries, except India and Thailand, have limited experience of carrying out public–private partnership (PPP) projects in transport infrastructure. These countries are at a nascent stage of PPP readiness. Some have set up PPP units—Bangladesh in 2010 and Bhutan in 2017—and Myanmar and Nepal are in the process of doing this. India and Thailand stand apart in their rich experience in transport infrastructure PPPs. A review of cross-border projects in the BIMSTEC region shows they have been executed only by the engineering procurement construction and item-rate contract mode utilizing government budgetary support (from any one of two participating countries in the case of multicountry projects) or through multilateral or bilateral concessional loans and grants. The Association of Southeast Asian Nations (ASEAN), the European Union (EU), and the Greater Mekong Subregion (GMS) have implemented regional projects through PPP modes.

Regional institutional structure and soft system bottlenecks. In the BIMSTEC region, a focus on coordinating individual projects rather than an overarching framework for undertaking groups of projects negatively affects preparation and implementation timelines for many regional transport infrastructure projects. One of the reasons for this is the limited institutional capacity to plan, prepare, implement, and monitor projects. Other regional groupings, such as ASEAN, the EU, and the GMS, have robust institutional mechanisms for identifying, preparing, and implementing projects. Heterogenous technical standards and differences in policy and regulatory environments across BIMSTEC countries make the implementation of regional projects difficult.

Project bankability is important for attracting project financing. A project can become bankable if there are reliable mechanisms within a favorable enabling environment to capture its economic value and for it to acquire sufficient income to cover capital and operating costs. In the BIMSTEC region, traditional funding sources (i.e., government budgets) are constrained by rising government debt and fiscal deficits. Projects need to explore other funding sources beyond the traditional ones.

Levying user charges is one way of funding transport infrastructure projects. For cross-border projects, participating governments should agree on the pricing of toll or user fees as a means of funding, and tolling guidelines formulated. User fees need to be based on the true cost of using, maintaining, and improving infrastructure, as well as the benefits accruing to stakeholders, subject to the impact on total logistics costs for the movement. This addresses any affordability and willingness-to-pay concerns for infrastructure users.

Transport projects potentially have multiple benefits, including reduced accidents, increased employment, higher land values, and lower carbon emissions, which benefit both the economy in general and project proponents. Economic benefit analyses are important for the effective development of transport infrastructure projects, particularly cross-border projects where the economic benefits and associated costs are split among countries. No formal institutionalized mechanisms exist in BIMSTEC countries for evaluating the economic impact of these projects and the sharing of benefits among participating countries. BIMSTEC countries could adopt a standard economic analysis framework to identify and measure economic benefits. The proposed framework in the 2017 institutional document *Guidelines for the Economic Analysis of Projects of the Asian Development Bank (ADB)** could be used for guidance.

Instances have occurred where cross-subsidies are provided by a more affluent country to a less affluent one to cover operational costs for cross-border projects. Similar interventions could be explored as a financing solution in the BIMSTEC region.

Other levers that can be explored are improving the commercial viability of projects to provide capital support in the form of a one-time or deferred capital grant and operational support from a revenue or foreign exchange risk guarantee. Because of budget constraints, it will be difficult for the governments of BIMSTEC countries to provide capital and operational support across multiple projects. To resolve this, at least to some degree, asset recycling and securitization, among other mechanisms, can be explored to raise funds for capital and operational subsidies. Project authorities can explore ways to enhance revenue—e.g., land-value capture and non-toll revenue, such as advertising, privately owned public spaces, targeted taxation (vehicle and fuel surcharges, congestion charges, among other options), as well as newer tools, such as carbon pricing.

An enabling environment is needed to improve the bankability of regional projects. Three key potential interventions to enhance bankability are (i) standardizing coordination and decision-making processes, as done by ASEAN, the EU, and the GMS; (ii) overall capacity building by encouraging BIMSTEC countries to formulate transnational regulatory regimes, preparing standardized contract agreements, and harmonizing technical standards; and (iii) recognizing master plan projects in the pipeline of priority projects of BIMSTEC countries.

Ring-fenced funding sources need to be considered for cross-border transport infrastructure projects, especially when they are perceived to be of high risk by commercial financers. From a commercial viability perspective, there could potentially be three types of projects that may be in the pipeline of the BIMSTEC Transport Connectivity Master Plan: (i) projects with significant regional, economic, or social benefit but limited commercial viability where private sector financing may not be feasible for whole or part of the project; (ii) projects that require some degree of support in terms of low cost of financing sources in order to crowd in private sector financing—these may also include projects where certain trunk infrastructure may need to be supported through public/concessional sources in order to attract private investments in rest-of-project components; and (iii) projects with standalone commercial viability and ability to attract private sector financing.

Identifying financing for projects in categories (i) and (ii) above would be critical for the successful implementation of projects in the transport master plan. With this in view, two fund options can be explored, with the focus on specific project categories. Further, given that BIMSTEC leadership is already exploring the creation of the BIMSTEC Development Fund (BDF), these two fund options can be evaluated to come under this broader mandate.

Fund A would look to address the objective of supporting regional projects with limited commercial viability but significant social and economic benefits. Regional projects often compete with other budgetary demands from domestic infrastructure projects, which are often given a higher priority by local governments. The focus of this fund would be to have contributory grant corpus by each government for identified cross-border projects with management services provided by the BDF. Doing this would strengthen BIMSTEC's influence on the approval, time frames, and specifications of projects, because it would involve a BIMSTEC-administered fund. This fund would perform two key functions. First, it will act as a sinking fund to provide grants to support commercially

* Asian Development Bank (ADB). 2017. Manila. *Guidelines for the Economic Analysis of Projects.* https://www.adb.org/sites/default/files/institutional-document/32256/economic-analysis-projects.pdf.

unviable projects. Second, it would provide assistance on project preparation and capacity building through various mechanisms.

For the second category of projects, commercial financing sources that can provide low-cost and long-tenure capital need to be explored. While country-specific finance sector reforms and capital market development will be vital for improving the materiality of existing financial institutions, a separate fund to focus on BIMSTEC regional transport projects can be evaluated under the BDF with the core objective of having the credit rating or cost of funding superior to individual participating countries. This could be explored through various mechanisms, like multilateral institutions having majority ownership (51% or above) to enhance the sovereign credit ratings, provision of multilateral/bilateral guarantees, and establishment of low-cost currency swaps through country-level partnerships with other nations with an interest in development of strong BIMSTEC trade and the region becoming an integrated part of global value chains. Source of initial capital for such fund could include equity of BDF, debt raised through public or private markets and/or contribution from sovereign countries. An example of contribution from sovereign countries includes the pension fund contributions undertaken in Brazil's Banco Nacional De Desenvolvimento Economico e Social.

This proposed fund (Fund B) under the BDF would focus on transport and other infrastructure projects which improve transport connectivity in the BIMSTEC region with the ultimate objective to provide low-cost and long-term capital and attract private sector funding. Further, this fund could (i) provide syndication and co-lending services, assuming responsibility as a lead bank and leveraging cofinancing from commercial banks; (ii) develop guarantee products tailor-made for master plan projects; (iii) undertake project preparation and have the expertise to assess regional projects; (iv) conduct project appraisals on behalf of consortium banks; (v) develop guidelines on the type of projects to be evaluated, formulate a project review mechanism, and set disbursement targets and timelines; and (vi) facilitate policy alignment to enable the revenue streams of operational projects flow to the BDF.

The nascent financial and capital markets of Bhutan, Myanmar, Nepal, and Sri Lanka prevent regional savings from being channeled into infrastructure investments, including transport. To tackle this, a regional financing hub—perhaps along the lines of Singapore's Asian Infrastructure Finance Hub—needs to be established in a developed financial market in the region. Mumbai, the financial capital of the region's largest economy, is a potential candidate. Gujarat's International Financial Services Centre at Gujarat International Finance Tec-city could also be explored as an option given the state's development plans. Once established, borrowers in BIMSTEC countries could issue bonds in the hub's capital market and attract institutional funds looking for long-term investments. India is already a top destination for foreign portfolio and institutional investors because of its developed primary and secondary capital markets.

The following actions would help advance the creation of a financing hub: (i) standardizing fund-raising mechanisms; (ii) facilitating the repatriation of funds—the Nepalese rupee and the Bhutanese ngultrum, for example, are pegged to the Indian rupee, which provides stability to the financial system, and similar pegs could be established between some BIMSTEC currencies, which would result in lower exchange rate risk; and (iii) synchronize taxation rules—e.g., India, has a comprehensive Double Taxation Avoidance Agreement with all BIMSTEC countries. To boost infrastructure investments, taxes imposed on projects funded through this mechanism could be similarly coordinated.

Developing national financing institutions requires country-based interventions to enhance financial regulations and build capacity. Multilateral and bilateral institutions can provide support to increase the project appraisal capacity of financing institutions. Because BIMSTEC countries are strong in some areas, cross-training in these areas will be useful. For the proposed BDF, multilateral development banks can provide support through credit and loan guarantee products to deepen the financing of institutional investors. Deepening capital markets would help grow these institutional investors.

Government project authorities in BIMSTEC countries need to acquire the capacity to conduct detailed financial and value-for-money assessment to determine the "PPP ability" of master plan projects. This will depend on certain project-specific factors being in place that enable private players to bring efficiency gains to PPPs, such as a minimum threshold for project size, proper construction and operation risk-sharing mechanisms, and the status of land acquisitions. The likelihood of project cash flow covering investment costs is also an important factor as governments have limits on the level of annuity payments that they can offer for PPP projects.

Project authorities need to develop the capability to evaluate and implement PPP projects. Key considerations for this include (i) robust project planning and preparation—ADB's Office of Markets Development and Public–Private Partnership provides project preparation assistance to clients in Asia and the Pacific; (ii) risk-sharing model concession agreements for different PPP modes in each sector (roads, ports, airports) that incorporate feedback from investors, developers, and project authorities; (iii) establishing legal structures in concession agreements to enable special purpose vehicles to pass through rights and obligations to a downstream structure of contracts; and (iv) setting up an effective system for dispute resolution and renegotiation.

The interventions proposed for developing PPPs in BIMSTEC countries will likely take time to implement. In the meantime, the following alternative approaches are proposed. For national transport infrastructure projects, governments can take on construction risks and provide upfront capital expenditure. Once projects are up and running, private players can be invited to participate in operation and maintenance activities. For regional projects, construction risk can be taken on by participating governments through ex ante agreements with joint project financing supported by MDBs and other concessional financial institutions. When the transport infrastructure asset becomes operational and traffic volumes increase, participating governments can monetize their part of the assets. Capital costs for the construction of regional projects can also be partly financed from a regional fund for transport infrastructure projects. The later monetization of assets could then be transmitted back to the regional fund. This could also create headroom for developing and financing more regional projects downstream.

A concerted effort from all stakeholders—project authorities, governments, BIMSTEC, ADB, among others—is needed to improve the bankability of projects. Simultaneously, the capacity of existing and new financing institutions, and capital markets, should be increased to help provide the funding required to finance transport infrastructure projects.

While the recommendations on developing an overall financing framework for transport infrastructure projects in the BIMSTEC region highlighted in this report need to be adopted over the next few years, an immediate priority for BIMSTEC countries, along with its Secretariat, is to identify key economic corridors and associated transport projects that will be critical for developing the region. It will be essential to undertake economic and financial analyses for the investments that will be needed for this. For these projects, recommendations are made for exploring user charges; adopting alternative financing tools, such as land-value capture; building the capacity of project implementation agencies; supporting government funding through guarantees and foreign exchange instruments; involving agencies that can contribute to the preparation of projects, such as ADB's Office of Markets Development and Public–Private Partnership; and setting up a fund for commercial unviable projects or project components and another one to provide the source of low-cost financing potentially through the BDF for timely implementation and financing of priority projects.

Introduction and Background

The Bay of Bengal Initiative for Multi-Sectoral Technical and Economic Cooperation (BIMSTEC) is a regional organization comprising seven countries in the littoral and adjacent areas of the Bay of Bengal. The countries constitute a contiguous regional unity. The BIMSTEC member states are Bangladesh, Bhutan, India, Nepal, and Sri Lanka from South Asia, and Myanmar and Thailand from Southeast Asia. BIMSTEC's objective is to enhance regional cooperation in mutual areas of interest, such as trade growth and connectivity, and to utilize regional resources and geographical advantages for accelerated economic growth.

To achieve this, BIMSTEC has prepared a master plan of 267 transport projects to enhance regional trade and improve the transport infrastructure of member states. Of the 267 projects, 216 are in transport infrastructure and the rest in soft infrastructure—e.g., process automation, single-window customs clearance, and capacity building (Figure 1). A review of the current status of transport infrastructure projects shows that about 60% of them—134 projects worth more than $89.9 billion[1]—are in the planning stage and will require financing to be secured.

Figure 1: Status of BIMSTEC Master Plan for Transport Connectivity Projects

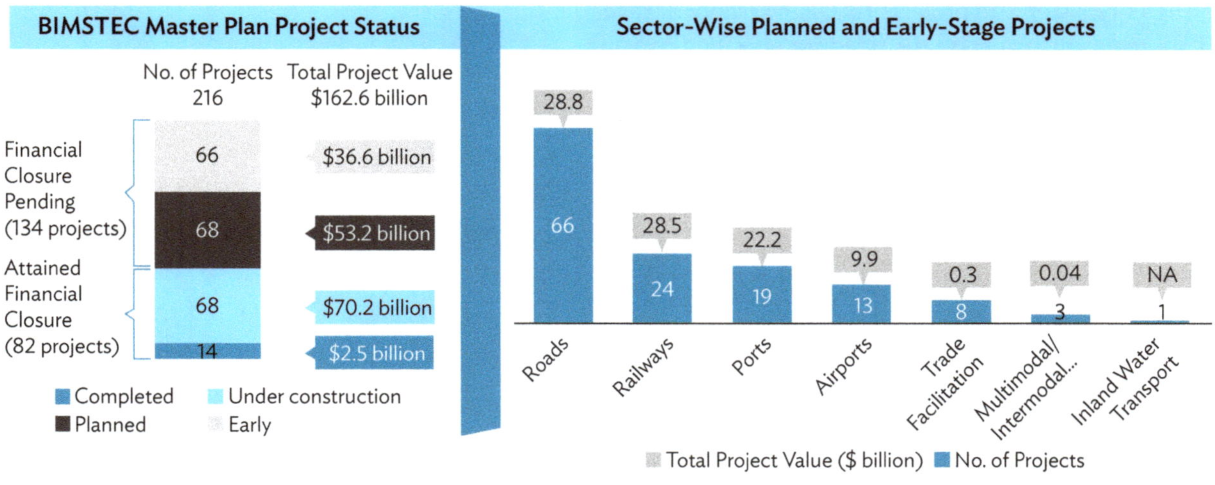

BIMSTEC = Bay of Bengal Initiative for Multi-Sectoral Technical and Economic Cooperation, NA = not available.

Note: Status of projects, as of March 2020, are from publicly available updates on official websites of ministries and government entities.

Source: Asian Development Bank. 2022. BIMSTEC Master Plan for Transport Connectivity. Manila. https://www.adb.org/documents/bimstec-master-plan-transport-connectivity.

[1] Project cost for some of the BIMSTEC master plan projects are not estimated yet (as of March 2020).

Although all master plan projects aim to improve regional connectivity, a closer look at project characteristics shows that some provide economic benefits almost entirely to the country where the project is located. Governments may give these projects a higher priority than projects where the in-country benefit is limited, but the regional benefit is large enough to justify participating in the project. These can be categorized as national and regional projects, as both need to be assessed separately (Figure 2).

Figure 2: Classification Framework of Regional Projects

Regional (R1) - Physical construction spanning across two or more countries leading to dependence on economic benefits realization	**Regional (R2)** - Subset of national projects whose economic viability is significantly dependent on BIMSTEC countries' trade	**National (N)** - Subset of national projects whose economic viability is significantly dependent on BIMSTEC countries' trade
Examples	**Examples**	**Examples**
* Road and rail projects spanning two neighboring countries, e.g., Akhaura (Bangladesh)–Agartala (India) rail link; * Trade facilitation projects spanning two countries, e.g., development of the Tamu (Myanmar)–Moreh (India) border crossing	* Border connecting roads, railway lines, waterways, e.g., development of National Waterway-2; two-laning of road from Dudhanai to Dalu * Land ports, e.g., Development of Nganglam Dry Port	* Roads/rail connecting major city/ports, e.g., Guwahati–Jorabat bypass * Ports/airports terminal development projects, e.g., construction of Laldia terminal, upgrading Gautam Buddha International Airport

BIMSTEC = Bay of Bengal Initiative for Multi-Sectoral Technical and Economic Cooperation.

Source: Study team.

Of the 134 master plan projects (early and planned stages), 70 are regional, indicating the need for specific financing-framework assessments for these projects (Figure 3).

This report conducts assessments for the following areas:

- The current financing landscape for national and regional transport infrastructure projects in the BIMSTEC region.
- The current landscape for public–private partnerships (PPPs) for transport infrastructure projects in BIMSTEC countries.
- Best practices and learning lessons from other regional groupings worldwide for national and regional recommendations for financing master plan projects.

Figure 3: BIMSTEC Master Plan for Transport Connectivity Regional and National Projects

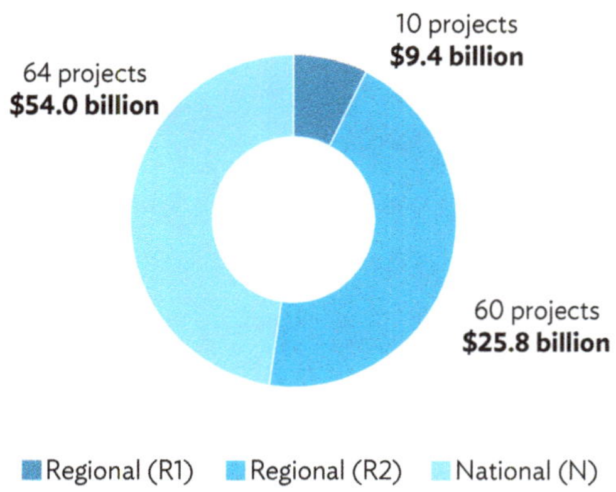

BIMSTEC = Bay of Bengal Initiative for Multi-Sectoral Technical and Economic Cooperation.

Source: Study team.

As-Is Assessment of the Transport Financing Landscape

The key components affecting the financing of transport infrastructure projects in the BIMSTEC region are shown in the financing framework below (Figure 4).

Figure 4: Key Components of a Financing Framework

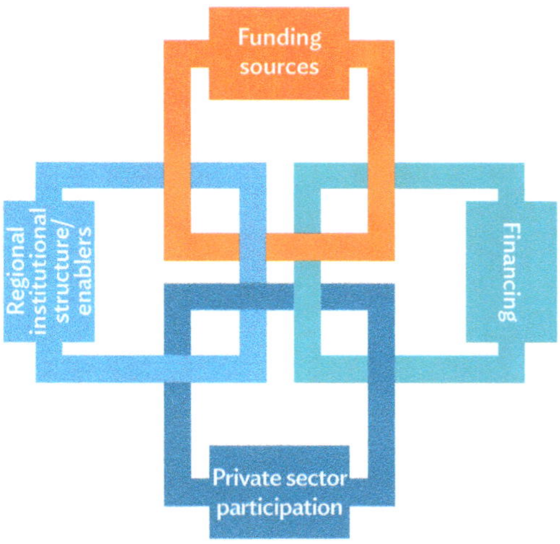

Key facets of issue identification framework

Funding sources
- Assessment of various ways of funding projects e.g., taxes, user charges

Financing
- Assessment of existing financing institutions (banks, NBFIs, etc) and their challenges
- Identifying/developing institutions to mitigate these challenges

Private sector participation
- Identifying projects that have potential to be executed via PPP mode
- Assessment of countries on readiness for PPP

Regional institution structure/enablers
- Assessment of institutional structures and mechanisms between member country governments which that impact planning and execution of projects

NBFI = nonbank financial institution, PPP = public–private partnership.

Source: Study team analysis.

Funding Sources

Government budgetary support is the primary funding source for regional transport projects in the BIMSTEC region. For national projects, some countries have set up user-pay mechanisms (e.g., toll roads in India). A view on the current and future funding capacities in BIMSTEC countries has been formulated, capturing the capacity of BIMSTEC countries to fund transport infrastructure projects through government budgetary sources, and the current utilization of user charges as a funding mechanism for transport infrastructure projects across BIMSTEC countries.

Government Capacity for Budgetary Allocations to Transport Infrastructure

Most BIMSTEC countries depend on government budget allocations and internal and extra budgetary resources of public sector entities to fund transport infrastructure projects.[2] The governments of these countries have set transport infrastructure or overall infrastructure investment targets. But the past trend of budget support for transport infrastructure shows that a significant funding gap needs to be bridged if the planned projects in general target plans are to be met within the timelines set (Figure 5).

Figure 5: Current and Planned Annual Expenditure for Transport Infrastructure in Bangladesh, Bhutan, India, and Myanmar, and Overall Infrastructure in Nepal, Sri Lanka, and Thailand

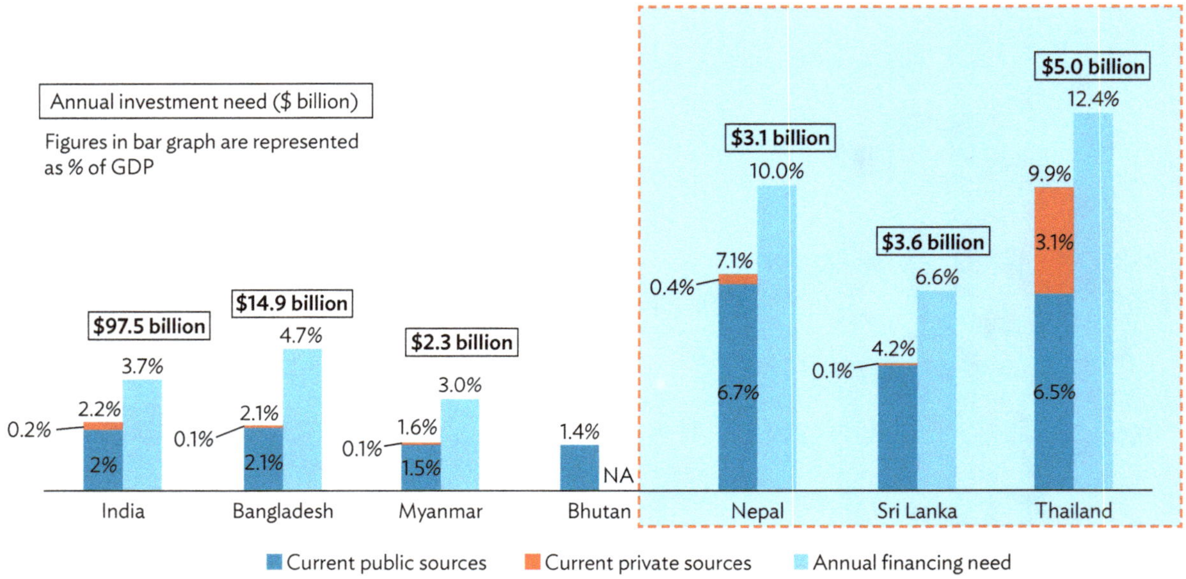

GDP = gross domestic product, NA = not available.

Notes:

For Nepal, Sri Lanka, and Thailand:

1. Current public sources include government budgetary allocations, internal and external sources, and state-owned enterprise investments.
2. Current private sources include investment using public–private partnership mode. It may include some government viability gap funding support. Numbers include average over 2010–2019.
3. Annual financing needs include investment envisaged under the countries' infrastructure pipeline projects.
4. Numbers of current public and private sources, and annual investment need, are for infrastructure; specific numbers not available.

Sources: India: National Infrastructure Pipeline; World Bank Private Participation in Infrastructure (PPI) database. Bangladesh: Ministry of Finance; PPI; Global Infrastructure Hub. Myanmar: National Transport Master Plan 2014; PPI. Bhutan: Ministry of Finance; National Budget of Bhutan. Nepal: Nepal Rastra Bank. Economic Survey 2019; PPI; Global Infrastructure Hub. Sri Lanka: Asian Development Bank. 2017. *Asia Infrastructure Needs*. Manila; Oxford Economics. 2017. *Global Infrastructure Outlook*; PPI. Thailand: Ministry of Transport calculations based on Financing Transport Action Plan 2008.

---

2 The internal resources of central public sector enterprises comprise mainly retained profits net of dividends to the government, depreciation provisions, and the carry-forward of reserves and surpluses. Extra budgetary resources are receipts from issue of bonds, debentures, external commercial borrowing, suppliers' credit, deposit receipts, and term loans from financial institutions.

The increase in budget allocations for transport infrastructure is likely to be constrained by the limited headroom for increasing government borrowing due to high ratios of debt-to-gross domestic product (GDP) and fiscal deficits, unfavorable sovereign rating outlooks by the global credit rating agencies, and government spending that is now focused on coronavirus disease (COVID-19) initiatives (Figure 6). Bhutan, Myanmar, and Nepal do not have a sovereign rating from the global credit rating agencies, which affects their ability to secure financing from foreign capital markets (Table 1). Interviews for this report with financing institutions indicated the need for having a sovereign rating from a reputable credit rating agency to attract investment from foreign institutional investors.

Figure 6: Government Debt and Fiscal Deficits, 2019

(% of GDP)

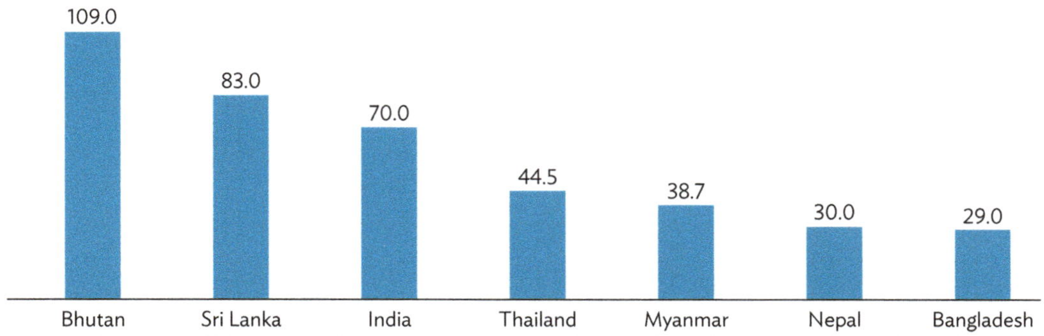

	Bhutan	Sri Lanka	India	Thailand	Myanmar	Nepal	Bangladesh
Fiscal deficit (as % of GDP)	2.0	6.8	3.3	–0.4	4.0	4.6	4.8

GDP = gross domestic product.

Note: Government debt of India comprises central government and state government debt.

Sources: Bangladesh: Bangladesh Bank; Bhutan: Royal Monetary Authority of Bhutan; India: Reserve Bank of India; Myanmar: Central Bank of Myanmar, secondary reports; Nepal: Nepal Rastra Bank; Sri Lanka: Central Bank of Sri Lanka; Thailand: Public Debt Management Office, Bank of Thailand.

Table 1: Credit Ratings and Outlooks

Country	Rating			Outlook		
	Fitch	Moody's	S&P	Fitch	Moody's	S&P
Bangladesh	Reaffimed BB-	Reaffimed Ba3	BB-	Stable	Stable	Stable
India	BBB-	Downgraded from Baa2 to Baa2	BBB- affirmed	Negative	Negative	Stable
Sri Lanka	Downgraded from B to B-	Downgraded from B2 to Caa1	Downgraded from B to B-	Negative	Stable	Stable
Thailand	BBB+ affirmed	Baa1 affirmed	BBB+ affirmed	From Positive to Stable	From Positive to Stable	From Positive to Stable
Bhutan	These countries do not have sovereign debt ratings					
Myanmar						
Nepal						

Sources: Sovereign rating updates from Fitch Ratings, Moody's Investors Service, and Standard and Poor's Global Ratings, as of June 2020.

Other Funding Mechanisms

Table 2 shows provisions for collecting direct user charges in five transport sectors in the BIMSTEC countries. Most countries have few national toll-based road projects. India and Thailand have significant experience in levying user charges for many road projects in the past, with revenue collection covering capital costs as well as maintenance. Myanmar had a large number of user-charged road projects, but user charges only partly cover maintenance costs and do not contribute to capital servicing. Bangladesh, Nepal, and Sri Lanka have explored user charges for only a few road projects. Revenue collected by user charges in Bangladesh and Nepal partly cover maintenance costs and do not contribute to capital servicing. Bhutan has not set guidelines for collecting tolls on roads. BIMSTEC countries have only very few toll-based regional road projects.

India and Thailand have significant experience in levying user charges for many road projects in the past, with revenue collection covering capital costs as well as maintenance.

Table 2: User Charges in Transport Infrastructure Projects

	Roadways (National)	Roadways (Regional)	Railways	Ports	Airports	Inland Waterways
Bangladesh	🟡	🟠	🟢	🟢	🟢	🟡
Bhutan	🟠	🟠	🟢	NA	🟢	NA
India	🟢	🟠	🟢	🟢	🟢	🟡
Myanmar	🟢	🟠	🟢	🟢	🟢	NA
Nepal	🟡	🟠	🟢	NA	🟢	NA
Sri Lanka	🟡	NA	🟢	🟢	🟢	NA
Thailand	🟢	🟠	🟢	🟢	🟢	NA

🟢 High number of projects 🟡 Select/few projects and toll guidelines/order exist 🟠 Negligible projects and/or no toll guidelines/order exist

NA = not available.

Sources: Bangladesh: Toll Policy 2014, news articles; Bhutan: Road Act, 2013, Road Rules and Regulations, 2016; India: National Highways Authority of India circular NHAI/1103/CGM (Fin)/ 2011; Myanmar: Asian Development Bank. 2016. Myanmar Transport Sector Policy Note. Manila; Nepal: Roads Board Nepal; Sri Lanka: Road Development Authority; Thailand: Expressway Authority of Thailand.

Apart from user charges, other possible funding sources, such as land-value capture and targeted taxation, are not used in the BIMSTEC region (Figure 7).

Figure 7: Infrastructure and Project Financing Sources by Region, 2019
(%)

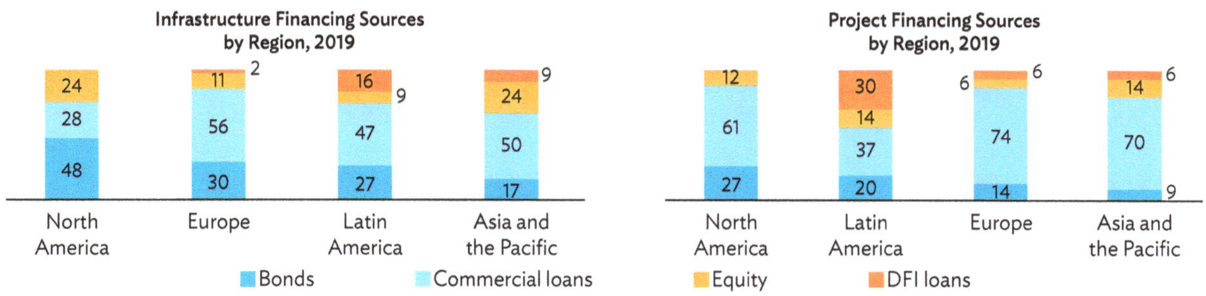

DFI = development finance institution.

Notes:
1. Commercial loans are predominantly provided by commercial banks.
2. DFI includes development banks, multilaterals. DFI loans represent noncommercial loans. Any commercial lending by DFI (if any) would fall in commercial loans.
3. Infrastructure or project finance is a form of finance that is fundamentally defined by recourse only to the transaction special purpose vehicle and the repayment of debt through the internal cash flows of that transaction.
4. Noncommercial finance is a type of transaction where the counterparties providing equity are predominantly state-owned and where debt (if any) is provided entirely by DFIs. It excludes funding from government budgetary sources.

Source: IJ Global—League tables 2020. https://www.ijglobal.com/league-tables.

Financing

Globally, bonds are major debt instruments for infrastructure and project financing. But bonds to finance infrastructure in Asia and the Pacific are not much used because of underdeveloped capital markets.

Commercial loans account for most infrastructure financing in Asia and the Pacific, accounting for 50% of overall sources of financing. For project finance, commercial loans dominate, accounting for 70% of overall sources of financing. Commercial loans in BIMSTEC countries are largely provided by commercial banks, which face inherent asset–liability mismatches and have limited project appraisal capabilities. Transport infrastructure projects typically have long gestation periods and require specific capabilities to be able to understand their construction and operational risks leading to asset liability mismatch (global approaches to address this issue detailed in Box 1).

Box 1: Approaches to Address Asset-Liability Mismatch

Most banks globally face asset–liability mismatches when financing infrastructure projects but approaches to financing these projects differ. In Japan, for example, deposit holders are generally willing to hold assets for longer, thereby reducing asset–liability mismatch risks. European banks either receive support from domestic development banks or successfully de-leverage, resulting in better capacity to finance infrastructure.

Banks based in the United Kingdom have shown less willingness to hold long-term debt, preferring to act as financial advisors offering shorter-term finance to cover the early stage construction risks faced by infrastructure projects. Once assets become operational and less risky, banks sell them to institutional investors.

Source: National Infrastructure Commission, Government of the United Kingdom. 2017. *Financing for Infrastructure*. London. https://nic.org.uk/studies-reports/national-infrastructure-assessment/national-infrastructure-assessment-1/financing-for-infrastructure-summary/.

Private investors regard regional transport infrastructure projects as high risk as the asset utilization depends on the political, diplomatic, and strategic dynamics of participating countries. Because of this, financing options, such as transport funds, regional financing hubs, and setting up a regional development fund, are explored later in this report.

Financing Institutions and Tools in BIMSTEC Countries

This report assesses the materiality of the key types of financing institutions and tools—commercial banks, nonbank financial institutions (NBFIs), insurance funds, pension funds, foreign direct investment (FDI), private equity, alternative investment funds, and other types of financing tools—in each BIMSTEC country to identify issues relevant to their use in infrastructure, including transport infrastructure.

Commercial banks. These are the largest financing institutions in BIMSTEC countries in terms of deposits as a percentage of GDP, but the lending exposure of these banks varies from country to country (Figure 8). The level is high in India and Sri Lanka compared with Bangladesh, Bhutan, Myanmar, and Nepal. Globally, commercial banks use different approaches to financing infrastructure projects.

Figure 8: Size and Contribution of Commercial Banks to Infrastructure

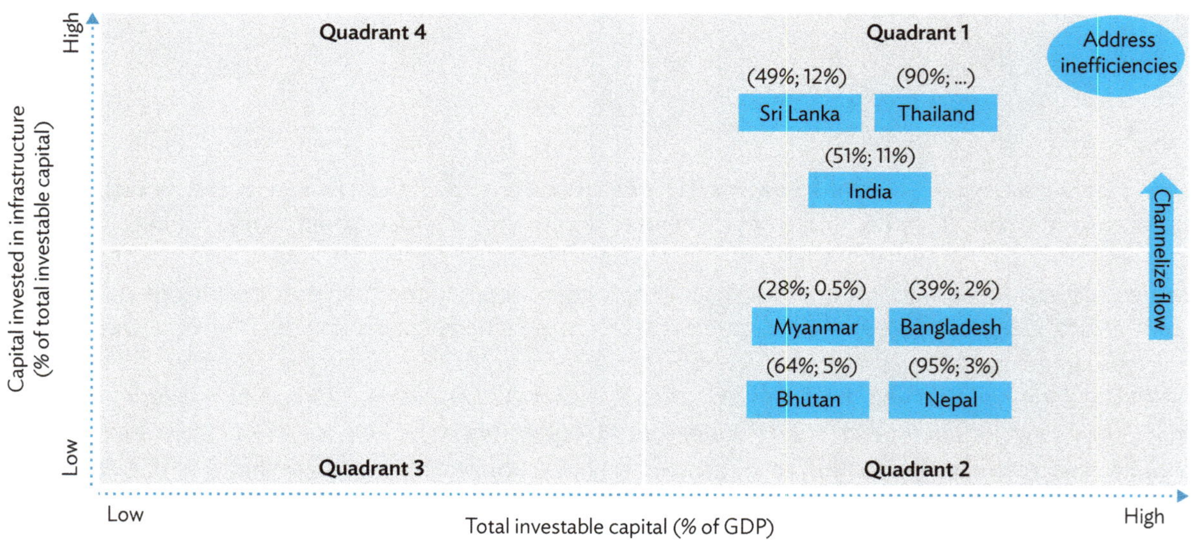

... = not available, GDP = gross domestic product.

Note: Institutions for which data are not available based on inputs from primary and secondary research.

Sources: 2019 data from the central banks of the seven countries.

In India, commercial banks play a significant role in the construction phase of infrastructure financing. In recent years, however, projects have been hit by rising nonperforming assets (NPAs), impairing the ability to finance projects because of stringent NPA recognition norms. These norms have put constraints on the credit allocated by banks for riskier infrastructure projects. Setting up credit guarantee funds or using loan guarantee instruments for infrastructure projects, such as the loan guarantees of the Multilateral Investment Guarantee Agency or the partial credit guarantee of the Asian Development Bank (ADB), will help reduce project risks. Addressing PPP infrastructure financing concerns, such as terminating payment risk, clarity on ways to refinance, and effective dispute resolution mechanisms, will improve the attractiveness of infrastructure projects. Enhancing liquidity in the secondary market for loans will create room for additional infrastructure financing by commercial banks.

In addition to asset–liability mismatches, commercial banks in Bangladesh and Nepal face inadequate track records, a lack of infrastructure PPP projects, and underdeveloped technical and project finance appraisal capabilities. Commercial banks in Bangladesh also face a cap on the maximum lending rate, which limits profitability and restricts infrastructure lending. Despite this constraint, Bangladesh's banks should strengthen corporate governance and improve commercial due diligence. Although commercial banks in Nepal have a high capital base of nearly 95% of GDP, they have limited capabilities for underwriting transport infrastructure projects during the construction stage. Because of this, their exposure to infrastructure loans is low, at 3% of the total capital base of commercial banks. Since most transport infrastructure projects are financed by the government, bank lending to the sector is limited. Myanmar's commercial banks have the lowest capital base in BIMSTEC countries and require government support for greater financial inclusion. Bhutan's commercial banks are constrained by high NPAs and limited technical capabilities for assessing infrastructure projects.

Country or regional project appraisals and capacity building using European Investment Bank (EIB) procedures would also help strengthen the technical capacity of commercial banks in the BIMSTEC region to be able to participate more in transport infrastructure financing.

Nonbank financial institutions. An NBFI has a principal business of receiving deposits under any scheme or arrangement by any mode (Figure 9). NBFIs are well developed in India. Like commercial banks there, these institutions face asset–liability mismatches due to short-term borrowing sourced mainly through banks and assets in the form of long-term loans to infrastructure projects. India is facing an NBFI crisis following the default of one

Figure 9: Size and Contribution of Nonbank Financial Companies to Infrastructure

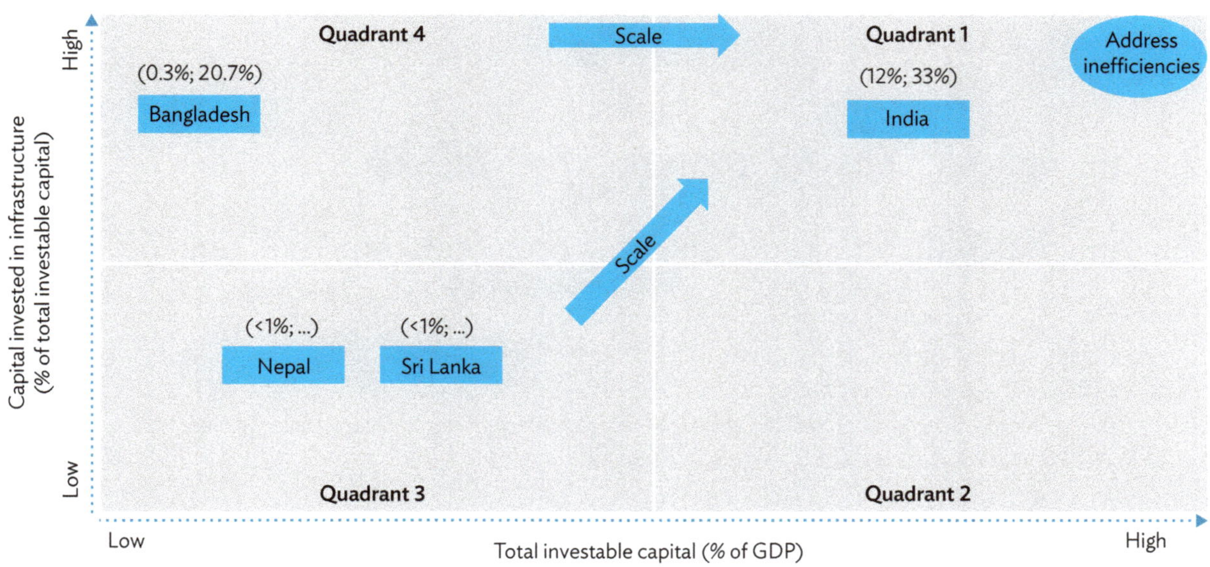

... = not available, GDP = gross domestic product.

Notes:

1. Total investable capital data for nonbank financial institutions in Bhutan, Myanmar, and Thailand is not available.
2. Institutions for which data are not available are placed based on inputs from primary and secondary research.

Source: 2019 data from the central banks of the four countries.

of its largest, Infrastructure Leasing & Financing Services Limited. Sri Lanka's NBFIs have recently come under pressure from deteriorating asset quality and low profitability. This has constrained NBFI lending, and a few of these companies, such as Infrastructure Leasing & Financing Services Limited, to be folded.

Bangladesh's NBFIs are highly concentrated in the power sector and, to a lesser extent, transport infrastructure. Development finance institutions (DFIs) and multilateral development banks (MDBs) provide longer-tenor loans for on-lending to transport infrastructure projects and can support NBFI financing on infrastructure projects other than those in the power sector. NBFIs in Nepal are small and focused on microfinance in rural areas.

Insurance funds. Among BIMSTEC countries, the insurance industry is well developed in India and Thailand. Bhutan, too, has a sizable insurance industry in relation to its GDP. The other BIMSTEC nations have much smaller insurance industries (Figure 10).

India's insurance industry draws heavily on the practices of other countries, particularly the United Kingdom (UK). In 1999, the Insurance Regulatory and Development Authority was constituted as an autonomous body to regulate and develop the insurance industry. The authority opened up the industry in 2000 to foreign companies, allowing ownership of up to 26%. This limit has since increased and is now at 74%.[3]

Figure 10: Size and Contribution of Insurance Funds to Infrastructure

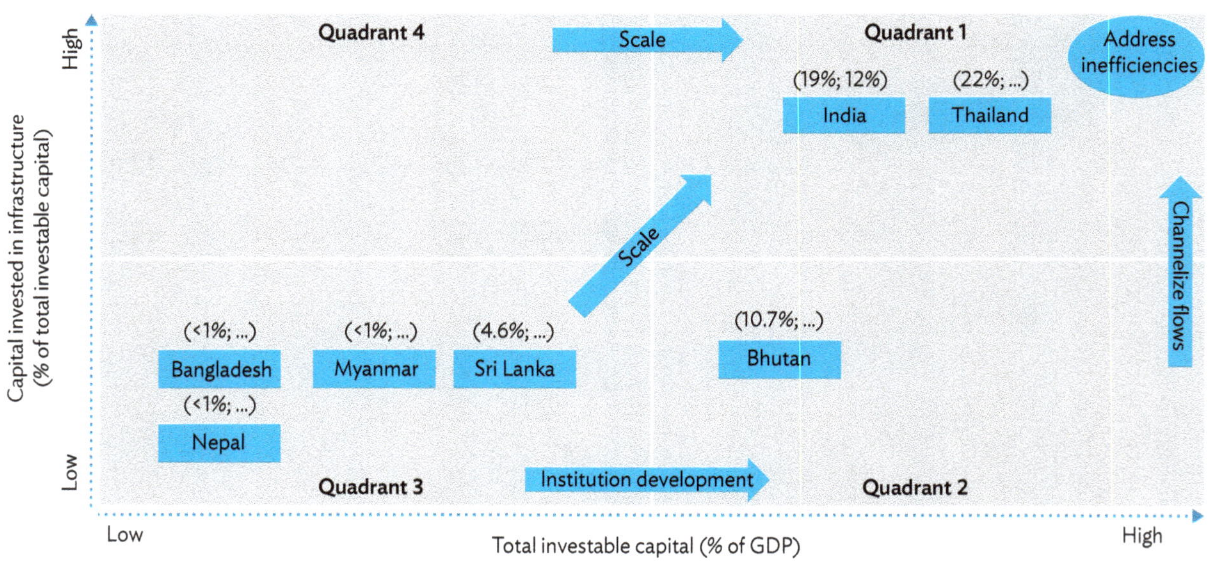

... = not available, GDP = gross domestic product.

Note: Institutions for which data are not available are placed based on inputs from primary and secondary research.

Source: 2019 data from insurance regulators in the seven countries.

3 *NDTV*. 2021. Budget 2021: FDI Limit in Insurance Hiked to 74%. 2 February. https://www.ndtv.com/business/finance-minister-hikes-fdi-limit-in-insurance-74-2361061.

Insurance players in India primarily invest in government securities and public sector bonds. As of 2018, life insurance companies invested 66% of their pool in public sector bonds, and just 14% in private bonds. By comparison, insurers in the UK invested nearly 47% of their pool in private bonds in 2018 (Figure 11).

Figure 11: Asset Allocation of Life Insurance Companies in Selected Countries (%)

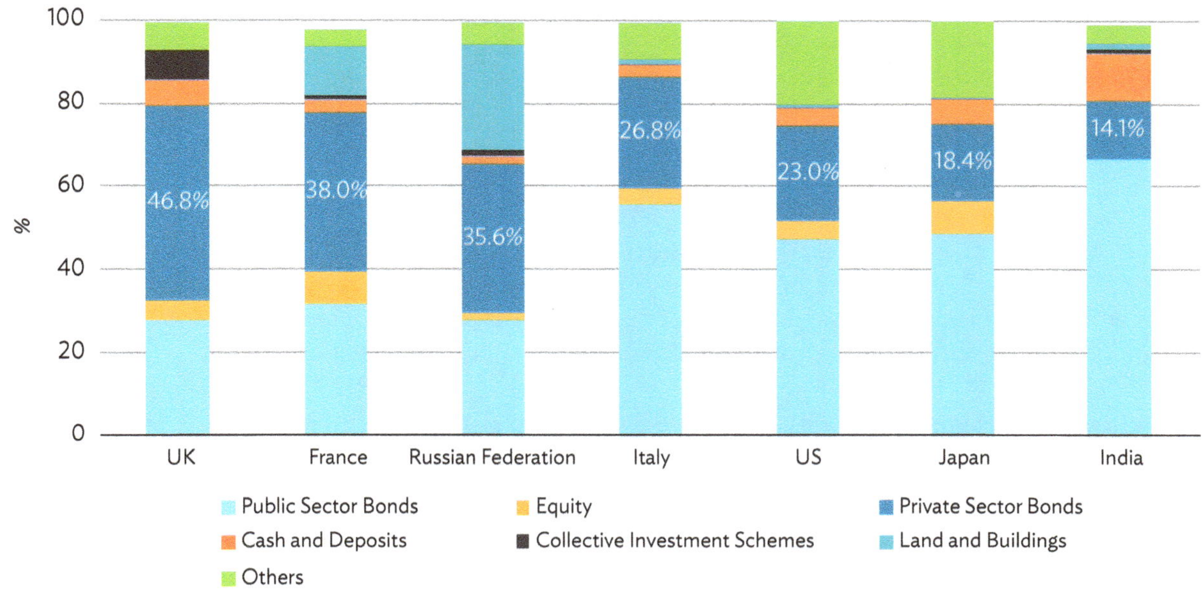

UK = United Kingdom, US = United States.

Source: Organisation for Economic Co-operation and Development. 2018. *Global Insurance Market Trends 2018*. Paris. https://www.oecd.org/daf/fin/insurance/Global-Insurance-Market-Trends-2018.pdf.

India's insurers are allowed to invest up to $14 billion annually in bonds at the current 15% regulatory threshold, but there are few infrastructure bonds to invest in, and less than 25% of infrastructure corporate bonds are rated above AA. The investment limits set by the Insurance Regulatory and Development Authority Act, 1999 for an insurance fund is 5% of a company's estimated annual accretion of funds and 10% for a single group. This cap on investments can be eased out in order to further increase the investments from insurance funds. Organisation for Economic Co-operation and Development (OECD) countries generally set limits on infrastructure investments.[4]

Supported by concerted government efforts, Thailand has a fast-growing insurance industry. Insurance penetration is high by regional standards, fueled by rising per capita income and expectations of long-term economic growth. The life sector dominates, accounting for 73% of the net premiums written. Most of these premiums are individual policies, largely endowment policies that have government tax incentives. Because of a well-developed corporate bond market, Thai insurers are significant infrastructure investors.

[4] Organisation for Economic Co-operation and Development. 2015. *Regulation of Insurance Company and Pension Fund Investment: OECD Report to G20 Finance Ministers and Central Bank Governors*. Paris. https://www.oecd.org/g20/summits/antalya/Regulation-of-Insurance-Company-and-Pension-Fund-Investment.pdf.

Bhutan has a significant insurance capital base, but the insurance industry does not invest in transport infrastructure. Because PPP projects are few and the bond market is underdeveloped, the scope is limited for the insurance industry to investment in transport infrastructure.

Nepal's insurance industry lacks experts, technical skills, research-based decision-making, and a rating mechanism to identify investment opportunities. Insurance companies may invest up to 20% of their total portfolio in infrastructure sectors, but this limit is not utilized because insurance companies prefer government securities and other fixed-income instruments, such as fixed deposits.

Bangladesh's insurance industry has low penetration. Insurance companies have mostly invested in government securities or kept their funds on Fixed Deposit Receipts (FDRs) in scheduled banks. However, 2019 regulations by the Insurance Development and Regulatory Authority have a provision that mandates 15% of the assets of insurance companies be invested in government infrastructure bonds. This should encourage insurance companies to invest in infrastructure projects.

The other BIMSTEC countries revise their investment guidelines for insurance companies from time to time. Revisions have included detailed rating methodologies for investment assessments, investment limits brought into line with other developing countries in the region, and guidelines for private insurers and FDI to increase insurance penetration. Developing the bond market in these countries will advance the industry's growth.

Pension funds. Globally, pension funds are major infrastructure financing tools. The United States (US) has the largest amount of assets in pension funds, at $18.8 trillion at the end of 2019, followed by the UK ($3.6 trillion), Australia ($1.8 trillion), the Netherlands ($ 1.7 trillion), Canada ($1.5 trillion), Japan ($1.4 trillion), and Switzerland ($1.0 trillion). In terms of the relative size of pension assets, pension funds in Scandinavian countries and the Netherlands are globally the highest, at nearly 200% of GDP (Figure 12).

Figure 12: Pension Assets as Percentage of Gross Domestic Product, 2019 or Later

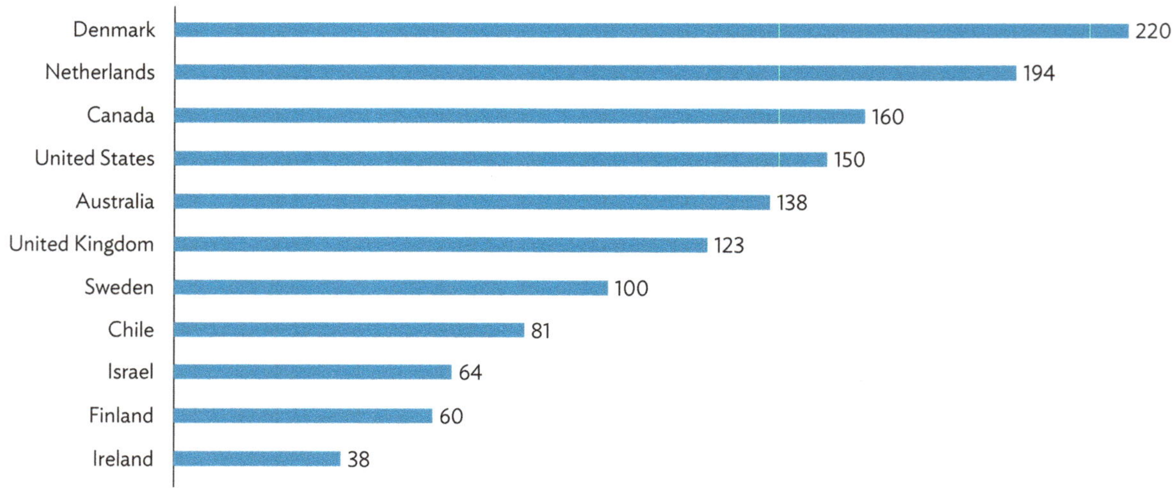

Source: Organisation for Economic Co-operation and Development. 2020. *Pension Markets in Focus*. Paris. https://www.oecd.org/daf/fin/private-pensions/Pension-Markets-in-Focus-2020.pdf.

Pension funds are invested for an average tenor of 25–30 years, which is suitable for long-term infrastructure investments. Australian superannuation funds, such as Australian Super, and Canadian pension funds, such as the Canada Pension Plan Investment Board and the Ontario Teachers' Pension Plan, have invested in infrastructure since the early 1990s, and are pioneers in this segment (Table 3). These countries have the world's highest asset allocation dedicated to infrastructure by pension funds, at about 10% compared with a global average of less than 5%.

Table 3: Infrastructure Allocation of Canadian Pension Funds, 2020

Pension Fund	Total Assets (Can$ billion)	Infrastructure Assets (Can$ billion)	% Infrastructure Assets
Ontario Teachers' Pension Plan	205	17	8.3
PSP Group	170	18	10.7
CPP Group	475	41	8.6
Ontario Municipal Employees Retirement System	105	21	20.0

Can$ = Canadian dollars, CPP = Canadian Pension Plan, PSP = Public Sector Pension.

Source: 2020 annual reports of the four insurance companies.

Australian superannuation funds invest in infrastructure primarily via infrastructure funds. As an example, Industry Funds Management is a specialist investment management company wholly owned by superannuation funds. Canadian pension funds focus on deals in North America and Western Europe, but they look at other regions on an opportunistic basis if they offer stable regulatory, economic, and political environments. Some prominent deals have been made by Canadian pension funds, including the Ontario Teachers' Pension Plan, the Ontario Municipal Employees Retirement System, the Canada Pension Plan Investment Board, and AIMCo. The Ontario Teachers' Pension Plan was one of the first pension funds in an OECD country to invest in unlisted infrastructure in Latin America, when it bought two Chilean water companies in 2007.

The pension sector in BIMSTEC countries is largely underdeveloped due to low awareness and coverage, except for Bhutan, Sri Lanka, and Thailand. Regulatory pushes through government reforms requiring mandatory contributions would help increase the pension sector—and this could help develop bond markets.

Reforms have been undertaken in Bhutan and Sri Lanka, creating a meaningful capital base for the pension sector. Indeed, the sector is now well developed in Bhutan, where pension and provident funds are mandatory in the private sector. Sri Lanka also has a solid capital base for the pension sector because of mandatory contribution plans. Thailand has a well-developed pension sector. The Government Pension Fund is the country's largest institutional investor, investing in infrastructure through equities and debt. Because of the social nature of pension funds, most of the fund's investments go into low-risk assets, such as government or Bank of Thailand bonds and US Treasury bills.

India's pension sector has a low base since a large part of the population is in the informal sector and not covered by pension plans.

The capacity for infrastructure financing in the BIMSTEC region through pension funds is constrained by not enough PPP projects, low pension coverage, and limited investable bonds in transport infrastructure. Like insurance funds, pension funds need developed bond markets to be able to invest in infrastructure. The growth of bond markets is positively associated with pension sector investment (Figure 13).

Figure 13: Size and Contribution of Pension Funds to Infrastructure

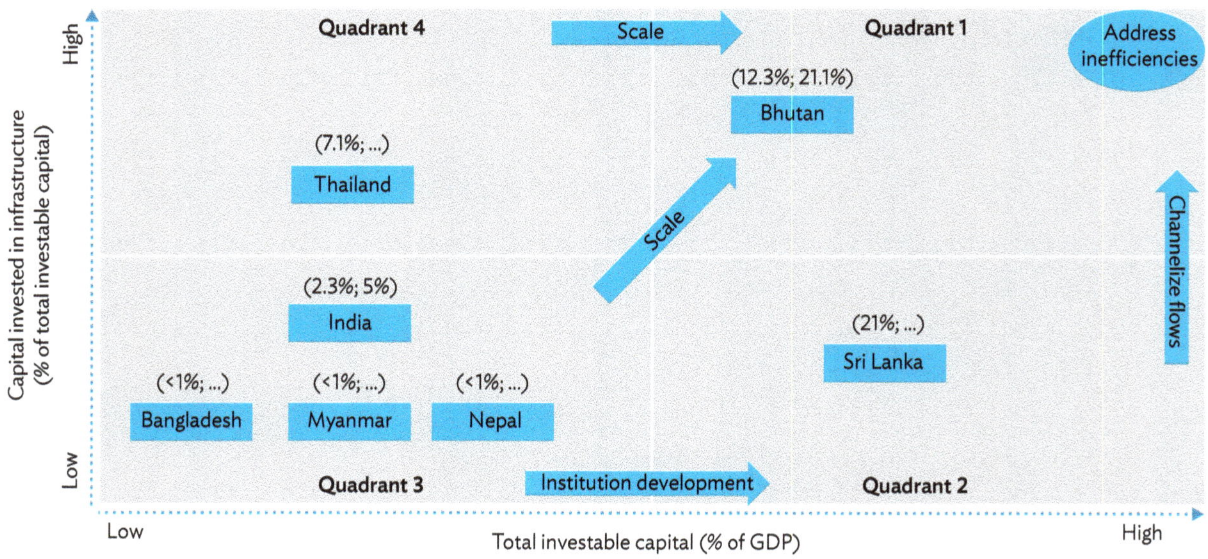

... = not available, GDP = gross domestic product.

Note: Institutions for which data are not available are placed based on inputs from primary and secondary research.

Source: 2019 data from pension fund regulators in the seven countries.

Foreign direct investment. BIMSTEC countries, except Thailand, allow 100% equity participation from foreign investors in transport infrastructure. These countries, however, face challenges from regulations, approval processes, and policies that hinder foreign investment (Figure 14).

In India, foreign exchange risks and the associated high hedging costs are the key FDI issues (Appendix 8 has a case study on the International Bank for Reconstruction and Development's Catastrophe Deferred Drawdown Option). In Bangladesh and Bhutan, lengthy approval processes are a major concern of foreign investors. In Nepal, it is the absence of an effective policy for trading partners and the lengthy approval processes. In Myanmar and Sri Lanka, most private financing in infrastructure comes from FDI. Myanmar's FDI in the infrastructure sector comes mainly from Hong Kong, China; the People's Republic of China; Singapore; and Thailand. In Myanmar, FDI projects included a new bridge over the Salween River in Kunlon and Kyaukphyu port. A relatively large share of Sri Lanka's FDI goes into infrastructure. FDI in 2018 mainly went to Hambantota International Port Group (Pvt) Limited, amounting to $828 million. Both Myanmar and Sri Lanka face challenges in attracting FDI. In Sri Lanka, frequent policy changes and slow project implementation both erode investor confidence.

Private equity and alternative investment funds. Private equity is an emerging alternative asset class in the BIMSTEC region. Typically, private equity funds do not take on construction-stage risks, but participate in operational infrastructure assets (Figure 15).

India has an active private equity market with many domestic and global funds investing in infrastructure assets. Global private equity players, including Macquarie and Brookfield, and domestic players, including Infrastructure Development Finance Company, operate in India. Private equity players in India face challenges, including demand risks from policy changes, and limited exit opportunities, making it difficult to churn assets. Private equity investments in port infrastructure have not had good exits because port traffic did not materialize due to

Figure 14: Size and Contribution of Foreign Direct Investment to Infrastructure

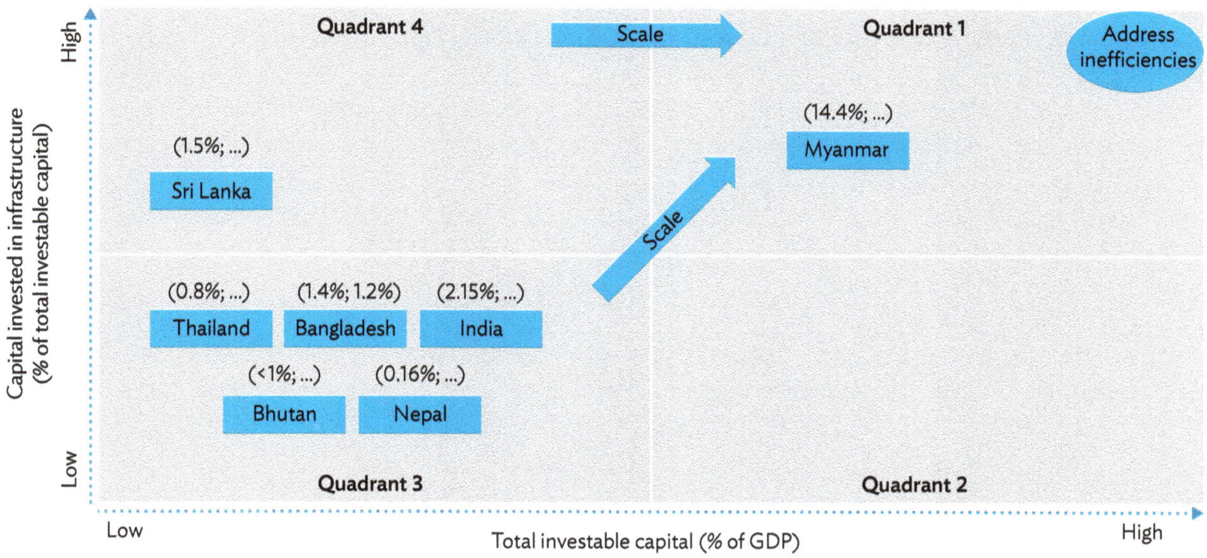

... = not available, GDP = gross domestic product.

Note: Institutions for which data are not available are placed based on inputs from primary and secondary research.

Source: Government reports from the seven countries.

Figure 15: Size and Contribution of Private Equity and Alternative Investment Funds to Infrastructure

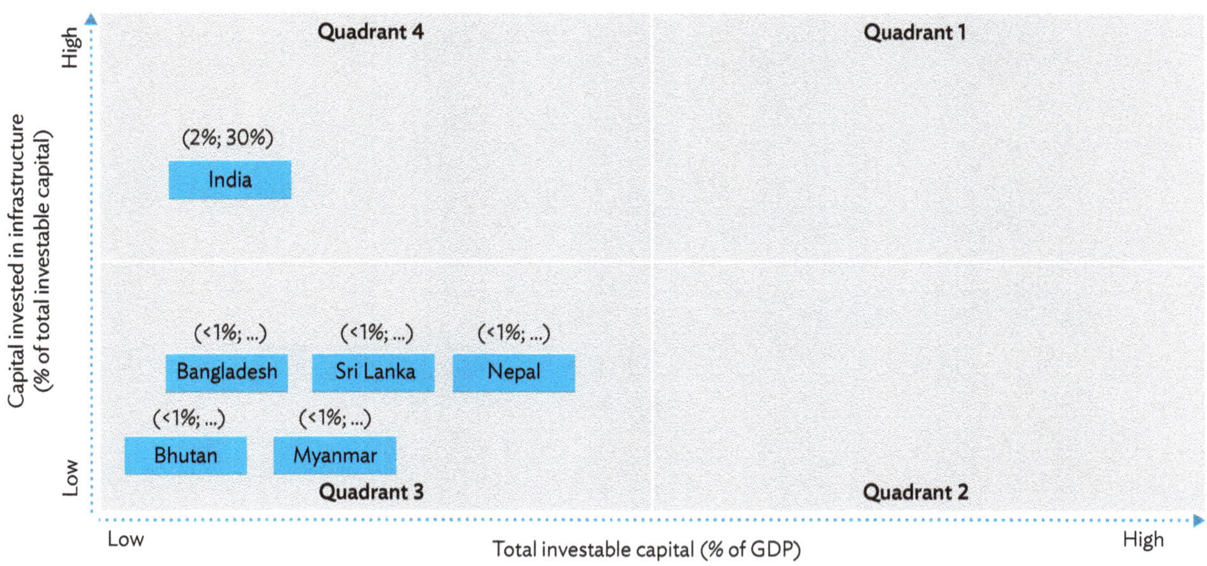

... = not available, GDP = gross domestic product.

Notes:
1. Institutions for which data are not available are placed based on inputs from primary and secondary research.
2. Total investable corpus for private equity funds in Thailand not available.

Source: 2019 industry reports from the six countries except Thailand.

overcapacity and policy changes. Asset churns have also been difficult in road projects. Hybrid annuity model concessions are generally not attractive for private equity investors.

Unlike India, other BIMSTEC countries do not have substantial private equity participation in infrastructure; both the corpus and investor participation are limited. Private equity players in Bangladesh are almost nonexistent and participation is mainly from start-ups. Nepal has only a few private equity players, such as the Dolma Fund and WLC Ventures, which are focused on small and medium-sized enterprises and providing growth capital.

Other financing tools and types. These include mutual funds, export credit agencies, and external commercial borrowing; they are not prominent in infrastructure investments in BIMSTEC countries or, for that matter, globally (Figure 16).

Using these financing tools would help develop equity and bond markets in BIMSTEC countries. Bangladesh, Bhutan, Myanmar, and Nepal should encourage retail participation in their capital markets. Growing government and corporate bond markets would also help develop these markets.

Increasing awareness on the different asset classes and introducing sophisticated financial products, such as derivatives and swaps, would help facilitate the increased use of these financing tools. Newer ones, such as infrastructure investment trusts (InvITs), could be developed to raise funds via public or private placements.

Figure 16: Size and Contribution of External Commercial Borrowing to Infrastructure

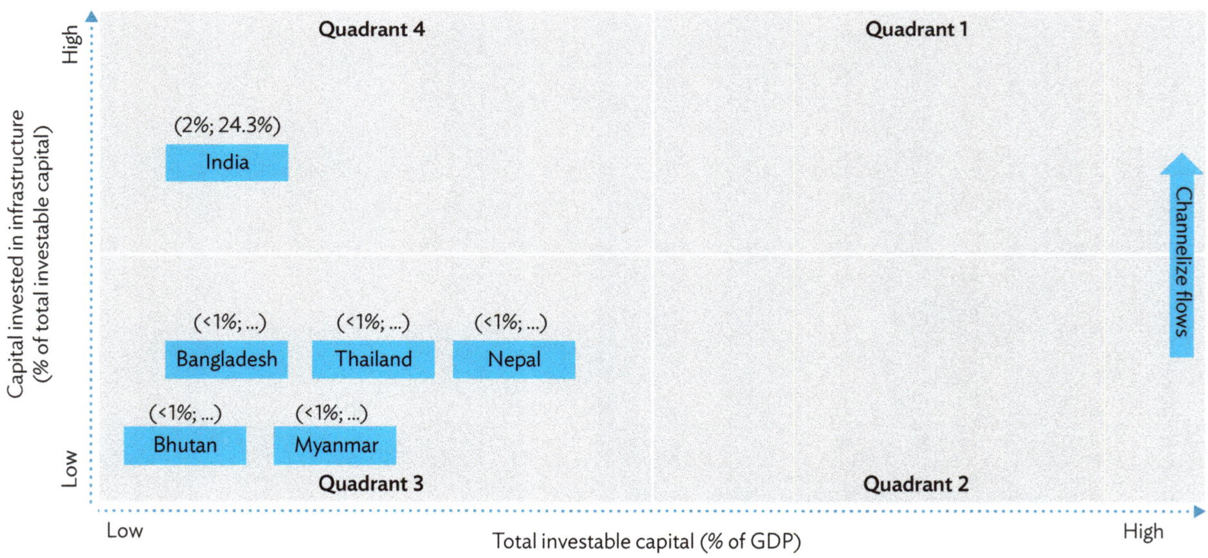

... = not available, GDP = gross domestic product.

Notes:
1. Institutions for which data are not available are placed based on inputs from primary and secondary research.
2. Total investable capital data for external commercial borrowings for Sri Lanka were not available.

Source: Industry reports from the six countries except Sri Lanka.

Developing a pipeline of PPP projects over the coming years could also help get these financing tools used for infrastructure investments . The governments of BIMSTEC countries can help the growth of these financing tools through an enabling policy and regulatory environment.

In sum, the participation of financing institutions in BIMSTEC countries in infrastructure has been limited, indicating the need for the region's financial markets to be broadened and deepened. Figure 17 shows the materiality of financing institutions in BIMSTEC countries.

Figure 17: Materiality of Financing Institutions

Financing Source	Bangladesh	Bhutan	India	Myanmar	Nepal	Sri Lanka	Thailand
Commercial banks	Medium	Medium	High	Medium	Medium	High	High
NBFIs	Medium	Low	High	Low	Low	Low	
Insurance funds	Low	Low	High	Low	Low	Low	High
Pension funds	Low	Medium	Low	Low	Low	Medium	Medium
FDI	Low	Low	Low	Medium	Low	Medium	Low
AIF/private equity	Low	Low	Medium	Low	Low	Low	–
Others (e.g., ECBs/ECAs)	Low	Low	Medium	Low	Low	–	–
Remarks	Two infra-focused NBFIs present but lack project finance capacity Encourages deepening of insurance and pension funds	Most institutions lack scale and capacity to finance infrastructure	Focus on channeling funds of pension, insurance funds to infrastructure	Most of the institutions lack scale and capacity to finance infrastructure	Most financial institutions lack scale and capacity Infra-focused NBFI formed in 2018	Barring central banks other institutions have low presence in infrastructure financing	Most pension and insurance funds along with infrastructure funds such as Thailand Future Fund are key private sources of infrastructure financing

Materiality: High, Medium, Low

– = not available, AIF = alternative investment fund, ECA = export credit agency, ECB = external commercial borrowing, FDI, = foreign direct investment, NBFI = nonbank financial institution.

Note: Materiality is based on total investable capital as a percentage of gross domestic product and percentage of capital in the infrastructure sector.

Source: Study team analysis.

Assessment of Capital Markets in BIMSTEC Countries

Capital markets in most BIMSTEC countries are nascent. But government bond markets are generally more developed than corporate bond markets for the following reasons:

(i) Sovereign status. The risk of sovereign default is typically low, making it an ideal instrument for market development

(ii) Homogeneity. Unlike corporate bonds, government securities are homogenous instruments from a single issuer

(iii) Frequency. Fiscal requirements create a regular source of issues in the government bond market. Despite the preference for government bonds, the market is underdeveloped (Figure 18).

Figure 18: Stages of Government and Corporate Bond Market Development

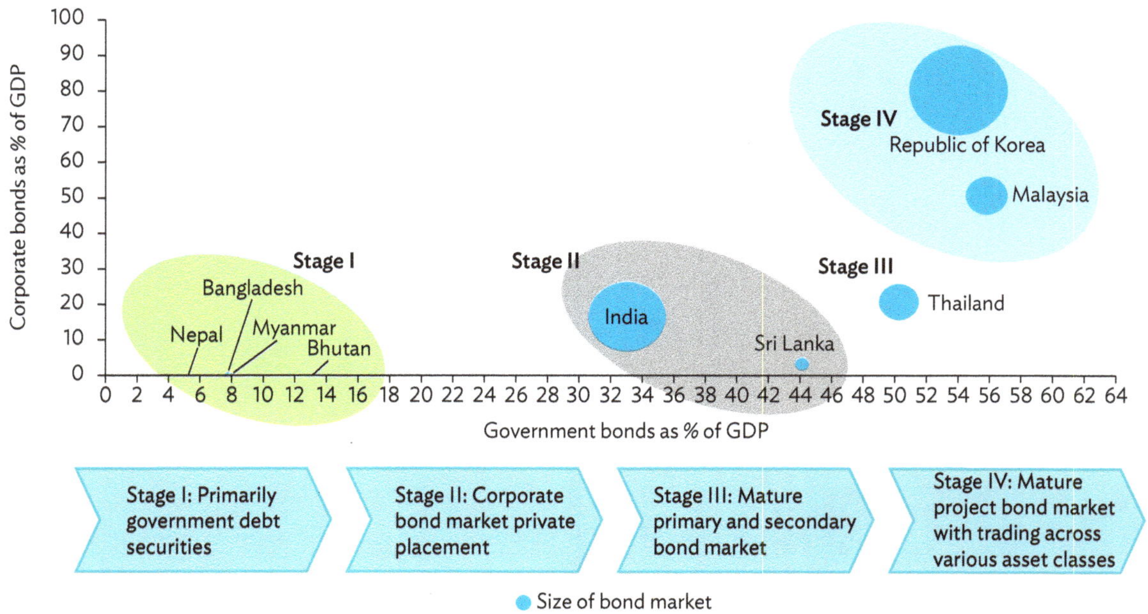

GDP = gross domestic product.

Note: : Government bonds include government and central bank issuances, Republic of Korea (2020), Thailand (2020), Malaysia (2020), India (2020), Sri Lanka (Domestic Government Bonds to GDP 2019, Corporate Bonds 2020), Bangladesh (2019), Myanmar (2019), Nepal (2019), Bhutan (2018).

Sources: Federal bank reports of BIMSTEC member countries; Asian Bonds Online web portal. https://asianbondsonline.adb.org/data-portal/; and study team analysis.

Suggested recommendations for developing the capital markets of BIMSTEC countries are summarized in the recommendations section of this report, and a detailed list of interventions are presented in the individual country sections.

Regional Institutional Structure and Soft System Bottlenecks

The following section examines the different types of soft system bottlenecks faced by transport infrastructure projects in the BIMSTEC region. These include challenges in institutional capacity as well as policy and regulatory framework in the region.

Limited coordination among BIMSTEC countries for implementation of regional transport infrastructure projects. This constraint is well recognized by member states. Indeed, many high-level meetings have been held on regional connectivity, but the importance given to this at these meetings has not been reflected during project implementation. The following regional transport projects, going by media reports, were delayed by 10–12 years because of inadequate coordination between the governments involved in these projects: (i) the construction of the Mechi Road Bridge connecting India and Nepal; (ii) the Akhaura–Agartala rail link connecting India and Bangladesh; and (iii) the new rail line linking Haldibari in India with Chilahati in Bangladesh.

Figure 19 compares the institutional structures of the European Commission, Association of Southeast Asian Nations (ASEAN), the Great Mekong Subregion (GMS), and BIMSTEC to identify institutional gaps.

Figure 19: Comparative Assessment of Regional Institutional Structures

	European Commission	ASEAN	GMS	BIMSTEC
Legal instrument/binding agreement (delineating roles and responsibilities of governing bodies/operational bodies)	✓	✓	✗[a]	✗
Well-defined and documented decision-making process	✓	✓	✓	✗
Availability of national interministerial committee coordinating activities in each country	✓	✓	✓	✗
Duration of highest-level meeting	At least once/week	Twice per year	Every 3 years	Four meetings happened since inception
Institutional arrangement for operationalizing master plan	✓	✓	✓	✗

ASEAN = Association of Southeast Asian Nations, BIMSTEC = Bay of Bengal Initiative for Multi-Sectoral Technical and Economic Cooperation, GMS = Greater Mekong Subregion.

[a] GMS leaders' summits culminate in a joint statement.

Sources: Official websites of ASEAN, BIMSTEC, the European Commission, and GMS, and various reports from secondary sources.

Limited institutional capacity in project preparation, planning, and monitoring. Most planning in the BIMSTEC region is done at the national level and is often presented in the form of time-based development plans—e.g., India's National Infrastructure Pipeline. National plans are a combination of ongoing projects, reflecting development demands identified at the national or local level, and the projected availability of funding. Because regional projects may not bring the economic returns to participating countries in proportion to their investment, they may not get due priority.

National plans do not generally include specific references to or relationships with the plans of neighboring countries. Transport infrastructure planning and development remain a national rather than bilateral, multilateral, or regional activity. Even so, there have been some regional initiatives in the transport infrastructure sector among BIMSTEC countries, such as the India–Myanmar–Thailand Trilateral Highway and programs under bilateral agreements. But even here, the development is dependent on timely budgetary allocations by each member country and priority accorded to the project. No regional mechanism exists to evaluate the economic impact, and to assess costs and benefits of a transport project in, say, country A on other countries in the region.

Limited implementation and monitoring of regional projects. Some line agencies and project authorities in the BIMSTEC region have limited capability to oversee regional projects, including the preparation of detailed project reports and conducting technical evaluations of project bids. This can lead to project delays. Some regional road projects have also been delayed because of ineffective project monitoring, e.g., the widening of the road linking Belhiya in India to Bhutwal in Nepal.

Differences in regulatory and policy frameworks. The complexity in most regional infrastructure projects is exacerbated by the multiple regulatory systems and policy frameworks that need to be navigated. Participating firms can face regulatory hurdles in one or more countries involved in a project, such as adverse or abrupt changes in laws and regulations, heterogenous technical standards (e.g., rail line gauge sizes), land acquisition risks, and the cancelation of licenses or approvals.

Thailand is the only BIMSTEC country with a developed international road transport sector with provisions for international licenses to allow Thai trucks to enter Cambodia and the Lao People's Democratic Republic (Lao PDR). Transporters in India can carry goods to and from Bhutan and Nepal, and vice versa under bilateral arrangements. Foreign transporters are not permitted to enter Bangladesh or Myanmar, other than at border transfer points, and Sri Lanka, as an island, has no international road transport requirements. The inability of road transporters to travel to neighboring countries could be considered a barrier to trade since it directly increases transport and transaction costs. The need to transship cargo at border crossings directly increases trade costs through additional border handling charges, as well as increasing the risk of damage and pilferage. In addition, the cost of hiring two separate transporters for shorter journeys is likely to be higher than the total cost of hiring a single carrier to convey goods from origin to destination.[5]

BIMSTEC countries do not follow the same technical standards in transport. India, for example, uses both broad- and dual-gauge railway tracks, but some tracks connecting Bangladesh to India are meter gauged. Variations in design specifications and material standards can become a critical problem, especially if a project is to be competitively tendered.

Land acquisitions in regional projects can be problematic during implementation because they are dependent on country-specific regulatory frameworks governing land and property rights. Differences in these frameworks can cause delays.

Model concession agreements that clearly delineate the roles and responsibilities of the government and private developers to ensure the equitable spread of project risk are not in place in BIMSTEC countries.

Regional projects seen as higher risk than domestic ones. This is because utilization of the regional transport infrastructure is dependent on the political, diplomatic, and strategic dynamics of participating countries. Broadly, regional projects are prone to two key risks:

(i) **Project risk.** Regional projects can have different foreign exchange, credit, and demand risks. Appropriate risk management instruments, such as demand guarantees, exchange rate guarantees, and currency hedging instruments, are needed to manage these risks. Guarantees on foreign exchange convertibility and transferability may be needed in cases where a project's main debt is denominated in one currency, but its revenue is denominated in another currency.

(ii) **Political risk.** Potential political risks include sociopolitical developments, such as conflicts or civil disturbances, contract breaches and sovereign debt default risks, and coordination risks across multiple government entities. Even when projects have dispute resolution agreements, the risks and costs of actually taking a state to court are considerable, and any ruling can be hard to enforce. Political election cycles and leadership changes can also result in sudden project cancellations.

[5] Asian Development Bank Institute. 2020. *Trade Impact of Reducing Time and Costs at Borders in the Central Asia Regional Economic Cooperation Region*. Tokyo.

Public–Private Partnership Readiness

BIMSTEC countries with the exceptions of India and Thailand have little experience in carrying out PPP projects in transportation infrastructure. These countries are at a nascent stage in terms of PPP readiness. Some of them have set up PPP units to facilitate partnership on transport infrastructure projects. Bangladesh did this in 2010 and Bhutan in 2017. Myanmar and Nepal are in the process of setting up PPP units. India and Thailand have rich experience in implementing PPP transport infrastructure projects (Figures 20 and 21).

Figure 20: Number of Public–Private Partnership Projects by Sector Achieving Financial Closure, 1996–2020

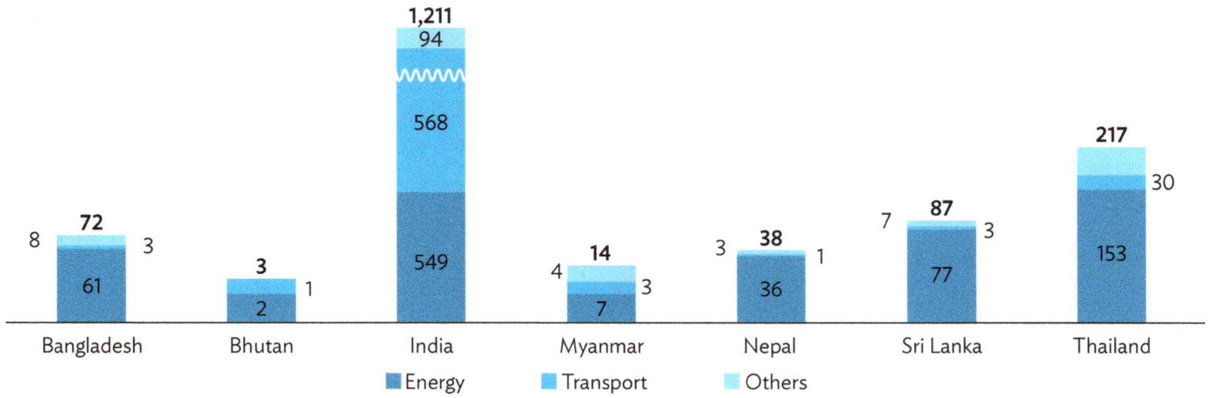

Notes:
1. Other sectors include information and communication technology, municipal solid water, and water and sewage.
2. India bar chart not to scale.

Source: World Bank. Private Participation in Infrastructure Database. https://ppi.worldbank.org/en/pp (accessed 15 May 2022).

Figure 21: Transport Infrastructure Public–Private Partnership Projects by Type Achieving Financial Closure, 1996–2020

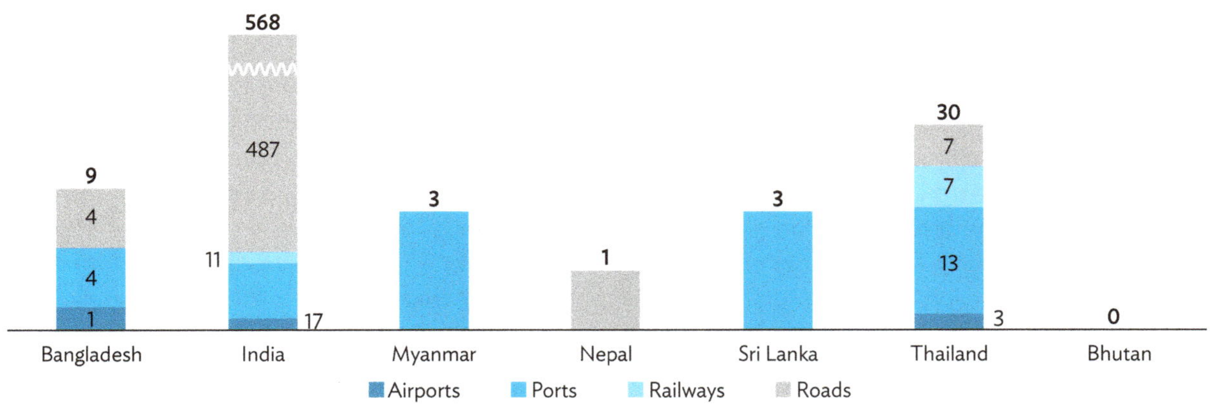

Note: India bar chart not to scale.

Source: World Bank. Private Participation in Infrastructure Database. https://ppi.worldbank.org/en/pp (accessed 10 April 2022).

A review of cross-border transport infrastructure projects in the BIMSTEC region shows that although participating countries may have implemented some national PPP projects, these have been executed using either the engineering procurement construction item-rate contract mode from government budgets or through multilateral or bilateral concessional loans or grants. In other regional groupings, including ASEAN, the EU, and the GMS, regional projects have been implemented through PPPs—e.g., the N4 toll road linking South Africa with Mozambique and the Malaysia–Singapore Second Link Bridge.

The World Bank's *Benchmarking Infrastructure Development 2020* report and the associated Benchmarking Infrastructure Development database provide useful country assessments of the enabling and management environment for PPPs, including for most BIMSTEC countries. The assessment covers four criteria: preparation, procurement, contract management, and unsolicited proposals. Table 4 shows the scores out of 100 for the six BIMSTEC countries covered by the assessment.

Table 4: Public–Private Partnership Scores of Six BIMSTEC Countries

Country	Preparation	Procurement	Contract Management	Unsolicited Proposals
Bangladesh	54	62	48	75
India	60	67	85	N/R
Myanmar	11	35	48	0
Nepal	33	47	58	42
Sri Lanka	22	54	57	92
Thailand	35	38	64	N/R

BIMSTEC = Bay of Bengal Initiative for Multi-Sectoral Technical and Economic Cooperation, N/R = not rated.

Note: Scores out of 100.

Source: World Bank. 2020. *Benchmarking Infrastructure Development 2020*. https://bpp.worldbank.org/ (accessed 5 April 2022).

Figure 22 shows six key determinants for a capacity assessment framework for PPPs. Figure 23 shows the PPP readiness of BIMSTEC countries. Each criterion is evaluated based on the output from a standard scoring matrix—Section I gives more details on this framework—which provides a score ranging from 0 to 3 for each determinant. The overall score of the government or project authority is the average score for each determinant. As the figure shows, a significant amount of work needs to be done to improve the PPP readiness of all BIMSTEC countries except for India and Thailand.

The above assessment sheds light on the following aspects of the PPP readiness of BIMSTEC countries:

(i) All BIMSTEC countries have PPP laws or policies. PPP policies in Bangladesh, Bhutan, Nepal, and Sri Lanka have provisions for dispute resolution. Thailand's latest PPP law was passed in 2019, but its provisions for dispute resolution—a major PPP issue there—are limited. Myanmar has PPP guidelines.

(ii) Although all BIMSTEC countries except India and Thailand have little experience in implementing PPP projects in transport infrastructure, all have set up national or project authority PPP units to enhance support from the public sector to carry out partnership projects. Capacity building is needed for these units, as is support for preparing sector-specific model concession agreements that capture local contexts.

(iii) India has provisions and approval processes for viability gap funding (VGF) on an institution-by-institution basis. Thailand's PPP law does not explicitly mention this form of funding, but VGF funding from the public sector has been used for PPP projects. Bhutan and Nepal have provisions for VGF in

Figure 22: Public–Private Partnership Capacity Assessment Framework

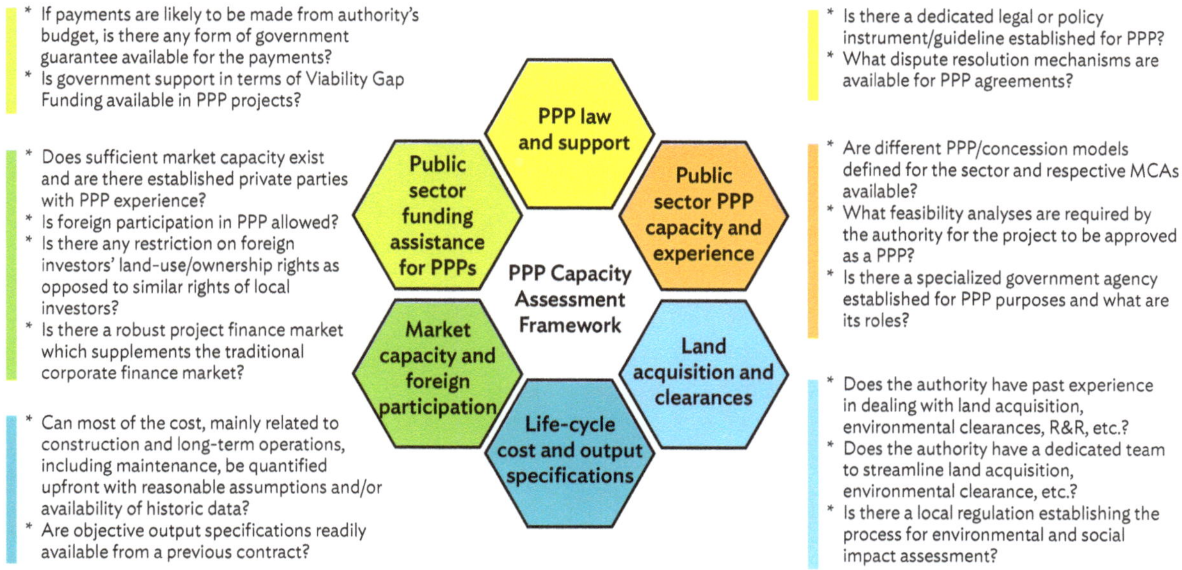

MCA = model concession agreement, PPP = public–private partnership, R&R = rehabilitation and resettlement.

Sources: Study team analysis; Asian Development Bank. 2017. *Public–Private Partnership Monitor*. Manila. https://www.adb.org/publications/public-private-partnership-monitor; World Bank. 2020. *Benchmarking Infrastructure Development 2020*. Washington, DC.

Figure 23: Public–Private Partnership Readiness

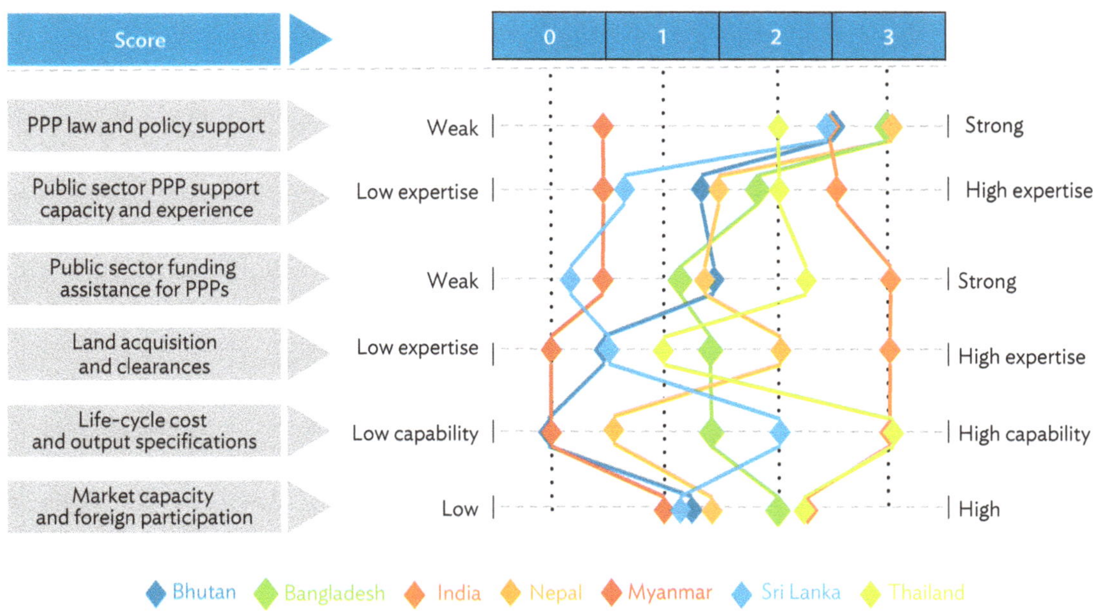

PPP = public–private partnership.

Sources: Asian Development Bank. 2017. *Public–Private Partnership Monitor*. Manila. https://www.adb.org/publications/public-private-partnership-monitor; feedback from and interviews with government agencies and other stakeholders; and information from secondary sources.

their PPP policies, but VGF in transport infrastructure does not seem to have been used. Myanmar and Sri Lanka have limited experience in funding projects through VGF.

(iv) BIMSTEC member countries except India and Thailand have limited provisions for credit guarantees for infrastructure projects.

(v) India and Nepal have set up dedicated units to handle land acquisition and social and environmental clearances to streamline these processes. Bangladesh and Thailand have experience in land acquisitions and clearances, but no procedures or dedicated units for PPP projects for either. Bhutan has strict processes for clearances, resulting in delays in most projects. Myanmar has no guidelines on land acquisitions or clearances specific to PPP projects, resulting in heavy delays.

(vi) Most of the project authorities in BIMSTEC countries (except Bhutan and Myanmar) have a good understanding of the costs and specifications for design and construction of transport infrastructure projects. However, the understanding of the long-term operational and life-cycle costs as well as output-based performance-orientated operational specifications, which are required for PPP projects in most BIMSTEC countries, are limited (except India and Thailand). Most infrastructure projects in Bhutan and Myanmar are developed through government-to-government agreements with neighboring countries and there is limited understanding of PPP projects in these countries.

(vii) Recent challenges in the award and execution of PPP projects in BIMSTEC countries highlight the need for increased market capacity to be able to implement these projects and enhance access to finance—e.g., Bangladesh's PPP authority database shows 20 approved transport projects, but only two are in the construction stage. PPPs were tried for Nepal's Kathmandu–Kulekhani–Hetauda Tunnel Highway and the Kathmandu–Terai/Madhes Fast Track Road Project, but there were no takers from the private sector.

Summary of As-Is Assessment

Figure 24 shows the severity of issues and challenges affecting the funding and financing of transport infrastructure framework in BIMSTEC countries at the national and regional levels across different elements of the identification framework.

These issues for each country in the region have been assessed to identify and understand the root causes and their severity.

(i) **Funding from government budgets.** Rising debt and fiscal deficit levels may constrain budget funding to transport infrastructure.

(ii) **Funding from alternative mechanisms.** Except for India and Thailand, BIMSTEC countries rarely use nonbudgetary funding sources; regional road projects are mainly funded by government budgets. Bhutan has no guidelines for collecting tolls on roads. Revenue from tolls in Bangladesh, Myanmar, and Nepal partly cover maintenance costs and do not contribute to capital servicing.

(iii) **Financing.** Financial markets in Bangladesh, Bhutan, Myanmar, and Nepal are underdeveloped, as are the capital markets of most BIMSTEC countries. Bhutan, Nepal, and Myanmar have no sovereign ratings. Financing institutions are either small or do not have exposure to the transport infrastructure sector.

(iv) **Institutional readiness and enablers.** BIMSTEC requires robust governance and institutional structures similar to ASEAN, the European Commission, and the GMS. ASEAN and the European Commission do corridor-level planning, and the GMS recently shifted from project to corridor planning. Project evaluations in BIMSTEC countries, however, do not consider wider economic impacts beyond the home country. There are differences in regulations, heterogenous technical standards, and limited capability to monitor the preparation of projects in the region.

(v) **PPP readiness.** Except for India and Thailand, BIMSTEC countries have considerably less experience in PPPs in transport infrastructure projects. PPPs have so far been not used in regional transport infrastructure projects.

Figure 24: Severity of Issues in the Identification Framework

Issue		Bangladesh	Bhutan	India	Myanmar	Nepal	Sri Lanka	Thailand	BIMSTEC
Funding	Inadequate government capacity	High	High	High	High	High	High	High	High
	Insufficient user pay	Medium	High	Low	Low	Medium	Medium	Low	High
	Availability of alternate funding sources	High	High	High	High	High	High	High	High
Financing	Materiality of financing institutions	Medium	High	Low	High	High	Medium	Low	High
	Capital market	High	High	Medium	High	High	Medium	Low	High
PPP readinesss		High	High	Low	High	High	High	Medium	High
Regional institutions structure/ enablers		–	–	–	–	–	–	–	High

Severity of issue: High, Medium, Low

– = not applicable, BIMSTEC = Bay of Bengal Initiative for Multi-Sectoral Technical and Economic Cooperation, PPP = public–private partnership.

Sources: Government capacity: central bank websites; User pay: toll guidelines, policy, and news articles; Alternative funding sources: primary interactions and, secondary sources; Materiality of financing institutions: central bank and other regulator websites; Capital market: market regulators; PPP readiness: primary interactions and secondary sources; Regional institution structure/enablers: regional grouping websites, various secondary sources.

Proposed Interventions for Improving the Delivery of Transport Infrastructure Projects

Bankable projects will be critical for attracting financing to master plan projects. A project can become bankable if there are funding mechanisms to capture its economic value and they are applied to various project aspects, including investment and a favorable enabling environment, such as low political risk, a transnational regulatory framework, and homogenous technical standards (Table 5). These funding mechanisms and enablers to make projects bankable are hardly used by BIMSTEC countries. This report explores interventions to make projects bankable and attract commercial financing. Interventions are proposed for financing national and regional projects, and improve the potential for PPPs to make efficiency gains.

Table 5: Four Facets of a Financing Framework

Funding	• Identify, measure, and capture economic value (user pay, tax pay) • Regional projects—Allocate cost among participating countries in line with economic benefits
Institutional coordination and enablers	• Implement institutional mechanism for better coordination • Support projects with various enablers—Formulate transnational regulatory environments, and create synergies between technical standards, guarantee instruments, capacity-building support, project preparation, and so on
Financing	• Identify capital sources and intermediaries for financing commercially viable and unviable projects
Enhance value through private sector participation	• Explore potential of private sector participation in projects for efficiency gains

Source: Study team analysis.

Funding

Most BIMSTEC countries traditionally use government budgets to fund projects. But this funding source, as discussed earlier, is constrained by rising government debt and fiscal deficits. Additional funding sources are needed.

In the current financing and funding landscape (user-pay norms), only a few transport infrastructure projects are commercially attractive. Figure 25 illustrates a high-level commercial viability assessment of two-lane road projects in the master plan; Appendix 17 lists the projects. At a user charge of $0.06 per vehicle-kilometer (km), only one project (project 19) is commercially viable. This indicates that interventions are needed to make projects commercially viable.

Traffic utilization rate for two-lane road projects is calculated considering the following three key data points:

- Past trade growth in the region (e.g., India–Bangladesh region for a road connecting India with Bangladesh)
- Traffic on the route (road), estimated by considering existing trade in the region, share of trade on each mode of transportation (road, rail, waterways, sea) in the region, trade split at each border trade location (border posts)
- Capacity of two-lane road project is 25,000 passenger–car units

Figure 25: Commercial Viability of Two-Lane Road Projects at a Toll Rate of $0.06 per Vehicle-Kilometer

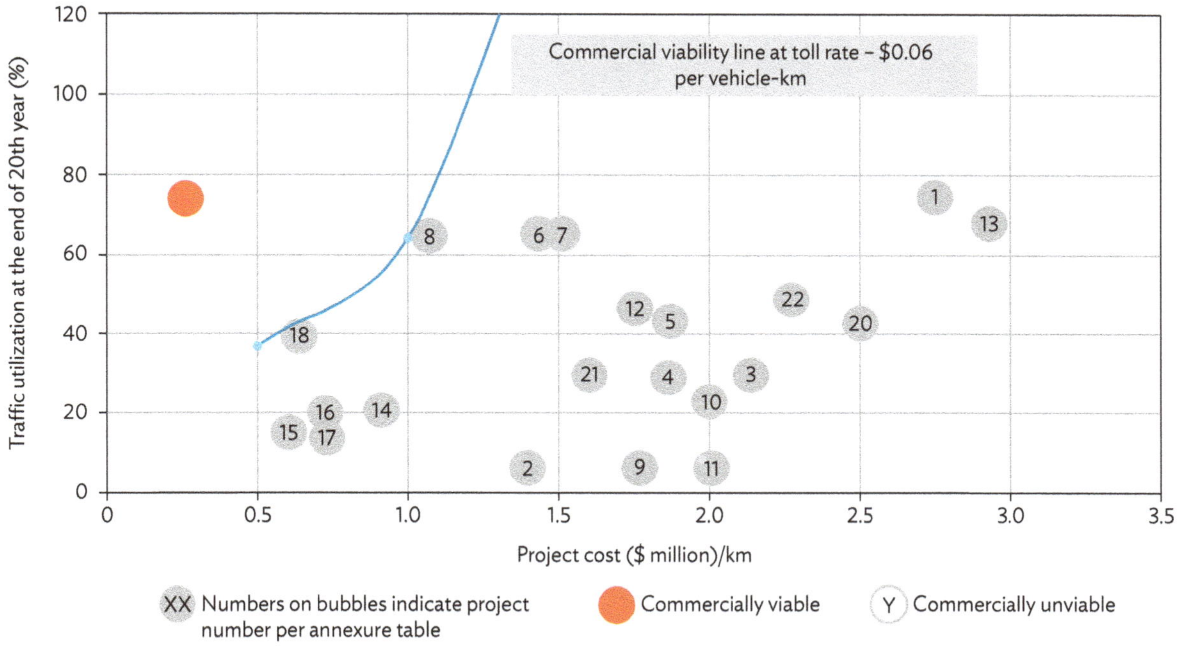

km = kilometer.

Notes:
1. Covers 22 projects.
2. Traffic utilization of two-lane projects calculated by project authorities based on traffic studies.

Sources: Study team analysis; various reports and news articles; International Trade Centre trade map; project cost estimated using data in BIMSTEC master plan and length of road data sourced from BIMSTEC Master Plan and secondary reports; RBSA Advisors. 2019. *Cost of Capital in India*. Hyderabad.

To increase the commercial viability of transport infrastructure projects, the following two key levers can be explored: lever 1—levying user charges in line with economic benefits accrued to the projects, and lever 2—providing a capital subsidy and/or an operational subsidy to make projects commercially viable.

Lever 1: Levying user charges captures a project's economic value and is a source of project revenue. As Figure 26 shows, increasing the toll rate shifts the commercial viability line toward the right, making more projects in the BIMSTEC master plan commercially viable.

Higher user charges in the BIMSTEC region can be explored. As Figure 27 shows, user charges for roads in Japan, the People's Republic of China, Spain, and the US are much higher than in most BIMSTEC countries. But user charges in Bangladesh, Myanmar, and Nepal are so low that they do not service capital costs and barely cover operation and maintenance (O&M) costs. Bhutan has no guidelines on user charges for roads or for charging user fees on road projects.

Figure 26: Commercial Viability of Two-Lane Road Projects Using Higher Toll Rates

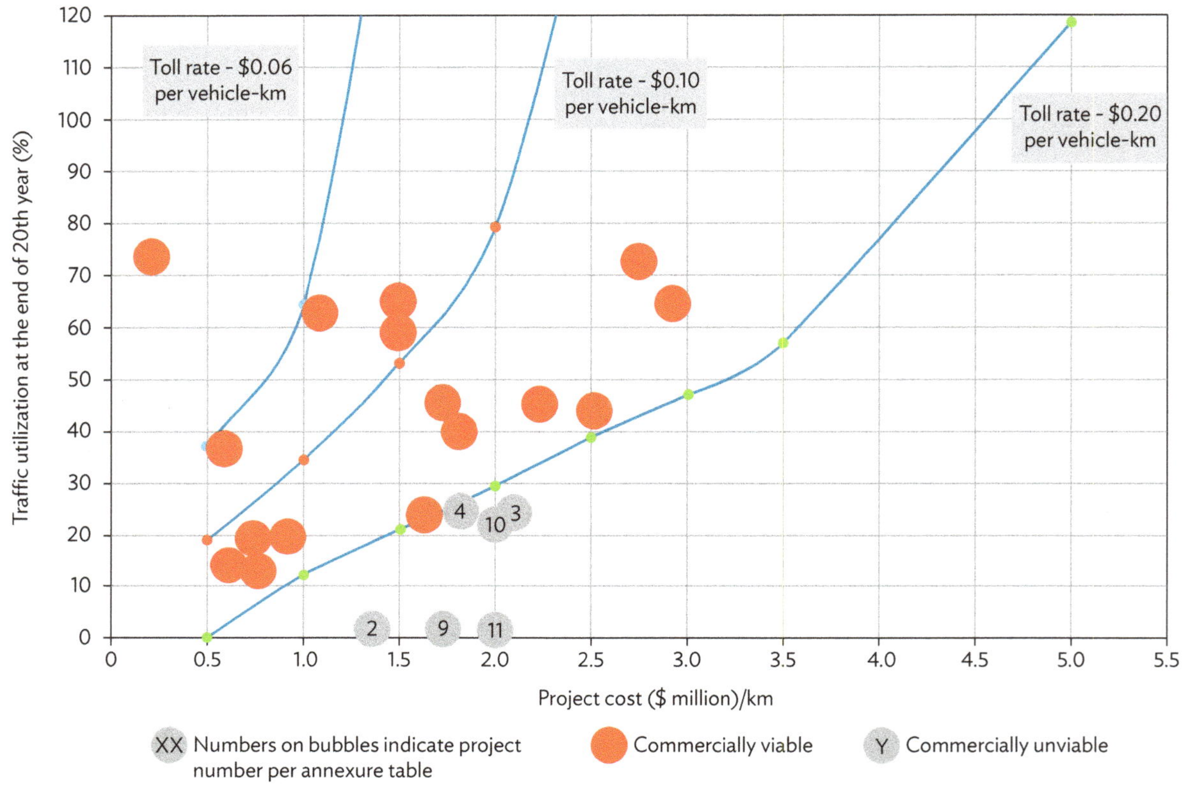

km = kilometer.

Note: In addition to the lever "levying user charge," which depends on the willingness of end users to pay, other complementary bankability-related interventions, such as the transnational regulatory environment and homogenous technical standards, need to be implemented to attract commercial financing.

Source: Study team analysis; RBSA Advisors. 2019. *Cost of Capital in India*. Hyderabad.

The affordability of user charges levied on road projects depends on the impact of these charges on overall logistics costs. Levying a user charge of $0.06 per vehicle-km on this route for transporting tea adds about 1.0% to the overall transportation cost and about 0.1% to the cargo value. The benefit to the end-user in terms of transportation and annual inventory cost savings is $0.10 per vehicle-km if an average speed on the route is 25 km an hour and $0.13 if average speed is 50 km an hour.

Figure 27: Toll Rates in BIMSTEC and Other Countries
(cents per vehicle-kilometer)

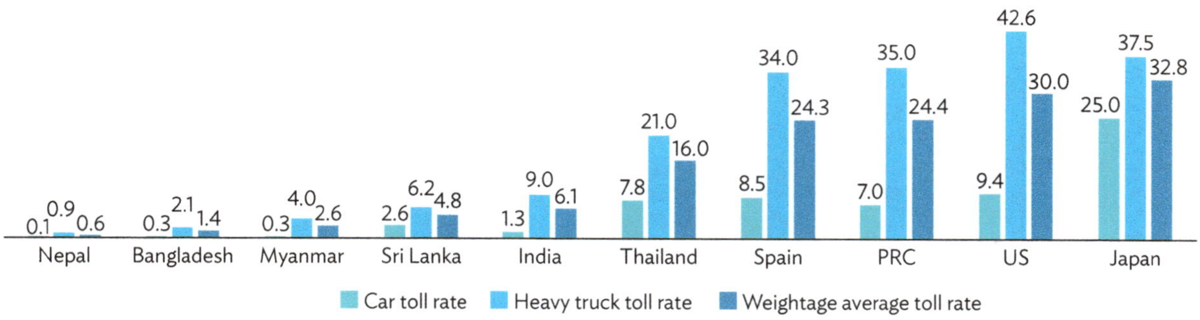

BIMSTEC = Bay of Bengal Initiative for Multi-Sectoral Technology and Economic Cooperation, PRC = People's Republic of China, US = United States.

Note: Bhutan has no guidelines on user charges for roads.

Source: Asian Development Bank. 2016. *Myanmar Transport Sector Policy Note: How to Improve Road User Charges.* Manila.

In addition to cost savings, other benefits include reduced accidents, increased employment, higher land values, and lower carbon emissions, all of which benefit the economy. Economic benefit analyses are needed so that governments can determine whether investing in a project would benefit the economy. Doing these analyses is even more important for regional projects where economic costs and benefits are split among multiple countries. In the BIMSTEC region, no mechanisms are in place that can make these evaluations. BIMSTEC countries should consider adopting a standard economic analysis framework to identify and measure the economic benefits of regional transport infrastructure projects. The economic analysis framework in ADB's 2017 institutional document *Guidelines for the Economic Analysis of Projects* could be used for guidance. Globally, there are instances where cross-subsidies are provided by a more affluent country to a less affluent one to cover operating costs—e.g., the N4 toll road linking South Africa and Mozambique. Similar interventions could be explored in BIMSTEC region as well (Table 6).

Table 6: Interventions for Improving the Delivery of Transport Infrastructure Projects

#	Interventions	Ownership
1	Agreement on evaluating toll/user fees as a means of funding by governments of the Bay of Bengal Initiative for Multi-Sectoral Technical and Economic Cooperation (BIMSTEC) countries User fees to be decided on the basis of the true cost of using, maintaining, and improving infrastructure, and the benefits accrued to stakeholders Example: M5 toll motorway, a regional road in Europe, adopted user fees as a means of funding Actions: • Relax national toll/user fee guidelines for BIMSTEC master plan projects to evaluate toll/user fees on the basis of true cost and benefits • Set regional toll guidelines/orders on the mechanism for charging toll rates on roads in line with economic benefits • Explore cross-subsidization (i.e., users from more affluent countries are charged higher user fees)	BIMSTEC Secretariat and member countries

continued on next page

Table 6 *continued*

#	Interventions	Ownership
2	Develop a regional cost-benefit sharing arrangement (multilateral development banks and the BIMSTEC Secretariat can play a role in cost allocation and responsibilities) Example: Asian Development Bank (ADB)-assisted in the cost-sharing arrangement basis to benefit accrual for the Great Mekong Subregion's Northern Economic Corridor project Actions: • Conduct economic and distribution analyses of projects during the project preparation stage • A framework on economic costs and benefits can be developed for each sector and agreed on by BIMSTEC countries • ADB's *2017 Guidelines for the Economic Analysis of Projects* is a useful reference for developing a framework	ADB, BIMSTEC Secretariat, project authorities

Source: Study team analysis.

Lever 2: Providing capital support can be a capital grant, one-time or deferred; operational support can be a revenue guarantee, foreign exchange risk instrument, or taxation. A capital subsidy to improve commercial viability for a two-lane road project that can cover 40% of the project cost.

The governments of BIMSTEC countries will find it difficult to provide capital and operational support to transport infrastructure projects because of budget constraints. To resolve this, at least to some extent, governments can explore asset recycling to raise funds for providing capital and operating subsidies. Here, governments can concession out the private sector operational projects that have stable cash flows and unlock the capital invested for further investment. An example of this is the National Highways Authority of India (NHAI) transferring some projects with stable cash flows to private concessionaires under the toll-operate-transfer PPP mode. Major ports in India are exploring transferring their operational projects to private players. The Lever 2 lessons for BIMSTEC countries are:

(i) The asset recycling of road assets is relevant for India as the country has a large and growing stock of revenue-generating public road assets. The NHAI, at the time of writing, held four phases of toll-operate-transfer bidding and the fifth is ongoing. The NHAI has conducted four phases of toll-operate-transfer bidding and unlocked invested capital worth about $1.9 billion.[6] The NHAI is looking to raise $11.6 billion by offering 6,165 km of highways using toll-operate-transfer bidding by 2024.

(ii) Most roads in Bhutan and Myanmar are funded by the government with or without support from MDBs. But either the number of toll-based brownfield roads or the quantum of toll collection is not sufficient to attract private investors in these asset recycling initiatives.

(iii) In Bangladesh, Nepal, Sri Lanka, and Thailand, brownfield toll roads are sometimes pooled together by governments for asset recycling, as was the case for 401 km of expressways and motorways in Thailand.

6 Press Information Bureau, Government of India. 2019. Cabinet Approves Amendments and Modifications in the Toll-Operate-Transfer Model and Securitization of User Fee Receipts of NH. Press release. 20 November. https://pib.gov.in/Pressreleaseshare.aspx?PRID=1592544; Cement Manufacturers Association. n.d. Highways from Canceled TOT Bundle on the Road Again. https://www.cmaindia.org/updates-trends/highways-from-cancelled-tot-bundle-on-the-road-again/; *Construction Week*. 2020. NHAI receives Rs5,011 cr from Cube Highways towards TOT Bundle. 24 October. https://www.constructionweekonline.in/business/15520-nhai-receives-rs-5011-cr-from-cube-highways-towards-tot-bundle-3; *India Infrahub*. 2020. NHAI Scraps Fourth TOT Bundle, Invites Bids for Fifth TOT Bundle with 20 Years Concession Period. 30 September. https://indiainfrahub.com/2020/roads/nhai-scraps-fourth-tot-bundle-invites-bids-for-fifth-tot-bundle-with-20-years-concession-period/; and *Economic Times*. 2021. Adani, DP Jain & Co Emerge Highest Bidders for NHAI's TOT-5 Bundle. 19 February. https://economictimes.indiatimes.com/industry/indl-goods/svs/construction/adani-dp-jain-co-emerge-highest-bidders-for-nhais-tot-5-bundle/articleshow/81114714.cms?from=mdr.

(iv) 170 km of expressways classified as class E roads by the Road Development Authority of Sri Lanka; three toll roads with a total length of 137 km in Bangladesh that includes the 13.7 km Chattogram Port Access Road and a 74 km stretch of the Dhaka–Sylhet highway. These are all part of the BIMSTEC master plan projects.[7]

Another avenue of funding transport infrastructure projects is through monetization of transportation assets, which has taken place to a certain extent in the BIMSTEC region:

(i) In India, 50-year contracts to private players for operating six brownfield airports were bid out in 2019. The Airport Authority of India plans to privatize more airports, and major ports in India are also exploring the transfer of operational projects to the private sector.
(ii) Bangladesh, Myanmar, Sri Lanka, and Thailand have large coastal areas and a large number of commercial ports. The governments of these countries could identify nonstrategic ports and recycle these assets.
(iii) Myanmar has privatized its international airports and plans to privatize 30-plus domestic airports. The other BIMSTEC countries could evaluate their international airports by pooling them and offering them for private participation, e.g., the six international airports—Don Mueang, Phuket, Chiang Mai, Hat Yai, Chiang Rai, and Suvarnabhumi—operated by the Airports of Thailand Public Company Limited, a public sector company. The government and the airports authority could consider privatizing the operations of these airports.

Asset-backed securitization is another way of raising funds on receipts estimated to be received in the future. The securitization proceeds can then be invested in other projects. This is an effective tool for governments and project authorities to unlock their invested capital and reinvest in existing or new projects. The NHAI raises long-term finance from banks by securitizing the user-fee receipts from plazas as a means of monetizing assets.

The Thailand Future Fund is both a mutual trust and a trust that invests in infrastructure by pooling multiple projects under an entity that is legally separate from the project entity. This enables the wider and longer-term refinancing of existing infrastructure projects and frees up the developers' capital to reinvestment in new projects. India's InvITs work like mutual funds and are designed to pool small sums of money from investors in assets that give cash flow over time. Part of this cash flow is distributed as a dividend to investors. These trusts are a good way to monetize revenue-generating infrastructure assets, the proceeds of which can be used by sponsors to either pay off interest payments in the initial period of low cash flow or invest in new projects. These trusts are currently used by private developers, but the NHAI is also exploring this option. Project authorities in the BIMSTEC countries should explore this funding option.

The authorities should also explore ways for revenue enhancement to increase their investable capital and improve the viability of projects (Table 7). Ways to enhance revenue include LVC; non-toll revenue, such as advertisements and privately owned public spaces; targeted taxation, such as vehicle fuel surcharges and congestion charges; and newer tools, like carbon pricing (carbon taxes and cap-and-trade systems). Some countries are already using innovative ways for generating revenue from existing infrastructure, such as solar panels on highways in Germany, the US, and Switzerland; branded toll plazas in Malaysia and Nigeria; roundabout sponsorships in Uganda and the UK; and associations with highways in India. Non-toll revenue is not featured prominently in either the master plan or the national plans of transport authorities in BIMSTEC countries. This could be explored for the BIMSTEC master plan projects as shown:

7 T. S. Adhikary. 2021. Dhaka-Mawa-Bhanga Expressway: Toll Collection Likely to Start from July. *The Daily Star*. 8 February. https://www.thedailystar.net/frontpage/news/dhaka-mawa-bhanga-expressway-toll-collection-likely-start-july-2040869.

(i) Of the 66 planned road projects in the master plan, 30-plus projects are within or connect to a sizable city or a region in close proximity to the proposed industrial parks.
(ii) Illustrative examples of BIMSTEC projects that can explore LVC are:
  (a) Tax Increment Financing for projects with significant upside, such as the Guwahati and Jorabat bypass (India) and the Bago National Highway (NH) 1 bypass (Myanmar).
  (b) Selling transferable development rights in city projects, such as the elevated expressway to Chennai port (India).
  (c) Relaxing floor space index[8] and increasing the stamp duty for projects connecting two key parts of a city, like the Dhaka–Ashulia elevated expressway (Bangladesh).

Table 7: Actions for Increasing Alternative Revenue Sources

#	Interventions	Ownership
1	Conduct knowledge workshops with the Bay of Bengal Initiative for Multi-Sectoral Technical and Economic Cooperation (BIMSTEC) program for the project authorities of member countries on alternative revenue sources. Prepare guidelines on the criteria for including alternative revenue sources in projects, and the structure and process for transferring revenue generated from alternative sources to a fund.	BIMSTEC member countries
2	Monetize existing assets, for instance by levying user charges in BIMSTEC master plan operational projects. Fourteen master plan projects worth $2.5 billion are operational and can be explored for asset monetization. Sixty-eight master plan projects worth $70.2 billion are under construction and can also be explored for asset monetization once operational. Ring-fence revenue from asset monetization for developing master plan projects.	BIMSTEC Member Countries

Source: Study team analysis.

Institutional Structure and Enablers to Finance Regional Transport Infrastructure Projects

In addition to establishing a funding mechanism for projects, an enabling environment will be needed to improve their bankability. Regional transport infrastructure projects face various transnational factors that make them more complex to implement and underwrite than domestic ones. For example, regional infrastructure projects often have—or are perceived to have—a political component that may require additional institutional arrangements. Decisions on a project's design, financing, construction, and operations need to be coordinated across sovereign governments and their respective agencies—and any differences in operational modalities need to be bridged. Added to this are the additional challenges stemming from the technical complexities of a project.

The following interventions are proposed to create a robust enabling environment for regional infrastructure projects:

Implement the master plan. Member countries should prioritize master plan projects that are economically beneficial for more than one country. To this end, BIMSTEC should set up a database of the project planning

[8] Floor Space Index (FSI), also known as Floor Area Ratio (FAR), is a parameter used in urban planning to determine the permissible construction density on a plot of land. It represents the ratio of the total built-up area allowed on a plot to the area of the plot itself.

information and related data in each member country—e.g., on development time frames and network characteristics, such as traffic and the condition of infrastructure of regional significance—that are included in national development plans. The GMS program has an online database of project-related data, including the current status of projects, a projects' web map, and geodata. The data are open to GMS member governments and other stakeholders.

Standardize coordination and decision-making processes. Other regional groupings do this to reduce construction-stage risks. This will also ensure that regional projects are implemented in a coordinated and timely manner by promoting governance and convening power in these institutions. BIMSTEC's compares regional institutions with those of other regional groupings. Table 8 shows the interventions that will be needed to create a robust institutional structure for the BIMSTEC region.

Table 8: Interventions for a Robust Institutional Structure

#	Interventions	Ownership
1	Bay of Bengal Initiative for Multi-Sectoral Technical and Economic Cooperation (BIMSTEC) countries implement the BIMSTEC Master Plan for Transport Connectivity projects and include them in national development plans	BIMSTEC member countries
2	BIMSTEC could implement the following measures to strengthen institutional structures: • Adopt a regional charter or treaty clearly delineating the roles and responsibilities of various bodies • Create a well-defined and documented decision-making process • Set up a national interministerial committee coordinating activities in each country • Hold regular meetings of sector-specific working groups of line agency officials • Hold regular meetings of heads of government for reviewing progress and providing strategic direction • Set up institutional arrangements to strengthen the operational plans of transport projects • Strengthen institutional arrangements at the project level for better implementation Adopting these measures would improve coordination among BIMSTEC member countries to promote the timely execution of projects.	BIMSTEC Secretariat

Source: Study team analysis.

Enabling regulatory environments and harmonizing technical standards. Both are imperative for attracting private developers to regional projects. BIMSTEC should encourage member states to create enabling transnational regulatory environments, prepare standard contractual agreements, and harmonize technical standards. This approach has been pursued in various initiatives by other regional groupings, e.g., the GMS's cross-border trade agreement and ASEAN transport facilitation agreements (Table 9).

Table 9: Interventions to Enable Regulatory Environments

#	Interventions	Ownership
1	The Bay of Bengal Initiative for Multi-Sectoral Technical and Economic Cooperation (BIMSTEC) should encourage member states to create enabling transnational regulatory environments, prepare standard contractual agreements, and harmonize technical standards.	Asian Development Bank/BIMSTEC Secretariat

continued on next page

Table 9 *continued*

#	Interventions	Ownership
	Set up an institutional structure to ratify mutual agreements, such as the Agreement for the Use of Chattogram and Mongla Ports, the Protocol on Inland Water Transit and Trade, the Agreement on Coastal Shipping, and the Motor Vehicles Agreement between Bangladesh, Bhutan, India, and Nepal, addressing all key nonphysical bottlenecks, including transnational regulatory frameworks and the harmonization of technical standards for efficient cross-border movements. Develop a standardized shadow cost model to determine value for money. An analysis of the operational regional projects could also help refine life-cycle cost assessments.	Asian Development Bank/BIMSTEC Secretariat
2	Set tariffs following the General Agreement on Tariffs and Trade principles. Countries need to ensure that tariffs charged for transit cargo are similar to their own export-import cargo, and that the tariffs charged for additional services are reasonable.	BIMSTEC member countries

Source: Study team analysis.

Financing

BIMSTEC regional projects often lack commercial viability and financing options and therefore depend on government budgetary support for funding. Regional projects often compete with other budgetary demands from wholly domestic infrastructure projects, with the latter often given a higher priority by local governments leading to delays in funding and hence implementation. For example, the construction of the Belahiya–Butwal highway, a key trade highway between Nepal and India has been delayed for 10 years because of budget constraints.

As a step to improve the implementation of regional projects, BIMSTEC is planning to develop a BIMSTEC Development Fund (BDF) with a focus toward development of cross-border transport infrastructure. Presently, the planned concept of the fund is in line with ASEAN's infrastructure fund and the SAARC development fund, and will operate with a planned initial capital infusion by the member states followed by voluntary contributions from the member states.

The regional projects in the pipeline of the BIMSTEC Transport Connectivity Master Plan can be categorized into three types of projects from a commercial viability perspective:

(i) **Category I:** Projects with significant regional, economic, or social benefit but limited commercial viability where private sector financing may not be feasible;
(ii) **Category II:** Projects that require some degree of support in terms of low cost of financing sources in order to crowd in private sector financing. These may also include projects where certain trunk infrastructure may need to be supported through public/concessional sources in order to attract private investments in rest of project components; and
(iii) **Category III:** Projects with standalone commercial viability and ability to attract private sector financing.

Identifying financing mechanisms for projects in categories I & II would be critical for successful implementation of projects in the transport master plan. With this in view, two fund options can be explored with focus on specific project categories. Further, given that BIMSTEC leadership is already exploring the creation of the BDF, these two fund options can be evaluated to come under a broader mandate. The proposed financing mechanisms for implementation of these three regional project categories is shown in Table 10.

Table 10: Regional Transport Infrastructure Financing Framework

<table>
<tr><th>Regional Project Category</th><th>Category I
Projects with significant regional, economic, or social benefit but limited commercial viability where private sector financing may not be feasible for project/ project components</th><th>Category II
Projects that require some degree of support in terms of low cost of financing sources in order to crowd in private sector financing</th><th>Category III
Projects with standalone commercial viability to attract private sector financing</th></tr>
<tr><td>Proposed Fund</td><td>Fund A</td><td>Fund B</td><td rowspan="5">Improve overall access to capital in BIMSTEC countries
• Standardize fund-raising mechanisms
• Facilitate the repatriation of funds to provide stability to the financial system and lower exchange rate risk
• Synchronize taxation rules to boost infrastructure investments</td></tr>
<tr><td>Key Objective</td><td>Support regional projects with limited commercial viability but significant social and economic benefits</td><td>Support with long term capital and crowd in of commercial lending for regional projects</td></tr>
<tr><td>Source of Capital</td><td>Grants by respective government</td><td>• Equity of BIMSTEC Development Fund (DBF)
• Debt raised through capital markets
• Contribution from sovereign countries</td></tr>
<tr><td>Salient Features</td><td>• Ownership: Management services provided by DBF
• Returns: No return expectation</td><td>• Ownership: Multilateral development bank majority ownership, rest by countries, bilateral/multilateral guarantees, low-cost currency swaps
• Returns: Market based (concessional compared to commercial lending)
• Credit rating/cost of funding superior to participating countries
• Local currency trade and regional financial market</td></tr>
<tr><td>Responsibilities</td><td>• Sinking fund: Grants to support commercially unviable projects (similar to viability gap funding in function but managed by a professional manager for better coordination for cross-border projects)
• Assistance for project preparation and capacity building</td><td>• Provide low-cost and long-term capital to attract private sector funding
• Add-ons like guarantee products tailor-made for master plan projects
• Syndication and co-lending services: Lead financial institution leverages cofinancing from commercial banks
• Project appraisal on behalf of consortium banks
• Develops guidelines on the projects to be evaluated</td></tr>
<tr><td></td><td colspan="3">BIMSTEC Development Fund acts as the fund manager and the overarching financing institution under a broader mandate</td></tr>
</table>

Source: Study team analysis.

These identified interventions and necessary steps to achieve implementation of regional connectivity projects in the financing framework are discussed in this section.

Developing Fund A for Category I Projects

As discussed, regional projects are often underprioritized over domestic infrastructure projects by local governments leading to delays in funding and implementation. Fund A would support regional projects with limited commercial viability but significant social and economic benefits.

The focus of this fund would be to have contributory grant corpus by each government for identified cross-border projects with management services provided by BDF similar to the South Asian Association for Regional Cooperation (SAARC) Development Fund (SDF) detailed in Box 3.1. This would also strengthen BIMSTEC's influence over the approval, time frames, and specifications of projects as it would be involved in administering the fund.

Box 3.1: South Asian Association for Regional Cooperation Development Fund

The South Asian Association for Regional Cooperation (SAARC) Development Fund (SDF) Secretariat was established and inaugurated in 2010 by heads of states/governments during the 16th SAARC Summit held in Thimphu, Bhutan. The fund serves as the umbrella financial institution for SAARC projects and programs that are in fulfilment of the objectives of the SAARC Charter. It aims to contribute towards regional cooperation and integration through project collaboration.

The SDF has three funding windows: **social, economic, and infrastructure.**

The Social Window primarily funds projects on poverty alleviation; social development focusing on education; health; human resources development; support to vulnerable/disadvantaged segments of society; funding needs of communities; micro-enterprises; and rural infrastructure development.

The Economic Window extends funding to non-infrastructural projects related to trade and industrial development, agriculture, services, science and technology, and other non-infrastructure areas. Under the Economic Window, the SDF proposes funding micro, small, and medium enterprises programs in SAARC member states. Approval of an SDF scheme to do this was approved at the 30th SDF Board meeting on December 2018.

The Infrastructure Window is primarily utilized to fund projects in areas such as energy, power, transportation, telecommunications, environment, tourism, and other infrastructure areas.

Currently, the SDF is involved with over 95 Board-approved projects across SAARC member states. There are 95 projects (under 15 areas) approved under the Social Window with a total fund commitment of US$91.58 million. Of this, over US$53 million have already been disbursed. Under the Economic and Infrastructure windows, the fund commitment is US$43 million, of which US$13 million has been disbursed to finance for ATR aircraft for Drukair Corporation, Bhutan. The cumulative fund committed for projects under the three funding windows is around US$134.58 million.

In terms of promoting commercial financing, the SDF has established and strengthened its relationship with partners to co-finance its cross-border regional projects. The SDF has developed a solid working relationship with various multinational development banks, international organizations, financial institutions, regional banks, micro, small, and medium-sized enterprises banks, chambers of commerce and industries, and trade and investment promotion agencies.

Source: SAARC Development Fund (SDF). https://www.sdfsec.org/about-sdf.

Globally, regional financing institutions have set up similar funds for regional projects (Appendix 5 on the Connecting Europe Facility). There are two key proposed functions of Fund A:

(i) The fund could act as a sinking fund to provide grants to commercially unviable projects or project components. This could help make projects/project components bankable, especially once construction activities and risks are addressed. Financing institutions in most BIMSTEC countries are underdeveloped, and it will take time to deepen finance sectors through reforms, as discussed later in this section. An alternative option to finance such regional projects is for governments to shoulder construction risks by agreements in advance. Governments can also consider monetizing project assets once projects are operational and develop additional trade volume. The capital from monetizing assets could then be pooled back into the regional transport fund by governments, and these funds could be used to develop and finance more regional projects downstream.

(ii) The fund could assist in project preparation and capacity building through various mechanisms. This could be achieved by the following interventions:
   (a) Setting up a dedicated fund to provide grants to support project preparation and capacity-building activities, like the African Development Bank's Middle Income Country Technical Assistance Fund and the New Development Fund's Project Preparation Fund.
   (b) Create dedicated programs and provide hands-on support during different project phases, like the EIB's Joint Assistance to Support Projects in European regions and the African Development Bank's African Legal Support Facility.

Table 11: Interventions to Set Up Fund A

Intervention	Ownership
Countries in the Bay of Bengal Initiative for Multi-Sectoral Technical and Economic Cooperation (BIMSTEC) forge an agreement to set up a regional connectivity funding corpus or fund to be managed by a trustee called the BIMSTEC Development Fund (BDF). Ring-fence the funding requirement of regional projects and pool funds in the regional fund. Capital for the regional fund could be provided by governments through advance commitments; capital contributions could also be sought from developed countries, such as Japan and Singapore. Capital drawn for funding regional projects should be disbursed using well-defined procedures. For example, Connecting Europe Facility grants are awarded through competitive calls for project proposals launched by the European Commission on the basis of Annual and Multi-Annual Work Programmes in which specific objectives, priorities, and budgets are defined. For each call, the commission assesses each proposal according to the defined award criteria (relevance, maturity, impact, and quality) and proposes the projects to be supported and the amount of funding to be allocated to each project.	BIMSTEC Secretariat / BIMSTEC Development Fund (BDF) and member countries

Source: Study team analysis.

Developing Fund B for Category II Projects

For the second category of projects, commercial financing sources that can provide low-cost and long-tenure capital need to be explored. While country-specific financial sector reforms and capital market development will be vital for improving the materiality of existing financial institutions, a dedicated fund to focus on BIMSTEC regional transport projects can be evaluated under the BDF with the core objective of having a credit rating or cost of funding superior to individual participating countries.

This could be explored through various mechanisms like multilateral institutions having majority ownership (51% or above) to enhance the sovereign credit ratings, provision of multilateral/bilateral guarantees, and establishment of low-cost currency swaps through country-level partnerships with other nations who may have key interest in development of strong BIMSTEC trade and the region becoming an integrated part of global value chains. Source of initial capital for such a fund could include equity of BDF, debt raised through public or private markets, and/or contributions from sovereign countries, like pension fund contributions done in Brazil's Banco Nacional de Desenvolvimento Econômico e Social.

This BDF fund would focus on transport and other infrastructure projects that improve transport connectivity in the BIMSTEC region, with an ultimate objective of providing low-cost and long-term capital and to attract private sector funding. The core functions of the proposed fund would include:

(i) **Providing low-cost capital.** Mechanisms described above could help ensure a strong credit rating for this fund. Once the fund has been set up, its credit rating will depend both on its shareholder ownership and its business performance. It would have to do risk assessments and select projects that generate cash flows in the long run to service debt. Doing this will enable the proposed fund to establish a credible track record for long-term financial sustainability. A high credit rating would enable it to raise low-cost capital from the international market.

    The EIB is rated AAA by Standard and Poor's Global Ratings (S&P) and Fitch Ratings, the New Development Bank is rated AA+ by S&P and Fitch, and the European Bank for Reconstruction and Development is rated AAA by S&P and Fitch—high ratings because of their promoter profiles, compliance to standard evaluation procedures, and their development of risk-mitigation instruments, among other factors. All of this has enabled these regional development funds to raise capital at a lower cost than would have been available in their regions.

(ii) **Attracting private investors.** The high credibility of regional financing institutions is an incentive to private financing institutions to participate in regional projects. The EIB, for example, plays a major role in attracting private capital in regional projects.

(iii) **Private sector windows.** ADB and other development institutions have private sector windows that have provisions for commercial financing. This financing corpus can also be used for regional projects.

(iv) **Project appraisals and evaluation.** These is needed for project preparation, coordination, and monitoring for the timely implementation of projects. Support is also needed for building the capacity of project authorities.

Further, the proposed fund can undertake development of non-fund-based functions as it evolves to increase private sector participation including:

(i) **Syndication and co-lending services:** The leading financing institution can leverage cofinancing from other financial institutions and arrange syndicated loans for regional projects similar to Development Bank of Japan's Role as Lead Arranger in a Loan Syndication detailed in Box 3.2.

Box 3.2: Development Bank of Japan's Role as Lead Arranger in a Loan Syndication

The DBJ and Japan Wind entered into a cooperation in 2016 as part of Japan's first capital-recycling model to expand the use of wind power. This approach promoted the utilization of private finance for the wind power project.

For DBJ, promoting a capital-recycling program throughout the renewable energy field was an important means of giving financial support to proprietors wanting to speed up investment and reduce project costs.

DBJ works alongside other financial institutions to arrange syndicated loans for infrastructure projects, including renewable energy, road and airport concessions. It promotes the construction stage by providing loans to projects.

Japan Bank for International Cooperation provides guarantees against risks, such as currency conversion, transfer, and country risks. This approach enables Japanese private financial institutions to provide medium- to long-term financing for developing economies, supporting the efforts of these economies to attract private capital, and help private companies expanding their international business.

Source: Asia-Pacific Economic Cooperation/Organisation for Economic Co-operation and Development. 2019. *Financing Infrastructure in APEC Economies: APEC/OECD Report on Selected Effective Approaches*. Paris.

(ii) **Guarantee products** of MDBs and other financing institutions could be used to leverage private capital into infrastructure projects. The following are key considerations:
   (a) Ensure the coverage of guarantee products to commercial lenders financing regional projects (nonrecourse basis) and involve all participating governments.
   (b) Explore development of guarantee products that are calibrated to master plan projects (e.g., the Loan Guarantee Instrument for Trans-European Networks Transport of the EIB ensures coverage of Trans-European Networks Transport planned connectivity projects).
   (c) Rationalize guarantee commission by exploring funding from concessional ordinary capital resources for regional projects. Pooled guarantee corpus to optimize the guarantee commission rate for BIMSTEC.
   (d) Adequate marketing to communicate the benefits of guarantee products (e.g., flexibility and leveraging private capital) over traditional loans to governments and project authorities.
   (e) Optimal coverage (i.e., a percentage of the project cost) ensuring comfort to private lenders and avoiding moral hazard.
   (f) Project authorities will need to assess the incremental cost of one or more guarantees in a project and add this to the project cost to provide a fuller picture of commercial viability. The cost of a guarantee is typically 1.0%–1.2% of the total project cost .

(iii) **Develop guidelines:** The BDF would need to identify and define the type of projects that will be evaluated, project review mechanisms, and the targets to be achieved and timelines for disbursement to provide comfort to lenders.

In addition, Fund B could be complemented by setting up Fund A, as they could take on both construction-stage risk and the financing of bankable projects. Globally, regional financing institutions are not a burden on government budgets other than for their initial seed funding. Historically, the initial capital contribution for similar funds come from countries in the institution's region. Once the proposed fund is operational and has proved its credibility in the market, its source of funding mainly comes from borrowings in the capital market and it has a lesser reliance on shareholder funds.

It should be noted that, for the proposed fund to be able to generate cash flow, a mechanism should be in place that converts the economic value of projects into financial value in the form of user charges and/or tax payments. The fund would then be able to service its debt from these projects. Because user-fee charging has been little used in BIMSTEC regional connectivity projects, levying direct or indirect user fees will need to be considered for future financially viable transport infrastructure projects.

Table 12 illustrates some of the user-fees mechanisms used in three PPP transport infrastructure projects financed by similar regional infrastructure funds. It should be noted that not all regional projects will become commercially viable through user charges because these charges are limited by the ability of users to pay and costs to trade. Because of this, government support may still be needed depending on a project's financial and economic viability.

Table 12: Public–Private Partnership Projects Financed by Regional Financing Institutions

Project	Region	Financing	Structure
Beiras Litoral and Alta Shadow Toll Road (€1.1 billion)	Europe	Debt: European Investment Bank loan and other private investors	Project was implemented via the public–private partnership design–build–finance–operate mode Adopted shadow toll regime to reduce uncertainty from traffic forecasts under a fully tolled (user pay) regime
N4 toll road ($660 million)	Africa (South Africa and Mozambique)	Debt: Development Bank of South Africa and four commercial banks Equity: Sponsors The Governments of South Africa and Mozambique provided joint and severable guarantees of the project debt	Project implemented via public–private partnership build–operate–transfer–toll mode Tolls collected used to repay debt holders
M5 toll motorway (€853 million)	Europe	Debt: European Reconstruction and Development Bank and commercial banks Equity: Sponsors	Project was initially implemented via the public–private partnership build–operate–transfer–toll mode Because traffic volumes were below expectation, the concessionaire requested support from the revenue shortfall mechanism in the agreement to operate the motorway. This allowed the concessionaire to draw support from the government for several years and repay senior lenders Motorway now financed through availability payments, independent of traffic flows, thus eliminating user risks of the operator

Source: Study team analysis.

In addition, the involvement of a government and/or MDB-backed entity in any regional development fund is seen as a quality stamp that will help the project attract additional investors. Figure 28 shows some of the ways that the proposed Fund B can be involved in projects.

Figure 28: Financial Products Offered by Regional Development Finance Institutions

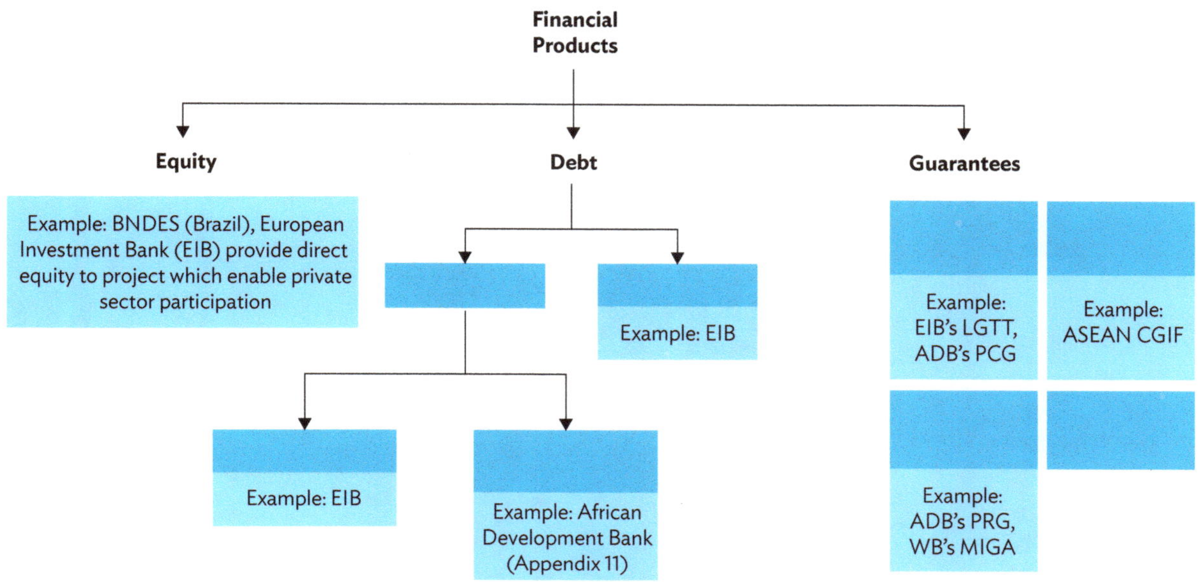

ADB = Asian Development Bank, ASEAN = Association of Southeast Asian Nations, BNDES = Banco Nacional de Desenvolvimento Econômico e Social (National Bank for Economic and Social Development), CGIF = credit guarantee and investment facility, EIB = European Investment Bank, FX = foreign exchange, LGTT = loan guarantee instrument for TEN-T projects, MIGA = Multilateral Investment Guarantee Agency, PCG = partial credit guarantee, PRG = political risk guarantee.

Source: Study team analysis.

With that said, there are concerns in setting up such a fund under BDF, including the following:

(i) The negotiations, planning, and implementation of the proposed Fund B could be lengthy and possibly less cost effective than using existing institutions. The more detailed concerns on this point are:
  (a) It may take some time for multiple members to agree on the operational characteristics of the proposed fund.
  (b) Operating costs have exceeded operating income in the past for some of the regional financing institutions (e.g., ADB's operating ratio was 111.66% in 2015)—so care needs to be taken to ensure the operating costs of the proposed fund are under control.
  (c) The initial set-up costs are likely to be significant.
  (d) Multilateral and bilateral banks will need to agree to take majority ownership of Fund B to balance out the "negative" impact of shareholders with lower or no sovereign credit ratings, such as Bangladesh, Bhutan, and Nepal. These institutions will all have a higher credit rating—e.g., ADB is rated AAA by Moody's Investors Service.

(ii) The proposed fund would need to establish a credible track record to ensure trust and confidence among its members and their private sectors. It may take time for this to happen and to develop a loan portfolio that generates the income needed to support the fund's operations.

Box 3.3: Indonesia Infrastructure Finance

Indonesia Infrastructure Finance (IIF) offers fund based, non-fund-based, and fee-based services, including syndication and financial advisory services, in order to meet the long-term financing needs of infrastructure projects in Indonesia. IIF ensures that its business strategy complements existing players and fills the gap of financing needs in the market.

Financing Products Offered by Indonesia Infrastructure Finance Across Project Stages

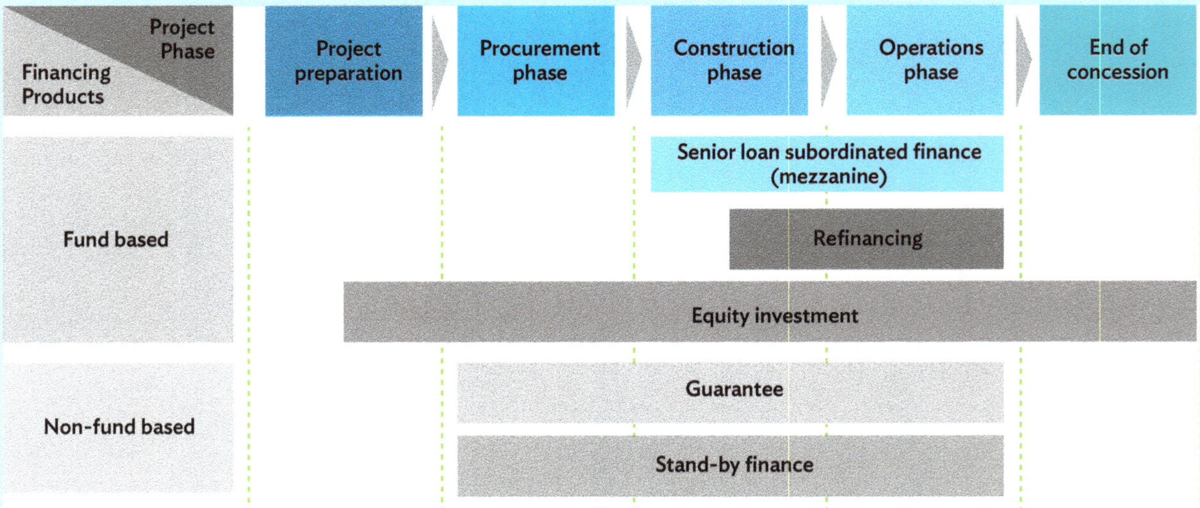

As shown above, the financing products offered by the IIF include long-term products spanning the construction and operations phase of an infrastructure project. These investments are primarily aimed at increasing viability of the infrastructure projects and attracting private sector participation.

Source: Indonesia Infrastructure Finance (IIF). https://iif.co.id/en/about-us/overview/.

The objectives and project selection criteria for Fund B need to be clearly defined so as not to crowd-out the commercial finance available for financially viable transport infrastructure projects (Table 13).

Improve Access to Capital in the BIMSTEC Region

On the demand side, 134 projects worth about $90 billion in the master plan had not achieved financial closure as of March 2020 (Appendix 20). BIMSTEC countries also have their own national infrastructure development plans, which should be added to the total investment requirement of the BIMSTEC region. Supply will mainly come from regional savings and international capital. Gross savings in the BIMSTEC region in 2018 totaled $1.2 trillion, which, if channeled to financing institutions, could support transport infrastructure financing.

In some BIMSTEC countries, including Bhutan, Myanmar, and Nepal, a major portion of savings go into physical assets, such as real estate and gold. Bank deposits form a moderate share of total savings, but pension and insurance funds have a low corpus in these countries. Apart from savings, other sources of capital include international capital and foreign exchange reserves. The absence of sovereign credit ratings and limited investor-centric regulations may be factors for not attracting foreign investors in some BIMSTEC countries, including Bhutan, Myanmar, and Nepal.

Table 13: Interventions Needed to Set Up the Fund B for Category II Projects

#	Interventions	Ownership
1	Fund B under the BIMSTEC Development Fund (BDF) needs the following: • **Mandate.** Should have a regional outlook, participation, and coordination, among other things, be able to evaluate the impact of cross-border projects. • **Convening power.** All BIMSTEC member countries should be able to provide exemptions for infrastructure investments (e.g., the Asian Development Bank gets tax exemption in India). • **Source of capital.** Initial seed capital to be provided by the governments of BIMSTEC members and multilateral development banks. The government guarantee fee should be waived to enable capital sourcing. • **Superior credit rating.** Multilateral agencies (an AAA-rated agency, such as ADB as per Fitch Ratings) could take majority ownership (51% or above) for piercing the ceilings of sovereign ratings of BIMSTEC countries so they can access low-cost, long-term capital from the market. Other options would include provision of multilateral/bilateral guarantees and establishment of low-cost currency swaps. • **Credible track record.** This needs to be established for long-term financial sustainability. To this end, BDF would need to undertake prudent risk assessments and select projects that generate cash flows in the long run to service debt. • **Policy.** Policy alignment is needed for revenue streams of operational projects to flow to the proposed fund. Policy should prioritize the financing of regional connectivity projects requiring some degree of support in terms of low cost of financing sources in order to crowd in private sector financing. Project appraisals need to be done on behalf of a consortium of lenders when requested by project proponents. • **Guidelines.** These need to identify what type of projects will be evaluated, project review mechanisms, the targets to be achieved, and timelines for disbursement.	BIMSTEC Secretariat/ BDF
2	The guarantee products of multilateral development banks and other financing institutions could be used to leverage private capital into infrastructure projects. The following are key considerations: • Ensure the coverage of guarantee products to commercial lenders financing regional projects (nonrecourse basis) and involve all participating governments. • Develop guarantee products that are calibrated to master plan projects (e.g., the Loan Guarantee Instrument for Trans-European Networks Transport of the European Investment Bank ensures coverage of planned connectivity projects). • Rationalize guarantee commission by exploring funding from concessional ordinary capital resources for regional projects. Pool guarantee corpus to optimize the guarantee commission rate for BIMSTEC. • Adequate marketing to communicate the benefits of guarantee products (e.g., flexibility and leveraging private capital) over traditional loans to governments and project authorities. • Optimal coverage (i.e., a percentage of the project cost) ensuring comfort to private lenders and avoiding moral hazard. • Project authorities will need to assess the incremental cost of one or more guarantees in a project and add this to the project cost to provide a fuller picture of commercial viability. The cost of a guarantee is typically 1.0%–1.2% of the total project cost.[a]	BIMSTEC Secretariat/ BDF

[a] Government of India, Ministry of Finance. Memorandum.

Source: Study team analysis.

India and Thailand are the most developed financial markets in the BIMSTEC region. India's savings rate is about 30% of GDP, which compares well with other countries with a similar level of economic development. India has financing intermediaries to channel savings—50% of savings in financial assets are with banks and about 25% with insurance and pension funds. Alternative and external commercial borrowing regulations allow for the easy inflow and outflow of infrastructure capital (Figure 29).

Figure 29: Investment Demand and Supply of Capital

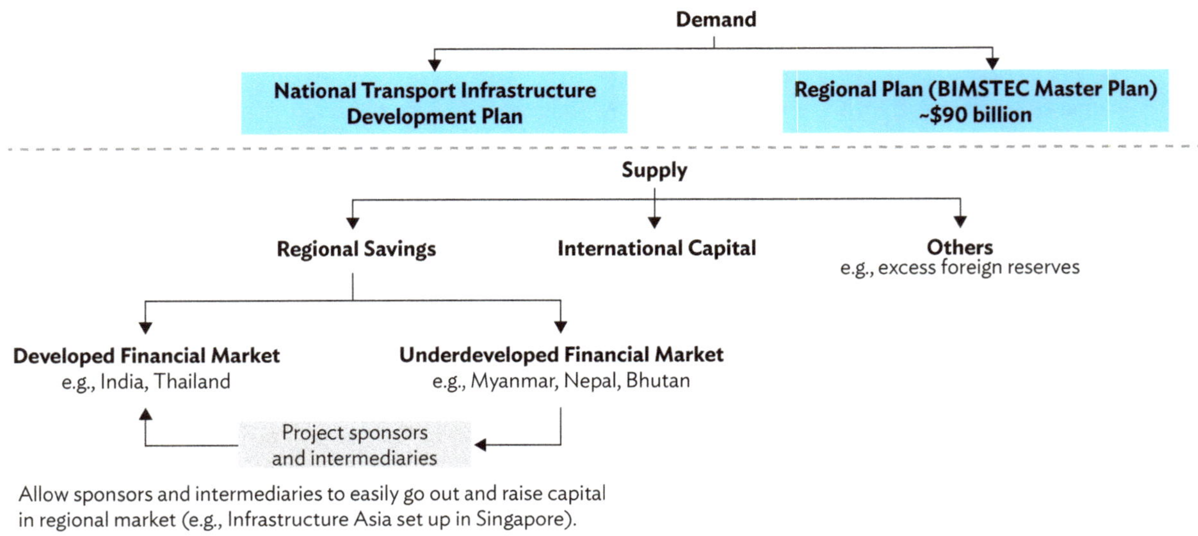

BIMSTEC = Bay of Bengal Initiative for Multi-Sectoral Technical and Economic Cooperation.

Note: Total investment requirement for transport infrastructure at the national level for all BIMSTEC member countries. Projects in national development plans may overlap with the BIMSTEC master plan.

Sources: BIMSTEC Master Plan for Transport Connectivity; study team analysis.

As Figure 29 shows, the nascent financial markets in Bhutan, Myanmar, and Nepal prevents the channeling of regional savings to infrastructure projects, including transport infrastructure. Establishing a regional financing hub in the BIMSTEC region, preferably in an already developed financial market center, would address this challenge (Appendix 5 has a case study on Singapore's Infrastructure Asia Finance Hub). Box 3.5 shows proposed interventions to develop a regional financing hub for the BIMSTEC countries while Table 14 shows how to develop financing institutions in the construction stage, and Table 15 shows how to develop them in the operation stage.

Among major cities in the BIMSTEC region, Mumbai could fill this role. The city is already the financial capital of the region's largest economy. Gujarat's International Financial Services Centre at GIFT (Box 3.4) could also be explored as an option given the development plans for the state. Borrowers from BIMSTEC countries could issue bonds in the hub capital market and attract institutional funds looking for long-term investments. India is already a top destination for foreign portfolio and institutional investors due to its developed primary and secondary markets. As a step in this direction, India enacted the National Bank for Financing Infrastructure and Development bill in 2021 for setting up a national infrastructure financing institution. In fiscal year 2021 (ended 31 March of that year), foreign portfolio investments in India totaled ₹25 million. Adopting the following actions would help develop a financing hub for the BIMSTEC region:

(i) **Standardized fundraising mechanism.** The governments of BIMSTEC region could collaborate on developing a fundraising mechanism through the regional hub and prepare standardized documents. The mechanism should, among other things, include the roles and responsibilities of governments and a mechanism to repatriate the funds. Standardizing this could expedite the fundraising process for project developers.

(ii) **Repatriation of funds.** This means pegging of currencies which results in lower exchange rate risk. The Nepalese rupee's peg to the Indian rupee provides stability to the financial system, and similar pegs could be adopted for the currencies of other BIMSTEC countries.

(iii) **Taxation.** The tax regime on infrastructure investments is an important factor for private participation. India has a comprehensive Double Tax Avoidance Agreement with BIMSTEC countries. To boost infrastructure investments in the BIMSTEC region, taxes on these projects could be reduced.

Box 3.4: International Financial Services Centre at Multi Services Special Economic Zone in Gujarat

The Government of India operationalized the International Financial Services Centre at Gujarat International Finance Tec-City (GIFT) Multi Services Special Economic Zone (SEZ) in April 2015. The Union Budget 2016 provided a competitive tax regime for the center, which has emerged as a hub for international financial services activities.

The Ministry of Finance effectively provided a new initiative for undertaking international financial services business in India. Regulators, namely, the Reserve Bank of India, Securities & Exchange Board of India, and the Insurance Regulatory & Development Authority of India, issued regulations allowing Indian and foreign institutions to open their offices at the center, which aspires to become India's gateway for inbound and outbound international financial services.

Sources: GIFT SEZ. https://giftsez.com/; International Financial Services Centre Authority. https://www.ifsca.gov.in/.

Box 3.5: Intervention to Develop a Regional Financing Hub for BIMSTEC Countries

Interventions	Ownership
Setting up a regional financial hub for the Bay of Bengal Initiative for Multi-Sectoral Technical and Economic Cooperation (BIMSTEC) that is similar to Singapore's Infrastructure Asia. This intervention would require: • Provisions for raising finance in the hub market for investments in BIMSTEC national and regional projects (e.g., bonds) with suitable taxation and repatriation norms. • For the repatriation of funds, currencies could be pegged, resulting in lower exchange rate risk; the Nepalese rupee and the Bhutanese ngultrum could be pegged to the Indian rupee. • To boost infrastructure investments in the BIMSTEC region, taxes on projects funded through a standardized fundraising mechanism can be reduced. • Additional support for early project scoping, best-practice sharing, deal brokering, and harnessing the existing financial infrastructure ecosystem of advanced member countries. • Mumbai and Gujarat could be a regional financial hub for BIMSTEC given the well-developed infrastructure of both cities. • Borrowers in BIMSTEC countries could issues bonds in hub capital market to attract institutional funds looking for long-term investments.	BIMSTEC Secretariat and regulators in BIMSTEC member countries

Source: Study team analysis.

Table 14: Developing Construction-Stage Financing Institutions

Construction- Stage Financial Institutions	Supply-Side Challenges	Interventions
Bangladesh		
NBFIs (e.g., IDCOL, BIFFL): Limited institutions in infrastructure sector	Cap on lending rates (may prevent NBFIs from taking on construction risks) Limited capital for investment in transport infrastructure Only collateralized-based lending	Ease of lending restrictions for infrastructure projects Enabling regulation to raise long-term sources of capital for financing infrastructure projects (e.g., commercial banks in India are allowed to raise bonds specially for infrastructure financing)
Commercial banks (e.g., City Bank): Limited experience in transport infrastructure	Asset–liability mismatch Cap on lending rates (may prevent banks taking on construction risks) Limited project appraisal capabilities (collateral-based lending to industry and retail sector)	Developing regulations for setting up NBFIs by private players (e.g., NBFI–IFC regulations in India) Avenues for refinancing (e.g., bridge-to-bond financing, take-out financing, secondary loan market) Providing capacity-building support for project financing
Bhutan		
Commercial banks: Limited experience in transport infrastructure No infrastructure-focused NBFIs	Asset–liability mismatch Limited project appraisal capability (collateral-based lending) No regulation for infrastructure-focused NBFIs	Enabling regulation to raise long-term sources of capital for financing infrastructure projects (e.g., commercial banks in India are allowed to raise bonds specially for infrastructure financing) Developing regulations for setting up NBFIs by private players (e.g., NBFI–IFC regulations in India) Avenues for refinancing (e.g., bridge-to-bond financing, take-out financing, secondary loan market) Capacity building for project financing
India		
Commercial banks (e.g., State Bank of India): Major private sector lender in transport infrastructure	Asset–liability mismatch No active secondary market for refinancing	Avenues for refinancing (e.g., bridge-to-bond financing, take-out financing, secondary loan market) Institutionalizing secondary market for loans by creating a centralized platform for auctions and sales of loan assets, standardizing documents and market practices Ensure enablers to facilitate capital—raising through bonds (e.g., credit rating-enhancement instruments to raise the ratings of issuers and facilitate capital-raising through bonds) Capacity building for NBFIs for project financing
NBFIs (e.g., IIFCL): Low exposure to transport infrastructure	Asset–liability mismatch for infrastructure-focused NBFIs (excluding government-owned, power sector-focused NBFIs) Limited project appraisal capability IIFCL: Lending cap of 20% of total project cost and does not have provision to take lead role in project due diligence and financing	

continued on next page

Table 14 *continued*

Construction- Stage Financial Institutions	Supply-Side Challenges	Interventions
Myanmar		
Commercial banks: Very limited experience in infrastructure No infrastructure-focused NBFIs	Asset–liability mismatch Low financial inclusion Cap on lending rates (may prevent banks taking on construction risks) Limited project appraisal capabilities (collateral lending) No regulation for infrastructure-focused NBFIs	Enabling regulation to raise long-term sources of capital for financing infrastructure projects (e.g., commercial banks in India are allowed to raise bonds specially for infrastructure financing) Developing regulations for setting up NBFIs by private players (e.g., NBFI–IFC regulations in India) Avenues for refinancing (e.g., bridge-to-bond financing, take-out financing, secondary loan market) Step up financial inclusion drive Ease of lending restrictions for infrastructure projects Capacity building for project financing
Nepal		
NBFIs (NIFRA): Only one infrastructure-focused NBFI at initial stage of development	Limited bankable projects	Technical assistance for project preparation (e.g., OPPP and ADB have expressed interest in helping to introduce PPP contracts for O&M of airport terminals in Nepal) Enabling regulation to raise long-term sources of capital for financing infrastructure projects (e.g., commercial banks in India are allowed to raise bonds specially for infrastructure financing) Developing regulations for setting up NBFIs by private players (e.g., NBFI–IFC regulations in India) Avenues for refinancing (e.g., bridge-to-bond financing, take-out financing, secondary loan market) Capacity building for project financing for commercial banks
Commercial banks (e.g., Nepal Rastra Bank): Limited experience in transport infrastructure	Asset–liability mismatch Limited project appraisal capabilities (collateral lending)	
Sri Lanka		
Commercial banks (e.g., Commercial Bank of Ceylon)	Asset–liability mismatch Cap on lending rates	Enabling regulation to raise long-term sources of capital for financing infrastructure projects (e.g., commercial banks in India are allowed to raise bonds specially for infrastructure financing) Developing regulations for setting up NBFIs by private players (e.g., NBFI–IFC regulations in India) Avenues for refinancing (e.g., bridge-to-bond financing, take-out financing, secondary loan market) Ease of lending restrictions for infrastructure projects Capacity building for project financing
NBFIs: Very limited experience in infrastructure sector	Cap on lending rates Prefer other sectors	

continued on next page

Table 14 *continued*

Construction- Stage Financial Institutions	Supply-Side Challenges	Interventions
Thailand		
Commercial banks (e.g., Bangkok Bank, Kasikorn Bank, Krung Thai Bank)	Decreasing deposit tenure leading to increase in asset–liability mismatch	Avenues for refinancing (e.g., bridge-to-bond financing, InvIT structure, take-out financing, secondary loan market)

ADB = Asian Development Bank, BIFFL = Bangladesh Infrastructure Finance Fund Limited, IDCOL = Infrastructure Development Company Limited, IFC = International Finance Corporation, IIFCL = India Infrastructure Finance Company Limited, InvIT = infrastructure investment trust, NBFI = nonbank financial institution, NIFRA = Nepal Infrastructure Bank Limited, O&M = operation and maintenance, OMDP = Office of Markets Development and Public–Private Partnership, PPP = public–private partnership, SBI = State Bank of India.

Source: Study team analysis.

Table 15: Developing Operation-Stage Financing Institutions

Operation Stage Financial Institutions	Supply-Side Challenges	Key Intervention Areas
Bangladesh		
Insurance funds (e.g., JBC, SBC): Low penetration	• Low premium per capita due to limited awareness of insurance products, and limited skills and knowledge to provide insurance services • Insolvency-related risk • Lack of trust • Underdeveloped capital market • Absence of AA and above-rated bonds	• Bancassurance opportunity (i.e., selling insurance products in partnership with banks and taking advantage of bank networks, and technological and human resources) • Need for insurance products in agriculture and health sectors • Regulations that focus on reducing the risk of insolvency that use international standards
Pension funds: Low penetration	• Low pension coverage • Large workforce in informal sector deprived of pension benefits due to lack of legal structure • Underdeveloped capital market	• Create awareness about pension and retirement planning • Bring informal workers under a legal structure with pension and gratuity benefits • Improve capital markets
Private equity funds	• Focused on start-ups	
Bhutan		
Insurance funds: (RICBL & BIL): Only two funds	• Limited understanding of insurance products • Underdeveloped capital market and limited investable bonds leading to investments in short-term loans	• Awareness-raising campaign for different insurance products available in the market • Improve capital markets
Pension funds (NPPF): Only one fund	• Underdeveloped capital market and limited investable bonds, leading to investment in short-term loans	• Improvement of capital markets
India		
Insurance funds (e.g., life insurance companies): Limited investment in infrastructure	• Absence of AA and above-rated bonds • Single and group borrower limits	• Phase out borrower limits to increase investments (OECD countries do not have these limits) • Create awareness about pension and retirement planning • Mandatory participation in defined contribution plans • Banks need to flip assets to other institutions • Explore options for institutionalizing an active secondary market for loans
Pension funds (e.g. National Pension Scheme): Limited investment in infrastructure	• Large population part of informal sector and not covered by pension plans • Absence of AA and above-rated bonds	

continued on next page

Table 15 *continued*

Operation Stage Financial Institutions	Supply-Side Challenges	Key Intervention Areas
NBFI-infrastructure development funds (e.g., NIIF Infrastructure Finance Limited)	• Low supply of viable and good quality operational projects	
Private equity/AIFs (e.g., Brookfield, Macquaire, IDFC private equity)	• Limited exit opportunities	• Concession-agreement flexibility in clauses for refinancing obligations, termination payment, demand risks
InvIT (e.g., IRB InvIT fund)	• Secondary market for InvIT is illiquid	• Educate retail investors and reduce lot size
Myanmar		
Insurance funds (e.g., Aung Thitsar Oo Insurance): Low penetration	• Limited product awareness, leading to low premium/capita • Underdeveloped capital market	• Expand products offering in agriculture, health, and microinsurance • Awareness-raising campaign for different insurance products • Improve capital markets
Pension funds: Low penetration	• Low pension coverage • Underdeveloped capital market	• Regulatory push requiring mandatory contributions can help increase the corpus • Improve capital markets
Nepal		
Insurance funds: Low penetration	• Not enough experts and inadequate rating methodology for assessing investment opportunities • Underdeveloped capital market	• Detailed rating methodology for assessing investments • Train agents • Create awareness about pension and retirement planning • Bring informal workers under a legal structure with pension and gratuity benefits
Pension funds: Low penetration	• Low pension coverage • Underdeveloped capital market	
Private equity funds (e.g., Dolma funds)	• Few private equity funds focused on SMEs	
Sri Lanka		
Insurance funds Pension funds (e.g., public service pension scheme)	• Central bank regulation does not allow banks to sell insurance products directly	• Enable regulations to allow bancassurance
Thailand		
Insurance funds (e.g., Bangkok Insurance Public Company)	• Nonlife insurance market is intensely competitive, which can result in the erosion of underwriting discipline and create solvency problems	• Industry consolidation to mitigate these pressures • TFFIF to increase its portfolio of infrastructure assets
Pension funds (e.g., government pension fund)	• Bulk of investment in low-risk assets	
InvIT (e.g., TFFIF)	• Limited operation history and dependent on EXAT for the operation of expressways and the collection and delivery of the transfer revenue to TFFIF	

AIF = alternative infrastructure fund, BIL = Bhutan Insurance Limited, EXAT = Expressway Authority of Thailand, IDF = infrastructure development fund, IDFC = Infrastructure Development Finance Company, IFL = India Finsec Limited, InvIT = infrastructure investment trust, JBC = Jiban Bima Corporation, NBFI = nonbank financial institution, NIIF = National Investment and Infrastructure Fund, NPPF = National Pension and Provident Fund, OECD = Organisation for Economic Co-operation and Development, RICBL = Royal Insurance Corporation of Bhutan Limited, SBC = Sadharan Bima Corporation, SMEs = small and medium-sized enterprises, TFFIF =Thailand Future Fund.

Source: Study team analysis.

Developing Capital Markets. Strong transport infrastructure needs to be backed and financed by a developed capital market. India needs interventions to develop its corporate bond market by tackling supply-side constraints—e.g., reducing timelines, meeting public listing compliance requirements for debt issues, credit enhancement for lower-rated infrastructure bonds, enhancing the depth of the government securities market to create a reliable benchmark yield curve, improving market infrastructure (developing an electronic request for proposal-based trading platform for corporate bonds, for instance), and demand-side measures, such as encouraging the participation of pension and insurance funds through enhanced ratings. Pooling assets, credit guarantee funds, and infrastructure ratings, among other innovations, are critical for enhancing the supply of bonds and financing national infrastructure pipelines. Implementing these measures will encourage a conducive route for domestic and foreign institutional investors to deepen their exposure in infrastructure projects.

In Bangladesh, developing the capital market for government and commercial bonds needs to be prioritized for channeling investments through this route, as does the issuance of long-term securities. Benchmark securities need to be identified and marketable government bonds increased to ensure a minimum net issuance every year. A 2019 Bangladesh Bank report sets out in detail the areas of the country's capital market that need to be developed. Adopting these measures will help promote a strong government bond market, creating the base for corporate issuances, including for infrastructure projects.

Bhutan needs to develop a sovereign bond market for financing its domestic expenditure. Budget deficits are financed entirely by Treasury bills. The Royal Monetary Authority of Bhutan could look at developing a secondary market for Treasury bills by dematerializing them. Initiatives are also needed to develop market infrastructure (e.g., primary dealers) and demand, as institutional investors are not present and this is preventing an active government bond market.

Myanmar's and Nepal's nascent bond markets are characterized by their low number of issuance of government securities. The bond markets of both countries need to develop market infrastructure (e.g., scripless clearing and a settlement system), and establish intermediaries (e.g., regulations for primary dealers and brokerage houses). They need to address supply-side issues—both governments, for instance, need to increase the tenor, quantum, and frequency of bond issues, implement demand-side measures by encouraging banks to trade actively in the bonds in their books, and encourage institutional investors and mutual funds to participate in the bond market.

Sri Lanka's bond market consists of government securities (Treasury bills and bonds), corporate and bank bonds listed on the stock exchange, and unlisted corporate bonds. Sri Lanka has active primary and secondary markets in government securities and overseas issuances of sovereign debt. The country's sovereign rating risk is a concern for capital markets as the government's fiscal stimulus has been criticized by credit rating agencies. Sri Lanka has an active primary market for corporate bonds, but the secondary market for corporate bonds is fairly inactive. Sri Lanka's capital market has yet to venture beyond traditional instruments, such as stocks and bonds, into derivatives, commodities, and other more sophisticated instruments. But introducing these products would encourage the further development of the country's capital market.

Thailand's bond market has made remarkable progress since the Asian financial crisis. Government securities and corporate debt securities are actively traded, and the market is a significant source of funding for the government, the corporate sector, and the central bank's management of monetary policy. Thailand needs to balance further bond market development with maintaining fiscal stability. This will require increasing nonresident issuances in domestic markets, and encouraging bond issuances by onshore and offshore issuers. In line with the Securities and Exchange Commission Strategic Plan, 2021–2023, Thailand should focus on building an ecosystem for a sustainable capital market, encourage accessibility, and provide investor protection and education.

The nascent or early development stage of the capital markets of most BIMSTEC countries inhibits certain financing institutions, such as insurance and pension funds, from participating in infrastructure financing as the capital market route is a major investment route for them. And the challenges facing other financing institutions, such as commercial banks and NBFIs, are hindering the development and deepening of the capital markets of BIMSTEC countries. The country sections later in this report discuss these challenges in detail and recommend remedial actions that can be taken by financing institutions (Table 16).

Table 16: Actions to Develop Capital Markets

#	Interventions	Ownership
1	Develop national financial intermediaries through country-level interventions for strengthening regulation and capacity building.	Finance regulators from Bay of Bengal Initiative for Multi-Sectoral Technical and Economic Cooperation (BIMSTEC) member countries
2	Develop financial intermediaries for construction-stage financing tools, involving the capacity building of commercial banks and nonbank financial institutions for project financing; technical assistance can be provided by multilateral and bilateral institutions. Impact: Development of specialized capabilities to identify, evaluate, and price construction-period risks.	Multilateral development banks
3	Develop financial intermediaries for operational-stage financing tools by introducing credit and loan guarantee products to deepen institutional investors' financing. Impact: More investable bonds with minimum AA credit rating for institutional funds.	Multilateral development banks/ regional infrastructure funds
4	Develop capital markets.	Financing regulators of BIMSTEC countries

Source: Study team analysis.

Private Sector Participation

Being able to use PPPs depends on project-specific factors that affect the efficiency contributions that private sector participation can bring to a project. These include having a threshold project—a project of sufficient size that it can go to a private partner—and whether there are significant construction and operational risks that are not under the direct control of the private partner. The likelihood of a project's cash flow covering an investment is an important criterion, more so as certain countries like India have limits on annuity payments. In addition, the capability of government and project authorities to plan and prepare an appropriate PPP structure (i.e., a capacity assessment framework) would be critical for successful implementation of PPPs. Table 17 details the project-specific factors that authorities can use to identify a project's PPP "ability."

Table 17: Parameters to Evaluate Public–Private Partnership Projects

Parameter	Criteria	BIMSTEC Master Plan Projects' Assessment
Scope of private sector in operations stage	This filters out small sections of railways (operations difficult to hand over to private players) and port dredging projects (no operations component)	25+ projects in master plan (e.g., expansion of inner-harbor basin at Paradip port, India)
Threshold size of projects	This ensures a minimum private investment to garner interest from private players (e.g., projects under $55 million not considered for PPP in Nepal; NHAI has minimum project size of $150 million for PPPs; project capacity as a proxy)	100+ projects in master plan can be taken up for PPP, subject to meeting criteria
Potential for coverage of cash flows by government support	If projects are not viable for financing through user fees, government agencies could look at supporting the projects through annuity payments. However, there would be policy and fiscal considerations for such arrangements, with certain countries/their agencies already setting overarching limits to such payments (e.g., In India, MORTH has explored a 20% ceiling of annual capex for road annuity projects).	High-level assessment indicates that about 44 projects may be explored for provision of government support in the form of annuity payments. PPP project authorities can identify the projects that can be taken up using the annuity mode based on their assessment of maximum permissible annuity commitments.
Construction and operation risks not under direct control of private player[a]	In difficult terrains and strike-prone regions (e.g., some parts of India's North Eastern Region) or projects with land acquisition issues, private players may participate only in item-rate contracts	Due diligence by project authorities and adequate project preparation, including land acquisition
Legal and regulatory barriers (e.g., government restrictions in border areas)	Some border road projects may not be awarded to private sector due to national security concerns	Not highlighted as a concern for master plan projects

BIMSTEC = Bay of Bengal Initiative for Multi-Sectoral Technical and Economic Cooperation, MORTH = Ministry of Road Transport and Highways, NHAI = National Highways Authority of India, PPP = public–private partnership.

[a] For example, land acquisition status and perceptions, intermodal competition, support infrastructure, technical feasibility, and safeguard concerns.

Source: Study team analysis.

Project authorities need the capability to evaluate and implement PPP projects—and where these are missing, to be able to develop them. In addition to the above considerations for project authorities, secondary interventions to the overall PPP regime can be undertaken to improve private sector participation:

(i) **Conduct detailed financial assessment and value-for-money assessment.** A detailed financial feasibility assessment for transport projects can explore the possibility of developing the project through various PPP modes. In addition, a value-for-money assessment can be undertaken to understand the overall economic benefit of a regional transport projects.

(ii) **Adopt phased approach to introducing PPPs in BIMSTEC member states lacking PPP experience.** Some BIMSTEC member states such as Bhutan, Myanmar, and Nepal are at an early stage in their use of PPP for implementation of transport projects. Initially, private sector participation through operation and maintenance (O&M) contracts can be explored. As the project authorities and private sector players in these member states gain PPP experience, PPP models with more shared risk allocations can be used to implement transport projects.

(iii) **Bundle projects to diversify risks, leverage synergies, and manage procurement costs and timelines.** Some regional transport projects in the BIMSTEC region are unattractive for PPP due to reasons such as lack of demand, low capital cost and returns, and high risk due to geopolitical scenarios. Bundling similar transport projects can lead to benefits lowering demand risk, higher capital cost and returns, lower procurement costs, time and cost savings, and improved efficiencies in project implementation. In addition, project authorities can leverage synergies between bundled projects to achieve faster implementation and improved PPP-ability.

(iv) **Robust project planning and preparation.** Project authorities or PPP units should create a pipeline of investable PPP projects. This requires inputs from transport master plans and assessments by project authorities to determine whether projects can be PPPs. Necessary project preparation efforts, such as developing detailed project reports, and social and environment impact assessments, should be done before projects are evaluated by prospective investors, including multilateral and bilateral financing institutions.

Quasi-independent and trusted third parties, such as development finance institutions (DFIs), may be needed for capacity-building programs for project authorities to help them with project preparation. ADB's Office of Markets Development and Public–Private Partnership, for instance, provides project preparation assistance to clients in Asia and the Pacific. Some DFIs, including ADB and the EIB, provide advisory support which includes knowledge and capacity building, project preparation and implementation, and environmental, climate, and social impact assessment, as well as advising project authorities on procurement and regulatory rules to project authorities. Some DFIs have dedicated funds for advisory support.

(v) **Preparing model concession agreements.** Preparation of model concession agreements that achieve fair risk allocation among the project stakeholders for different PPP modes in each transport sector (roads, ports, airports), incorporating feedback from investors, developers, and project authorities. MDBs can provide capacity-building support for this.

(vi) **Legal structures.** These are needed in concession agreements for special purpose vehicles to pass rights and obligations to downstream contracts—e.g., intergovernmental agreements and additional support agreements to lenders.

(vii) **Dispute resolution and renegotiation.** A sound, clear, and fast dispute resolution mechanism is needed to avoid time and cost overruns in case an infrastructure project is halted due to dispute between various parties.

The proposed interventions (Table 18) for private sector participation will likely take time to implement in BIMSTEC countries. In the meantime, the following approaches could be considered:

(i) For national projects, governments can shoulder construction risks. Once a project becomes operational, the private sector can be invited to participate in O&M.

(ii) For regional projects, construction risks could be shouldered by participating governments through in-advance agreements to finance the development of regional projects with the support of MDBs or DFIs. When assets are operational, participating governments can then monetize their side of these assets. The capital cost for the construction of regional projects can come from setting up regional funds. As discussed in Section C, two fund options can be explored to cater to this capital cost of regional projects. Given that BIMSTEC leadership is already exploring the creation of BDF, these two fund options can be evaluated to come under this broader mandate. Fund A would support regional projects with limited commercial viability but significant social and economic benefits. Fund B would focus on transport and other infrastructure projects that improve transport connectivity in the BIMSTEC region, with the ultimate objective to provide low-cost and long-term capital and attract private sector funding. The monetized assets could then be pooled back to Fund A by governments. Doing this could create more headroom for developing and financing more regional projects downstream.

Table 18: Interventions to Enhance Private Participation

#	Interventions	Ownership
1	Prepare bankable projects: • For project preparation, multilateral development banks can provide capacity building and transaction advisory services • Prepare bankable model concession agreements for public–private partnership (PPP) models with balanced risk-sharing arrangements in each sector (roads, ports, airports) incorporating feedback from investors, developers, and project authorities • Periodically update model concession agreements to take account of changing business environments • Establish a legal structure in concession agreements for special purpose vehicles to pass rights and obligations to downstream contracts (e.g., intergovernmental and additional sponsor support agreements to lenders) • Dispute resolution and renegotiation considerations	Asian Development Bank, Office of Markets Development and Public–Private Partnership, other multilateral development banks, and regional financing institutions
2	Conduct detailed financial assessment and value-for-money assessment to determine PPP-ability of projects	Project authorities of Bay of Bengal Initiative for Multi-Sectoral Technical and Economic Cooperation (BIMSTEC) countries
3	Adopt phased approach to introducing PPPs in Bhutan, Myanmar, Nepal, and Sri Lanka, which are at an early stage in their use of these partnerships for transport projects. Initially, private sector participation through operation and maintenance contracts can be explored	
4	Bundle projects to diversify risks, leverage synergies, and manage procurement costs and timelines	BIMSTEC member countries

Source: Study team analysis.

Action Plan

Table 19 is an action plan based on the interventions proposed in the previous section. The prospects of achieving each action is assessed over the short, medium, and long term.

Table 19: Transport Infrastructure Financing Action Plan

#	Actions	Owner	Impact of Actions		
			Short-term (0 – 2 years)	Medium-term (2 – 5 years)	Long-term (> 5 years)
Funding					
1	Levy user charges.				
	Agree on evaluation of toll or user fee as means of funding by governments.	BIMSTEC countries			
	Develop a framework on the economic benefits and costs for each transport sector, agreed by BIMSTEC countries.	MDBs and BIMSTEC countries			
	Relax existing national toll and user fee guidelines for BIMSTEC Master Plan for Transport Connectivity projects to evaluate their true cost and benefits.	BIMSTEC countries and Secretariat			
	Introduce regional toll guidelines or orders setting out the mechanism for charging toll rates on roads in line with economic benefits.	BIMSTEC countries and Secretariat			
2	BIMSTEC governments should explore an alternative revenue mechanism to raise funds for capital and operational subsidies.				
	Conduct knowledge workshops with members to explore a mechanism for alternative revenue sources.	BIMSTEC Secretariat and ADB/MDBs			
	Prepare guidelines on the criteria for inclusion of the alternative revenue sources mechanism in projects, and the structure and process of transferring revenue generated from the mechanism to a fund.	BIMSTEC countries			
	Monetize operational assets, including projects in the master plan.	BIMSTEC countries			
	Ring-fence revenue from asset monetization for master plan project development.	BIMSTEC countries			

continued on next page

Table 19 *continued*

#	Actions	Owner	Impact of Actions		
			Short-term (0 – 2 years)	Medium-term (2 – 5 years)	Long-term (> 5 years)
Regional Institutional Structure and Enablers					
3	Create a robust regional institutional structure—e.g., a regional charter treaty delineating the roles and responsibilities of concerned agencies and a well-defined and documented decision-making process.	BIMSTEC countries	■		
4	Identify transport corridors with a list of projects critical for regional development through economic and financial analysis to identify the impacts of corridor planning. Identify priority projects in corridor planning for implementation and financing.	BIMSTEC countries	■		
5	BIMSTEC countries should include master plan projects in their national development plans.	BIMSTEC Secretariat	■		
6	Encourage member states to formulate transnational regulatory environments, prepare standard contractual agreements, and harmonize technical standards.	BIMSTEC Secretariat		■	
7	Set up an institutional structure to ratify mutual agreements, such as ACMP, PIWTT, ACS, BBIN, and MVA, addressing all key nonphysical bottlenecks. The structure should include a transnational regulatory framework and harmonization of technical standards for efficient cross-border movement.	BIMSTEC Secretariat	■		
8	Develop a standardized shadow-cost model to be able to compare value for money. The analysis of operational regional projects can help refine life-cycle cost assessments.	BIMSTEC countries and Secretariat	■		
9	Set tariffs following General Agreement on Tariffs and Trade principles. Countries need to ensure that tariffs charged for transit cargo are similar to their own export–import cargo and that tariffs charged for any additional services are rational.	BIMSTEC countries and Secretariat	■		
Financing					
10	Set up regional fund (Fund A) under BDF.				
	Finance projects where construction risks are borne by governments and operation and maintenance is done by a private party.	BIMSTEC countries and Secretariat	■		
	Fund commercially unviable projects through grants.	BIMSTEC countries and Secretariat	■		
11	Set up another regional fund (Fund B under BDF) focusing on infrastructure projects and regional transport connectivity projects that require some degree of support in terms of low cost of financing sources in order to crowd in private sector financing.	BIMSTEC Secretariat and MDBs			■
12	Use guarantee products of MDBs and other financial institutions to leverage private capital into infrastructure projects.	MDBs	■		

continued on next page

Table 19 *continued*

#	Actions	Owner	Impact of Actions		
			Short-term (0 – 2 years)	Medium-term (2 – 5 years)	Long-term (> 5 years)
13	Establish a financial hub in the BIMSTEC region.	BIMSTEC countries and Secretariat			
14	Strengthen national financing institutions.	BIMSTEC member countries			
	Country-level interventions related to regulations and capacity building.	Finance regulators of BIMSTEC countries			
	Capacity building of commercial banks and nonbank financial institutions for project financing. Technical assistance can be provided by multilateral and bilateral institutions.	MDBs			
	Introduce credit and loan guarantee products to deepen the financing of institutional investors.	MDBs/ DFIs			
15	Deepen capital markets.	Finance regulators of BIMSTEC countries			
Private sector participation					
16	Provide capacity-building support for project authorities for carrying out PPP projects. Project authorities participating in the development of the identified corridors could be prioritized for capacity-building support.	MDBs			
17	Conduct detailed financial assessment and value for money assessment to determine the PPP-ability of projects.	BIMSTEC countries			
18	Prepare bankable projects—e.g., bankable risk-sharing model concession agreements for different PPP models in each sector and a dispute resolution mechanism.	BIMSTEC countries and MDBs			
19	Use a phased approach to introducing PPP in Bhutan, Myanmar, Nepal, and Sri Lanka, where PPPs are at a nascent stage. Explore private participation in O&M contracts. DFIs, such as ADB's Office of Markets Development and Public–Private Partnership, can provide transaction advice on the O&M component.	BIMSTEC countries and MDBs			
20	Bundle projects to diversify risks, leverage synergies, and manage procurement costs and timelines.	BIMSTEC countries			
21	Standardize output specifications for O&M of transport infrastructure projects in key sub-sectors.				

ACMP = Agreement for the Use of the Chattogram and Mongla Ports, ACS = Agreement on Coastal Shipping, ADB = Asian Development Bank, BBIN = Bangladesh-Bhutan-India-Nepal, BDF = BIMSTEC Development Fund, BIMSTEC = Bay of Bengal Initiative for Multi-Sectoral Technical and Economic Cooperation, DFI = development finance institution, MDB = multilateral development bank, MVA = Motor Vehicle Act, O&M = operation and maintenance, PIWTT = Protocol for Inland Water Trade & Transit , PPP = public–private partnership.

Source: Study team analysis.

APPENDIX 1

Regional Projects Assessment

Classification of Regional Projects

While all Bay of Bengal Initiative for Multi-Sectoral Technical and Economic Cooperation (BIMSTEC) Master Plan projects aim to improve regional connectivity, a closer review of project characteristics shows that some projects would provide economic benefits almost entirely to the country where the project is located, without much dependence on cross-border trade. These projects may get higher prioritization for development by the governments than projects that are regional in nature. Regional projects are inherently complex to plan and execute because of the direct or indirect involvement of multiple governments. Because of this, these projects need a special focus to identify an optimal institutional structure and financing mechanisms. Table A1.1's classification framework identifies regional projects in the master plan.

Table A1.1: Regional Projects Classification Framework

Classification	Characteristics	BIMSTEC Project Illustration
Regional (R1)	Projects that involve physical construction works and/or coordinated policies and procedures spanning two or more neighboring countries.	Road and rail projects spanning two or more neighboring countries. For example: • Akhaura (Bangladesh)–Agartala (India) rail link • Construction of Mechi bridge connecting India and Nepal
Regional (R2)	National infrastructure projects that have a significant cross-border impact. These projects are: • designed to connect to the network of a neighboring or third country; • involve planning and implementation that requires cooperation or coordination with one or more countries; and • aim to add economic value to two or more countries in the BIMSTEC region.	

BIMSTEC = Bay of Bengal Initiative for Multi-Sectoral Technical and Economic Cooperation.

Source: Study team analysis.

The characteristics of each project are then assessed using this framework, and this separates regional from national projects. Of the 134 projects in planning stage, 70 of them, worth $35.2 billion, are regional. Ten of these projects, worth $9.4 billion, are construction works spanning multiple countries.

For R1 regional category projects (Table A1.1), eight out of a total of 10 projects in this category are in roads and railways. These are construction projects spanning two countries. Two projects are in trade facilitation to develop border-crossing infrastructure and facilities. For R2 regional category projects, 52 out of a total 60 projects (85%)

are roads and railways. These projects include border roads and railway lines. One of these projects is the National Waterway-2 connecting Bangladesh and India. Six are dry ports, integrated check posts, and inland container depots at borders. One of these projects is a transport hub in Bhutan. The projects in these two categories and their details are in Appendix 19.

Challenges in Regional Projects, Proposed Interventions

Studies have sought to quantify the potentially significant benefits of developing cross-border infrastructure in Asia and the Pacific.[1] Despite the benefits, developing and financing projects for this remains a considerable challenge, largely because cross-border infrastructure projects have to contend with various transnational factors that make them more complex to implement and underwrite.

A key determinant of success is having a shared regional vision across countries and a strategic framework to realize a regional vision, region-wide planning and coordination mechanisms, a financing mechanism of sharing costs to align with economic value-sharing, and enablers, such as risk guarantee instruments and harmonized regulatory environments. Figure A1.1 identifies the key facets in these four areas.

Figure A1.1: Key Facets of Implementing Regional Projects

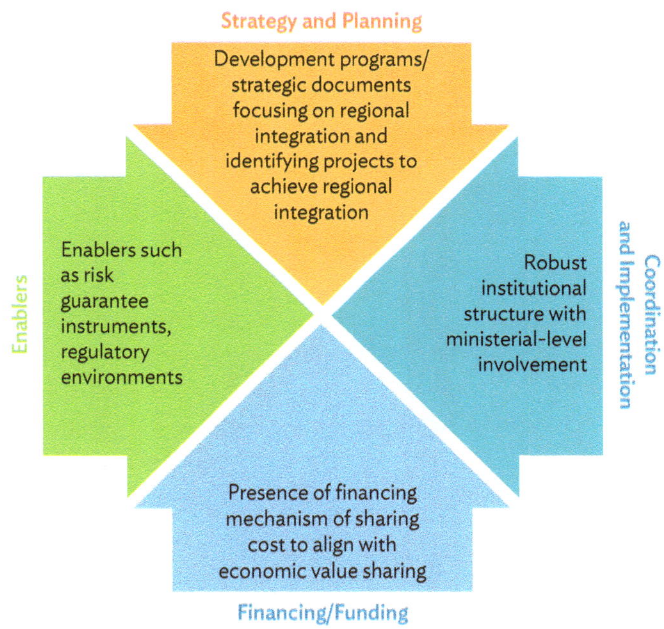

Source: Study team analysis.

Strategy and planning. Most transport infrastructure planning in the Bay of Bengal Initiative for Multi-Sectoral Technical and Economic Cooperation (BIMSTEC) region is done at the national level and is often presented in the form of time-based development plans (e.g., India's National Infrastructure Pipeline). These national road plans include a combination of ongoing projects, reflecting development demands identified at the national or local level, and the projected availability of funding. Regional projects that may not bring economic value to a country in proportion with the required investments may not get due priority in these plans.

National plans do not generally include specific references to or relationships with the plans of neighboring countries. Road planning and development remains a national rather than a bilateral, multilateral, or regional activity. That said, there have been some regional initiatives, such as the India–Myanmar–Thailand Trilateral

[1] E.g., John Gilbert and Nilanjan Banik. 2012. Socio-Economic Impacts of Regional Transport Infrastructure. In Biswa Nath Bhattacharyay, Masahiro Kawai, and Rajat M. Nag, eds. *Infrastructure for Asian Connectivity*. Cheltenham, United Kingdom: Edward Elgar; Susan Stone, Anna Strutt, and Thomas Hertel. Socio-Economic Impact of Regional Transport Infrastructure in the Greater Mekong Subregion; and Fan Zhai. 2012. Benefits of Infrastructure Investment: An Empirical Analysis, also in *Infrastructure for Asian Connectivity*.

Highway and programs under various bilateral agreements. But even in these cases, the development may be dependent on budgetary allocations approval by the countries involved and priority accorded to the project by the countries involved.

For master plan projects, the issue on the prioritization of regional projects may partially get resolved once BIMSTEC member countries ratify the master plan. Once ratified, master plan projects need to be included in national development plans and a mechanism developed to keep members informed of ongoing or planned developments in other member countries that might affect the planning or scheduling of each other's projects.

Member countries should ratify the master plan and push for the implementation of projects that are economically beneficial for more than one country—e.g., the Rosso Bridge Construction Project between Senegal and Mauritania was included in the master plans of both the countries and recognized as strategic project by both.[2]

BIMSTEC should set up a database so that member countries can exchange project planning data of regional significance (e.g., time frames and network characteristics, such as the condition of infrastructure) and include national development plans in the database. The Greater Mekong Subregion (GMS) program, for example, has an online project database that includes the current status of projects, a projects' web map, and geodata. The database is open to officials in the GMS countries and stakeholders.

Coordination and implementation. In the BIMSTEC region, there is little coordination among countries on implementing regional projects, as widely recognized by the government of member states. Many high-level meetings have been held on regional connectivity, but that spirit has not been reflected during the implementation of projects. Indeed, coordination issues among BIMSTEC countries on regional projects have caused significant delays.

Interventions. It is important that a regional financing institution (the BIMSTEC Development Fund [BDF] with a broader mandate) has an adequate governance mechanism and is empowered to ensure regional projects are implemented in a coordinated and timely manner. The BDF can be compared with other regional institutions, such as the Association of Southeast Asian Nations (ASEAN), the European Commission, and the GMS program to arrive at gaps and possible solutions. Appendix 3 gives a detailed comparative review of these regional institutions. The following are interventions needed to create a robust institutional structure for the proposed regional financing institution the BDF:

(i) A regional charter or treaty that clearly delineates the roles and responsibilities of various bodies;
(ii) A well-defined and documented decision-making process;
(iii) A national interministerial committee coordinating activities in each country;
(iv) Sector-specific working groups of line agency officials to conduct regular meetings;
(v) Regular meetings held at the highest level (heads of governments) for reviewing progress and providing strategic direction;
(vi) An institutional arrangement for strengthening the operational plan of transport projects; and
(vii) Strong institutional arrangements at the project level for better implementation.

The GMS provides an example of how to do this (Box A1.1).

2 African Development Bank. Data Portal. Rosso Bridge Construction Project. https://projectsportal.afdb.org/dataportal/VProject/show/P-Z1-D00-037#home (accessed January 2021).

Box A1.1: Institutional Structure of the Greater Mekong Subregion Program's Sector Approach

In 2002, the Greater Mekong Subregion (GMS) countries put the various sector approaches to their programs and projects into a comprehensive strategic framework for subregional development—the GMS Strategic Framework 2002–2012 and 2012–2020—with a focus on the following five strategic thrusts:

- strengthening infrastructure linkages (transport, energy, telecommunications, agriculture);
- facilitating cross-border trade, investment, and tourism—this involves promoting and facilitating intra- and extra-GMS trade, investment, and tourism;
- enhancing private sector participation and competitiveness;
- developing human resources; and
- protecting the environment and promoting the sustainable use of shared natural resources.

GMS countries set up sector forums and working groups to design each of the framework's strategic thrusts and help ensure their effective implementation.

Since 2012, the identification and prioritization of GMS investment projects in a sector has been conducted as part of overall subregional investment programming under the GMS Regional Investment Framework (RIF) mechanism. The instituted a process allowing GMS countries to review and refine the pipeline of projects in the GMS program regularly.

The RIF's implementation plans is reviewed and updated regularly to ensure its continued relevance. The progress of transport projects in the framework's implementation plan is also monitored and reviewed regularly by the GMS Subregional Transport Forum with the assistance of the GMS Secretariat.

Developing transport infrastructure in tandem with policies and the procedures for crossing borders and promoting trade has been central to efforts to interconnect GMS countries. The Transport Sector Strategy 2030 provides a common framework for GMS cooperation in this sector. GMS investments in transport projects have been undertaken as part of overall subregional investment programing under the RIF since 2012.

To operationalize Transport Sector Strategy 2030, it will be necessary to translate its strategic thrusts and priorities into an action program consisting of projects that will be a component of the RIF. The figure shows a breakdown of the RIF's funding sources, totaling $55.6 million as of November 2020.

Greater Mekong Subregion Investment Framework Funding Sources
(%)

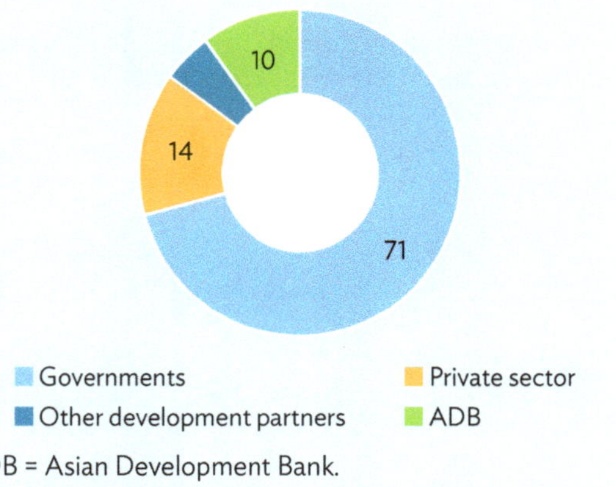

ADB = Asian Development Bank.

Source: ADB. 2016. *Study on Strengthening the Greater Mekong Subregion Program's Institutional Framework*. Manila.

The Subregional Transport Forum reviews, coordinates, and monitors the regional transport plans and projects of GMS member countries.

Private financing has grown from 8% of total financing in 2017 to 14% in 2020. For example, financing from the Asian Development Bank's private sector operations and Japan Bank for International Cooperation catalyzed greater amounts of private sector funding for the Nam Ngiep 1 Hydropower Project, with $564 million of the $977 million total project cost financed by private investors. In general, private sector financing appears to be limited to transport and energy investments.

The GMS initially had a two-tiered structure: ministerial-level for policy and working groups for operations. The GMS Strategic Framework, 2002–2012 rationalized and unified all GMS projects into broadly defined strategic thrusts. But in doing this, the GMS program evolved into a more complex cooperation arrangement.

continued on next page

Box A1.1 *continued*

While retaining its pragmatic and results-oriented modality, the program started to take on more complex policy initiatives, such as the Cross-Border Transport Facilitation Agreement and the Intergovernmental Agreement on Power Interconnection and Trade. As a result, the program's institutional structure became somewhat similar to that of the Association of Southeast Asian Nations and the Asia-Pacific Economic Cooperation, which are driven by agreements and policies rather than projects. Thus, the GMS program's institutional structure has evolved with an increasing focus on policy-oriented tasks.

GMS countries have strong ownership of the program. This is pursued through a GMS leaders' summit at the political level, a ministerial conference supported by a meeting of senior officials at the policy level, and sector forums and working groups at the project and operational levels. A national interministerial committee, assisted by a focal point or national secretariat, coordinates GMS activities in each country (see below chart).

Organization Structure of the Greater Mekong Subregion

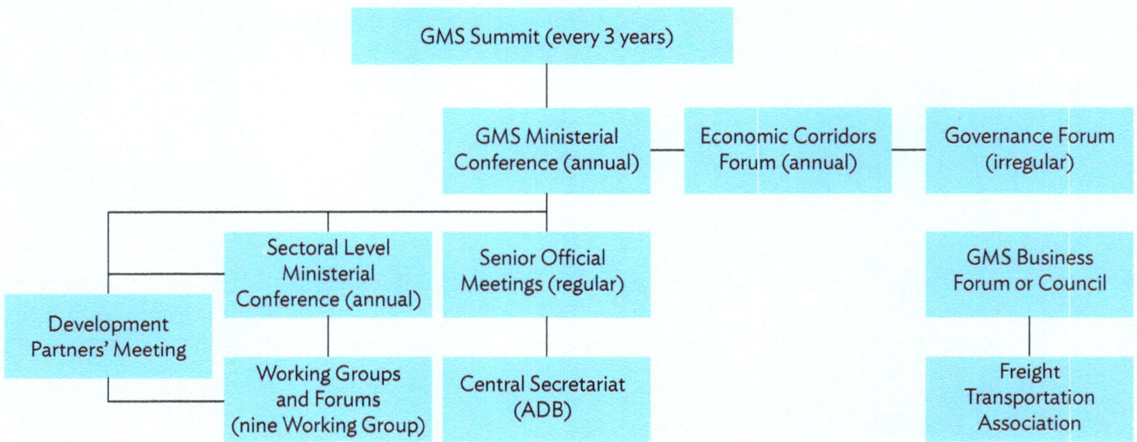

ADB = Asian Development Bank, GMS = Greater Meong Subregion.

Source: ADB. 2016. *Study on Strengthening the Greater Mekong Subregion Program's Institutional Framework*. Manila.

An Asian Development Bank unit at headquarters provides secretariat support to the GMS program in coordination with national secretariats in the GMS countries.

According to the Regional Investment Framework 2022, out of a total of 210 projects worth $78.3 billion, more than half (121) were either completed or ongoing as of October 2020.

Institutional Structure of Cross-Border Projects in Other Regions

Project Name	Project Structure	Region	Institutional Structure
N4 Toll Road ($660 million)	PPP (BOT)	Africa (Mozambique and South Africa)	Two-tier structure comprising: (i) Executing agency: South Africa's Department of Transportation appointed the South African National Road Agency Limited and Mozambique's Department of Roads and Bridges created the Administração Nacional de Estradas to oversee project progress.

continued on next page

Box A1.1 *continued*

Project Name	Project Structure	Region	Institutional Structure
			(ii) Implementing agency: South Africa's Department of Transport and the Department of Roads and Bridges in Mozambique entered into a protocol agreement to establish an implementing authority. The authority drew up the concession contract documents and the tender process. The idea was to have one government counterpart for the private operator to simplify and streamline contract negotiations, construction oversight, and progress reporting. The bidding process closed in 8 months.
Malaysia–Singapore Second Link ($340 billion for Malaysia; $450 million for Singapore)	PPP (BOT)	Asia (Malaysia and Singapore)	Intergovernmental agreement: This was signed between the two governments setting out their responsibilities for the design, construction, and operation and maintenance of the second link. Joint committee: This has representatives from both governments, and was set up to supervise the project implementation.
Lake Chad Basin Regional Road Network Integration Project (construction of bridge over Logone between Yagoua, Cameroon and Bongor, Chad) (XUA93 million)	EPC	Africa (Cameroon and Chad)	Bilateral project steering agreement, signed between Cameroon and Chad in 2014, established a bilateral project monitoring committee as the project's executing agency.
Rosso Bridge Construction Project (€88 million)	EPC	Africa (and Mauritania and Senegal)	Project ad hoc committee: Memorandum of understanding signed to set this up for the project's operations; committee includes department-level representatives of both countries (e.g., environment and local authorities); committee seen as essential for coordination. Program management unit: Based in Rosso, Mauritania, comprising members from both countries. Responsible for: (i) preparing procurement documents, bids assessment reports, and draft procurement documents and contracts to be submitted to authorities for approval and for obtaining no-objection notification from donors; (ii) forwarding an original and a copy of procurement documents and contracts to the two countries and donors; (iii) ensuring adherence to the project implementation schedule; (iv) monitoring operations; (v) preparing annual work program and project progress reports; (vi) preparing counterpart budgets and ensuring their timely availability; (vii) financial management of the project; and (viii) monitoring and evaluation.

BOT = build-operate-transfer, EPC = engineering procurement construction, PPP = public–private partnership.

Source: Reports in the public domain.

Limited institutional capacity. Because of the inherent complexity of regional projects, their development can put a high degree of pressure on the capacities of participating countries' state institutions. In the BIMSTEC region, some line agencies and project authorities have limited capacity to oversee the implementation of regional projects, including the preparation of detailed project reports and technical evaluation of project bids.

A solution to this would be to use quasi-independent and trusted third parties, such as regional financing institutions, to do the capacity building and project preparation programs for project authorities. Various regional financial institutions, including ADB and the European Investment Bank (EIB), provide advisory support for knowledge and capacity building, project preparation and implementation, and environmental, climate, and social impact assessments, as well as advising project authorities on procurement and regulatory rules. Some financial institutions have dedicated funds for providing advisory support. This should lead to a reduction in time and cost overruns while implementing a transport infrastructure project.

Enabling environment. The level of complexity in most regional infrastructure projects is exacerbated by the multiple regulatory systems and policy frameworks that need to be navigated. Participating firms may face regulatory hurdles in one or more countries, such as adverse and abrupt changes in laws and regulations, heterogenous technical standards (e.g., gauge of lines), land acquisition risks, and the cancelation of licenses or approvals.

In the BIMSTEC region, Thailand is the only country with an identifiable international road transport sector, with specific international licenses required to allow Thai trucks to enter Cambodia and the Lao PDR while engaged in an international transport operation. Indian transporters can carry goods to and from Bhutan and Nepal, and vice versa under bilateral arrangements. Foreign transporters are not permitted to enter Bangladesh or Myanmar, other than at border transfer points, and Sri Lanka as an island has no international road transport requirements. The inability of road transporters to travel into neighboring countries may be considered a trade restriction, since it directly increases transport and transaction costs. The need to transship cargo at border crossings directly increases trade costs through additional border handling charges, as well as increasing the risk of damage and pilferage. In addition, the cost of hiring two separate transporters with shorter journeys is likely to be higher than the total cost of hiring a single carrier to convey the goods from origin to destination.[3]

Countries in the BIMSTEC region also do not follow the same technical standards. For instance, India has either broad or dual gauge railway tracks whereas some of the tracks connecting Bangladesh to India are meter gauge tracks. Variations in design specifications and material standards can become a critical problem, especially if the project is to be competitively tendered.

In addition, land acquisition in the case of regional projects causes problems during project implementation. As land acquisition of a project is dependent on country-specific regulatory frameworks regulating land and property rights, difference in regulatory frameworks causes delay.

BIMSTEC could encourage member states to take actions that foster a conducive transnational regulatory environment, prepare standard contractual agreements, and harmonize technical standards. This approach has been followed in various regional initiatives, such as the cross-border trade agreements established under ASEAN and GMS transport facilitation agreements. Box A1.2 looks at the GMS's 2003 Cross-Border Trade Agreement. This could lead to improved returns for private investors and may reduce cost overruns.

3 Asian Development Bank Institute. 2020. *Trade Impact of Reducing Time and Costs at Borders in the Central Asia Regional Economic Cooperation Region*. Tokyo. https://www.adb.org/publications/trade-impact-reducing-time-costs-borders-carec-region.

Box A1.2: Greater Mekong Subregion's 2003 Cross-Border Trade Agreement

The Cross-Border Trade Agreement of the Greater Mekong Subregion (GMS), signed in 2003, is a landmark accord that consolidates in a single legal instrument all key nonphysical measures for efficient cross-border land transport. The agreement has mechanisms for the following:

- **Facilitating cross-border formalities.** This is done through a single-window and single-stop inspections, and reduced documentation and procedures for cross-border traffic.
- **Cross-border transport for goods.** This is facilitated by exemptions from routine physical inspections at borders. Transit traffic is exempt from customs duties and taxes, and clearances of perishables goods are prioritized.
- **Requirements for road vehicles.** Vehicles (on designated open routes), drivers (with mutual recognition of driving licenses and visa facilitation), and goods (with regimes for dangerous and perishable goods) can cross national borders through the GMS road transport permit system; technical requirements of vehicles need to satisfy agreed standards.
- **Infrastructure.** Design standards for roads and bridges, border-crossing facilities, and roads signs and signals.
- **Institutional framework.** National transport facilitation committees, chaired by a minister, and a joint committee of representatives of national committees oversee activities under the agreement as shown in the following detailed institutional structure.

Institutional Structure of Cross-Border Trade Agreement

Ministerial-Level Conference (annual)	• Joint committee makes recommendations to the Ministerial-Level Conference on issues regarding the implementation of the agreement and its annexes and protocols.
Joint Committee (as and when required)	• Representatives of the respective National Transport Facilitation Committees form together the Joint Committee. • The Joint Committee monitors and assesses the functioning of the agreement. • It serves as a platform for discussion, a forum for amicable settlement of disputes, and it may address advice to and formulate proposals for contracting parties and formulate proposals for amendments to the agreement.
Subcommittees (as and when required)	• The Joint Committee establishes subcommittees, including (i) transport, (ii) customs, (iii) health inspection (sanitary/phytosanitary/quarantine), and (iv) immigration. • Working under the guidance of the Joint Committee, the subcommittees are responsible for (i) discussing implementation-related issues, and (ii) making recommendations to the Joint Committee on how to resolve these issues.
National Transport Facilitation Committee	• The contracting parties each establish a permanent National Transport Facilitation Committee chaired by a Minister, vice Minister, or equivalent. • It brings together representatives of all parties concerned with the implementation of the agreement.

GMS = Greater Mekong Subregion.

Source: GMS Cross-Border Trade Agreement. https://www.adb.org/sites/default/files/publication/29294/gms-cbta-instruments-history.pdf.

Financing and funding challenges. Regional BIMSTEC transport infrastructure projects have been done through engineering procurement and item-rate contracts, with funding support from government budgets and concessional loans and grants from multilateral institutions. Funding from multilateral sources, however, puts additional stress on government borrowing. There have also been too few initiatives to assess these regional projects from a commercial perspective.

Regional projects are also likely to be perceived as highly risky by private investors as demand realization depends on the political, diplomatic, and strategic dynamics of participating countries. Regional financing institutions play a central role in overcoming these challenges. Data from regional financial institutions worldwide indicate a lesser reliance on shareholder funds once these institutions reach maturity (Appendix 4).

The proposed regional financing institution (the BDF, with a broader mandate) would need to invest in cash flow-generating projects. Because BIMSTEC countries have little experience in charging user fees for regional connectivity projects levying direct or indirect user fees will need to be considered for future projects wherever financially viable. For a regional financing institution to be able to generate cash flow, a mechanism is needed so that the economic value of projects gets converted into financial value in the form of user charges and tax payments. These financial institutions would be able to service debt from these projects and therefore to service the debt of their lenders. Risk-mitigating instruments will be needed to tackle the inherent riskiness of regional projects and to raise the credit rating of a regional development fund. Providing risk-mitigation instruments, such as loan guarantees, credit enhancement, and foreign currency hedging, can provide a level of comfort to private investors. Globally, regional financial institutions use various instruments as safeguards to the interests of private investors in projects. These instruments differ depending on the nature of risk—project-related or political, for example (Box A1.3).

From a commercial viability perspective, there three potential types of projects that may be in the pipeline of the BIMSTEC Transport Connectivity Master Plan: (i) projects with significant regional, economic, or social benefit but limited commercial viability where private sector financing may not be feasible; (ii) projects that require some degree of support in terms of low cost of financing sources in order to crowd in private sector financing—these may also include projects where certain trunk infrastructure may need to be supported through public/concessional sources in order to attract private investments in rest-of-project components; and (iii) projects with standalone commercial viability and ability to attract private sector financing.

Box A1.3: Examples of Risk-Mitigating Instruments Provided by Development Finance Institutions

The examples of Project-level risk mitigating instruments provided by financial institutions can be evaluated for transport sector projects.

- **Loan guarantees**
  - The Loan Guarantee Instrument for Trans-European Transport Network Projects, administered by the European Commission and the European Investment Bank (EIB), favors commercial banks that provide standby facilities in addition to the usual project finance. The standby facility can be drawn by the project company if traffic revenue falls during the ramp-up period to service senior debt. This is repaid by the project company on a subordinate basis. If an amount is still outstanding under the standby facility after the ramp-up period, the EIB reimburses the facility's providers and becomes subordinated lender.
  - The Asian Development Bank's private sector window
  - The International Development Association's private sector window
  - Partial credit guarantees of the African Development Bank; these cover a portion of scheduled repayments of private loans or bonds against all risks.
- **Credit rating enhancement instruments**
  - The Association of Southeast Asian Nations' Credit Guarantee and Investment Facility provides credit enhancement for issuers with lower credit ratings to raise long-term financing both in their domestic market and in the region. The EIB's Project Bond Initiative of the European Commission is a similar instrument.
- **Foreign exchange risk guarantee instruments**
  - The local currency solution of the Asian Development Bank's private sector window mitigates the potential losses of commercial lenders from local currency exposure.
- **Political risks instruments**
  - The African Development Bank's partial risk guarantees cover private lenders against government risks or a government agency failing to perform its obligations to a private project.

Source: Secondary sources about the institutions in this box.

Identifying financing for projects in category (i) and (ii) above will be critical for successful implementation of projects in the transport master plan. With this in view, two fund options can be explored for project category (i) and (ii) respectively. Further, given that BIMSTEC leadership is already exploring the creation of the BDF, these two fund options can be evaluated to come under this broader mandate. Box A1.4 and Box A1.5 detailed examples of similar regional transport development funds and financing instruments in Europe and South-east Asia.

Box A1.4: Loan Guarantee Instrument for Trans-European Transport Network Projects

The Loan Guarantee Instrument for Trans-European Transport Network Projects (LGTT) of the European Investment Bank (EIB) and European Commission facilitates the greater participation of the private sector in the Trans-European Transport Network (TEN-T), a network of transportation, energy, and communications in the European Union (EU).

The LGTT facilitates the private sector's involvement in core EU transport infrastructure, which often finds it difficult to attract private sector financing due to the relatively high levels of revenue risk in a project's early operating stages.

The LGTT partially covers these risks and consequently and significantly improves the financial viability of TEN-T projects. The LGTT is financed with a capital contribution of €1 billion—€500 million each from the European Commission and the EIB—to support up to €20 billion of senior loans.

The LGTT aims to facilitate investment in TEN-T projects by significantly improving the ability of borrowers to service senior debt during a project's initial operating period, or ramp-up phase, irrespective of initial traffic revenue. Its design substantially enhances the credit quality of senior credit facilities, thereby encouraging a reduction of risk margins applied to senior loans to projects. These savings should surpass the cost to the borrower of the guarantee, resulting in financial value-added for the project.

The standby liquidity facility guaranteed by the LGTT should not exceed 10% of the total amount of the senior debt. This is 20% in duly justified cases—i.e., high-traffic volatility during the ramp-up period with a strong indication of stabilized traffic and acceptable debt service capacity post-ramp up. The amount of the guarantee is subject to a maximum ceiling of €200 million per project under EIB-structured finance facility rules (Appendix 12). This is the EIB's main facility for increased risk taking, established to support projects of importance to the EU, including large infrastructure.

Structure of Loan Guarantee Instrument for Trans-European Transport Network Projects

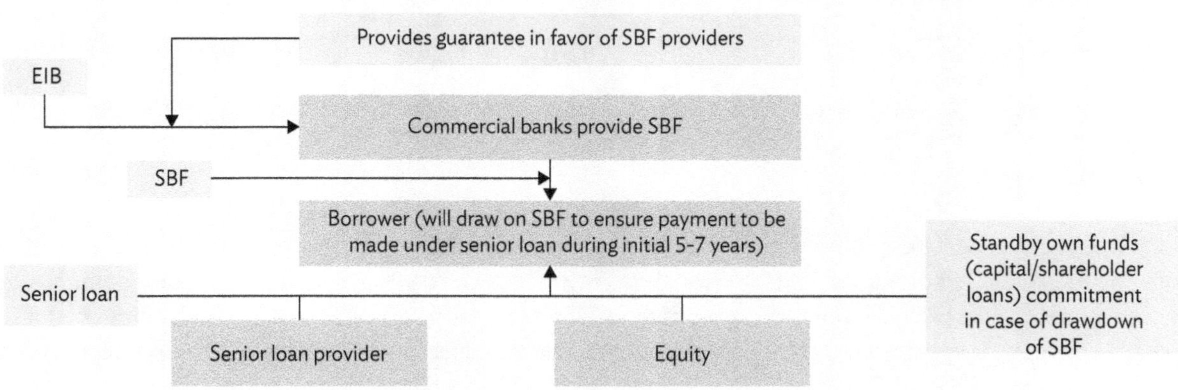

EIB = European Investment Bank, SBF = standby facility.

According to a 2014 operations evaluation report, seven TEN-T projects—five in roads—used LGTTs. A sample of five projects scored satisfactory on project relevance and effectiveness.

Source: European Investment Bank (EIB). 2019. *The Loan Guarantee Instrument for TEN-T Projects (LGTT)*. London. https://www.eib.org/attachments/ev/ev_lgtt_en.pdf

Box A1.5: Credit Guarantee and Investment Facility for Countries in the Association of Southeast Asian Nations Plus 3 Program

The Credit Guarantee Investment Facility (CGIF) was setup in November 2010 to promote financial stability and to boost long-term investments in ASEAN+3—the 10 countries of the Association of Southeast Asian Nations plus Japan, the People's Republic of China, and the Republic of Korea. The CGIF provides guarantees on local currency-denominated bonds issued by companies in the ASEAN+3 region (Appendix 13).

These guarantees make it easier for corporations to issue local currency bonds with longer maturities. This helps reduce the currency and maturity mismatches that caused the Asian financial crisis and make the region's financial system more resilient to volatile global capital flows and external shocks. The CGIF provides guarantees for local currency denominated bonds issued by investment-grade corporations in the region. The CGIF got an initial capital contribution of $700 million from ASEAN, the plus three countries, and the Asian Development Bank. As of August 2020, the CGIF's capitalization was $1.1 billion following a capital increase.

The CGIF aims to help companies that would otherwise have difficulty tapping local bond markets to secure longer-term financing, and reduce their dependency on short-term foreign currency borrowings to mitigate currency and maturity mismatches. Increased issuance of local currency bonds will promote financial stability in the ASEAN+3 region and aid the development of bond markets in ASEAN countries.

Structure of the Credit Guarantee Investment Facility

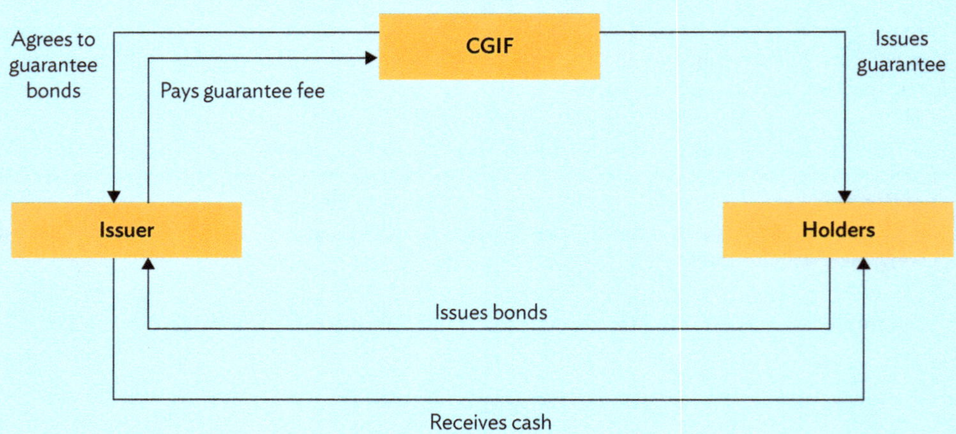

Source: European Investment Bank.

Fund A would look to address the objective of supporting regional projects with limited commercial viability but significant social and economic benefits. Regional projects often compete with other budgetary demands from domestic infrastructure projects, which are often given a higher priority by local governments. The focus of this fund is to have contributory grant corpus by each government for identified cross-border projects with management services provided by the BDF. Doing this would strengthen BIMSTEC's influence on the approval, time frames, and specifications of projects because it would involve a BIMSTEC-administered fund.

This fund would perform two key functions. First, it would act as a sinking fund to provide grants to support commercially unviable projects. Second, it would provide assistance for project preparation and capacity building through various mechanisms. Further, the fund may explore an alternative option for governments to take on construction risks by entering into in advance agreements and have the fund provide project development financing.

The monetization of assets can be considered by governments once a project is operational and additional trade volumes are developed. The capital received from the future monetization of assets could then be pooled back into the fund by participating governments.

Fund B of the BDF would focus on transport and other infrastructure projects that improve transport connectivity in the BIMSTEC region, with the ultimate objective to provide low-cost and long-term capital and attract private sector funding. Box A1.6 and Box A1.7 details out other infrastructure development funds similar institutional structure to the proposed Fund B. The core functions of the proposed fund is to improve the implementation of regional projects and would include:

(i) **Providing low-cost capital.** The mechanisms described above could help ensure a strong credit rating for this fund. Once the fund has been set up, its credit rating will depend both on its shareholder ownership and its business performance. It would have to do risk assessments and select projects that generate cash flows in the long run to service debt. Doing this will enable the proposed fund to establish a credible track record for long-term financial sustainability. A high credit rating would enable it to raise low-cost capital from the international market.
The EIB is rated AAA by Standard and Poor's Global Ratings (S&P) and Fitch Ratings, the New Development Bank is rated AA+ by S&P and Fitch, and the European Bank for Reconstruction and Development is rated AAA by S&P and Fitch—high ratings because of their promoter profiles, compliance to standard evaluation procedures, and their development of risk-mitigation instruments, among other factors. This has enabled these regional development funds to raise capital at a lower cost than would have been available in their regions.
(ii) **Attracting private investors.** The high credibility of regional financing institutions is an incentive to private financing institutions to participate in regional projects. The EIB, for example, plays a major role in attracting private capital in regional projects.
(iii) **Private sector windows.** ADB and other development institutions have private sector windows that have provisions for commercial financing. This financing corpus can also be used for regional projects.
(iv) **Project appraisals and evaluation.** These are needed for project preparation, coordination, and monitoring for the timely implementation of projects. Support is also needed for building the capacity of project authorities.

Further, the proposed fund can undertake development of nonfund-based functions as it evolves to increase private sector participation:

(i) **Syndication and co-lending services:** The leading financing institution can leverage cofinancing from other financial institutions and arrange syndicated loans for the regional projects
(ii) **Guarantee products** of MDBs and other financing institutions could be used to leverage private capital into infrastructure projects. The following are key considerations for this:
    (a) Ensure the coverage of guarantee products to commercial lenders financing regional projects (nonrecourse basis) and involves all participating governments.
    (b) Develop guarantee products that are calibrated to master plan projects (e.g., The Loan Guarantee Instrument for Trans-European Networks Transport [LGTT] of the EIB ensures coverage of Trans-European Networks Transport planned connectivity projects).
    (c) Rationalize guarantee commission by exploring funding from concessional ordinary capital resources (OCR) for regional projects. Pooled guarantee corpus to optimize the guarantee commission rate for BIMSTEC.
    (d) Adequate marketing to communicate the benefits of guarantee products (e.g., flexibility and leveraging private capital) over traditional loans to governments and project authorities.

(e) Optimal coverage (i.e., a percentage of the project cost) ensuring comfort to private lenders and avoiding moral hazard.

(f) Project authorities will need to assess the incremental cost of one or more guarantees in a project and add this to the project cost to provide a fuller picture of commercial viability. The cost of a guarantee is typically 1.0%–1.2% of the total project cost.[4]

(iii) **Develops guidelines**: The BDF would need to identify and define the type of projects that will be evaluated, project review mechanisms, targets to be achieved, and timelines for disbursement to provide comfort to lenders.

Box A1.6: Association of Southeast Asian Nations Infrastructure Fund

The ASEAN Infrastructure Fund (AIF) is Southeast Asia's largest infrastructure financing initiative for infrastructure based on funding contributions of the member countries of the Association of Southeast Asian (ASEAN). The AIF was set up in 2011 by ASEAN's 10 member countries and the Asian Development Bank (ADB). The fund's total equity is $485.3 million.

The AIF started lending in 2013, offering loans to ASEAN member countries for infrastructure projects. To date, the AIF has committed financing to nine projects, with a total portfolio size of about $3 billion cofinanced with ADB for infrastructure development in energy, water, transport, and urban development, among other areas. ADB involvement eases the risk concerns of investors, enabling the AIF to establish a credible track record.

The AIF's board of directors includes nominees of the ministries of finance of ASEAN countries; the board meets at least twice a year.

ASEAN Infrastructure Fund Commitments

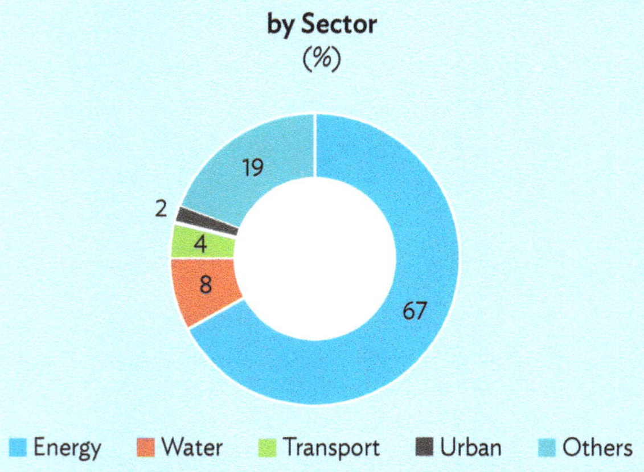

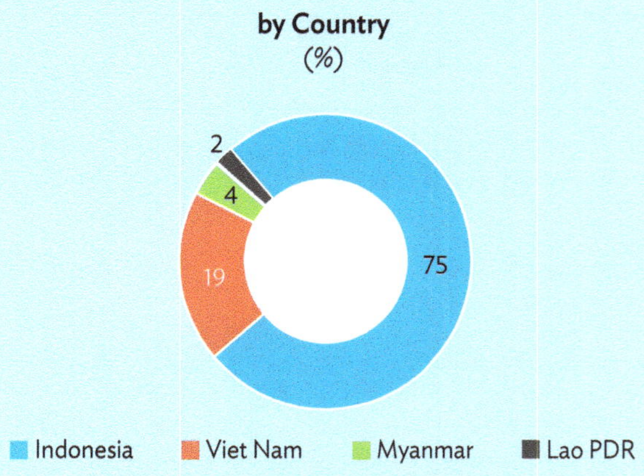

ASEAN = Association of Southeast Asian Nations, Lao PDR = Lao People's Democratic Republic.

Source: ADB. 2019. *ASEAN Infrastructure Fund, Financing Infrastructure for Growth & Development*. Manila.

continued on next page

[4] Ministry of Finance, India Memorandum.

Box A1.6 *continued*

Profile of the ASEAN Infrastructure Fund

Equity	$485 million in initial equity contribution.
Debt	Debt will eventually be issued to leverage 1.5 times equity, with about $162 million in hybrid capital (perpetual bonds), targeting high investment-grade credit ratings. Central banks and other institutions, including private sector investors, will purchase the debt after the ASEAN Infrastructure Fund (AIF) has established a clear track-record and sufficient lending volume.
Financing mechanisms and lending limit	$300 million a year.
Qualifying projects	Adaptation, energy, energy efficiency, infrastructure, mitigation, renewable energy, technology, transport, urban, waste management, water, water efficiency.
Eligibility	National and subregional projects in ASEAN's developing member countries are eligible for AIF funding. These are Brunei Darussalam, Cambodia, Indonesia, the Lao People's Democratic Republic, Malaysia, the Philippines, Singapore, Thailand, and Viet Nam.

Example: the Greater Mekong Subregion East–West Economic Corridor Eindu to Kawkareik Road Improvement Project. Funding totaled $100 million, with an interest rate of 1.5% and a $20 million ADB concessionary loan with an interest rate of London Inter-Bank Offered Rate +1.4% by the AIF.

ASEAN Infrastructure Fund Structure

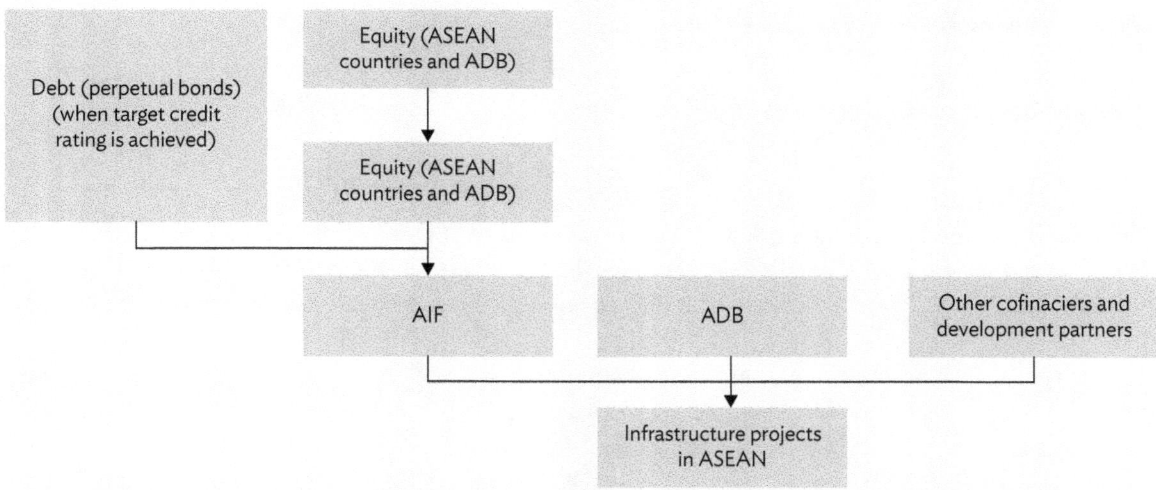

ADB = Asian Development Bank, AIF = ASEAN Infrastructure Fund, ASEAN = Association of Southeast Asan Nations.

AIF lending terms

- AIF loans are similar to ADB loans based on the LIBOR, with a floating rate based on 6-month LIBOR plus a fixed spread and a maturity premium where applicable that is fixed over the life of the loan.
- All AIF loans are denominated in dollars.
- Under the AIF's Green and Inclusive Infrastructure Window, opened in 2019, attractive loan terms apply to projects that meet certain criteria.

Asian Development Bank Role

- The ADB plays an important role in the AIF through its contribution as a shareholder, cofinancer, and administrator.
- As cofinancer and lender of record, ADB helps attract additional resources and eases the risk concerns of investors, enabling the AIF to establish a credible track record.

continued on next page

Box A1.6 *continued*

- As administrator, ADB is responsible for managing and disbursing all AIF resources and for ensuring that projects comply with the bank's policies and safeguards.
- ADB designs and structures AIF projects, and shares the substantial costs linked to their preparation and implementation, thereby freeing up more AIF resources for investment. ADB reports regularly on the AIF's operations to the fund's board.

Source: ADB. 2019. *ASEAN Infrastructure Fund: Financing Infrastructure for Growth and Development*. Manila. https://www.adb.org/publications/asean-infrastructure-fund-brochure.

Box A1.7: ADB's Private Sector Window

The Private Sector Window of the Asian Development Bank (ADB) is a blended-finance solution that aims to improve the risk–return profiles of commercial financiers, helps crowd in private capital, de-risk investments, close viability gaps, and advance well-designed transactions that would not otherwise proceed in absence of any concessionality.

Since 2012, ADB has financed 16 private sector window transactions—$500 million by ADB and $170 million by other multilateral development institutions—using a blended-finance approach and mobilized some $1.2 billion in commercial financing.

An example of a project financed using the private sector window is the 216-megawatt run-of-river Upper Trishuli-1 Hydropower Project in Nepal. Because the private sector market was not able to manage the political, economic, and regulatory country risks, blended finance was instrumental in making the project bankable.

Source: ADB. Private Sector Financing. https://www.adb.org/what-we-do/private-sector-financing.

Insufficiently developed financial markets. The capital markets of most BIMSTEC countries are at a nascent stage of development. In capital markets, government bond markets develop before the market for corporate bonds. In Bangladesh, Bhutan, Nepal, and Myanmar, a government bond market has yet to develop.

Institutional funds, such as insurance funds and pension funds, hold patient capital, which is ideal for long-term investments. One of the major investment routes for institutional funds is through the capital market. The underdeveloped capital markets in the BIMSTEC region hinders the entry of these funds.

To help remedy this, a financial hub could be established to raise finance for projects and programs in the BIMSTEC region. A hub could facilitate investments in regional infrastructure projects based on a market-driven approach as seen in other regional development funds detailed in Box A1.8 and Box A1.9. As noted earlier, Mumbai could fulfill this role because it is already the financial capital of BIMSTEC's largest economy. Borrowers in the BIMSTEC region could issue bonds in Mumbai to attract institutional funds looking for long-term investments. India is already a top destination for foreign portfolio and institutional investors because of its developed primary and secondary markets. In fiscal year 2021, foreign portfolio investors invested ₹25 million. Adopting the following actions would enable the development of a regional financing hub:

(i) **Standardize fund raising mechanism.** Respective governments can collaborate to develop a fundraising mechanism through the regional hub and prepare standardized documents. The mechanism shall include the roles and responsibilities of the governments, a mechanism to repatriate the funds, etc. Standardizing the processes can expediate the fundraising process by the project developers.

(ii) **Repatriation of funds.** The Nepali rupee is pegged with the Indian rupee which provides stability to the financial system. Similarly, a currency can be pegged with other BIMSTEC countries resulting in lower exchange rate risk.

(iii) **Taxation.** India has a comprehensive Double Tax Avoid Agreement with all the BIMSTEC countries. To boost infrastructure investments in the BIMSTEC region, taxes imposed on projects funded through this mechanism can be reduced.

Box A1.8: Singapore's Infrastructure Asia Finance Hub

Singapore is strategically positioned at the heart of the Southeast Asia region, and has a strong corpus of infrastructure development companies, financing and risk management institutions, consultancies, and law firms. More than 200 international asset management firms are in Singapore, as are many of the world's leading names in insurance broking and captive and risk management. All this makes Singapore well placed to share its expertise with the region's stakeholders.

Singapore has an infrastructure office, Infrastructure Asia, to support infrastructure development in the region by bringing together local and international partners across the infrastructure value chain, including developers, institutional investors, multilaterals, and legal, accounting, and financial services providers. Infrastructure Asia is open for partnerships with foreign governments or companies (local and foreign) looking to participate in regional infrastructure projects.

Infrastructure Asia can connect governments in Asia with domain experts (subsegment champions) among developers and professional services, as well as with technical and financing solutions to meet specific project needs. It can bring parties together with the required expertise with project partners to bridge knowledge gaps and raise capabilities in project development, financing, and implementation. It also provides advisory services on project scoping and conceptual structuring to improve the viability and success of projects.

Through Infrastructure Asia, Singapore has positioned itself as a broker for regional infrastructure investments by leveraging its experience as global financial hub.

Source: Infrastructure Asia. https://www.infrastructureasia.org/.

Box A1.9: Regional Funds in Europe and Africa

The following are examples of regional funds used in Europe, under a regional institution, and Africa, under a regional financing institution:

Funds under the European Commission

- **Connecting Europe Facility:** This is for transport infrastructure projects; it provides financial support (grants, loans) with a maximum cofinancing of 50% of project costs. The European Commission has considerable influence on approvals and project time frames, which ensures that priority projects are not hit by delays.
- **European Structural and Investment Funds:** These include the following:
  Cohesion Fund: This supports grant projects to reduce economic and social disparities and promote sustainable development in 15 Cohesion Fund member states. Maximum cofinancing is 85%.
  European Regional Development Fund: This aims to strengthen economic and social cohesion in the European Union by correcting imbalances between regions using grants. Maximum cofinancing is 85%.
  European Fund for Strategic Investment: This supports investment in key sectors through financial guarantees.
  Horizon 2020: This provides funding for research and development projects with the aim of transferring great ideas from the lab to the market.

Fund under a regional financing institution

- **African Development Fund:** This is the concessional window of the African Development Bank.

Source: Secondary sources on the regional institutions.

Delays in meeting project timelines. Regional transport infrastructure projects in the BIMSTEC region are generally carried out using engineering procurement or item-rate contracts. Because of this, projects depend on government budgetary support for funding—and, as noted earlier, regional projects often compete with other budgetary demands from wholly domestic infrastructure projects, with the latter often given a higher priority by local governments.

APPENDIX 2

Country Assessments

Public–Private Partnership Capacity Assessment Framework

Table A2.1 shows the determinants and their respective criteria used to assess the public–private partnership (PPP) capacity of Bay of Bengal Initiative for Multi-Sectoral Technical and Economic Cooperation (BIMSTEC) countries. The scoring is the same as that used in Table A2.122.

Table A2.1: Public–Private Partnership Capacity Assessment Framework

Area	#	Determinants	Relevance	Criteria	0	1	2	3
PPP law, policy support	1	Is there a dedicated legal or policy instrument or guideline for PPPs?	High		No	Yes, general or sector-specific PPP guidelines for some transport infrastructure sectors.	Yes, general and sector- specific PPP guidelines exist for some or all transport infrastructure sectors. Guidelines cover various PPP models (e.g., BOT, joint venture).	Yes, PPP guidelines with legislation covering all sectors and various PPP models (e.g., BOT, joint venture).
PPP law, policy support	2	What dispute resolution mechanisms are available for PPP agreements?	Medium		Dispute resolution not available.	Dispute resolution mechanisms are not well defined and time-bound; no dedicated tribunal or authority.	Well-defined mechanisms for dispute resolution, along with defined authority and compensation rules.	Well-defined dispute resolution mechanism with compensation rules, at country level as well as international arbitration.
Public sector PPP capacity and experience	3	Are different PPP/concession models defined for the sector and are sector-specific model concession agreements available?	Medium	Use of standard procurement documents and contracts with no negotiation can reduce transaction costs. These are most likely to be suitable for greenfield projects that follow a standard design for which previous PPPs have previously been successfully awarded.	No	Yes, model concession agreement, model request for quote, and model request for proposal are available for some PPP or concession models.	Yes, model concession agreement, model request for quote, and model request for proposal available.	Yes, model concession agreement, model request for quote, and model request for proposal available, and strictly adhered to in implementation.

continued on next page

Table A2.1 *continued*

Area	#	Determinants	Relevance	Criteria	0	1	2	3
Public sector PPP capacity and experience	4	Is a streamlined approval process followed by the authority for the project to be approved as a PPP?	Medium					
	a	Technical feasibility			No			Yes
	b	Financial feasibility			No			Yes
	c	Legal feasibility			No			Yes
	d	Environmental and social sustainability			No			Yes
	e	Value-for-money assessment			No			Yes
	f	Fiscal affordability assessment			No			Yes
	g	PPP structuring and risk allocation			No			Yes
	h	Initial market testing			No			Yes
Land acquisition and clearances	5	Does the authority have experience in dealing with land acquisitions, environmental clearances, and R&R?	High	This reflects the authority's knowledge of terms of the processes and protocols, along with the knowledge of procedural issues. This will help the authority to develop a more effective plan to deal with these aspects.	For less than five projects.	For 5–10 projects.	For 10–15 projects.	For more than 15 projects.
Land acquisition and clearances	6	Does the authority have a dedicated team to streamline land acquisitions and environmental clearances, and the experience to handle these areas?	High	Presence of a dedicated team creates accountability and necessary bandwidth, which can essentially expedite the process.	No			Yes, a dedicated team has a thorough understanding of the process and has considerable experience in obtaining clearances.

continued on next page

Table A2.1 *continued*

Area	#	Determinants	Relevance	Criteria	0	1	2	3
Public sector PPP capacity and experience	7	Is there a specialized government agency (or agencies) established for PPP purposes (e.g., PPP unit), and what are its roles?	Medium	Defined PPP government mechanisms in place to coordinate needs.	No PPP focal point.			
	a	Guidance and coordination between other government agencies	High		No			Yes
	b	Support (e.g., PPP project preparation, appointment of advisers, running project development fund)	High		No			Yes
	c	Appraisal of PPP project feasibility studies	High		No			Yes
	d	Approval of PPP projects	High		No			Yes
	e	Procurement	High		No			Yes
	f	Managing, monitoring, and enforcing ongoing PPP contracts	High		No			Yes
Public sector PPP capacity and experience	8	Does the sponsoring agency have experience with PPPs?	High		No experience.	Experience in two or more PPP projects that are under procurement.	Experience in two or more PPP projects that are under construction.	Experience in two or more PPP projects that became operational in last 3 years.
Creditworthiness of the authority	9	If payment is likely to be made by the parent government, what is the credit rating of the parent government?	Medium	Creditworthiness reduces revenue risk and encourages competition in the sector, enticing many bidders to participate.	Below B	BB or B	A or BBB	AAA or AA

continued on next page

Table A2.1 *continued*

Area	#	Determinants	Relevance	Criteria	0	1	2	3
Creditworthiness of the authority	10	If payments are likely to be made from authority's budget, is there any form of government guarantee available for the payments?	Medium	Creditworthiness reduces revenue risk and encourages competition in the sector, enticing many bidders to participate.				
	a	Currency inconvertibility and transfer risk	Medium		No			Yes
	b	Foreign exchange risk	Medium		No			Yes
	c	War and civil disturbance risk	Low		No			Yes
	d	Breach-of-contract risk	Low		No			Yes
	e	Regulatory risk	Medium		No			Yes
	f	Expropriation risk	Low		No			Yes
	g	Government payment obligation guarantee	Medium		No			Yes
	h	Credit guarantees	High		No			Yes
	i	Minimum demand/revenue guarantee	High		No			Yes
Public sector funding assistance for PPPs	11	Is government support for viability gap funding available for PPP projects?	High	Government support or assistance can help make projects attractive for private sector.	No	0%–20% of project capital cost.	20%–35% of project capital cost.	35%–50% of project capital cost.
Life-cycle cost	12	Can most of the costs, mainly related to construction and long-term operations, including maintenance, be quantified upfront with reasonable assumptions, and are historical data available?	High	Better estimation of life-cycle costs would support private concessionaires to make more informed bids.	Project life-cycle costs are not well understood and cannot be estimated by the public authority.	Limited understanding of life-cycle costs, and costs cannot be accurately estimated by the public authority.	Project life-cycle costs are well understood, and can be somewhat accurately estimated by the public authority.	Project life-cycle costs are well understood, and can be accurately estimated by the public authority.

continued on next page

Table A2.1 *continued*

Area	#	Determinants	Relevance	Criteria	0	1	2	3
Market capacity and interest	13	Is there sufficient market capacity and are there private parties with PPP experience?	High		No market capacity and no private players to participate.	Some market capacity and interest of private players can be brought in through market outreach.	Established market capacity and interest of private players can be brought in through market outreach.	Established market capacity and interested private players.
Output specifications	14	Are objective output specifications readily available from a previous contract?	Medium	Presence of readily available output specifications tested in other projects improves the possibility of successful PPPs.	No			Yes
Foreign participation	15	Is foreign participation in PPPs allowed?	Country specific		Foreign participation not allowed.	Foreign participation allowed with some limitations.	Foreign participation allowed with no limitations	Foreign participation allowed freely, and actively sought and encouraged.
Foreign participation	16	Is the exchange rate stable?	Country specific	Exchange rate risk can reduce foreign participation in PPPs.	No			Yes
Foreign participation	17	Are there restrictions on foreign investors' land use/ ownership rights (i.e., are they the same as for local investors)?	Country specific	Land user/ ownership restrictions can hamper development during project construction phase.	Yes			No
Access to finance	18	Is there a robust project finance market, which supplements the traditional corporate finance market?	Medium	Access to finance is critical for timely financial closure at a low cost.	No			Yes
Access to finance	19	Are debt instruments available for different project needs, such as senior, mezzanine, and subordinate debt, and take-out financing?	Medium	Debt instruments are critical for meeting the long-term financing needs of infrastructure PPP projects.	No			Yes

BOT = build-operate-transfer, JV = joint venture, PPP = public–private partnership, R&R = rehabilitation and resettlement.

Source: Asian Development Bank. 2017. *Public–Private Partnership Monitor*. Manila. https://www.adb.org/publications/public-private-partnership-monitor; World Bank. 2016. *Country Readiness Diagnostic for Public–Private Partnerships*. Washington, DC. https://pubdocs.worldbank.org/en/943711467733900102/Country-PPP-Readiness-Diagnostic-Tool.pdf; and study team analysis.

Bangladesh

Transport Infrastructure Financing Landscape

Sources of Transport Infrastructure Financing

Bangladesh will require an annual investment of $14.9 billion, 4.7% of gross domestic product (GDP), according to the Global Infrastructure Hub Report. The International Monetary Fund's World Economic Outlook Database shows multilateral and bilateral funding for transport infrastructure was, as of October 2017, 1.4%–1.8% of GDP. Current public–private funding sources, including multilateral and bilateral loans, cover only 2.1% of GDP out of an annual investment need of 4.7% of GDP for financing transport infrastructure (Figure A2.1). Because of the high annual investment requirement and limited budgetary support from the government, Bangladesh's dependence on other financing instruments for developing transport infrastructure will increase.

Figure A2.1: Sources of Infrastructure Investments in Bangladesh
(% of GDP)

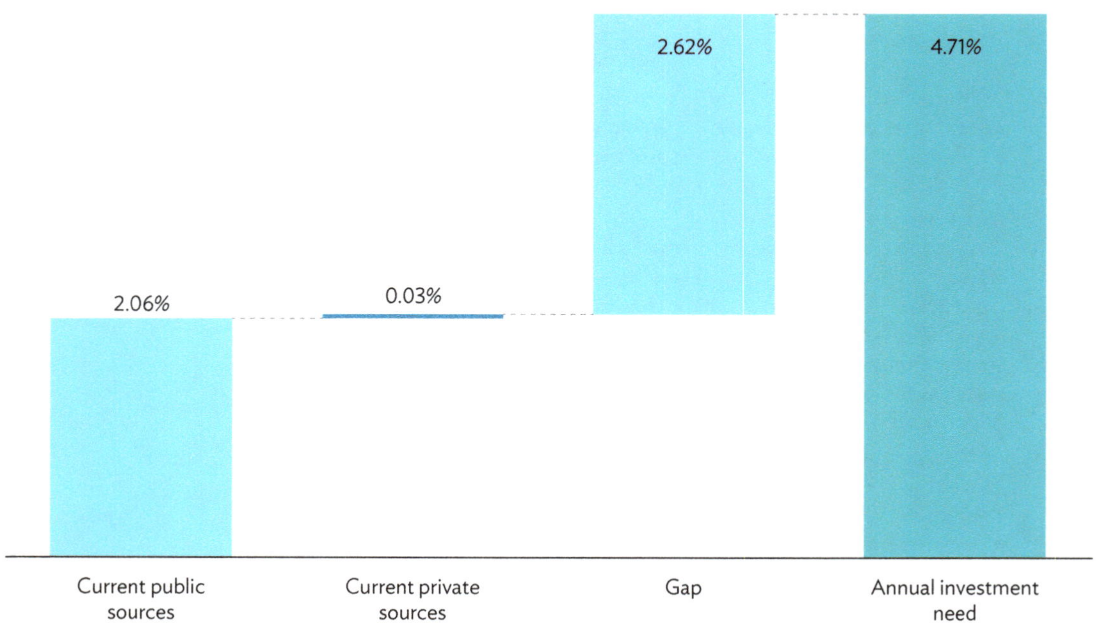

GDP = gross domestic product.

Sources: Global Infrastructure Hub; Ministry of Finance; and World Bank data.

Moody's Investors Service expects the government's debt burden to remain low, at 35%–37% of GDP over the coming years. Government revenue, at 12.6% of GDP as of June 2019, is the lowest of any country in the world.

As Figures A2.2 and A2.3 show, the fiscal deficit is less than 5% and government debt as ratios of GDP less than 30%. The government aimed to limit these fiscal ratios to 5.5% and 35.0% in fiscal year (FY)2020 (ending 30 June) to limit future budget growth. The fiscal deficit target for FY2021 is 6%. Fitch Ratings expects fiscal deficits of under 50% of GDP for the next few years. Bangladesh's debt-to-GDP ratio has been around 35% since FY2019 due to moderate revenue shortfalls, the right mix of credit, and a stable exchange rate.

Figure A2.2: Bangladesh Central Government Fiscal Deficit, FY2015–FY2019
(% of GDP)

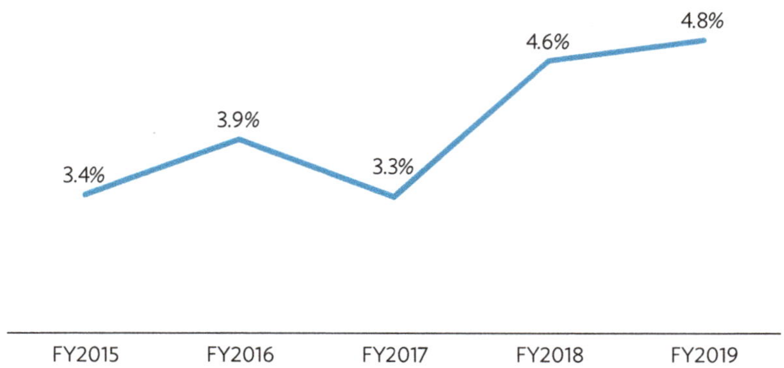

FY = fiscal year, GDP = gross domestic product.

Note: FY ends 30 June.

Sources: Bangladesh Bank; and Ministry of Finance.

Figure A2.3: Bangladesh Government Debt, FY2014–FY2019
(% of GDP)

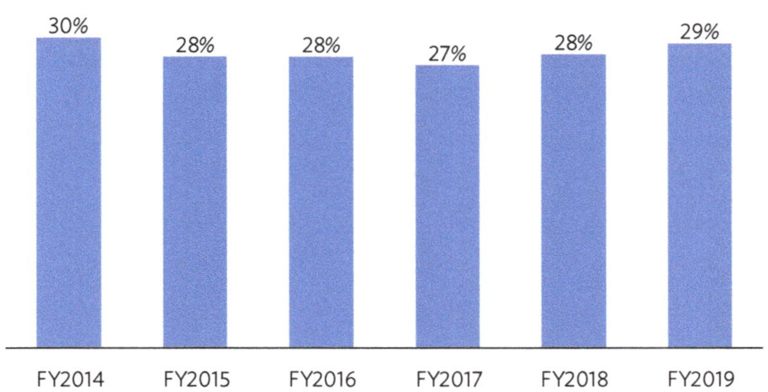

FY = fiscal year, GDP = gross domestic product.

Note: FY ends 30 June.

Sources: Bangladesh Bank; and Ministry of Finance.

In FY2020, the government launched various stimulus packages totaling $12 billion—3.7% of GDP—to tackle the economic impact of coronavirus disease (COVID-19). The economic slowdown caused by the pandemic has been an additional stress on government borrowing and the fiscal deficit target.[1] Fitch Ratings, Moody's Investors Service, and Standard and Poor's Global Ratings expect the economy to continue growing by 7%–8% over the next few years, underpinned by its globally competitive ready-made garments industry and supported by macroeconomic and external stability. Table A2.2 shows the ratings outlook from the three credit rating agencies.

Table A2.2: Bangladesh's Sovereign Ratings and Outlook by Global Credit Rating Agencies

Agency	Rating	Outlook	Date
Fitch	Reaffirmed BB–	Stable	25 Nov 2019
Moody's	Reaffirmed Ba3	Stable	19 Mar 2020
Standard and Poor	BB–	Stable	Oct 2019

Sources: Fitch Ratings; Moody's Investors Service; and Standard & Poor's Global Ratings.

Because investment and foreign direct investment (FDI) has been primarily in high-growth sectors, such as garments, pharmaceuticals, and agriculture, encouraging investment on infrastructure and transport will be required in the near future.

Bridging the Financing Gap

Bangladesh's commercial banks have a low share of infrastructure loans and primarily lend to the manufacturing sector. Limits on the cost of lending imposed by Bangladesh Bank is a major factor dampening lending to infrastructure projects. The country's large nonbanking financial institutions (NBFIs), such as Infrastructure Development Company Limited (IDCOL), get concessional funds from multilateral sources channeled through the government, but this carries a foreign exchange risk. IDCOL on-lends to private infrastructure developers based on collateral. Other financial institutions, including insurance and pension funds, are at a nascent stage and need to be developed to create alternative financing sources for infrastructure.

Figure A2.4 shows the total investable capital, as a percentage of GDP, of Bangladesh's financial institutions and their contribution to infrastructure financing, as a percentage of their capital base.

1 *Daily Star*. 2020. Bangladesh's Stimulus Package Second Highest among Peer Countries. 15 June. https://www.thedailystar.net/business/news/bangladeshs-stimulus-package-second-highest-among-peer-countries-1914621.

Figure A2.4: Size and Contribution of Bangladesh's Financial Institutions to Infrastructure

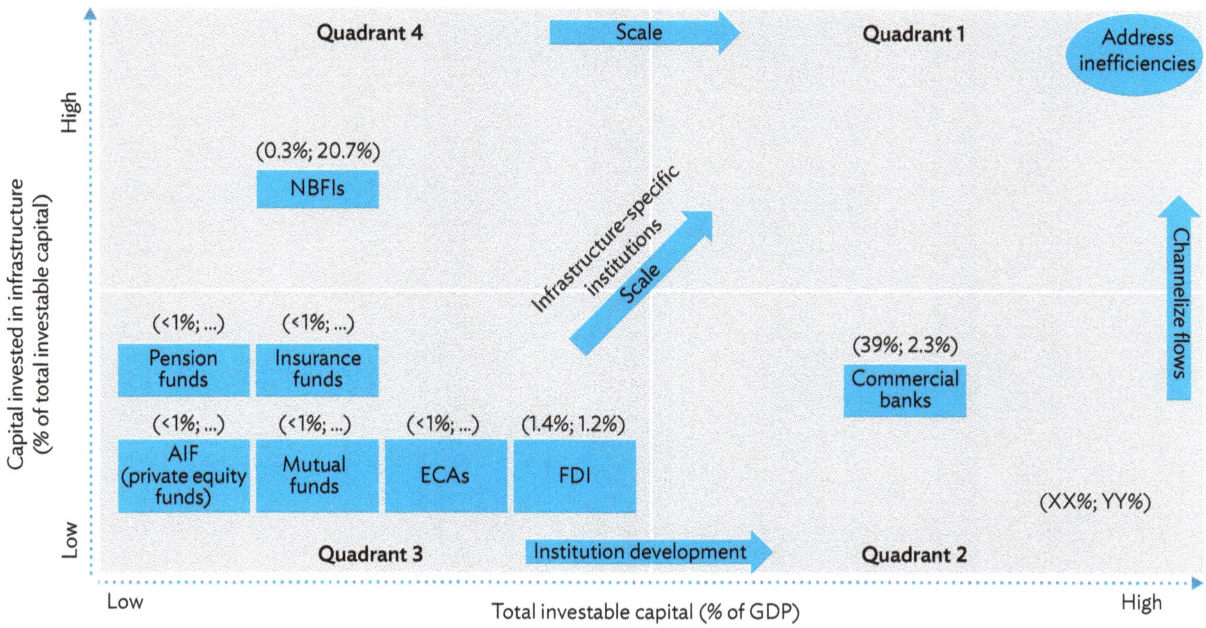

... = not available, AIF = alternative investment fund, ECA = export credit agency, FDI = foreign direct investment, GDP = gross domestic product, NBFI = nonbank financial institution.

Notes:

1. Percentage figures provide a comparative measure and are based on most recent data as available.
2. Institutions where data is not available are placed based on a general understanding from primary and secondary research.

Sources: Bank of Bangladesh; and secondary sources.

Challenges of Developing Bangladesh's Financing Institutions for Investing in Transport Infrastructure

The following assessment of Bangladesh's financial institutions has been done in two parts. The first identifies the challenges faced by these institutions in providing capital to infrastructure projects, and suggests interventions to overcome them. This essentially covers the supply-side of infrastructure financing. The second part identifies sector-related PPP challenges; this essentially covers the demand side of infrastructure financing.

Commercial Banks

Commercial banks are among the largest financial institutions in Bangladesh. As Figure A2.5 shows, the credit exposure of these banks to infrastructure is minimal, at 2.3%. They focus instead on high-growth sectors, such as textiles, agriculture, and services.

Figure A2.5: Infrastructure Exposure of Bangladesh Commercial Banks, FY2014–FY2019

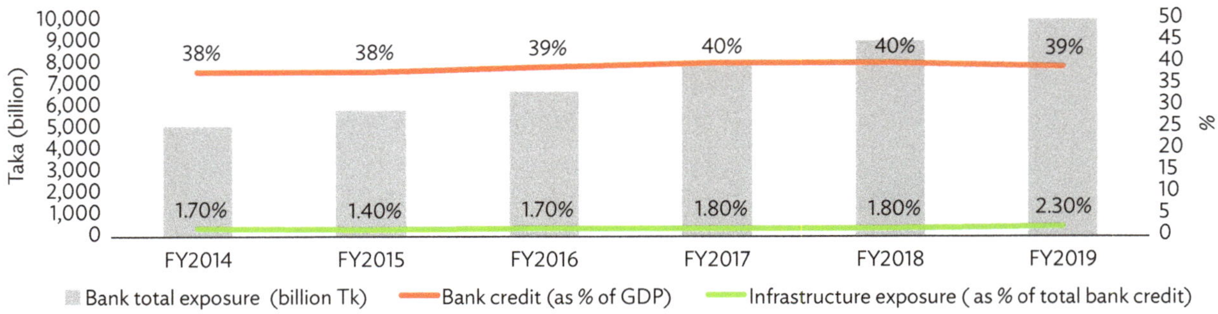

FY = fiscal year, GDP = gross domestic product, Tk = Bangladesh taka.

Note: FY ends 30 June.

Sources: Bangladesh Bank; and Ministry of Finance.

The following discusses the main issues for the low exposure of commercial banks in Bangladesh to transport infrastructure financing:

Rising nonperforming loans. High nonperforming loans (NPLs) in the banking system have restricted lending, especially to riskier infrastructure projects, and resulted in a low capital adequacy ratio.[2] Of Bangladesh's four types of bank (state commercial banks, private commercial banks, development finance institutions, and foreign commercial banks), with the second-largest market share in deposits (26%), have the highest NPL ratio, at 31%. Commercial banks face asset–liability mismatches due to the long-term nature of assets (loans) and the short-term nature of deposits (liabilities) (Figure A2.6).

Figure A2.6: Percentage of Bangladesh's Gross Nonperforming Loans to Total Loans by Bank Type, FY2013–FY2019

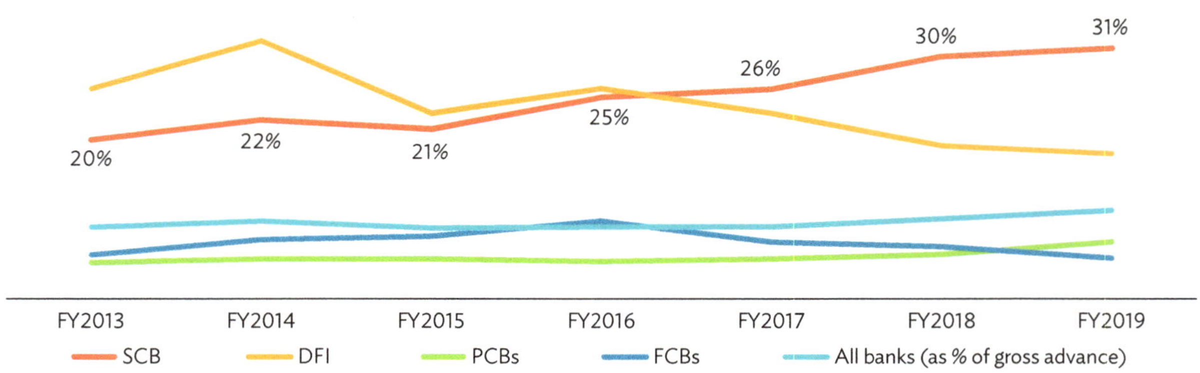

DFI = development finance institution, FCB = foreign commercial bank, FY = fiscal year, PCB = private commercial bank, SCB = state commercial bank.

Note: FY ends 30 June.

Sources: Bangladesh Bank; and Ministry of Finance.

2 The ratio of NPLs to total loans in 2017 was highest in India (10.0%), followed by Bangladesh (9.3%), Thailand (3.1%), Indonesia (2.6%), Viet Nam (2.3%), Sri Lanka (2.5%), and Malaysia (1.5%).

Table A2.3 outlines actions to reduce the high NPLs of commercial banks.

Table A2.3: Actions to Reduce Nonperforming Loans of Bangladesh's Commercial Banks

Action	Impact
Strengthen corporate governance and do careful due diligence. Loans should be made only on commercial considerations, with no external influences.	Reduced default risk and nonperforming loans.
Bankruptcy Act, 1997 should be strengthened. An insolvency and bankruptcy code, and timebound procedures, could be set up to provide better comfort to lenders.	Expedites the resolution and increased recovery of nonperforming loans.

Source: Study team analysis.

Upper limit on cost of lending. Because infrastructure projects are considered to be at a higher risk during the construction phase than the operational phase, the 9% upper limit on the cost of lending by Bangladesh Bank might not be able to cover project risks, especially time and cost overruns. The limit is a disincentive for investing in infrastructure. Box A2.1 is a short a case study from Kenya that is relevant to Bangladesh on this issue. Table A2.4 outlines actions to resolve the upper limit on the cost of lending in Bangladesh's commercial banks.

Box A2.1: Kenya's Interest Rate Cap

Kenya's Parliament passed a law capping interest rates on loans at 4% above the policy rate in September 2016. But the rate cap was removed in November 2019 because it caused significant harm to the economy.

As lending became unprofitable for banks, real credit growth turned from double-digit to negative almost immediately after the rate cap was implemented. Nonperforming loans surged from 6.8% in 2015 to 12.3% in 2017 because of the interruption to borrowers' working capital and capital expenditure needs. The figure shows real credit growth before and after the cap.

Kenya Real Credit Growth Before and After Lending Cap
(%)

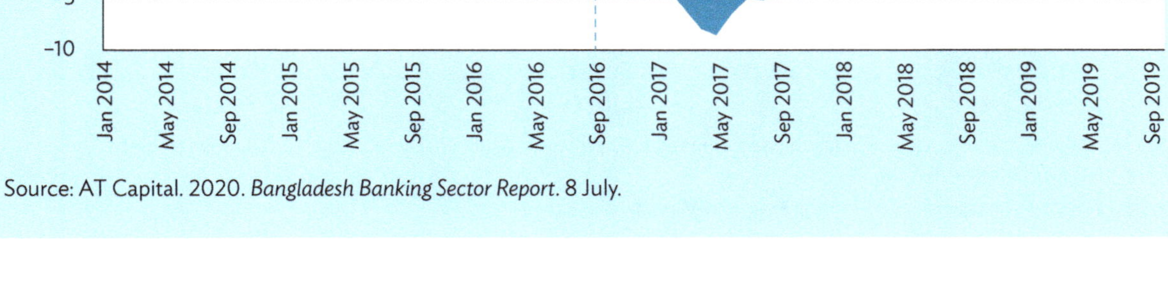

Source: AT Capital. 2020. *Bangladesh Banking Sector Report*. 8 July.

Table A2.4: Actions to Resolve the Cap on Cost Lending for Bangladesh Commercial Banks

Actions	Impact
For infrastructure projects, which typically have higher risk profiles, government could explore options for removing the 9% upper limit on the cost of lending on commercial bank lending rates Build the capacity of commercial banks to enable the pricing of loans based on the cost of funds and project risks	The proper pricing of loans and advances will help commercial banks cover costs and risks, improving lending profits

Source: Study team analysis.

Commercial banks have only limited capabilities to underwrite infrastructure projects. Because of this, NBFIs that are focused on infrastructure, such as IDCOL and Bangladesh Infrastructure Finance Fund Limited (BIFFL), should lead deal structuring while gradually involving commercial banks.

Nonbank Financial Institutions

Except for IDCOL and BIFFL, NBFIs primarily lend to the retail, pharmaceutical, and garment industries. IDCOL, with a loan portfolio of Tk60 billion (USD 542 million) in FY2018, is the country's largest NBFI and a major recipient of funding from multilateral agencies via the government for infrastructure investment. Most funding goes to power generation and renewable energy projects; 70% of these funds have maturities of less than 5 years. BIFFL, with a loan portfolio of Tk16 billion in FY2018, is the second largest. It invests mostly in ports, power, telecommunications, and renewable energy. Some 50% of funds have maturities of more than 5 years (Figure A2.7).

Figure A2.7: Infrastructure Exposure of Infrastructure Development Company and Bangladesh Infrastructure Finance Fund

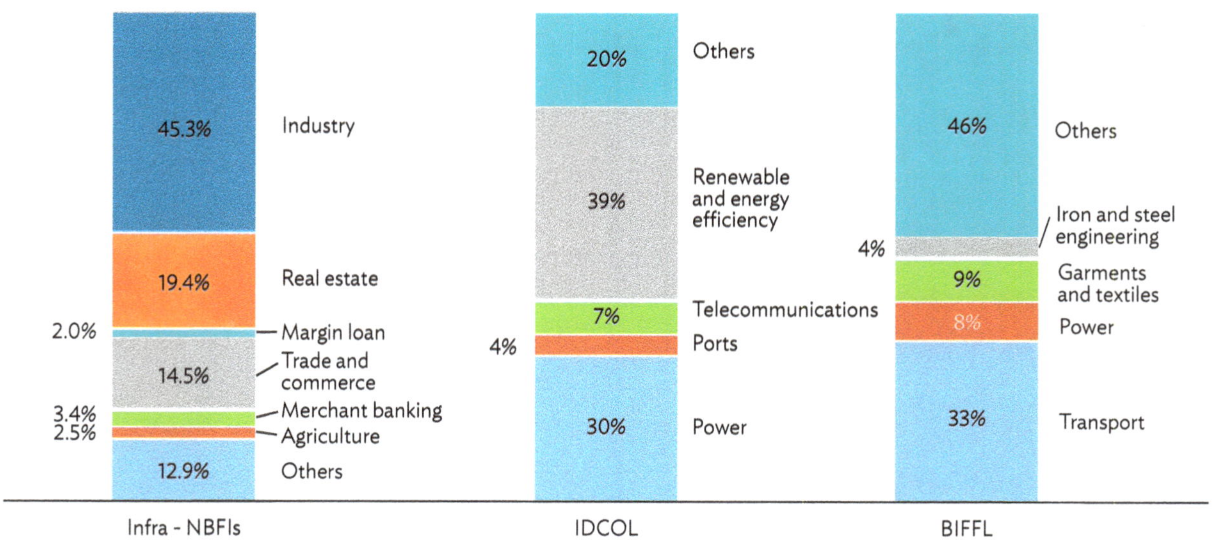

BIFFL = Bangladesh Infrastructure Finance Fund Limited, IDCOL = Infrastructure Development Company Limited, NBFI = nonbank financial institution.

Sources: 2018 annual reports of the companies; and Ministry of Finance.

Infrastructure-focused NBFIs face the following challenges: credit lines concentrated in just a few sectors, the 9% upper limit on the cost of lending; rising NPLs, and a lack of skills to underwrite transport infrastructure projects.

Sector concentration of credit lines. These are focused mainly on power, telecommunications, and manufacturing, according to interviews for this report with IDCOL and multilateral development banks, including the International Development Association, Japan International Cooperation Agency, and Germany's KfW, whose credit lines to NBFI infrastructure are mainly in these sectors. Table A2.5 outlines actions for increasing credit lines to transport infrastructure projects.

Table A2.5: Areas to Increase the Credit Lines of Bangladesh's Nonbank Financial Institutions

Actions	Impact
Government could work with development finance institutions (Appendix 14) to structure credit line for transport infrastructure projects.	Increased attractiveness of financing for transport infrastructure.
Nonbank financial institutions (NBFIs) focused on infrastructure can also explore alternative funding sources, such as borrowing through bonds. Because the corporate bond market is not developed in Bangladesh, NBFIs can raise funds by issuing bonds in regional financing hub.	NBFIs will be able to expand their exposure to other sectors including transport infrastructure.

Source: Study team analysis.

Upper limit on the cost of lending. The 9% cap that applies to commercial banks discussed earlier also applies to NBFIs. Table A2.6 outlines actions to resolve this.

Table A2.6: Actions to Resolve the Cap on Cost Lending for Bangladesh Nonbank Financial Institutions

Actions	Impact
For infrastructure projects, the government could explore options for removing the 9% limit on the cost of lending on nonbank financial institution (NBFI) lending rates, and allow these institutions to set rates based on the cost of funding, and the type of borrower and project.	Covering the cost and risks and thus maintaining the profitability of the banks and NBFIs through proper pricing of portfolio.
NBFIs should be allowed to flexibly price loans to cover risk during the construction phase; once projects become operational, interest rate revision needs to be taken up.	Proper pricing and covered risk in construction and operational phases reduce non-profitability risk.

Source: Study team analysis.

Foreign Direct Investment

To attract FDI, Bangladesh Bank in 2020 relaxed regulations on the repatriation of funds, allowing full repatriation of capital invested from foreign sources. Profits and dividends accruing to foreign investment can also be transferred in full. If foreign investors reinvest their dividends or retained earnings, these are treated as new investments.

Special facilities and venture capital support is provided to export-oriented industries. These so-called thrust sectors are primarily agricultural industries, information and technology, infrastructure, oil and gas, textiles, and tourism.

Full tax exemption on income and capital gains is given to certain PPPs for 10 years. In addition, 5 to 10 years of tax holiday and reduced tax depending on area is given. This incentive, according to the Bangladesh Development Authority, is not given to transport projects.

Full foreign equity ownership is allowed for FDI. Nonresident institutional and individual investors can make portfolio investments in Bangladesh's stock exchanges (Figure A2.8).

FDI growth doubled from FY2015 to FY2019, but as a percentage of GDP, growth has been nominal, at about 1.3%. About 90% of FDI is concentrated in export and thrust sectors. The transport sector, over the last decade, has attracted less than 1% (Figure A2.9). Table A2.7 outlines actions to increase FDI for developing infrastructure.

Figure A2.8: Foreign Direct Investment in Bangladesh, FY2013–FY2019

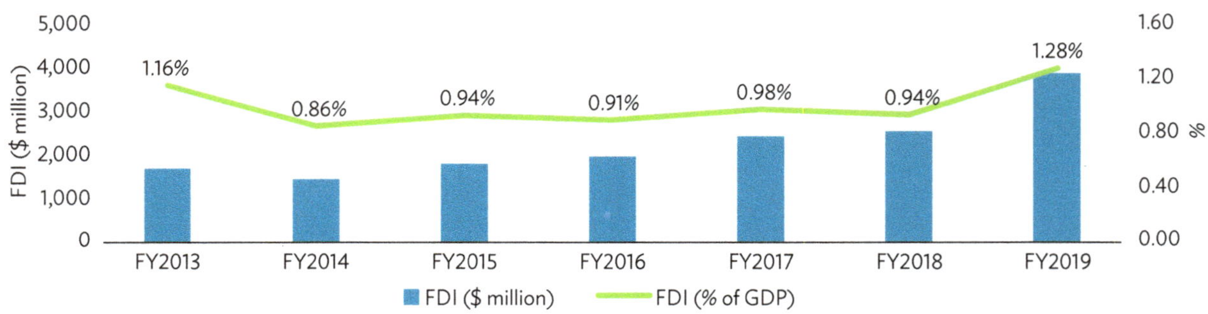

FDI = foreign direct investment, FY = fiscal year, GDP = gross domestic product.

Note: FY ends 30 June.

Sources: Bangladesh Bank; and Ministry of Finance.

Figure A2.9: Foreign Direct Investment in Bangladesh by Sector, FY2013–FY2019
(% of gross FDI)

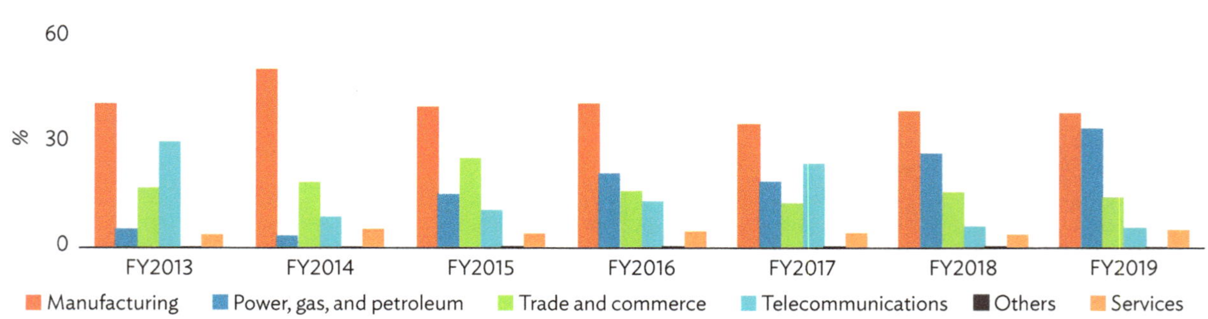

FDI = foreign direct investment, FY = fiscal year.

Note: FY ends 30 June.

Sources: Bangladesh Bank; and Ministry of Finance.

Table A2.7: Actions to Increase Foreign Direct Infrastructure Investment in Bangladesh

Actions	Impact
Agencies should be legally bound to follow One-Stop Service and provide more than 150 investment-related services, including timely repatriation, from multiple organizations (35 plus) through the online platform.	Attracts investors and makes it easier for them to start businesses in Bangladesh.
Improve brand image in terms of ease of doing business, create awareness of investment opportunities, and improve investment policies for existing and potential investors.	Boost foreign investment.

Source: Study team analysis.

Insurance Funds

The main issues here are not enough insurance funds, which reduces the availability of funds for infrastructure, and the absence of long-term debt instruments and high-quality bonds.

Too few insurance funds. Life insurance constitutes 73.5% of Bangladesh's insurance market and nonlife insurance the rest. As Figure A2.10 shows, insurance penetration—insurance premiums as a share of GDP—was 0.6% in 2018 and has mostly fallen since 2009.

Figure A2.10: Insurance Penetration in Bangladesh and Selected Economies (% of GDP)

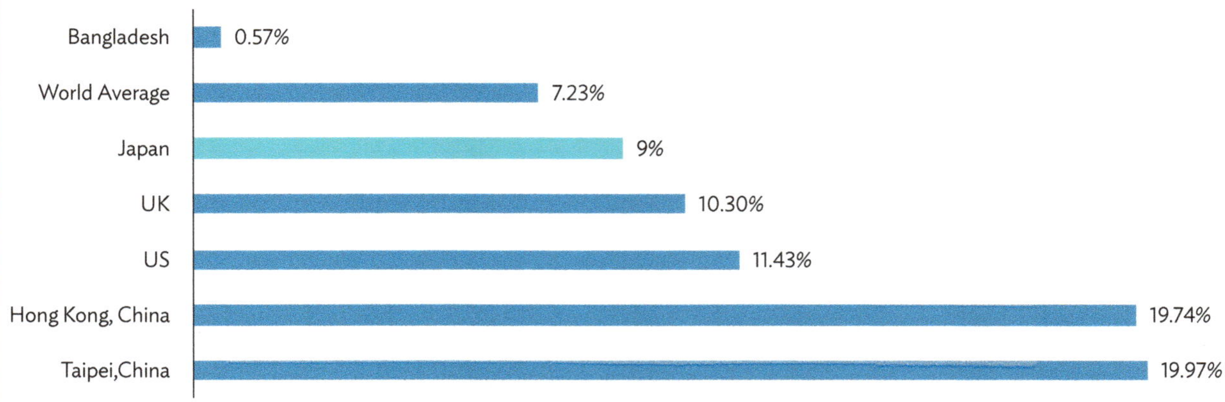

GDP = gross domestic product, UK = United Kingdom, US = United States.

Source: Statista 2019.

The growth of the insurance market in India using bancassurance and regulatory reforms in Egypt are experiences that could be useful for Bangladesh to increase its penetration of the insurance market (Appendix 5). Table A2.8 outlines actions to increase the pool of insurance funds in Bangladesh.

Table A2.8: Actions to Increase Insurance Funds in Bangladesh

Actions	Impact
Implement regulatory reforms similar to those undertaken by Egypt.	Significant growth in the insurance sector.
An opportunity for bancassurance: A partnership between an insurance company and a bank where the bank sells insurance product.	Customized products beneficial for customers, and all insurers and banks. Easy to grow business due to trust between customers and banks.

Source: Study team analysis.

Lack of long-term debt instruments and high-quality investable bonds. Insurance funds in Bangladesh can invest up to 15% of their total investments in infrastructure bonds with a minimum AA rating by a reputable and independent credit rating agency. Corporate bonds, however, are negligible in Bangladesh, with just a 0.01% share of total capital market. As Figure A2.11 shows, deposits with a share of 37% and bank loans at 32% dominate the long term debt instrument market. Table A2.9 outlines actions to remedy the lack of long-term debt instruments and high-quality investable bonds.

Figure A2.11: Size of Financial Instruments in Bangladesh
(%)

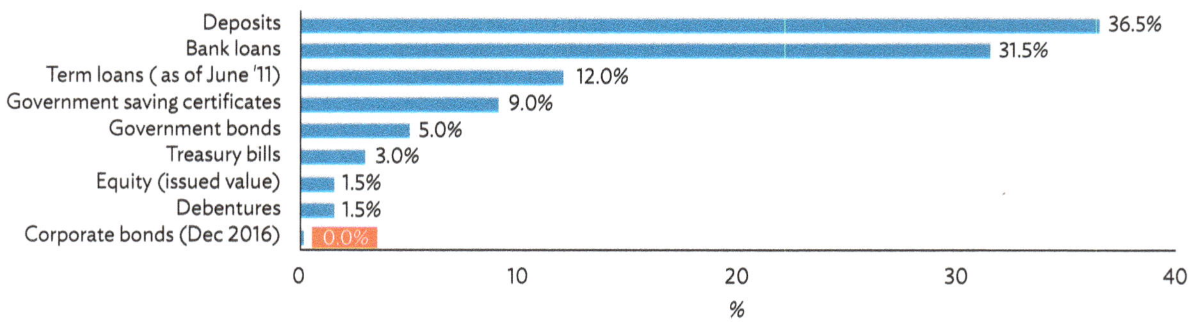

Source: Study team analysis.

Table A2.9: Actions to Remedy the Lack of Long-Term Debt Instruments and High-Quality Investible Bonds in Bangladesh

Actions	Impact
Increase promotion, education, and training programs on bonds among potential investors, including nonresident Bangladeshis.	Creates awareness and support for increasing the customer base.
Develop an online trading platform or long-term debt instruments to strengthen corporate governance and transparency.	Increased investor confidence.
Credit enhancement of bonds through guarantees and credit support; e.g., partial credit guarantees.	Better credit rating of bonds.

Source: Study team analysis.

Pension Funds

Bangladesh's informal economy provides employment for 87% of the workforce. About 2% of the workforce are in the government sector and are represented by Bangladesh's largest pension fund, Government Employees Pension and Provident Fund Scheme. Figure A2.12 shows zero coverage of Bangladesh's working population is covered by pensions, compared with selected developing and developed economies. Table A2.10 outlines actions to increase the corpus of pension funds in Bangladesh.

Figure A2.12: Working Population Covered by Pensions in Bangladesh and Selected Developed and Developing Economies
(%)

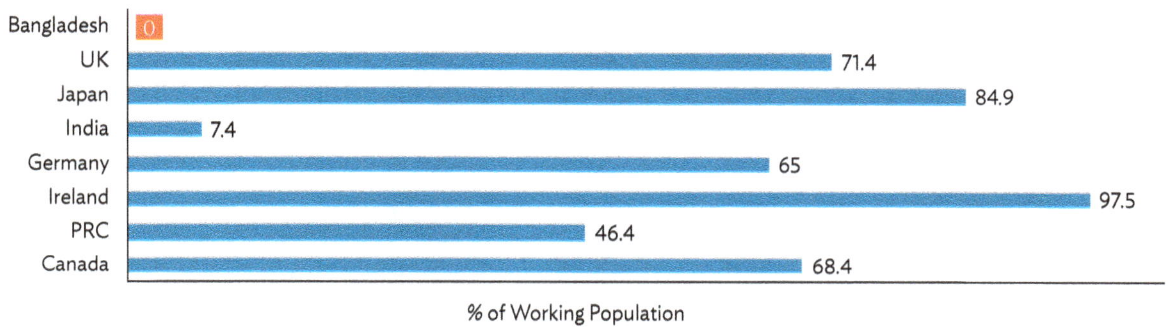

PRC = People's Republic of China, UK = United Kingdom.

Source: World Economic Forum. 2017. *Global Human Capital Report 2017*. Geneva. https://www.weforum.org/publications/the-global-human-capital-report-2017/.

Table A2.10: Actions to Increase the Corpus of Pension Funds in Bangladesh

Actions	Impact
Create awareness about pension and retirement planning.	Increased pension coverage for workers in the informal and private sectors.
Implement the 2014 Draft National Social Security Strategy, which includes pension policies for private sector employees.	Increased pension corpus.

Source: Study team analysis.

Debt Capital Market

Bangladesh needs to develop a debt capital market for both government securities and commercial bonds for attracting infrastructure investments. The market, as it stands, has insufficient corporate bond issuances. High fees and an absence of a yield curve deter investors, as does the market's overregulation. Table A2.11 outlines actions to develop the debt capital market.

Table A2.11: Actions to Develop Bangladesh's Debt Capital Market

	Market Parameter	Status	Actions
Market infrastructure	Central Counterparty or clearing house.	Delivery versus payment system used for transfers of government securities to avoid settlement risk.	Creation of a legal entity like Central Counterparty to mitigate counterparty default and settlement risks, especially for corporate bonds.
	Central security depository	Central Depository of Bangladesh operating since 2000.	Establish depository guidelines to ensure secure transfers of securities and secondary trading of government securities.
	Trading platform (stock exchange)	Chittagong and Dhaka Stock Exchanges are active but do not have trading platforms for fixed-income securities.	Stock exchanges could establish a separate platform for trading fixed-income securities. This would enhance liquidity and provide an exit route for investors.
Intermediaries	Primary dealers	Primary dealer system since 2003.	A system should be established to facilitate two-way price quotes, with primary dealers directed to quote two-way on a daily basis. Doing this would make the secondary market more efficient by bringing in more liquidity.
	Credit rating agencies	• Limited confidence in local credit rating agencies. • Most credit rating agencies do not have strategic partnerships with recognized international or regional credit rating agencies.	• A regulatory framework should be formulated for local credit rating agencies to establish strategic partnerships with recognized international rating agencies. • Bangladesh Bank should maintain and periodically update a list of approved credit rating agencies after evaluating their credentials.
	Brokerage houses	No dedicated fixed-income desk at brokerage houses.	Creating awareness and training among investors will help develop the bond market and enable the creation of a fixed-income desk.
Issuer	Government securities (reliable benchmark)	• Maturities are available for 2–20 years. • Insufficient instrument balance.	• Identify benchmark securities in the market and issue securities with suitable long tenors (e.g., 30, 40 years). • Increase the issuance of marketable government bonds to ensure a minimum net issuance every year. • State-owned enterprises, local government entities, and utility companies could issue bonds and develop instrument balance.
	T-Bonds auction calendar	No medium-term auction calendar.	Plan and publish an auction calendar at least on a half-yearly basis and hold auctions as per pre-announced auction calendar.
Investor	Commercial banks/primary dealers	Need for bank portfolio restructuring.	Based on market conditions, held-to-maturity and held-for-trading portfolios should be restructured and revised from time to time.

continued on next page

Table A2.11 *continued*

	Market Parameter	Status	Actions
	Pension, insurance, and mutual funds	Absence of established pension/provident funds.	• Set up pension funds for government employees. • Set up a separate regulatory body to formulate pension policies and regulate entities dealing with public and private pension funds. • Direct the government, semi-government entities, autonomous corporations, and private corporations and organizations to invest a certain percentage of their provident and gratuity funds in government bonds instead of National Savings Scheme certificates.
	Retail investors	Tax incentives for savings instruments lower demand for government debt instruments.	• Uniform tax treatment for all government debt instruments and other saving instruments for individual investors. • Government should sell National Savings Directorate instruments only to targeted groups, e.g., senior citizens, people on low incomes.
	Foreign institutional investors and portfolio	No foreign investors trading bonds on the exchange or over the counter market in fiscal year 2018.	• Allow government securities to be traded on the Dhaka Stock Exchange and Chittagong Stock Exchange platforms to make trading more convenient for institutional/individual/ foreign investors. • Introduce foreign currency-denominated government securities to attract foreign investors to increase inflow of foreign remittances and reduce pressure on the local money market.
External environment	Fiscal debt management	Fiscal policy guided by Public Money and Budget Management Act, 2009.	• The fiscal deficit widened to 4.6% of gross domestic product in fiscal year 2020. Government should take steps to reduce debt gradually, as stipulated in the act.
	Securities and exchange laws	Government securities operate under public debt (central government) rules from 1946.	• Regulations needed to clarify that if bonds are issued by a pass-through special purpose vehicle under the Trust Act, will be nominal stamp duty and the special purpose vehicle will be a non-taxable entity. • Trust structures and regulations are needed to guarantee incomes generated through assets.
	Treasury and cash management	Inadequate cash forecasting: this leads to frequent shifts/ instability in demand, hindering bond market development.	• Cash and Debt Management Committee should focus on developing the financial market and the cash and debt management of the government. • Government should adopt a clear issuance strategy and conduct cash forecasting in every financial year. • Ministry of Finance should establish a central information technology–based cash management cell.

Source: Study team analysis.

Insufficient corporate bond issuances. Because of limited transparency and the need to improve corporate governance standards, Bangladesh's corporate bond market remains small compared with other Asian bond markets (Figure A2.13). Table A2.12 outlines actions to develop this market.

Figure A2.13: Size of Corporate Bond Markets in Selected Asian Economies
(% of GDP)

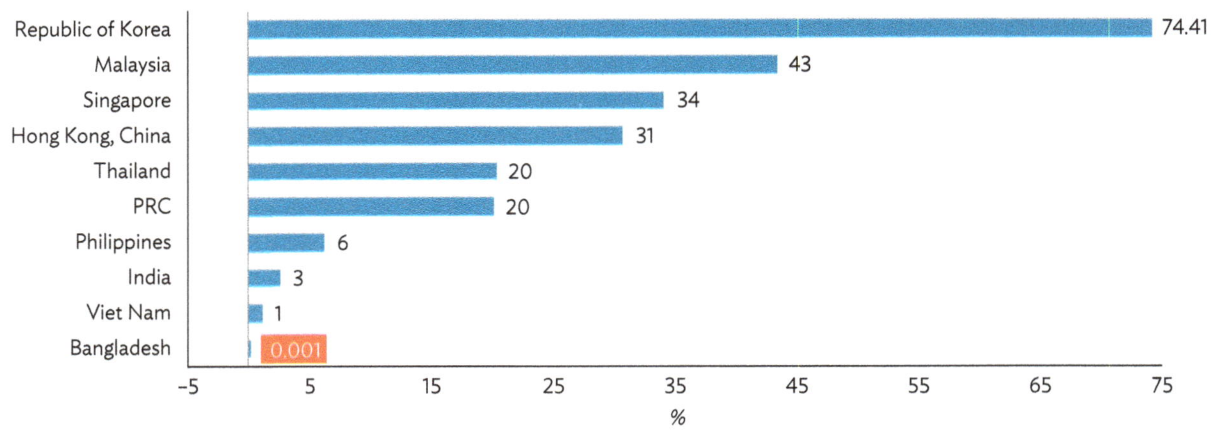

GDP = gross domestic product, PRC = People's Republic of China.

Source: Akter, A., R. H. Himo, and A. B. Siddik. 2019. *Corporate Bond Market: The Case of Bangladesh*. World Review of Business Research. Volume 9. No. 1. March. pp.20-38.

Table A2.12: Actions to Develop Bangladesh's Corporate Bond Market

Actions	Impact
Strengthen corporate governance and transparency.	Increased investor confidence of investors.
Develop a secondary market for corporate bonds that has instruments traded through an electronic platform.	Resolved illiquidity problem would attract more investors.

Source: Study team analysis.

High fees and absence of yield curve deter investors. High upfront commissions and charges during prospectus filing from, among other things, trustee deed stamp duties raise the cost of funding for issuers. Some 1.5%–2.0% of the total issuance cost is spent on registration fees, stamp duties, trustee fees, issue manager fees, underwriting fees (for a public issue of bonds), getting a credit rating, legal and audit fees, central depository fees, listing fees, printing of prospectuses, application fees, and certificates. Trustee costs can rise to 5% of the total amount raised. These charges have already been waived for mutual fund issuances. Registration fees for issuing debentures are also lower than bond issues.

Bond investors do not want their holdings stuck in illiquid instruments for tenures of more than 3 years, as this results in high opportunity cost and missing out on other investments with better returns. Table A2.13 outlines actions areas to tackle these issues.

Table A2.13: Actions for Pricing and Yield Curve Problems in Bond Issues in Bangladesh

Actions	Impact
Develop other mechanisms to benchmark a bond; e.g., using sovereign ratings for indicative indices (regulators have indicated support for setting this up).	Develops a credible yield curve and participants will have mark-to-market valuation of bonds. Supports development of secondary bond market.
Coordinate efforts with stakeholders, especially the Bangladesh Securities and Exchange Commission and the National Board of Revenue, to reduce high upfront commissions or charges during prospectus filing.	Parity with other financial instruments, such as mutual funds.

Source: Study team analysis.

Restrictive regulations, limited market infrastructure. Bond investors perceive the market to be overly regulated by restrictions on investing in corporate bonds and certain sectors (Table A2.14). Funding from capital markets is allowed only for projects that have been operating for at least 3 years, and is prohibited for greenfield projects.

Companies and high net worth individuals get tax benefits from investing in bonds, but banks and other financial institutions do not. The National Board of Revenue has tax benefit schemes for individuals investing in debt securities, but these are not available for banks, financial institutions, or insurance companies.

Corporate governance for private players is low and there is little accountability. This leads to defaults in interest payments on bonds raised, which has led to low investor confidence.

Table A2.14: Actions for Easing Restrictive Bond Market Regulations and Strengthening Market Infrastructure in Bangladesh

Actions	Impact
Coordinated effort from various stakeholders—Ministry of Finance, Prime Minister's Office, Bangladesh Bank, Bangladesh Securities and Exchange Commission, Bangladesh Investment Development Authority, public-private partnership Authority, and sector regulators—to develop a clear set of market regulation procedures for financing transport infrastructure projects through bonds. Developing a framework based on credit rating agencies, experience, financial strength so that funding can be extended to greenfield projects.	Increased supply of funds from bond market and, in turn, demand base.
Develop options so that tax benefit incentives can be extended to banks and financial institutions.	Increased investor base.
Ensure bonds are raised by companies that are leaders in their respective market segments and have a good credit profile, based on their past performance and financial strength. These issues should be structured and marketed well.	Increases the credibility and confidence of investors.

Source: Study team analysis.

Private Equity and Venture Capital Funds

Both are at a nascent state of development. Bangladesh's private equity funds primarily invest in high-growth sectors, such as information and communication technology, e-commerce, manufacturing, and energy. Investor confidence in these sectors is high due to their strong historical performance and growth prospects. The government has made information and communications technology and energy priority sectors, further driving interest in both.

The Securities and Exchange Commission, in 2015, issued the Alternative Investment Rules that are applicable to private equity and venture capital funds. The main players in infrastructure-focused private equity funds are Brummer and Partners, SEAF Bangladesh Ventures, and Islamic Infrastructure Fund. The effective tax rate on the profits and income of private equity investors is high: 35% corporate tax and a 2% stamp duty on a fund's total capital. Table A2.15 outlines actions to develop the market of both fund types.

Table A2.15: Actions to Develop Private Equity and Venture Capital Funds in Bangladesh

Actions	Impact
Private equity and venture capital funds should be exempted from stamp duty and get a tax holiday on management fees.	Incentivized investors.
Create awareness programs, such as road shows, on investment opportunities in both fund types.	Improved project attractiveness for investors.
Enhance and develop the capability of private equity and venture capital fund managers.	Increased investor confidence and stronger institutions.
Reduce the lock-in period of initial public offering from 3 years to 1 year for Bangladesh Securities and Exchange Commission–licensed private equity investors. Create an investment environment suitable for exit strategies.	Increased interest from local and foreign investors.

Source: Study team analysis.

Challenges in Public–Private Partnership Projects: Limited Capability within Banks to Underwrite Infrastructure Projects and Other Design Issues in Public–Private Partnership Projects Needing to be Addressed by Government

Undertaking PPP projects in Bangladesh is a challenge. Banks have little capacity to underwrite projects. Although about Tk40 billion is allocated to infrastructure projects per year, most of these funds are unspent.[3] The following discussion looks at how these challenges affect road and road transport PPP projects.

A key challenge is unfamiliarity with the PPP concept. Building the capacity and capability to use PPP modes does take time, and it took about a decade to fully take off in the United Kingdom. Even so, a systematic approach to PPPs is lacking in Bangladesh. PPPs have been most successful in power generation, because of the legal and regulatory framework for this sector, transparent procurement processes, efficient off-take guarantees, and the creation of sector-specific PPPs, such as the Power Cell and PPP office.[4] But the overall performance of PPPs in

3 *Financial Express*. 2020. Effective Strategy to Make PPP Initiatives Successful. 14 May. https://thefinancialexpress.com.bd/views/effective-strategy-to-make-ppp-initiatives-successful-1589384293.

4 http://www.powercell.gov.bd/; http://www.pppo.gov.bd/.

terms of implementation and operational success stories has been underwhelming. In other infrastructure sectors, such as roads, no PPPs have been successfully developed.[5]

For PPPs, the legal framework to distribute risks is limited, as are resources and rewards for public and private partners. Procedural delays have hit PPPs in the past, becoming a hurdle for more private participation in infrastructure projects. The lack of PPP guidelines and slow progress in implementing PPP projects have become disincentives for foreign investment in Bangladesh, as the case studies on the construction of the Dhaka–Chittagong National Highway and the Khanpur Inland Container Terminal Project show.

The construction of the Dhaka–Chittagong National Highway stalled due to the unavailability of the required technical assistance fund for upfront project development activities.[6] The Asian Development Bank (ADB) has taken up this project and plan to progress it forward. The Khanpur Inland Container Terminal Project implementation faced problems as public sector officials did not having a clear understanding about the procurement process of such private sector infrastructure projects. There were also delays in decision-making by the procuring agency, leading to investors losing interest in the project.

Canada, India, Singapore, and the United Kingdom have instituted rigorous regulatory frameworks and responsible public bureaucracies for implementation of PPP projects. For Bangladesh, the main concerns here are weak governance and the lack of transparency and accountability in PPP contracts.

The following interventions could help tackle Bangladesh's PPP challenges:[7]

(i) Strong governance structures and clear rules and regulations for allocating project risk, including construction and interface risk, between public and private partners and other stakeholders; and
(ii) Project authorities setting up a PPP cell to perform a wide range of services to develop PPP policies and legislation; formulating model contracts, manuals, and processes for identifying and developing PPPs; and setting up clearance and approval functions during the procurement and construction stage of PPPs. Sources of expertise need to be developed for PPP procurement and management, training programs, dissemination of PPP information, and assessing the fiscal costs (direct and contingent) of PPPs.
(iii) Extensive stakeholder consultations and PPP training on commercial, financial, legal, and negotiating aspects of these partnerships to strengthen the PPP ecosystem.
(iv) Detailed technical, financial, legal, environmental and social due diligence by agencies engaged during feasibility study, covering both the sponsor and the project.

Public–Private Partnership Capacity Assessment

To understand the capacity and experience of Bangladesh, and the areas that need to be improved to encourage private participation, this section contains a PPP capacity assessment using determinants under six defining areas to rate the country.

5 Bdnew24.com. 2016. Potentials and Challenges of Public–Private Partnership. 28 March. https://opinion.bdnews24.com/2016/03/28/potentials-and-challenges-of-public-private-partnership/.

6 ADB. 2017. *Public–Private Partnership Monitor.* Manila. https://www.researchgate.net/publication/309207990_The_Performances_and_Challenges_of_Public-Private_Partnership_PPP_Projects_in_Bangladesh.

7 The Performance and Challenges of Public-Private Partnership (PPP) Projects in Bangladesh, Md. Abu Rashed, PPP Advisor, PPP Office, Prime Minister's Office, Government of Bangladesh.

Public–Private Partnership Law and Policy Support Capacity

Table A2.16: Ratings for PPP Law and Policy Support Capacity in Bangladesh

#	Determinant	Rating
1	Is there a dedicated legal or policy instrument/guideline for PPPs?	3
2	What dispute resolution mechanisms are available for PPP agreements?	2

PPP = public–private partnership.

Source: Study team analysis.

Determinant 1: The government passed the Bangladesh PPP Act in September 2015 with the help of ADB's Office of Markets Development and Public–Private Partnership to facilitate the development of public infrastructure projects in sectors important to the people of Bangladesh. The law replaced a 2010 policy and strategy for PPPs. In 2017, a policy framework for implementing PPPs through government-to-government partnerships (either through state-owned enterprises or private enterprises) was completed.

Determinant 2: The PPP Act states that disputes arising from the application or interpretation of PPP agreement provisions should be settled by mutual agreement between the parties. If this does not work, the law provides for an expert mediator to be called in. If this fails, the case goes to arbitration.

Public Sector Public–Private Partnership Support Capacity and Experience

Determinant 3: Fitch Ratings, Moody's Investors Service, and S&P Global Ratings expect the economy to continue growing by 7%–8% over the next few years, underpinned by its globally competitive ready-made garments industry and supported by macroeconomic and external stability.

Table A2.17: Ratings for Public Sector Public–Private Partnership Support Capacity and Experience in Bangladesh

#	Determinant	Rating
3	If payment is likely to be made by the parent government, what is the credit rating of the parent government?	1
4	Is there a specialized government agency (or agencies) established for PPP purposes (e.g., PPP unit) and what are its roles?	3
5	Is there a streamlined approval process for PPP projects?	3
6	Does the sponsoring agency have previous experience with PPPs?	2
7	Are different PPP concession models defined for the sector and are model concession agreements available?	0

PPP = public–private partnership.

Source: Study team analysis.

Determinants 4 and 5: Various agencies have been set up by the government to enhance and streamline PPP processes for project preparation, decision-making, and overall monitoring, as shown in Table A2.18.

Table A2.18: Bangladesh Government Agencies Facilitating Public–Private Partnerships

Agency	Role in Promoting PPPs
Cabinet Committee on Economic Affairs	Responsible for providing in-principle approval and final approval for PPP projects for the contracting authority to enter into a contract with the preferred bidder or the project company.
Office of PPP	The Public–Private Partnership (PPP) Authority was set up in 2010 under the Prime Minister's Office to promote PPPs. Under the PPP Act, 2015 the office was made a statutory authority. Its powers and functions are set out in the act. They include decisions on financial and government participation in PPP projects, technical and best-practice requirements, prequalification and bidding documents, approving bidders and the model for PPP contracts, and terminating contracts.
Line ministry, implementing agency, or contracting authority	These are responsible for the identification, formulation, prequalification, tendering, contract award, and overseeing the implementation of PPP projects as per the contract.
Ministry of Finance, PPP Unit	The unit is part of the ministry's Finance Division and is responsible for overseeing the fiscal viability of PPP projects and sanctioning support funding for their development and financing. It also manages three key funds: the PPP Technical Assistance Fund, the Viability Gap Fund, and Bangladesh Infrastructure Finance Fund.

PPP = public–private partnership.

Source: Bangladesh Public-Private Partnership Act, 2015. https://www.pppo.gov.bd/download/ppp_office/PPP_Law_2015_(Approved_Translation).pdf.

Determinant 6: Only nine transport infrastructure PPP projects have achieved financial closure since 1996. The government is exploring further transport PPP projects.

Determinant 7: Bangladesh has no transport sector-specific model concession agreements—e.g., for roads and ports—to provide a framework for PPP agreements. Having one would encourage the participation of private players.

Public Sector Funding Assistance for Public–Private Partnerships

Determinant 8: In Bangladesh, viability gap funding is only available for build–operate–transfer projects. It comes in the form of a capital grant and must not exceed 30% of the total estimated project cost. This is equivalent to the lowest offer in the competitive tender for a capital subsidy or annuity. The following criteria must be met for a project to be eligible for viability gap funding:

(i) The project is implemented through a competitive tendering process;
(ii) The economic rate of return of a project meets the threshold level specified by the Ministry of Finance's PPP unit;
(iii) The project is in one of the sectors in the Policy and Strategy for Public–Private Partnerships, 2010; and
(iv) The project provides a service against payment of a predetermined tariff or user charge.

Table A2.19: Ratings for Public Sector Funding Assistance in Public–Private Partnerships in Bangladesh

#	Determinant	Rating
8	Is government support for viability gap funding available for PPP projects?	2

PPP = public–private partnership.

Source: Study team analysis.

Table A2.20 shows the number of PPP projects receiving government support from 1990 to 2017.

Table A2.20: Government Supported Public–Private Partnership Projects in Bangladesh, 1990–2017

Funding Type	1990–2017
Viability gap funding	0
Government guarantees	22
Availability-based payments	65

Source: Asian Development Bank. 2017. *Public-Private Partnership Monitor*. Manila. https://www.adb.org/publications/public-private-partnership-monitor.

Availability-based payments have so far not been used in transport projects. Most of the projects using this are in power generation. A PPP roads project to improve the Hatirjheel–Shekherjaiga–Amulia–Demra road using this mechanism however is currently in the procurement stage.

Land Acquisition and Environmental and Social Clearances

Determinant 9: Bangladesh's PPP framework has no specific regulations for land acquisitions. According to a review by the United Nations Conference on Trade and Development of the country's investment policy, access to land titles and land registration are subject to many laws and regulations, including the Transfer of Property Act, 1882; the Registration Act, 1908; and the Land Reforms Board Act, 1989. These laws and regulations make the administration of land rights complex, long, and costly.

Table A2.21: Ratings for Land Acquisition and Environmental and Social Clearances in Bangladesh

#	Determinant	Rating
9	Does the authority have experience in dealing with land acquisitions, environmental clearances, and rehabilitation and resettlement?	3
10	Does the authority have a dedicated team to streamline land acquisitions and environmental clearances, and the experience to handle these areas?	0

Source: Study team analysis.

Table A2.22: Government Land Acquisition Support in Bangladesh

Support type	✓/×
Resettlement and compensation costs to residents	✓
Imposed limits on time frame to complete land acquisitions	×
Dedicated agency to streamline land acquisitions	×
Exemption from or reduction of land use fees	×

Source: Asian Development Bank. *Public–Private Partnership Monitor*. Manila. https://www.adb.org/publications/public-private-partnership-monitor.

Foreign entities can own land only by incorporating a company in Bangladesh. In many cases, land owned by municipal corporations is leased out for long periods, but there are restrictions on lease transfer to foreign entities.

Determinant 10: The Environmental Conservation Rules, 1997 define the procedures that industrial investors must follow to get an environmental clearance certificate. Feasibility studies for PPP projects identify environmental and social issues that may need to be addressed, and the law also requires an environmental impact assessment to be carried out. This assesses the direct and indirect effects of a project on humans, fauna and flora, soil, water, air, climate, and the countryside, as well as material assets and cultural heritage.

No special regulations cover land clearances, but the government has the right to take ownership of private land by compulsory purchase. This practice has been used for a number of projects, including social infrastructure and transportation projects.

Market Capacity and Foreign Participation

Determinant 11: Market capacity for carrying out transport infrastructure PPPs in Bangladesh is inadequate. Local private players have little PPP experience in this sector. Most transport PPP projects are developed by private players from neighboring countries.

Table A2.23: Ratings for Market Capacity and Foreign Participation in Bangladesh

#	Determinant	Rating
11	Is there sufficient market capacity and do private players have PPP experience?	1
12	Is foreign participation in PPP allowed?	3
13	Are there any restrictions on foreign investors' land use and/or ownership (i.e., do foreign investors have the same rights as locals?)	3
14	If payments are likely to be made from the authority's budget, is there any form of government guarantee available for these payments?	1
15	Is the exchange rate stable?	3
16	Is there a robust project finance market, which supplements the traditional corporate finance market?	1
17	Are debt instruments available for different project needs, such as senior, mezzanine, and subordinate debt, and take-out financing?	1

PPP = public–private partnership.

Source: Study team analysis.

Determinant 12: Only a few sectors are closed to foreign investors. Among reserved sectors are the arms industry and nuclear power. There is no limitation on foreign-equity stakes in non-reserved sectors. Here, a foreign investment can either be 100% owned or be a joint venture with a local or foreign partner.

PPPs in Bangladesh that have reached financial closure were owned by foreign entities; these have included PPP projects in transport (airports and ports), energy (thermal power generation), and social infrastructure (health).

Determinant 13: The Foreign Private Investment Promotion and Protection Act, 1980 enables the government to regulate foreign investment and provides for fair and equitable treatment, protection from expropriation, and provisions for foreign exchange. Foreign exchange regulations restrict the repatriation of divestment proceeds to the net asset value. The repatriation of capital and capital gains is subject to strict reporting requirements or authorization by Bangladesh Bank.

Determinant 14: A major issue raised during interviews for this report is the need for government credit guarantees for projects in the BIMSTEC master plan to secure revenue from these projects. Bangladesh provides these guarantees based on the result of feasibility studies for proposed PPP projects and negotiation between the project authority and private players. Table A2.24 shows risks covered by government guarantees.

Table A2.24: Risks Covered by Government Credit Guarantees in Bangladesh

Risk	✓/×
Currency inconvertibility and transfer risk	×
Foreign exchange risk	×
War and civil disturbance risk	×
Breach of contract risk	×
Regulatory risk	×
Expropriation risk	×
Government payment obligation guarantee	✓
Credit guarantees	×
Minimum demand/revenue guarantee	×

Source: Asian Development Bank. 2017. *Public–Private Partnership Monitor*. Manila. https://www.adb.org/publications/public-private-partnership-monitor.

Determinant 15: As for exchange rate risks, Bangladesh has very low currency fluctuations and volatility historically.

Determinant 16: Most transport infrastructure projects in Bangladesh are financed through budgetary allocations and MDBs. ADB is a major player in infrastructure financing for PPP projects in the country, and has been providing long-term loans for PPP projects since 2008 through the Infrastructure Development Company Limited, a state-owned firm specializing in infrastructure financing.

Loan tenures offered by banks in Bangladesh are too short to meet the needs of large, capital-intensive infrastructure PPP projects. These projects, when financed by banks, are usually transacted through simple, organically available equity and plain debt. Domestic project financing is a hybrid between project finance and commercial debt transactions. It includes taking security on project assets or corporate guarantees from a parent company.

Many infrastructure projects in Bangladesh have been financed by the Investment Promotion and Financing Facility Project managed by Bangladesh Bank, with the financial assistance of the International Development Association. Bangladesh Bank allocates funds from the Investment Promotion and Financing Facility Project fund to local financial institutions, which then lends to the infrastructure project. Table A2.25 shows three other project development funds for financing transport infrastructure PPPs.

Determinant 17: Bangladesh has no active market makers or fixed-income funds in its bond market; hence, issuers face challenges in collecting funds and issuing bonds. Because the bond market is small and nascent, it is unable to support the financing of large infrastructure projects.

The low number of issuers in the bond market is because of the excessive dependence on bank credit. It is easier for corporate borrowers to get credit from banks than to comply with the governance standards required for raising funds through the bond market or to meet the disclosure requirements for listing on one of the country's

Table A2.25: Development Funds for Financing Public–Private Partnership Transport Infrastructure Projects in Bangladesh

Institution	Role in Promoting PPP
Investment Promotion and Financing Facility	This financing facility was set up with a $105.2 million fund for infrastructure, comprising a $102.7 million financing facility and a $2.5 million technical assistance fund. The World Bank contributed $50 million and the Government of Bangladesh and the Participatory Financing Institution contributed $55.2 million.
Infrastructure Development Company Limited	This nonbank financial institution was created to develop medium and large infrastructure with loans from the World Bank's Private Sector Infrastructure Development Fund ($80 million). It aims to develop private sector participation in infrastructure through subloans.
Industrial and Infrastructure Development Finance Company	The objective of this public limited company is to promote and finance investments in infrastructure and industry. The company is active in arranging syndicated finance for large infrastructure projects.

PPP = public–private partnership.

Source: Study team analysis.

exchanges. It takes about 25–30 weeks to complete the legal formalities to issue a bond in Bangladesh—a much more cumbersome and longer process than taking out a bank loan.

Life-Cycle Cost and Output Specifications

Determinants 18 and 19: Bangladesh has enough experience in transport infrastructure projects to be able to quantify construction and long-term operational costs, as well as output specifications.

Table A2.26: Ratings for Life-Cycle Cost and Output Specifications in Bangladesh

#	Determinant	Rating
18	Can most of the costs, mainly related to construction and long-term operations, including maintenance, be quantified upfront with reasonable assumptions, and are historical data available?	3
19	Are objective output specifications readily available from a previous contract?	3

Source: Study team analysis.

Recommended Interventions for Bangladesh

Bangladesh could adopt the following approaches to tackle the investment gap in its transport infrastructure sector: (i) increase private investment in transport infrastructure by addressing the issues hindering the development and deepening of financing institutions; (ii) explore avenues for revenue enhancement (e.g., land-value capture [LVC], non-toll revenue, such as advertisements and privately owned public spaces) to increase the government's investable capital, improve project viability, and unlock capital investment in operational projects through asset securitization (e.g., infrastructure investment trusts and toll securitization) and asset recycling (e.g., toll–operate–transfer).

Brownfield toll roads can be pooled by the government for potential asset recycling. For example, three toll roads of approximately 137 km (including the 50 km Hatikumrul–Bonpara Highway, 13.7 km Chattogram Port Access Road, and a 74 km stretch of the Dhaka–Sylhet Highway) in Bangladesh are already collecting tolls and may be pooled together for asset recycling. In years to come, approximately 21,525 km of roads are set to come under toll collection by the government.[8] These roads would also present a case for asset recycling once they achieve a stable revenue stream. Table A2.27 summarizes the key recommended interventions to augment the use of financing tools, banks and other financial institutions, and the capital market to reduce PPP-related risks in Bangladesh.

Table A2.27:Summary of Recommended Finance Sector Interventions for Bangladesh

Finance Sector	Issues	Actions
Commercial banks	Increasing nonperforming loans in the banking system, restricting lending to riskier infrastructure projects	Strengthen corporate governance and careful due diligence. Loans to be made only on commercial considerations (i.e., not external ones).
		Strengthen Bankruptcy Act, 1997. Establish an insolvency and bankruptcy code and timebound procedures for lender comfort.
	Upper limit of 9% on the cost of lending, limiting profitability opportunities and reducing investment in infrastructure	For infrastructure projects, which typically have higher risk profiles, government could explore removing the cap. Further capacity building of institutions needed to enable loans to be priced on the basis of fund and project risks.
Nonbank financial institutions (NBFIs)	Credit line ring-fenced to power, telecommunications, manufacturing; no credit line ring-fenced for transport projects	Government could work with development agencies and structure credit-line ring-fencing for transport infrastructure projects.
		NBFIs could look for cofinancing transport projects with development agencies.
	Rising nonperforming loans (9%–11%) of NBFI limits profitability and lending corpus, especially to riskier infrastructure projects	Strengthen corporate governance and conduct due diligence; should be based only on commercial considerations.
		Set up of credit guarantee funds for infrastructure projects.
		Strengthen Bankruptcy Act, 1997. Set up insolvency and bankruptcy code and timebound procedures.
	Upper limit of 9% on the cost of lending constrains profitability opportunities of NBFIs, reducing investment in infrastructure	For infrastructure projects, government could explore options to remove the cap. NBFI lending decisions should be based on cost of fund, type of borrower, and project.
		Flexibility of pricing loans to cover risk during construction phase should be available for commercial banks. Once projects are operational, the interest rate can be revised.
Foreign direct investment (FDI)	FDI growth has doubled from fiscal year 2015 to fiscal year 2019, but percentage of gross domestic product has been nominal, at 1.3%. Also, more than 90% of FDI is dominated by export-oriented and thrust sectors, including manufacturing, power, trade and commerce, and telecommunications	Investors should be legally bound to follow one-stop service for project-related services to provide some 150 services, including timely repatriation through the online platform.
		Improve brand image for ease of doing business, create awareness of investment opportunities, improve policies for existing and potential investors.

continued on next page

8 *Maritime Gateway*. 2020. 21,595 km Roads To Come Under Tolls in Bangladesh. November 9. https://www.maritimegateway.com/industrialists-ludhiana-seek-resumption-freight-services-2/.

Table A2.27 *continued*

Finance Sector	Issues	Actions
Insurance funds	Low overall insurance funds leading to lower availability of funds for infrastructure	Implement regulatory reforms like Egypt.
		Create bancassurance opportunities.
	Absence of sufficient long-term debt instruments and high-quality investable bonds in infrastructure with minimum AA rating	Increase promotion, education, and training programs on bonds for potential investors, including nonresident Bangladeshis.
		Develop online and electronic system for long-term debt instruments to strengthen corporate governance and transparency.
		Provide credit enhancement for bonds through guarantees and credit support, e.g., partial credit guarantees.
FDI	High currency hedging costs affect FDI returns	Provide government or multilateral development bank-sponsored hedging facility, along with tolls and tariffs linked to inflation or any indicator that gradually passes through the foreign exchange risk.
Pension funds	Limited corpus leading to lower available funds for infrastructure	Create awareness about pension and retirement planning.
		Implement 2014 Draft National Social Security Strategy, which includes pension policies for private sector employees.
Bond market	Major issues in developing bond market include insufficient bond issuances, low investor base, limited investor awareness, and absence of promotional activities and marketing	Increase promotion, education, and training programs on bonds for potential investors, including nonresident Bangladeshis.
		Develop online system for long-term debt instruments.
		Develop a secondary market with instruments that are traded through an electronic platform.
	Absence of yield curve. Pricing issues (lower returns compared with anticipated risks) further deters the investment	Develop other mechanisms to benchmark bonds (e.g., using sovereign ratings for indicative indices). Regulators have indicated support for this.
		Coordinated stakeholder effort needed, especially by the Bangladesh Securities and Exchange Commission and National Board of Revenue, to relax high upfront commissions and charges during prospectus filing (e.g., in the form of trustee deeds and stamp duties).
	Weak regulation and limited market infrastructure	Coordinated stakeholder effort needed (Ministry of Finance, Prime Minister's Office, Bangladesh Bank, Bangladesh Securities and Exchange Commission, Bangladesh Investment Development Authority, PPP Authority, sector regulators) to develop a clear set of market regulations and procedures. Develop a framework based on ones used by credit rating agencies, past experience, and financial strength so that funding can be extended to greenfield projects.
		Develop options for tax-benefit incentives to be extended to banks and financial institutions.
		Ensure bonds are raised by companies that are leaders in their respective market segments and have good credit profiles based on their performance and financial strength. Issues should be well structured and marketed.

continued on next page

Table A2.27 *continued*

Finance Sector	Issues	Actions
Private equity funds	Private equity and venture capital funds at nascent stage	Alternative investment funds could be exempted from stamp duty and a tax holiday on management fees.
		Create awareness program road shows on investment opportunities to attract potential investors.
		Enhance and develop the capability of fund managers.
		Reduced initial public offerings' 3-year lock-in period to 1 year for Bangladesh Securities and Exchange Commission-licensed private equity investors. Create investment environment suitable for exit strategies.
Challenges in public–private partnership (PPP) projects	Limited capability of banks to underwrite infrastructure projects and other PPP design issues	Strong governance structures and clear rules and regulations need to be set allocating multiple risks, including construction, interface, and corruption risks among the government, the private sector, and other stakeholders. Establish sector-focused PPP unit to perform a wide range of services, including developing PPP policies and legislation; standard contracts; manuals and processes for identifying and developing PPPs; clearance and approval functions; source of expertise in one or more aspects of PPP procurement and management; developing training programs; disseminating information on PPPs; and assessing the fiscal costs (direct and contingent) of PPPs. Set up a central PPP unit within a ministry and supplement the capacities of the ministry. It can be set up as an autonomous entity, attached to but not fully part of the bureaucracy. Alternatively, a central PPP unit overseeing country-wide activities could be set up. The unit can be framed as a government-owned company overseen by public or private board. Extensive stakeholder consultations and PPP training on the commercial, financial, legal, and negotiation aspects required to strengthen and develop skills within institutions. Conduct detailed technical, financial, legal, environmental, and social due diligence, covering both the sponsor and the project.

Source: Study team analysis.

Bhutan

Transport Infrastructure Financing Landscape

Sources of Infrastructure Financing

The government is the main source of infrastructure funding. Because the private sector is small, the government also relies on development assistance in the form of loans from multilateral and bilateral financial institutions, and government-to-government credit lines. India is Bhutan's largest development partner, with large Indian private sector players as well as the government investing primarily in energy infrastructure. External grants are expected to decline due to project delays, and India has stopped excise duty refunds from FY2020, which may affect trade between the countries. External borrowing, in the form of grants and concessional loans, are also sourced from ADB and the World Bank for financing investment projects and supporting programs.

Fiscal Support to Infrastructure

In FY2021 (ending 31 March), the government allocated nearly 6% (Nu4.2 billion) of the total budget for the construction and maintenance of roads (Figure A2.14). The new construction of roads and bridges constitutes only 32% of allocated funds; most (68%) goes to the maintenance and repair of infrastructure (Figure A2.15).

Figure A2.14: Budget Allocation for Roads in Bhutan, FY2018–FY2021
(% of total budget)

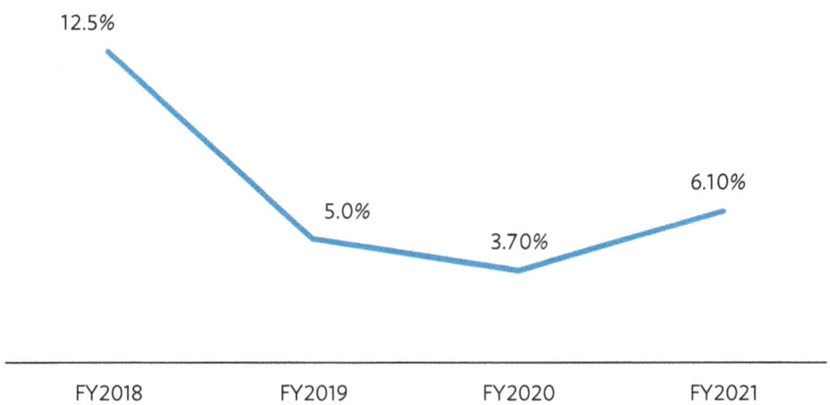

FY = fiscal year.

Note: FY ends 30 June.

Source: Royal Monetary Authority of Bhutan.

Figure A2.15: Budget Allocation for Road Subsectors in Bhutan, FY2021
(% of road budget)

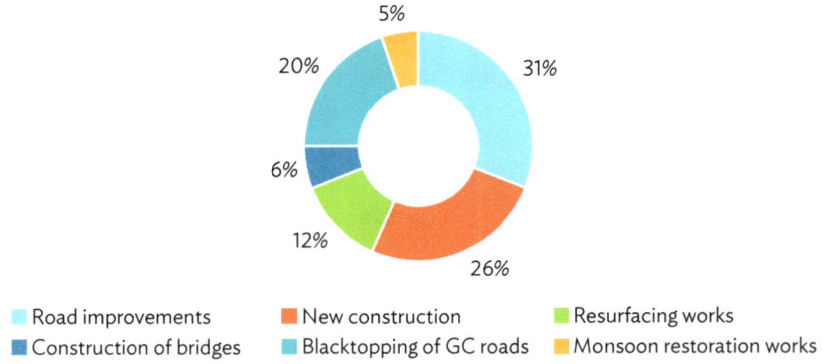

FY = fiscal year, GC = Gewog Center.

Note: FY ends 15 July.

Source: Royal Monetary Authority of Bhutan.

Increasing the budget allocation for road projects was constrained by the 12th Five-Year Plan, 2018–2023's fiscal target and the economic impact of coronavirus disease (COVID-19). The plan's fiscal target is to maintain the average fiscal deficit within 3% of GDP, with a fiscal target of 5% for FY2021. The current projected fiscal deficit for FY2021 is 7.4% of GDP, primarily due to the impact of COVID-19 (Figure A2.16).[9]

Figure A2.16: Government of Bhutan's Fiscal Deficit, FY2015–FY2019
(% of GDP)

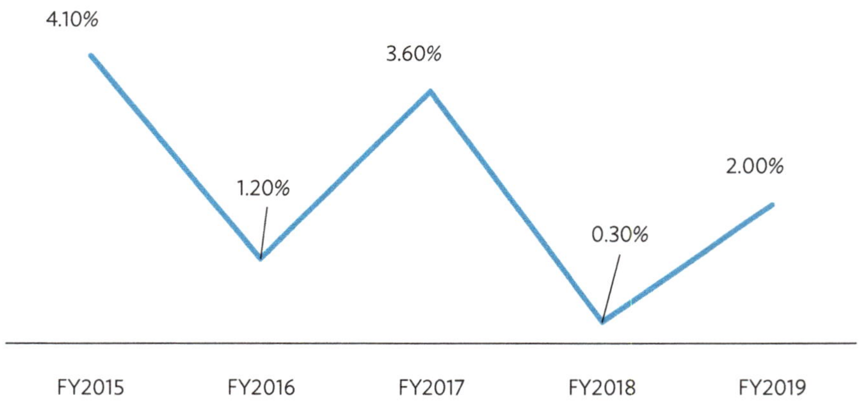

FY = fiscal year, GDP = gross domestic product.

Note: FY ends 15 July.

Source: Royal Monetary Authority of Bhutan.

---

9 United Nations Economic and Social Commission for Asia and the Pacific. 2020. Bhutan's First Sovereign Bond: Financing Lessons during the Pandemic. 6 October. https://www.unescap.org/blog/bhutans-first-sovereign-bond.

Consolidated government debt is already more than 100% of GDP (Figure A2.17). External borrowing is constrained by the limit on external debt imposed by the Public Debt Policy, 2016. Here, the annual debt service obligation of total external debt must not exceed 25% of total exports of goods and services, which limits government borrowing.

Figure A2.17: Government of Bhutan Consolidated Debt, FY2014–FY2019
(as % of GDP)

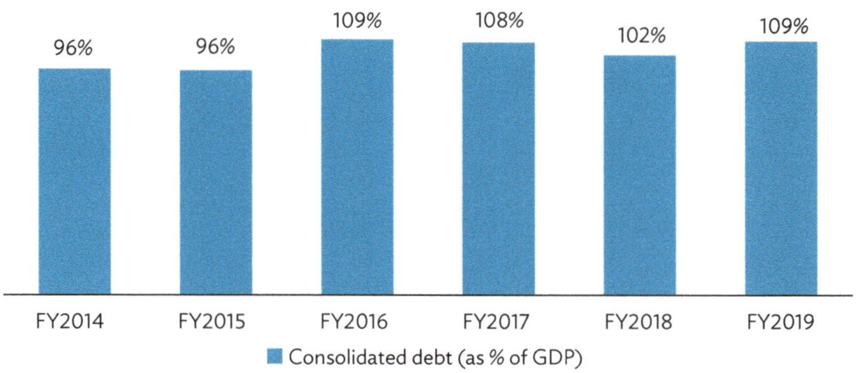

FY = fiscal year, GDP = gross domestic product.

Source: Royal Monetary Authority of Bhutan.

In 2020, Bhutan completed its first sovereign bond offering, a 3-year Series RGOB001 bond totaling Nu3 billion. The country does not, however, have a sovereign rating from an international credit rating agency. A favorable rating would make it easier for the government to raise further capital in the international market. Bhutan needs to develop and deepen its financial market. With concessional financing expected to decline, it will need steady and efficient sources of domestic financing for its infrastructure needs.[10] This could be provided by a well-functioning public debt market, along with innovative methods of project financing.

Bridging the Financing Gap

Because fiscal support is unlikely to increase in the near term, Bhutan needs to encourage the private sector to supplement government sources of infrastructure financing. Figure A2.18 depicts Bhutan's financial institutions based on their total investable capital, as a percentage of GDP, and their contribution to infrastructure financing, as a percentage of their capital base.

Bhutan's finance sector consists of five commercial banks, four NBFIs (three insurance companies and one pension fund), and six microfinance institutions.[11] The National Pension and Provident Fund, which manages retirement accounts and was set up in 2000, is one of the country's largest real estate developers. Bhutan Insurance has a substantial capacity and plays a key role in deepening the insurance sector.

[10] ADB. 2019. *Country Partnership Strategy: Bhutan, 2019–2023—Fostering Diversification and Reducing Disparities.* Manila. https://www.adb.org/sites/default/files/institutional-document/526656/cps-bhu-2019-2023.pdf.

[11] Royal Monetary Authority Bhutan. 2019. *Annual Report 2019.* Thimphu. https://www.rma.org.bt/RMA%20Publication/Annual%20Report/Annual%20Report%202019.pdf.

Figure A2.18: Bhutan Financial Institution Mapping

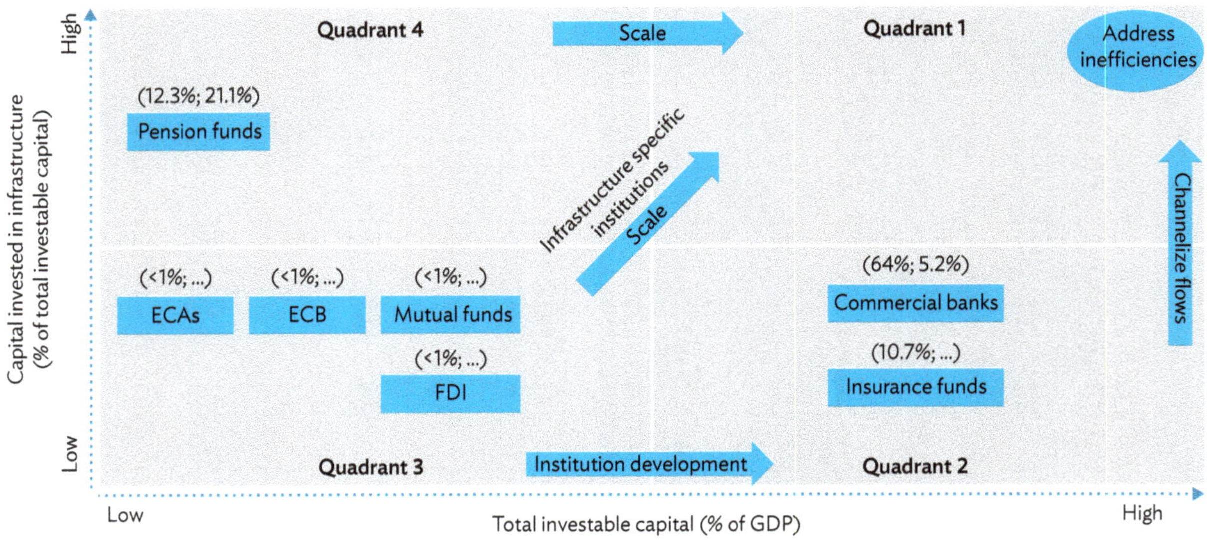

... = not available, ECA = export credit agency, ECB = external commercial borrowing, FDI= foreign direct investment , GDP = gross domestic product.

Notes

1. Percentage figures provide a comparative measure and are based on latest available data.
2. Institutions where data is not available are placed based on a general understanding from primary and secondary research.

Sources: Royal Monetary Authority of Bhutan; and secondary sources.

Challenges of Developing Bhutan's Financing Institutions for Investing in Transport Infrastructure

Commercial Banks

Bhutan's commercial banks have significant exposure to infrastructure, at about 5% of their total loans and advances. Lending is focused on hydropower projects; exposure to transport infrastructure is low. Commercial banks are small in terms of their asset bases, and their returns on assets are low. They face three key challenges that hinder investments in infrastructure projects: high nonperforming assets (NPAs) and a substandard credit appraisal mechanism, low loans and advances to the transport infrastructure, and limited financing capability to take on PPP projects.

High nonperforming assets and a substandard credit appraisal mechanism. This limits profitability opportunities and so reduces the loans and advances available for riskier assets, such as transport infrastructure. The NPAs of Bhutan's commercial banks as a percentage of gross loans are the highest among BIMSTEC countries. This affects the circulation of money, as affected borrowers are not able to pay their loans back and this, in turn, prevents them from lending more.

NPAs are mostly in services and tourism, and totaled Nu8.5 billion (31.7% of total NPLs) as of June 2020, followed by bad loans in trade and commerce, at Nu4.9 billion (18.2%), housing (Nu3.7 billion, 14.0%), and production and manufacturing (Nu3.6 billion, 13.5%). The cause of NPAs is banks' lack of adherence to basic appraisal standards. Most commercial bank lending is collateralized. Thimphu, Paro, and other urban areas have a markedly disproportionate share of financial banking services, especially in credit dissemination. Table A2.28 outlines actions to reduce NPAs.

Table A2.28: Actions to Reduce Nonperforming Assets of Bhutan's Commercial Banks

Actions	Impact
Strengthen corporate governance and due diligence. Strategy needed for ensuring transparency in project lending	Reduced default risk and nonperforming loans
Royal Monetary Authority of Bhutan needs to formulate rules and policies to make nonperforming assets less frequent	Reduced nonperforming assets
Diversify asset portfolios across sectors and geography to reduce concentration of risk, as lending focused on housing and hydropower	Reduced concentration of risk and, simultaneously, increased profitability
Instead of fixed pricing, allow banks to charge borrowers different rates for the same credit product, based on the riskiness of the borrower and the loan	Flexible pricing policy will reduce the risk of nonperformance and increase profitability

Source: Study team analysis.

Low loans and advances to the transport infrastructure. Bhutan Development Bank Limited is the country's biggest commercial bank, with an 80% share of total deposits and 70% of loans. It was formerly Bhutan Development Finance Corporation Limited, which was set up with ADB support to serve the needs of small and medium-sized enterprises. It became a commercial bank in 2010. Bhutan Development Bank contributes 6%–7% to transport infrastructure financing. Figure A2.19 gives a breakdown of the deposits and loans of Bhutan's commercial banks and Figure A2.20 shows the breakdown of Bhutan Development Bank's lending by sector.

Figure A2.19: Deposits and Credit of Bhutan's Commercial Banks, 2019
(% of gross deposits and credit)

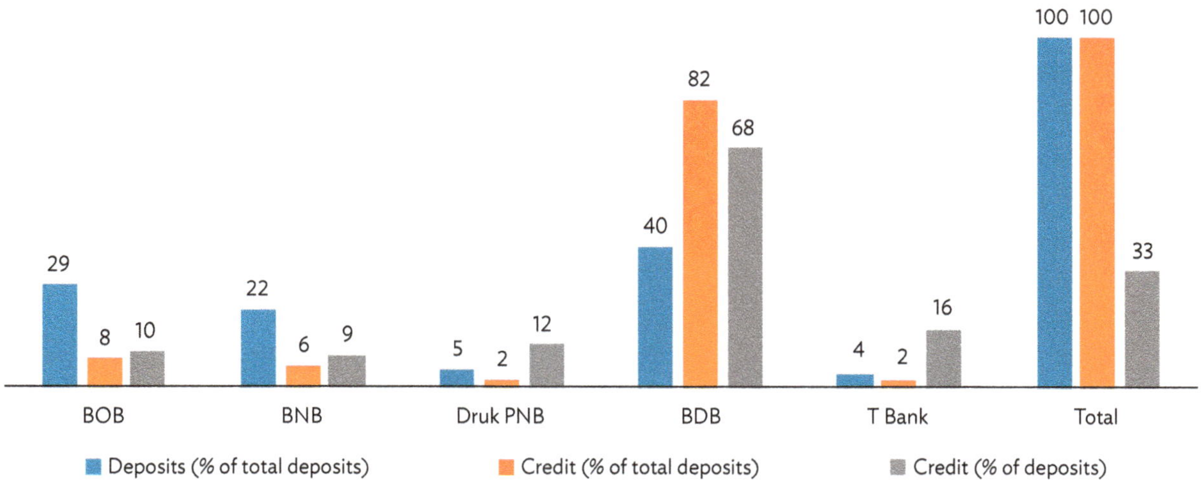

BDB = Bhutan Development Bank, BNB = Bhutan National Bank, BOB = Bank of Bhutan, Druk PNB = Druk Punjab National Bank.

Source: Roderick Wijunamai. 2020. *Banking Infrastructure in Bhutan: An Assessment of Commercial Bank Branches.* Thimpu. https://papers.ssrn.com/sol3/papers.cfm?abstract_id=3689397.

Figure A2.20: Bhutan Development Bank Sector Lending
(% of total loans)

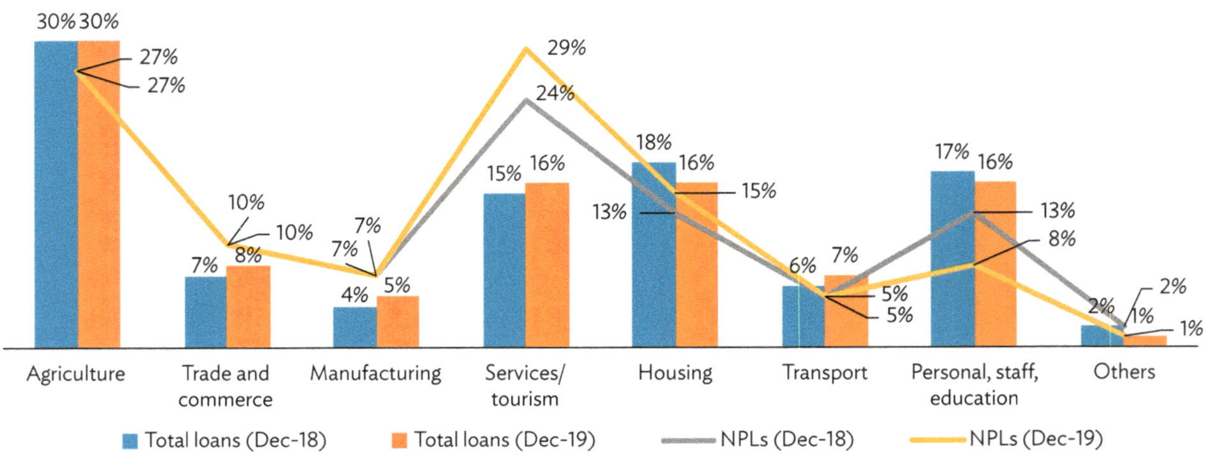

NPL = nonperforming loan.

Source: Roderick Wijunamai. 2020. *Banking Infrastructure in Bhutan: An Assessment of Commercial Bank Branches*. Thimpu.

A financing institution dedicated to funding infrastructure projects could be developed in Bhutan along the lines of Power Finance Corporation in India, the Bangladesh Infrastructure Finance Fund and Infrastructure Development Company (Bangladesh), and Nepal Infrastructure Bank Limited. Bhutan should look at developing similar institutions so that it has a dedicated source for financing in transport projects, which are seen as high risk projects. Table A2.29 looks at other actions that could help address this issue.

Limited financing capability of banks to take on PPP projects. Bhutan's state-owned enterprises operate in key areas of the economy, including energy, banking, manufacturing, transport, telecommunications, and infrastructure, and contribute about 40% of government revenue. The public sector dominates hydropower development; the private sector is concentrated in ferro-alloys, food and beverages, and tourism, among other areas.

Table A2.29: Actions to Stimulate Lending to Transport Infrastructure Projects by Bhutan's Development Financial Institutions

Actions	Impact
National Development Bank can catalyze the participation of commercial banks in lending for infrastructure projects by being lead arrangers for loan syndicates (Box A2.2)	Greater participation of commercial banks in infrastructure lending
Blended finance can be used to attract financing from commercial banks (Box A2.3)	Greater participation of commercial banks in infrastructure lending

Source: Study team analysis.

Box A2.2: Development Bank of Japan's Role as Lead Arranger in a Loan Syndication

A cooperation between the government-owned Development Bank of Japan (DBJ) and the Japan Wind Development Co. Limited was entered into in 2016 as part of Japan's first capital-recycling model to expand the use of wind power. This approach promoted the utilization of private finance for the wind power project.

For DBJ, promoting a capital-recycling program throughout the renewable energy field was an important means of giving financial support to proprietors wanting to speed up investment and reduce project costs.

DBJ works alongside other financial institutions to arrange syndicated loans for infrastructure projects, including renewable energy, roads, and airport concessions. It promotes the construction stage by providing loans to projects.

Japan Bank for International Cooperation provides guarantees against risks, such as currency conversion, transfer, and country risks. This approach enables Japanese private financial institutions to provide medium- to long-term financing for developing economies, supporting the efforts of these economies to attract private capital, and helping private companies expanding their international business.

Source: Asia-Pacific Economic Cooperation/Organisation for Economic Co-operation and Development. 2019. *Financing Infrastructure in APEC Economies: APEC/OECD Report on Selected Effective Approaches*. Paris. https://www.oecd.org/finance/private-pensions/Financing-infrastructure-in-APEC-economies-selected-effective-approaches-2019.pdf.

Box A2.3: Philippine Water Revolving Fund Project Use of Blended Finance

The main objective of the Philippine Water Revolving Fund Project (PWRF) is to encourage private sector participation in financing water sector projects. The fund's cofinancing mechanism allows interest rates to be reduced to end-borrowers by blending official development assistance funds with money from private financial institutions.

The PWRF is implemented by the Development Bank of the Philippines (DBP) and involves the participation of Japan International Cooperation Agency and United States Agency for International Development. Japan International Cooperation Agency allocated an initial ¥1.5 billion concessional loan to DBP with a 30-year maturity (inclusive of a 10-year grace period), combined with cofinancing from private finance initiative (PFI) funds. These were then on-lent to public (local governments and water districts) and private water service providers.

The financing mix between the DBP and the PFIs is set at a 75:25 ratio of the approved loan amount. The facility can provide tenors of up to 20 years at a fixed interest rate, allowing water service providers to better manage their debt.

Concurrently, the PFIs applied for a credit risk guarantee covering a maximum of 85% of their exposure. The guarantee was issued by the local government guarantee corporation, a private entity. This was backed by a co-guarantee facility provided by United States Agency for International Development's Credit Authority. This led to a reduction in the credit risk exposure of the PFIs and incentivized lending to the water sector.

A DBP impact study reported that the PWRF project resulted in 225,594 households being connected to water services, as of October 2015.

Source: Organisation for Economic Co-operation and Development. 2019. *Making Blended Finance Work for Water and Sanitation: Unlocking Commercial Finance for SDG 6*. Paris. https://www.oecd.org/environment/resources/making-blended-finance-work-for-sdg-6-5efc8950-en.htm.

Weak Private Sector

The World Bank has supported the streamlining of business registration processes, improving the efficiency and access to financial services, and improving the investment climate for private sector growth and job creation in Bhutan. It has also strengthened the institutional and legal framework of the country's financial infrastructure. Despite these interventions, Bhutan's regulatory environment governing businesses needs further improvement. Bhutan's evolution from being a market participant to a policymaker is still ongoing. The World Bank and International Finance Corporation have collaborated closely in assisting Bhutan in developing sector policies, improving the investment climate, and strengthening financial services.[12]

Private participation in public projects was going on before Bhutan adopted a PPP policy in 2019—e.g., the 126 megawatt Dagachhu hydropower project, the country's first such project to be implemented using the PPP model, Thimphu TechPark, and Thimphu Thromde's two multilevel car parks. But there have so far been no transport sector PPPs, except these car parks.

Because of the size of PPP investments, the 2019 policy provides for grants, subsidies, and other financing support to make projects viable for investors and bankable for financers. But additional capital is generally needed for PPP projects to take off. Subsidies are performance-driven, based on the private party achieving certain outputs. Where possible, subsidies are targeted at disadvantaged users or groups of users.

Bhutan's PPP Contract Monitoring Unit, an agency under the PPP Authority, monitors all PPP contracts. Because of limited government resources, only the highest priority projects get financial assistance. In sum, there has not been much growth in PPP projects.

Because PPPs are a relatively a new concept in Bhutan, the technical capacity of stakeholders, including government agencies, and the financial capacity of the private sector need strengthening to be able to expand the use of PPPs.

Technical capacity. Although Bhutan lacks the skills and expertise to scale up PPP projects, there are concerns within the domestic population about recruiting foreign workers. Bhutan's labor regulations make it difficult for firms to recruit foreign workers. Regulations on hiring nonnationals, which are set out in the *Handbook on Recruitment and Employment of Foreign Workers* by the Ministry of Labour and Human Resources, allow only Indian workers to be employed, impose a cap on the number of foreign workers, and bar firms from terminating the contracts of local employees. While Bhutan's foreign investment regulations allow greater flexibility for foreign firms, this does not appear to be the case in practice. Investors indicate they are subject to the standard regulations and find it difficult to hire foreign workers.

As of April 2016, 48,122 foreign workers were employed in Bhutan, comprising 19.8% of the workforce.[13] Most are less skilled, as indicated by their lower qualifications and wage levels (footnote 12). Almost all are Indian; only 323 were non-Indian. The cap on hiring foreign workers is preventing firms from filling skill shortages.[14]

---

12 International Development Association, International Finance Corporation, and Multilateral Investment Guarantee Agency. Performance and Learning Review of the Country Partnership Strategy for the Kingdom of Bhutan for the Period FY2015–2019. Report No. 110736-BT.

13 World Bank.2017. *Bhutan's Labor Market: Toward Gainful Quality Employment for All.* Washington, DC. https://elibrary.worldbank.org/doi/abs/10.1596/25703.

14 M. Santini, T. T. Tran, and A. Beath. 2017. *Investment Climate Assessment of Bhutan.* Washington, DC: World Bank. https://elibrary.worldbank.org/doi/abs/10.1596/28539.

Financial capacity of the private sector. Domestic credit to the private sector as a share of GDP increased rapidly from 2006 and 2019 (Figure A2.21). But the Royal Monetary Authority of Bhutan's 2019 annual report shows that this is primarily dominated by housing and personal loans (28.3% of total credit) due to higher demand for hotel and residential, services (26.9%), manufacturing (13.5%) trade (17.8%), transport (7.2%), and agriculture (5.8%) (Figure A2.22).

Figure A2.21: Domestic Credit to Private Sector in South Asia, 2005–2019
(% of GDP)

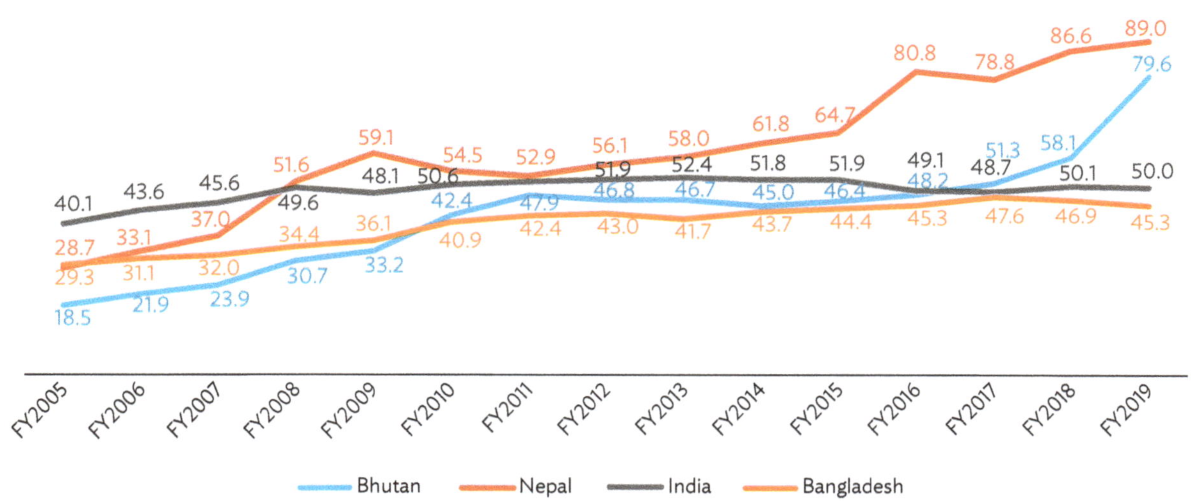

FY = fiscal year, GDP = gross domestic product.

Source: World Bank. World Development Indicators Database (accessed in 2020). https://databank.worldbank.org/source/world-development-indicators.

Figure A2.22: Credit by Sector in Bhutan
(% of total)

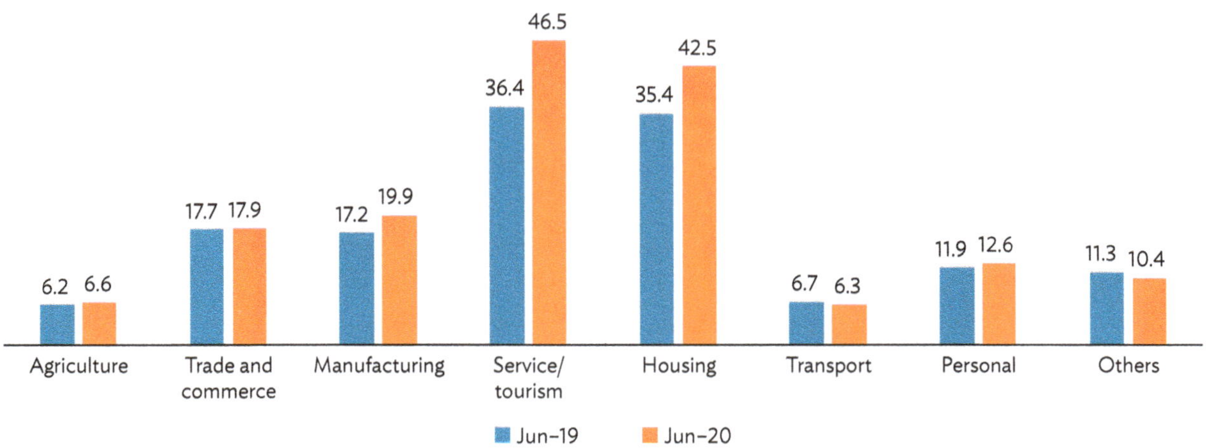

Source: Royal Monetary Authority. 2019. *Annual Report 2019*. Thimphu. https://www.rma.org.bt/RMA%20Publication/Annual%20Report/Annual%20Report%202019.pdf.

The government could initiate a partnership with ADB or the World Bank to enable them to offer credit enhancement products to Bhutan. These financial products reduce the nonpayment risk that a credit provider has on the entity that benefits from its financing. The credit enhancement products would involve credit and investment insurance and guarantee products, cofinancing loans of certain MDBs, and the guarantor-of-record schemes of ADB and Multilateral Investment Guarantee Agency (MIGA) under which these MDBs cooperate with private insurers.

The government should start a program to increase the access of Bhutan's financial markets to long-term finance. The government could seek a line of credit from MDBs and bilateral institutions. This could be extended to a designated national bank that could on-lend to projects. In the longer term, the government could also commission a technical program to develop financial market institutional arrangements for new financing instruments and long-term local currency financing for PPPs. Table A2.30 outlines actions to increase PPP investment in transport infrastructure projects.

Table A2.30: Actions to Increase Investment in Bhutan Public–Partnership Transport Projects

Actions	Impact
Government should use the credit enhancement products of multilateral development banks	Guarantees will increase funding for high-risk projects
The government should start a focused program to enable financial markets to use long-term financing	Increase the availability and source for domestic lending in infrastructure/transport projects
RMA should take steps to increase investment in private sector transport and infrastructure-related projects	Increased domestic lending in infrastructure transport projects
Banks, regulators, RMA, and other financial institutions should hold exchange programs across countries and workshops to develop the capability of their staff	Creates awareness of global developments in the PPP sector and enhances in-house capabilities
Banks, regulators, RMA, and other financial institutions should enhance the expertise of their staff in law, finance, accounting, development, and engineering	Increased in-house expertise, especially for handling riskier projects
The government and the Ministry of Labour and Human Resources should increase the upper limit on the number of foreign workers with specialized skills for analyzing and developing transport and infrastructure projects and incentivize them to attract a more skilled workforce	Increased in-house expertise in specialized areas, including infrastructure and transport-related projects

PPP = public–private partnership, RMA = Royal Monetary Authority of Bhutan.

Source: Study team analysis.

Foreign Direct Investment

The two key FDI issues are that these investments are low overall, particularly in infrastructure and transport, and no transport infrastructure project has been guaranteed by MIGA.

Low foreign direct investment. FDI inflows have averaged less than $20 million a year since 2010, and turned to a $13 million outflow in 2016, recovering to a $10 million inflow in 2017. FDI in Bhutan is significantly lower than in other South Asian countries (Figure A2.23).

Figure A2.23: Foreign Direct Investment in South Asian Countries, 2000, 2010, and 2018
($ million)

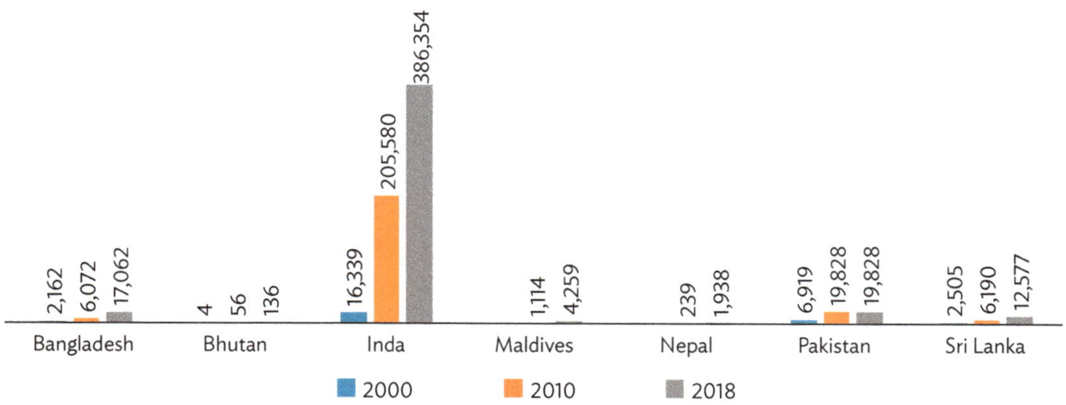

Source: United Nations Conference on Trade and Development. 2019. *World Investment Report 2019*. Geneva. https://unctad.org/system/files/official-document/wir2019_en.pdf.

In addition to weak FDI, Bhutan has faced a continual decline in external grants, and this was a key factor for plummeting capital expenditure in FY2019. To increase FDI, the approval processes for foreign investors need to be streamlined and a single window created for investors to interface with the Ministry of Economic Affairs. In 2019, the FDI division was authorized to function as an investment promotion agency and to be the point of contact for foreign investors. FDI services are provided online through an integrated business licensing system while the FDI division liaises with relevant agencies through focal officials to provide investor services. These endeavors have yet to see increased FDI.

Despite these services, Bhutan does not have a strategy to proactively target potential investors. New Zealand, a small and geographically isolated country, set up the New Zealand Trade and Enterprise to target investment in the government's priority growth sectors to develop a global network of investors and to attract and retain smart FDI in greenfield and brownfield projects. Table A2.31 outlines actions to increase FDI.

Table A2.31: Actions to Increase Foreign Direct Investment in Bhutan

Actions	Impact
The government should promote foreign direct investment (FDI) through a well-formulated promotion strategy, targeting niche markets in transport infrastructure and other sectors of the economy (e.g., medical, educational tourism, and niche agriculture products) • Short term: Promote investment opportunities to existing networks of investors • Medium term: Assess the need to create a standalone investment promotion unit with dedicated staff to conduct outreach	Enhanced attractiveness of Bhutan as an FDI destination that would increase investment in transport and other infrastructure sectors
Develop an effective market research team and investment promotion strategy for infrastructure projects. An investment summit could be launched (like the Gujarat Invest Summit), as could an agency similar to New Zealand Trade and Enterprise	Enhance the attractiveness of Bhutan as an FDI destination

continued on next page

Table A2.31 *continued*

Actions	Impact
Upgrade internet infrastructure through investments especially in cable and fiber optics to increase promotion and branding among foreign investors	Strengthen Bhutan's brand among foreign investors
Deepen value chains with India and Bangladesh, and strengthen bilateral relations with other countries	More focused investment in transport and other infrastructure projects

Source: Study team analysis.

No Multilateral Investment Guarantee Agency involvement in transport infrastructure. Bhutan completed the requirements to join the agency in 2014, becoming its 181st member country. Agency guarantees are available to support projects in the country. MIGA has so far only given guarantees to power projects (Tina Hydropower project in Solomon Islands, Salima Solar power station in South Africa, Ghoubet Djibouti Windfarm project in East Africa).

The government, with the support of the International Finance Corporation, should draw up a proposal to use MIGA for infrastructure projects. This would improve confidence for investing in projects in high-risk sectors.

Insurance Companies

Bhutan has two major insurance companies, Royal Insurance Corporation of Bhutan Limited (RICBL) and Bhutan Insurance Limited. The insurance industry in Bhutan has a small capital base—Nu12.8 billion in FY2019, about 5.13% of GDP.[15]

Low corpus of insurance funds. Bhutan's insurance companies face a low overall corpus of insurance and an extremely underdeveloped capital market marked by a lack of long-term debt instruments, leading to investments primarily financed through loans similar to commercial banks funds. The government should look at how India has grown bancassurance[16] and the regulatory reforms that Egypt has taken to increase its insurance market. Indeed, undertaking regulatory reforms similar to Egypt's could result in significant growth in Bhutan's insurance market for a bancassurance opportunity. The impact of this could be a win-win for insurers and banks, and customized insurance products that are beneficial for customers.

Extremely underdeveloped capital market; lack of long-term debt instruments. Because of insufficient traditional insurance company assets, RICBL primarily invests in loans, not unlike a commercial bank. Because of the dearth of long-term financial instruments to finance long-term liabilities, Bhutan's two insurance companies must fund their long-term liabilities with short-maturity loans—in direct competition with banks. Bhutan's pension funds are also in this situation. Figure A2.24 shows the large amount of assets invested in loans of both companies. Only 3% of Bhutan Insurance's total assets was invested in bonds in FY2019.

[15] Royal Monetary Authority of Bhutan. 2019. *Annual Report 2019*. Thimphu. https://www.rma.org.bt/RMA%20Publication/Annual%20Report/Annual%20Report%202019.pdf.

[16] Bancassurance is an arrangement between a bank and an insurance company allowing the insurance company to sell its products to the bank's client base.

Figure A2.24: Assets Invested in Loans by Royal Insurance Corporation of Bhutan and Bhutan Insurance, 2017–2019
(%)

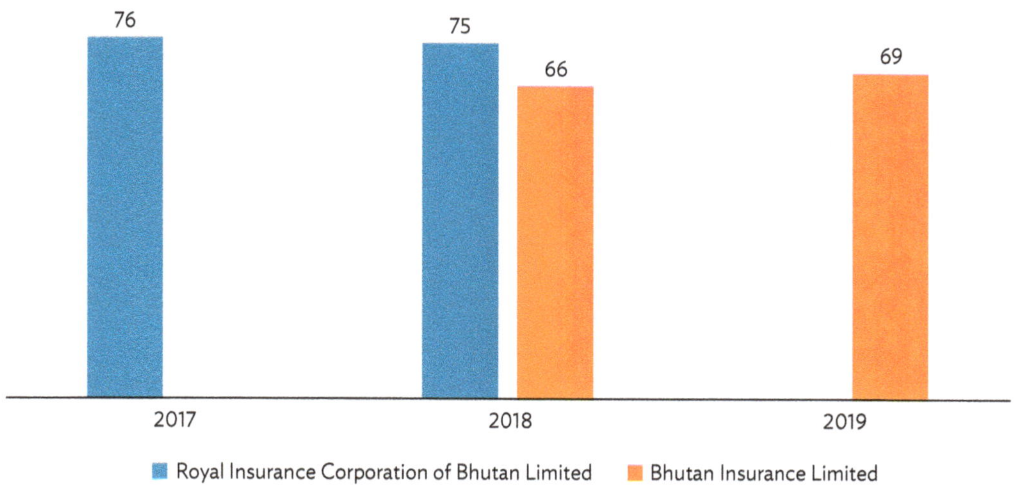

Note: Data for Bhutan Insurance in 2017 and Royal Insurance Corporation of Bhutan 2019 not available.

Source: Bhutan Insurance 2019 annual report. https://www.bhutaninsurance.com.bt/AnnualReport/11th_annual_report.pdf; and Royal Insurance 2018 annual report. https://www.ricb.bt/wp-content/uploads/2022/04/RICBL-Annual-Report-online-2019.pdf.

The same suggestion for Bhutan's debt capital market could also be used for the two insurance companies to tackle the lack of long-term debt instruments and high-quality investable bonds. To develop Bhutan insurance funds, the industry needs to increase promotion, education, and training programs on insurance funds among potential investors, including nonresident Bhutanese. This will create awareness of insurance products and increase the customer base. In addition, the country should develop an online and electronic system for long-term debt instruments to strengthen corporate governance and transparency and increase investor confidence.

Pension Fund: National Pension and Provident Fund

Limited corpus (Nu36 billion) leading to lower available funds for infrastructure. The National Pension and Provident Fund (NPPF), which manages public and private sector pensions, was created in March 2000. Before that, public pensions were managed by RICBL. To facilitate investment of pension assets, the NPPF was licensed by loans. NPPF is one of the largest real estate developers in Bhutan. Its fund size is the equivalent of 14.7% of GDP, according to its annual report for FY2019.

Because long-term financial instruments to finance long-term liabilities are insufficient, the NPPF, in a situation similar to Bhutan's life insurance funds, must fund its long-term liabilities with short-maturity loans, which is a problem for pension funds. In FY2019, only 13% of the NPPF's total assets were invested in bonds, while more than 70% were in term deposits and loans.[17] Awareness on retirement and pension planning needs to be raised in Bhutan. Doing this would result in more workers in the private and informal sector being covered by pensions.

[17] NPPF. 2019. *Annual Report 2019.* Thimpu.

Debt Capital Market

Bhutan needs to develop a sovereign bond market for budget financing. Currently, budget deficits are financed entirely through Treasury bills. The Royal Monetary Authority of Bhutan could look at developing a secondary market for Treasury bills by dematerializing these bills. Interventions are also needed to develop market infrastructure (e.g., primary dealers) and demand (e.g., institutional investors, which are lacking) for establishing an active government bond market. Table A2.32 outlines actions to develop the debt capital market.

Table A2.32: Actions to Develop Bhutan's Debt Capital Market

Item	Market Parameter	Status	Actions
Market infrastructure	Central counterparty or clearing house	Neither	Establish both Develop a scripless clearing and settlement system.
	Central security depository	None	Set up a central security depository for electronically registering securities
	Trading platform (stock exchange)	One stock exchange: Royal Securities Exchange of Bhutan About 20 listed companies listed	Royal Monetary Authority of Bhutan (RMA) needs to encourage more companies, especially state-owned enterprises, to list An infrastructure for government securities trading needs to be developed
Intermediaries	Primary dealers	Treasury bills issued by RMA No system of primary dealers	Introduce a primary dealer system to facilitate the auction of bills and, over the medium term, Treasury bonds
	Credit rating agencies (CRAs)	No international CRAs	The regulatory framework should be formulated for local CRAs to establish strategic partnerships with international CRAs
	Brokerage firms	Only a handful of brokerage firms	RMA needs to encourage a larger corpus of brokerage firms, and ensure that they are licensed and active
Issuer	Government securities (maturity range and liquidity)	Treasury bills, but no Treasury bonds	RMA needs to develop a secondary market for Treasury bills by dematerializing Treasury bills
	Securities auction calendar		
Investor	Commercial banks or primary dealers	Treasury bills held by banks	Develop and enhance the legal framework for secured transactions such as repurchase agreement (repo) transactions

continued on next page

Table A2.32 *continued*

Item	Market Parameter	Status	Actions
	Pension, insurance, and mutual funds	Absent from fixed-income securities	Develop a legal framework for investing pension and insurance funds in government securities; this will help create regulatory demand
	Retail investors	Absent from fixed-income securities	RMA needs to conduct programs for training and awareness on fixed-income securities
	Foreign institutional and portfolio investors	Absent from fixed-income securities	RMA needs to first develop a domestic institutional and retail investor base before creating a case for foreign investors
External environment	Fiscal debt management	Public Debt Policy formulated in 2016 The annual debt service obligations of total external debt must not exceed 25% of total exports of goods and services	The threshold for domestic debt needs to be determined to complement threshold for external debt The Public Debt Policy threshold should establish domestic limits and align borrowings accordingly
	Securities and exchange laws	No regulations	Need to establish regulatory framework for licensing merchant bankers, primary dealers, CRAs
	Treasury and cash management	Inadequate liquidity management and forecasting ability	RMA, in parallel with efforts to set up a liquidity management framework, should promote the gradual development of a functional money market
	Sovereign credit ratings from international CRAs (Fitch Ratings, Moody's Investors Service, and Standard and Poor's Global Ratings)	Not rated	Bhutan should strive to get rated by one of the three international CRAs

Source: Study team analysis.

Public–Private Partnership Capacity Assessment

Public–Private Partnership Law and Policy Support Capacity

Determinant 1: Bhutan enacted a PPP policy in 2016 that superseded the Private Participation in Infrastructure Framework, 2010. The policy's main objective is to build a sustainable PPP market in Bhutan by (i) facilitating and promoting a structured, institutionalized, and predictable approach to PPPs, and establishing uniform procedures across sectors; (ii) ensuring transparency in the structuring, procurement, and implementation of PPP projects; (iii) ensuring fair and equal access in the award of PPP projects; (iv) promoting priority projects that are affordable to the government and end-users, and that are value for money; (v) encouraging innovation in the provision of infrastructure and related services; (vi) clearly articulating accountability for outcomes; and (vii) supporting the development of viable PPP projects that offer reasonable returns to the private sector, while protecting the government from fiscal risks.

Determinant 2: Dispute settlements relating to PPP projects and programs are governed by the provisions of United Nations Commission on International Trade Law and the laws of Bhutan.

Table A2.33: Ratings for Public–Private Partnership Law and Policy Support Capacity in Bhutan

#	Determinant	Rating
1	Is there a dedicated legal or policy instrument/guideline for PPPs?	3
2	What dispute resolution mechanisms are available for PPP agreements?	2

PPP = public–private partnership.

Source: Study team analysis.

Public Sector Public–Private Partnership Support Capacity and Experience

Determinant 3: Bhutan does not have a sovereign debt rating by any of the international credit rating agencies.

Table A2.34: Ratings for Public Sector Public–Private Partnership Support Capacity and Experience in Bhutan

#	Determinant	Rating
3	If payment is likely to be made by the parent government, what is the credit rating of the parent government?	0
4	Is there a specialized government agency (or agencies) established for PPP purposes (e.g., PPP unit) and what are its roles?	3
5	Is there a streamlined approval process for PPP projects?	3
6	Does the sponsoring agency have previous experience with PPPs?	0
7	Are different PPP concession models defined for the sector and are model concession agreements available?	0

PPP = public–private partnership.

Source: Study team analysis.

Determinants 4 and 5: Bhutan has a specialized PPP agency to streamline PPP investment and procurement. Table A2.35 shows the feasibility analysis required for PPP projects by the government's Public–Private Partnership Agency.

Table A2.35: Feasibility Analyses Required for Public–Private Partnership Project Approvals in Bhutan

Feasibility	✓/✗
Technical feasibility	✓
Financial feasibility	✓
Legal feasibility	✓
Environmental and social sustainability	✓
Value for money assessment	✗
Fiscal affordability assessment	✗
PPP structuring and risk allocation	✗
Initial market testing	✗

PPP = public–private partnership.

Source: Asian Development Bank. 2017. *Public–Private Partnership Monitor*. Manila. https://www.adb.org/publications/public-private-partnership-monitor.

Determinant 6: No projects have achieved financial closure in the transport infrastructure sector since 1996 in Bhutan.

Determinant 7: Because no transport projects have been implemented in Bhutan using the PPP mode, there are no sector-specific model concession agreements to provide a framework for PPP agreements. Having these agreements could encourage private participation in transport infrastructure.

Public Sector Funding Assistance for Public–Private Partnerships

Determinant 8: The government, under the PPP law, provides subsidies or viability gap funding for PPP projects that are economically and socially justified, but this falls short of financial viability. This funding can be an explicit subsidy that is performance-driven (based on the private party achieving measurable outputs) and should be targeted toward socioeconomically disadvantaged users or groups of users. For this purpose, the Ministry of Finance has issued guidelines setting the criteria for eligibility to receive this funding and the procedure for applying, approving, disbursing, and monitoring the use of these funds.

Table A2.36: Ratings for Public Sector Funding Assistance in Public–Private Partnerships in Bhutan

#	Determinant	Rating
8	Is government support for viability gap funding available for PPP projects?	3

PPP = public–private partnership.

Source: Study team analysis.

Table A2.37: Ratings for Land Acquisition and Environmental and Social Clearances in Bhutan

#	Determinant	Rating
9	Does the authority have experience in dealing with land acquisitions, environmental clearances, and rehabilitation and resettlement?	1
10	Does the authority have a dedicated team to streamline land acquisitions and environmental clearances, and the experience to handle these areas?	0

Source: Study team analysis.

Land Acquisition, and Environmental and Social Clearances

Determinant 9: Bhutan has little experience in dealing with land acquisitions, environmental clearances, and rehabilitation and resettlement. Land lease periods are set in a way that recovers the cost of investments subject to provisions of the Land Act, 2007 and its amendments. Table A2.38 shows the support provided by the government in land acquisition to project developers.

Determinant 10: Environmental clearances for infrastructure projects require submitting a detailed proposal using the 2004 guidelines of the National Environment Commission. The social and resettlement process is overseen by the Ministry of Works and Human Settlement, which requires a detailed social impact assessment under its guidelines. Both these clearances are separate procedures, and the proposals are heavily scrutinized before PPP projects get the green light.

Table A2.38: Land Acquisition Support by the Government in Bhutan

Land Acquisition Support	✓/✗
Resettlement and compensation costs to residents	✓
Imposed limits on time frame to complete land acquisition	✗
Dedicated agency to streamline land acquisition	✗
Exemption from or reduction of land use fees	✗

Source: Asian Development Bank. 2017. *Public–Private Partnership Monitor*. Manila. https://www.adb.org/publications/public-private-partnership-monitor.

Market Capacity and Foreign Participation

Determinant 11: Private sector capacity in Bhutan to build transport infrastructure is negligible. Most PPP projects in the sector are implemented by private developers from India and other neighboring countries through item-rate contracts.

Determinants 12 and 13: Foreign participation is allowed and encouraged in Bhutan due to the lack of indigenous private developers in the country. There are restrictions in landownership rights for foreign investors in Bhutan. However, exemptions have been granted for infrastructure projects in the country.

Determinant 14: A major issue raised by foreign private developers during interviews for this report is the requirement for government credit guarantees for projects in the BIMSTEC master plan to secure revenue from these projects. Because Bhutan does not have a sovereign credit rating, the government provides no risk guarantees.[18]

Determinant 15: As for exchange rate risks, Bhutan has high currency fluctuations and volatility leading to higher hedging costs for long-term investments.

Determinant 16: Transport projects, as noted earlier, are financed predominantly through government budgetary sources, loans from multilateral and bilateral financial institutions, and government-to-government credit lines. Bhutan's capital market is still nascent and is not able to finance infrastructure projects that require long-term financing.

Table A2.39: Ratings for Market Capacity and Foreign Participation in Bhutan

#	Determinant	Rating
11	Is there sufficient market capacity and do private players have PPP experience?	0
12	Is foreign participation in PPP allowed?	3
13	Are there any restrictions on foreign investors' land use/ownership (i.e., do foreign investors have the same rights as locals?)	3
14	If payments are likely to be made from the authority's budget, is there any form of government guarantee available for these payments?	0
15	Is the exchange rate stable?	1
16	Is there a robust project finance market, which supplements the traditional corporate finance market?	1
17	Are debt instruments available for different project needs, such as senior, mezzanine, and subordinate debt, and take-out financing?	0

PPP = public–private partnership.

Source: Study team analysis.

[18] ADB. 2017. *Public–Private Partnership Monitor*. Manila. https://www.adb.org/publications/public-private-partnership-monitor.

Determinant 17: Bhutan has embarked on a program to develop its financial markets to increase access to long-term finance. As the first step in this process, the government has secured loans from multilateral institutions that can be extended to banks in Bhutan for on-lending to transport projects. The government has also secured support of ADB and the World Bank to enable them to offer credit enhancement products to Bhutan (risk-sharing and risk-mitigation instruments).

Life-Cycle Costs and Output Specifications

Determinants 18 and 19: Bhutan does not have enough experience in transport infrastructure projects to quantify construction and long-term operation costs, as well as output specifications.

Table A2.40: Ratings for Life-Cycle Cost and Output Specifications in Bhutan

#	Determinant	Rating
18	Can most of the costs, mainly related to construction and long-term operations, including maintenance, be quantified upfront with reasonable assumptions, and are historical data available?	0
19	Are objective output specifications readily available from a previous contract?	0

Source: Study team analysis.

Possible Interventions

Bhutan could adopt the following two approaches to address the investment gap in its transport infrastructure. First, increase private investment in transport infrastructure by tackling the issues hindering the development and deepening of its financing institutions. And second, it could explore avenues for revenue enhancement (e.g., LVC and non-toll revenue, such as advertisements and privately owned public spaces) to increase government investable capital, improve project viability, and unlock capital invested in existing operational projects through asset securitization (e.g., infrastructure investment trusts and toll securitization) and asset recycling (e.g., toll-operate-transfer).

Table A2.41 summarizes the key recommended interventions to augment the use of financing tools, banks and other financial institutions, and the capital market to reduce PPP-related risks in Bhutan.

Table A2.41: Summary of Recommended Finance Sector Interventions for Bhutan

#	Finance Sector	Issue	Actions
1	Commercial banks	High nonperforming assets and substandard credit appraisal process	Create stringent nonperforming asset recognition norms to identify stressed assets early. Option of setting up a national infrastructure development bank or, if it is created, use a regional development bank set up by countries in the Bay of Bengal Initiative for Multi-Sectoral Technical and Economic Cooperation.
2	Foreign direct investment (FDI)	Low overall FDI inflows and investment in infrastructure, including transport sector	Promote new FDI through a well-formulated promotion strategy, targeting niche markets in transport infrastructure sectors, as well as other sectors (e.g., medical, education, tourism, and niche agricultural products). Short term: Promote investment opportunities directly to existing networks of investors. Medium term: Assess the need to create a standalone investment promotion unit with dedicated staff to conduct outreach.
			Develop an effective market research team and investment promotion strategy for infrastructure projects. An investment summit could be held, perhaps along the lines of the Gujarat Invest Summit.
			Upgrade internet infrastructure through investments, especially in cable and fiber optics to increase promotion and branding among foreign investors.
			Deepen value chains with Bangladesh and India and strengthen bilateral relations with other countries.
3	Insurance funds	Low overall penetration of insurance funds leading to lower availability of these funds for infrastructure	Implement regulatory reforms like Egypt.
			Seek out bancassurance opportunities (i.e., partnership between an insurance company and a bank where the bank sells insurance products).
		Underdeveloped capital market and absence of sufficient long-term debt instruments, leading to investments primarily through loans similar to commercial banks	Increase promotion, education, and training programs about bonds for potential investors, including nonresident Bhutanis.
			Developed online and electronic system for long-term debt instruments to strengthen corporate governance and transparency.
4	Pension funds	Limited corpus (Nu36 billion); means lower available funds for infrastructure	Create awareness about pension and retirement planning.

continued on next page

Table A2.41 *continued*

#	Finance Sector	Issue	Actions
5	Government borrowing	Bhutan does not have a sovereign rating from any of the international credit rating agencies, which hinders the government's ability to secure financing from foreign capital markets	Bhutan should secure a sovereign credit rating from one of these agencies.
6	Private sector participation	Only a few public–private partnership (PPP) projects in transport infrastructure	Improve and strengthen the enabling environment for PPPs. This can be done through: **Robust project planning and preparation:** Project authorities or the PPP cells should work towards creating a pipeline of investable PPP projects. This would require inputs from transport master plans and subsequent assessment by project authorities to determine the projects that can be taken up on PPP mode. Necessary project preparation efforts such as developing detailed project reports, social and environment impact assessment, etc. should be undertaken and then projects put up for evaluation by prospective investors, including multilateral and/or bilateral financing institutions. **Developing suitable project structures:** Project authorities should build the capacity to develop suitable project structuring and risk-sharing models (e.g., exploring options of minimum revenue guarantees and annuity payments to cover demand risks if required). Model concession agreements for suitable PPP models should be prepared. **Increasing the investor base:** Concession agreements should allow for asset recycling so that investors who invest in operational assets are also eligible to participate in them. **Exploring ways to enhance revenue and asset securitization:** This will unlock invested capital in existing operational assets and increase cash inflows.

Source: Study team analysis.

India

Transport Infrastructure Financing Landscape

Sources of Transport Infrastructure Financing

India's transport infrastructure financing needs are primarily financed through government budgetary support. Apart from this, project authorities rely on internal and extra-budgetary resources. Project authorities raise funds through the sale of assets, such as bonds serviced by future cash flows. Insurance companies and pension and mutual funds are among the main subscribers to these bonds. These sources of financing for transport infrastructure contribute to about 2% of GDP annually.

The National Highways Authority of India (NHAI) relies on extra-budgetary resources for more than 60% of its financing needs (Figure A2.25). Figure A2.26 shows the financing sources of Indian Railways.

Figure A2.25: National Highways Authority of India Financing Sources, FY2019–FY2021
(₹ trillion)

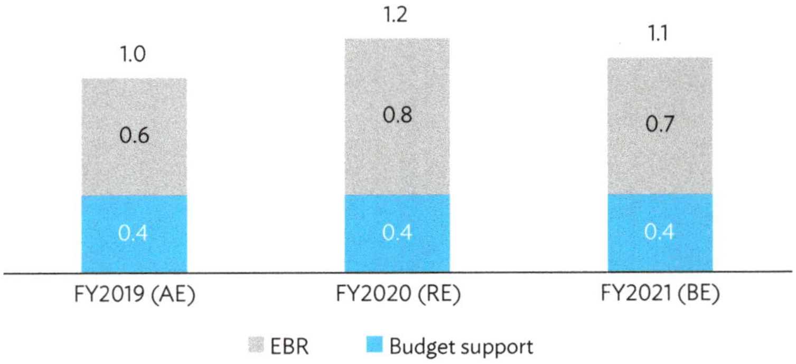

AE = actual expenditure, BE = budget estimates, EBR = external budgetary resource, FY = fiscal year, RE = revised expenditure

Note: FY ends 31 March.

Source: Government of India. Union Budget 2020–21. https://www.indiabudget.gov.in/budget2020-21/.

Figure A2.26: Indian Railways Financing Sources, FY2019–FY2021

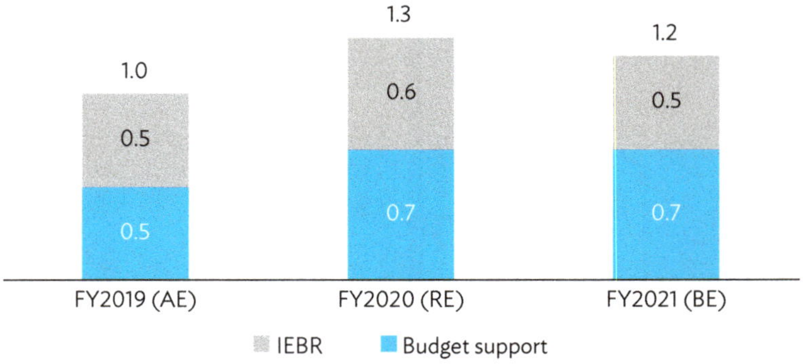

AE = actual expenditure, BE = budget estimate, FY = fiscal year, IEBR = internal and external budgetary resources, RE = revised expenditure.

Note: FY ends 31 March.

Source: Government of India. Union Budget 2020–21. https://www.indiabudget.gov.in/budget2020-21/.

The contribution of private sector investment to transport infrastructure is only about 0.2% of GDP, compared with an annual requirement of 3.7% in the National Infrastructure Pipeline. This ambitious pipeline of infrastructure projects has a total investment of ₹35 trillion from 2019 to 2025 (Figure A2.27).

Figure A2.27: India's Financing Sources and Annual Transport Infrastructure Financing Needs
(% of GDP)

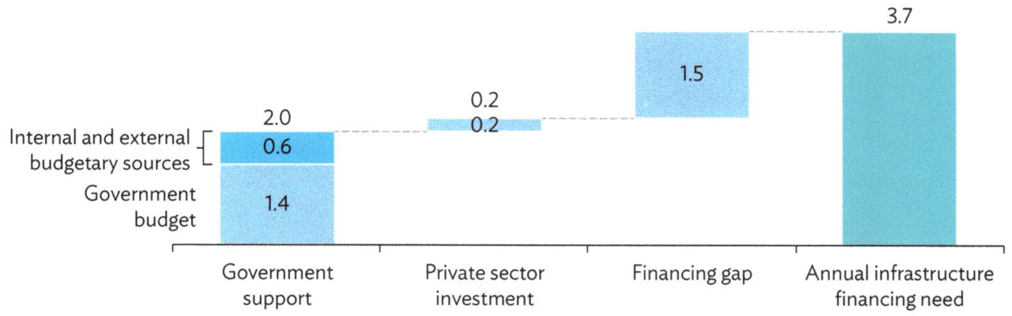

GDP = gross domestic product.

Sources: Government of India, National Infrastructure Pipeline. https://indiainvestmentgrid.gov.in/national-infrastructure-pipeline; and World Bank. Private Participation in Infrastructure database (Accessed in 2020). https://ppi.worldbank.org/en/ppi.

Fiscal Support to Infrastructure

The debt burden of the general government—combined central and state governments—is estimated at 72% of GDP in FY2019 (ended 31 March)—that is, before COVID-19. Moody's Investors Service expects the pandemic to have caused the debt burden to rise to about 84% of GDP in FY2020 (Figure A2.28).[19]

Figure A2.28: India Government Debt, FY2014–FY2019
(% of GDP)

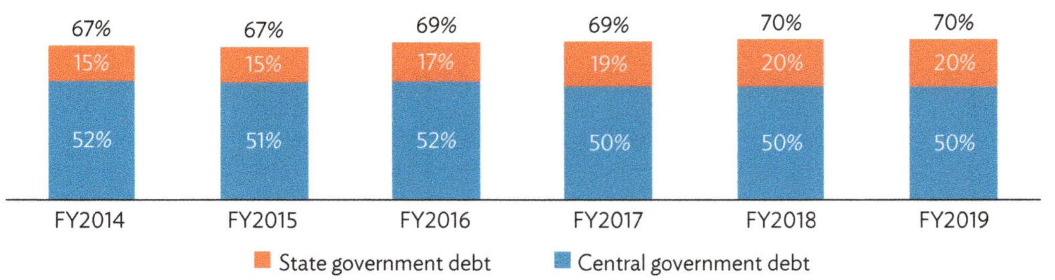

FY = fiscal year, GDP = gross domestic product.

Note: FY ends 31 March.

Source: Public Debt Statistics (2020-2021). Reserve bank of India. https://www.rbi.org.in/scripts/FS_PDS.aspx.

[19] *The Hindu*. 2020. Moody's Downgrades India's Rating to Baa3. 1 June. https://www.thehindubusinessline.com/economy/moodys-downgrades-indias-rating-to-baa3/article31725074.ece.

In 2020, India's sovereign credit rating outlook was revised to negative by two of the three global credit rating agencies (Table A2.42). India's rising ratio of debt-to-GDP, along with the ratings downgrade by Moody's Investors Service and Standard & Poor's Global Ratings is making it harder for the government to borrow internationally.

Table A2.42: India's Sovereign Credit Ratings and Outlook, 2020

Agency	Rating	Outlook	Rating Release Date
Fitch	BBB-	Negative	18 June 2020
Moody's	Downgraded from Baa2 to Baa3	Negative	1 June 2020
S&P	BBB- affirmed	Stable	10 June 2020

S&P = Standard & Poor's Global Ratings.

Sources: Rating updates from Fitch Ratings, Moody's Investors Service, Standard & Poor's Global Ratings.

With the scope for international borrowing reduced, India's transport budget has less scope for expansion. Since the last decade, the sector's budget has ranged 5%–6% of total budget allocation, with capital expenditure accounting for 80%–90% (Figure A2.29). Figure A2.30 shows transport budget expenditure by sector.

Figure A2.29: India's Budget Allocation on Transport Infrastructure by Expenditure Type, FY2016–FY2019

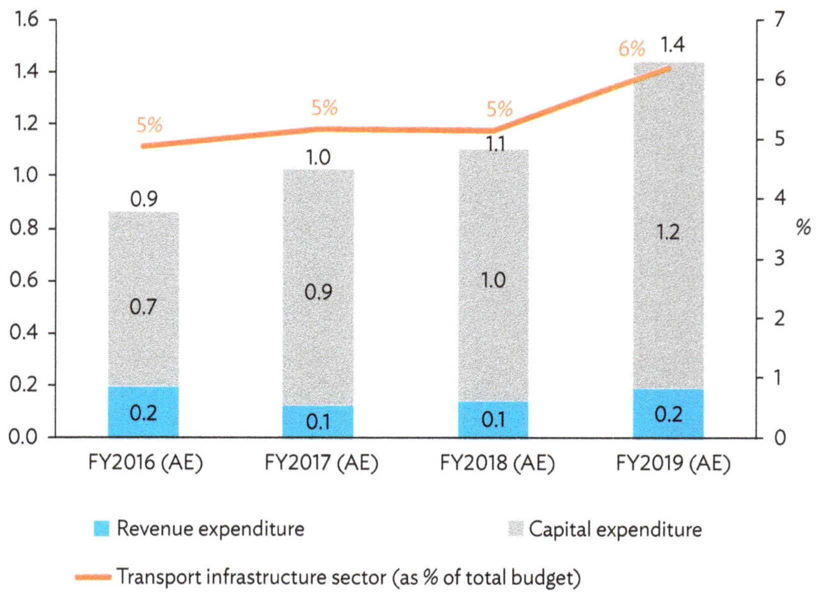

AE = actual expenditure, FY = fiscal year.

Note: FY ends 31 March.

Source: Government of India. Union Budget 2020–21. https://www.indiabudget.gov.in/budget2020-21/.

Figure A2.30: India's Budget Allocation for Transport Infrastructure by Sector, FY2016–FY2020
(₹ trillion)

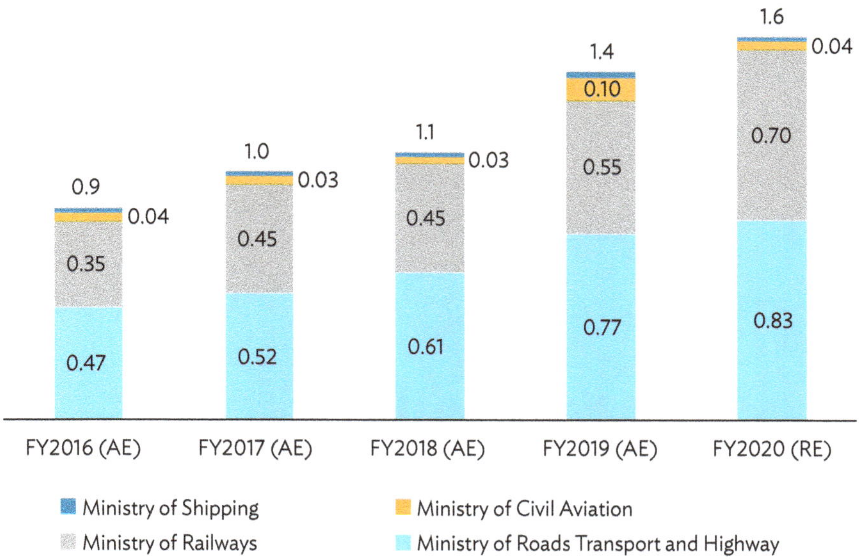

AE = actual expenditure, FY = fiscal year, RE = revised expenditure.

Note: FY ends 31 March.

Source: Government of India. Union Budget 2020–21. https://www.indiabudget.gov.in/budget2020-21/.

COVID-19 has further aggravated the fiscal situation. Because of the economic distress caused by the pandemic, the government, in May 2020, announced a special economic package totaling ₹21 trillion.[20] The package includes short- and long-term sector reforms, including labor and agriculture reforms, and encouraging private participation in strategic sectors.

The government's response to the COVID-19 economic impact has focused on recovery through reforms and monetary policy.

Bridging Financing Gaps

To bridge the financing gap, India could increase financing for transport infrastructure by improving the conditions for private investment in the sector. To do this, they can tackle the issues hindering the development and deepening of financing institutions and instruments, explore ways to enhance revenue by unlocking government capital blocked in operational projects, and secure loans from multilateral and bilateral financial institutions.

Figure A2.31 maps India's financial institutions based on their total investable capital, as a percentage of GDP, and their contribution to infrastructure financing, as a percentage of their capital base.

20 S. Sharma. 2020. *Financial Express*. 18 May. Modi's Rs 21 Lakh Cr Special Economic Package Actually Costs the Govt Only this Much. https://www.financialexpress.com/economy/narendra-modis-rs-21-lakh-cr-special-economic-package-actually-costs-the-govt-only-this-much-nirmala-sitharaman-relief-package/1962288/.

Figure A2.31: Financial Institution Mapping for India

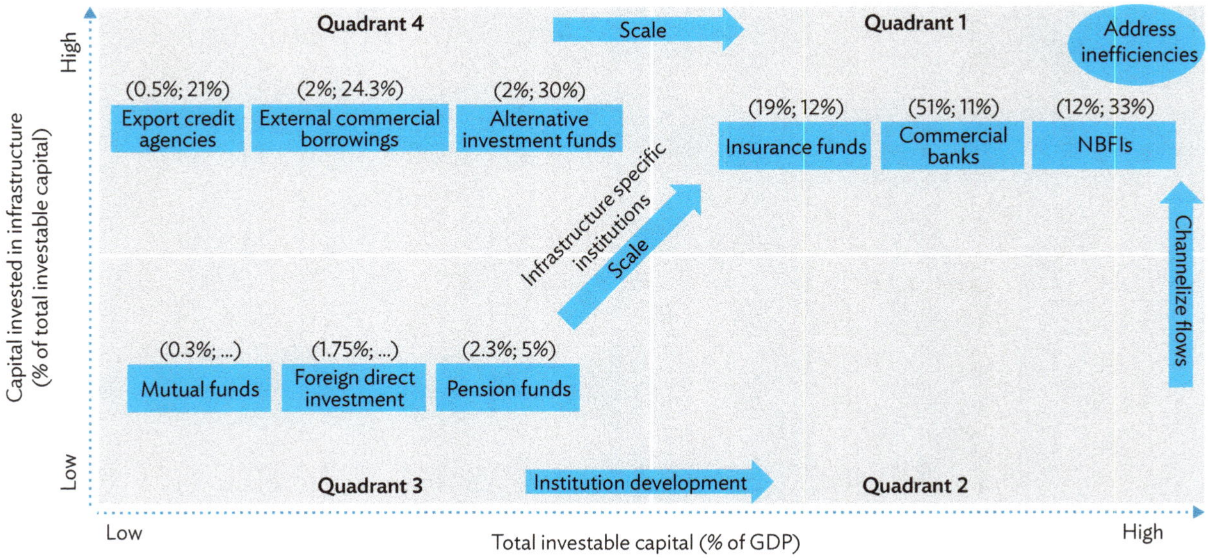

... = not available, GDP = gross domestic product, NBFI = nonbank financial institution.

Notes:

1. Percentage figures provide a comparative measure and are based on recent data as per availability.
2. Institutions for which data are not available are placed based on the general understanding from primary and secondary research.

Sources: Insurance and Pension Regulators Security Commission; and Reserve Bank of India.

India's commercial banks, insurance funds, and NBFIs have a large total investable capital base and play a key role in private infrastructure financing. Alternative investment funds, external commercial borrowing, and export credit agencies have a high share of infrastructure financing, but they do not have the scale to finance infrastructure in meaningful way. The continuing stress on banks and NBFIs constrains the supply of credit for consumption and investment. India needs to focus on channeling the funds of financing institutions, such as insurance and pension funds, to increase their contribution to infrastructure through the capital market.

Challenges Facing Financing Institutions for Investing in Transport Infrastructure

The assessment is done in two parts. In the first, the challenges faced by financing institutions in providing capital to infrastructure projects are identified along with possible interventions. This essentially covers the supply side of infrastructure financing. In the second part, PPP challenges by sector are identified; this essentially covers the demand side.

Commercial Banks

India has 12 public sector and 22 private sector banks under the category "scheduled commercial banks."[21] State Bank of India is the largest public sector bank; HDFC Bank is the largest private bank in terms of total assets.[22]

[21] Reserve Bank of India. List of Scheduled Commercial Banks. https://m.rbi.org.in/scripts/bs_viewcontent.aspx?Id=3657.
[22] Reserve Bank of India. Database on Indian Economy. (accessed July 2020). https://www.rbi.org.in/scripts/FS_PDS.aspx.

Commercial banks are the main private financing institutions for infrastructure. The outstanding loans and advances of these banks for infrastructure, as of March 2019, was ₹97.1 trillion, about 51% of GDP. Outstanding infrastructure loans totaled ₹10.4 trillion—about 11% of banks' total outstanding loans and advances.

India spends about $58 billion–$60 billion a year on transport infrastructure.[23] Under the National Infrastructure Pipeline it needs to spend $500 billion from FY2020 to FY2025—about $98 billion a year.[24] This implies a funding gap of $70 billion–$180 billion a year that needs to be bridged by the various financing tools available in India. However, the exposure of commercial banks to infrastructure, and particularly transport infrastructure, has declined since FY2015, as shown in Figure A2.32.

Figure A2.32: India Commercial Bank Credit to Transport Infrastructure, FY2015–FY2020
(% of total bank credit)

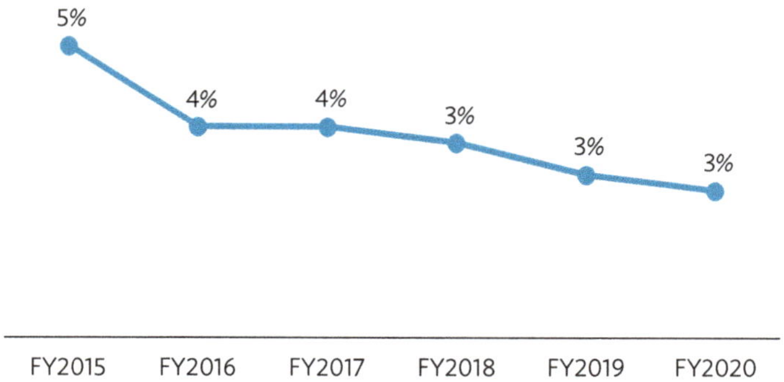

FY = fiscal year.

Note: FY ends 31 March. Figures calculated taking into account banks' exposure to roads and other transport sectors.

Source: Reserve Bank of India.

Reasons for the decrease include (i) asset–liability mismatches due to the long-term nature of the assets (loans) and the short-term nature of deposits (liabilities); (ii) increasing nonperforming loans (NPLs) and stringent recognition norms for nonperforming assets (NPAs), which are constraining the credit allocation of commercial banks for riskier infrastructure projects; and (iii) the design of PPP concession agreements and dispute resolution-related concerns. These three points are now discussed in more detail.

(i) **Asset–liability mismatches.** This occurs when infrastructure financing requires longer-tenure loans, which commercial banks need to finance by short-term borrowings, generally in the form of deposits. As Figure A2.33 shows, the share of term deposits with maturities of over 5 years was only 14% of the total term deposits of banks as of March 2019. But infrastructure lending by banks are for a tenure ranging from 10 to 12 years.[25]

[23] Government of India. Union Budget 2020–21; National Infrastructure Pipeline. https://indiainvestmentgrid.gov.in/national-infrastructure-pipeline; and World Bank. Public Private Participation in Infrastructure database (accessed July 2020) https://ppi.worldbank.org/en/ppi.

[24] Ministry of Finance. Economic Survey 2019–2020. https://www.indiabudget.gov.in/budget2020-21/economicsurvey/index.php.

[25] Interviews with commercial banks in India.

Figure A2.33: Maturity Pattern of Term Deposits of India's Commercial Banks

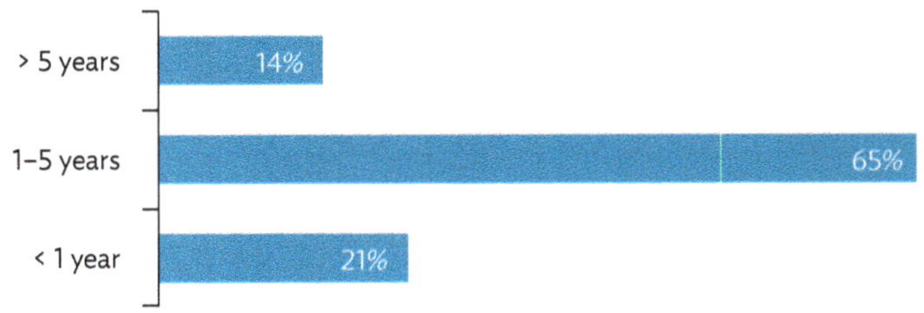

FY = fiscal year.

Note: FY ends 31 March.

Source: Reserve Bank of India.

State Bank of India has a lower quantum of deposits and borrowings compared with assets with maturities of over 5 years; this indicates that commercial banks are lending to long-term assets with short-term liabilities (Figure A2.34).

Figure A2.34: State Bank of India Assets and Liabilities with Average Maturity of Over 5 Years (₹ trillion)

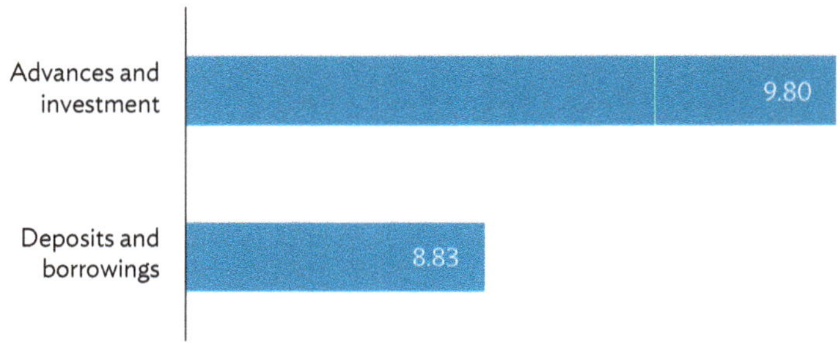

Source: State Bank of India. 2018–2019. *Annual Report*. Mumbai. https://sbi.co.in/corporate/AR1920/ ?Publishing location.

Long-term sources of borrowing, such as bond issues, remain low for commercial banks even though the Reserve Bank of India allows them to raise long-term bonds that have a minimum 7-year maturity.[26] For instance, State Bank of India's share of bonds to total deposits and borrowing was 2% as of March 2019.[27]

26 Reserve Bank of India Circular. DBOD.BP.BC.No.25/08.12.014/2014-15. 15. July 2014.

27 State Bank of India. 2018–2019. *Annual Report*. Mumbai

On the asset side, a secondary market for loans has not evolved to the scale of its potential because of the following reasons: (i) limited secondary deals due to a smaller number of secondary investors (insurance funds, NBFIs, and infrastructure development and pension funds); (ii) the reluctance of banks to flip good operational projects; (iii) the need for an effective, and reliable price discovery mechanism; (iv) the need for a systematic loan–sales platform; and (v) limited standardization in loan and transfer documentation. Several loan market associations, such as the Loan Syndications and Trading Association in the United States, the Loan Market Association with members in Africa, Europe, and the Middle East, and the Asia Pacific Loan Market Association, play an active role in developing secondary markets (Box A2.4). Project bonds are an effective financing instrument for refinancing commercial banks loans, as the example in Box A2.5 shows.

Box A2.4: Development of the Secondary Loan Market in Europe

The growth in borrowing requirements in Europe during the 1970s saw loan facilities traditionally provided on a bilateral basis increasingly replaced by larger credit lines from a pool of lenders, and then by loan facilities syndicated to the wider market.

Up to the mid-1990s, participation in Europe's secondary loan market was dominated by a small number of United States banks, predominantly investment banks, specialist debt traders, and vulture funds, with activity focused on the distressed debt market. But from the mid-1990s, institutional investors and other nonbank financial institutions increasingly looked to the secondary loan market to invest in.

Today's secondary loan market is used by a diverse and large number of participants, including investment banks; commercial banks; hedge, pension, and private equity funds; and specialist loan brokers, each looking to transact in par, near par, and distressed debt. Government agencies, such as the Irish National Asset Management Agency, bought up nonperforming debt as a result of the 2008–2009 global financial crisis.

To address the standardization of practices, a group of banks formed the Loan Market Association in 1996. Its loan volumes have increased significantly since then, and were at €1 trillion in 2018. The Loan Market Association is rules-based. The settlement time is 10–20 days and the enforcement mechanism used by the association for penalizing defaulters has led to a highly disciplined market. While due diligence is mostly undertaken before a trade is done, the time taken in settlement is reportedly due to documentation processes.

The Loan Market Association has some 600 members in 50 countries from bank and nonbank lenders, borrowers, law firms, credit rating agencies, and service providers. The association has expanded its activities to include all aspects of the primary and secondary syndicated loan market.

Source: Reserve Bank of India. 2019. *Report of the Task Force on the Development of Secondary Market for Corporate Loans*. Delhi. https://www.phdcci.in/wp-content/uploads/2022/01/RBI-releases-the-Report-of-the-Task-Force-on-the-Development-of-Secondary-Market-for-Corporate-Loans.pdf.

Box A2.5: Slovakia R1 Motorway Project Deal Refinancing

The R1 motorway between Nitra and Tekovske Nemce, as well as the Banska Bystrica Northern Bypass, covering a total length of 51.6-km, was the Slovak Republic's first public–private partnership. The project, executed in 2009, was based on the availability fee payments—in other words, there was no demand risk component. The total project cost was €1.3 billion, financed by a mix of senior debt (€981 million), shareholder funds (€149 million) and internally generated cash (€125 million a year, indexed).

continued on next page

Box A2.5 *continued*

The borrower wanted to refinance the senior debt in 2013 due to beneficial interest rate conditions. The purpose of going to the capital markets was to significantly extend maturities, where final maturity, after tough negotiations, reached 12 years, and to decrease interest expenses.

The European Bank for Reconstruction and Development came in as an anchor investor for the refinancing with a subscription of €200 million in a private placement of the project bond. Doing this triggered a reputational improvement and attracted a big pool of investors.

The use of project bonds in the refinancing structure was the preferred option by the borrowers due to the following factors: (i) the absence of construction risk facilitated an appropriate investment rating, resulting in a lower coupon rate than commercial banks could offer; (ii) the European Bank for Reconstruction and Development, being anchor investor, made the transaction even more bond-suitable and feasible (at that time, there was little willingness among banks to provide infrastructure refinancing for a very long tenor of 25 years and for €1.2 billion); and (iii) the project bond solution avoided certain provident fund covenants and strict dividend restrictions—another draw for the sponsor to go for a bond solution.

Source: APEC/OECD. 2019. *Financing Infrastructure in APEC Economies: APEC/OECD Report on Selected Effective Approaches*. Paris. https://www.oecd.org/finance/private-pensions/Financing-infrastructure-in-APEC-economies-selected-effective-approaches-2019.pdf.

Table A2.43 outlines actions that can be taken by India's commercial banks to resolve asset–liability mismatches and their possible impacts.

Table A2.43: Actions to Resolve Asset–Liability Mismatches in India's Commercial Banks

Actions	Impact
Encourage secondary deals that allow banks to recycle their exposure, post-commercial operations date; flip assets to long term-institutional investors or list project bonds (debt pricing should reflect this; i.e., the price of bank and institutional debt and corporate bonds cannot be the same—there should be a spread).	Secondary investors will have more operational assets to invest in refinancing through project bonds, which will help deepen the bond market.
Explore options for institutionalizing an active secondary loan market.	**Capital optimization:** Banks can unlock their capital by down selling their exposure to certain borrowers; this could help them to take advantage of new lending opportunities. **Liquidity management:** The secondary market can help banks manage asset–liability mismatches by facilitating the liquidation of long-term exposures and using those funds to meet unforeseen obligations. **Price discovery mechanism:** A well-developed secondary loan market can result in an efficient price discovery mechanism as the loan gets churned multiple times during its lifetime, thereby reflecting the prevailing market perceived price. This would in turn facilitate the appropriate pricing of future loan assets of the same borrower or sector. **Risk management:** Banks can mitigate their potential concentration risk for a specific borrower group, sector, geography, or maturity duration, which was not initially envisaged at the time of loan origination. **Refinancing options for borrowers:** Borrowers can also use this mechanism to retire loans and avail funds or debt at a lower cost.

Source: Study team analysis.

(ii) **Stringent nonperforming asset recognition norms.** NPAs have been rising and infrastructure assets are a significant contributor to this trend. The NPAs of commercial banks as a percentage of total gross advances rose from 2.4% in FY2011 to 9.1% in FY2019 (Figure A2.35). Because of higher NPAs in the infrastructure sector, banks have reduced lending to infrastructure projects. Banks have restricted their lending to mainly availability-based PPP road projects that are considered less risky than build–operate–transfer toll projects, where the demand risk is passed on to private players.

Figure A2.35: Nonperforming Assets of India's Commercial Banks, FY2011–FY2019
(% of total gross advances)

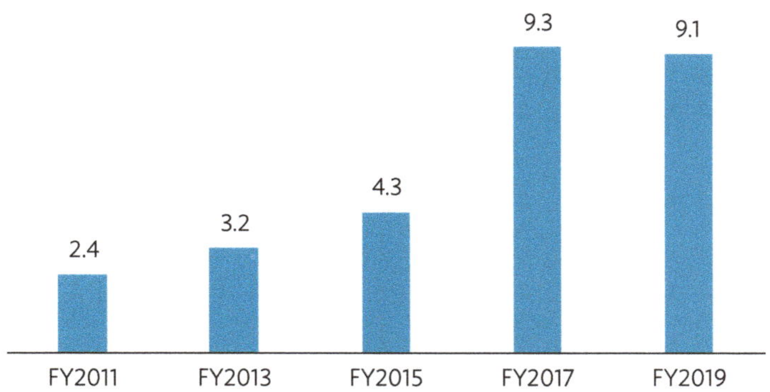

FY = fiscal year.

Note: Fiscal year ends March 31.

Source: Reserve Bank of India.

The rise in the NPAs of India's commercial banks was caused by the economic slowdown, PPP-related risks, and stringent NPA recognition norms. To resolve rising NPAs, some countries, including France, Finland, Germany, Indonesia, and Sweden, have set up bad banks to resolve or liquidate bad debts, a process initiated by US-based Mellon Bank in 1988.[28] Doing this has direct and indirect benefits, including allowing banks to clean up their balance sheets while enabling management to focus on growing bank business, bringing specialized knowledge to a bad bank, and preventing the "good" bank from being involved in troubled-asset workouts. The National Asset Reconstruction Company Limited was constituted by the Government of India in 2021 to deal with stressed assets in the Indian banking system. Commercial banks in India should also look into setting up bad banks to resolve or liquidate bad debts. Table A2.44 outlines actions to tackle the NPAs of commercial banks.

[28] Mellon Bank did this to hold its toxic assets by spinning off its own capital into the Grant Street National Bank. The bank did not take deposits from the public as normal banks do, but simply resolved or liquidated bad debt to recover as much money as it could. Grant Street was liquidated after it had served its purpose.

Table A2.44: Actions to Tackle Nonperforming Assets of India's Commercial Banks

#	Actions	Impact
1	Set up credit guarantee funds or introduce loan guarantee instruments for infrastructure projects (e.g., the Multilateral Loan Guarantee Agency's loan guarantee, Asian Development Bank's Partial Credit Guarantee)	• Lowers risk of outstanding loans becoming nonperforming • Might increase costs, but useful to address demand-risks without going for annuity-based models
2	Stabilize the Insolvency and Bankruptcy Code process	• Establishes case precedents on insolvency resolution and liquidation
3	Explore the larger role of specialized institutions, such as asset reconstruction agencies and bad banks, to resolve stressed assets	• Enables banks to focus on lending, rather than the rescue and recovery of distressed assets
4	Build capacity for lending to the infrastructure sector by disseminating global best practices via training, certification, and workshops	• Enhanced lending standards for infrastructure sector aligned to global benchmarks

Source: Study team analysis.

Nonbank Financial Institutions

NBFIs are the biggest financing institutions in India after commercial banks. The basic difference is that NBFIs cannot accept demand deposits from retail depositors. NBFIs have a special category of company for infrastructure finance that was created to meet the growing need for finance for infrastructure projects. Major NBFIs are Infrastructure Development Finance Company, India Infrastructure Finance Company Limited, L&T Infrastructure Finance Company Limited, Power Finance Corporation, and Rural Electrification Corporation (REC).

The outstanding loans and advances of NBFIs as of March 2019 was ₹22.8 trillion, 12.0% of GDP.[29] Outstanding infrastructure loans were ₹7.4 trillion, 32.6% of the total outstanding loans and advances of NBFIs. NBFIs have increased their lending sharply in line with the rising demand for financing power, telecommunications, and road projects (Figure A2.36).

Figure A2.36: Outstanding Infrastructure Loans of India's Nonbank Financial Institutions, FY2014–FY2019
(₹ trillion)

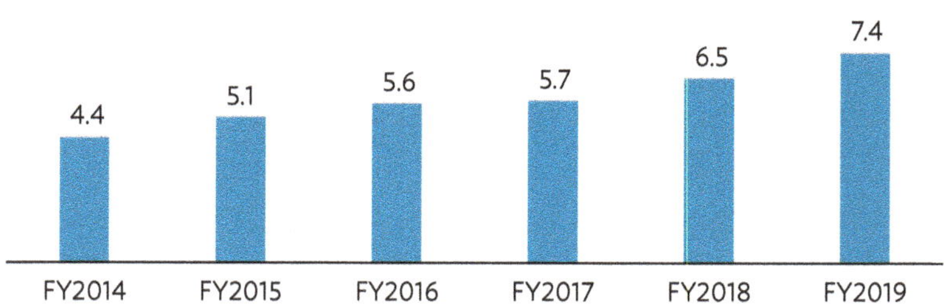

FY = fiscal year.
Note: FY ends 31 March.
Source: Reserve Bank of India.

[29] Reserve Bank of India. Non-Banking Financial Institutions. https://m.rbi.org.in/Scripts/PublicationsView.aspx?id=19367.

About one-third of NBFIs' total outstanding loans are in infrastructure—but their exposure to transport infrastructure is limited. Infrastructure-focused NBFIs are dominated by two government-backed companies specializing in the power sector: Power Finance Corporation and REC. They account for 85% of total NBFI infrastructure lending. NBFIs have only a small presence in transport infrastructure. India Infrastructure Finance Company and L&T are in this sector. Figure A2.37 shows that while infrastructure-focused NBFIs focus on power, commercial banks have more diverse portfolios.

Figure A2.37: Infrastructure Lending by India's Commercial Banks and Nonbank Financial Institutions, FY2019

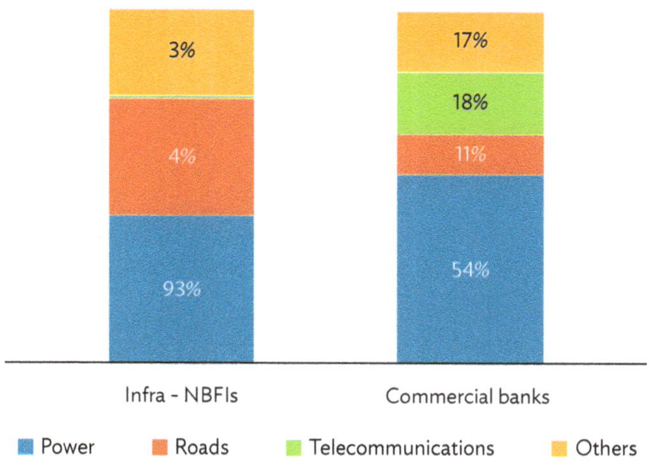

FY = fiscal year, NBFI= nonbank financial institution.

Source: Reserve bank of India; and secondary sources.

NBFI lending to infrastructure faces the following challenges: (i) asset-liability mismatches, because of the reliance on short-term sources of financing; (ii) a substantial rise in gross nonperforming infrastructure loans; (iii) a skills deficit for underwriting transport infrastructure projects; and (iv) a low supply of viable and good quality operational projects for infrastructure development funds. These four points are now discussed in more detail.

(iii) **Asset-liability mismatches.** Infrastructure financing requires longer-tenure loans that should ideally be financed by long-term borrowing. The borrowing of Power Finance Corporation and REC is 85% long-term bonds, but only 37% of the borrowing of other infrastructure NBFIs is long-term bonds; most of the rest comes from banks and short-term sources, such as commercial paper (Figure A2.38). Relying on these sources is not ideal for long-term financing. For instance, Infrastructure Leasing & Financial Services extended loans with its short-term borrowing, resulting in an asset-liability mismatch that caused a liquidity crisis at the firm. Table A2.45 outlines actions to resolve the asset-liability mismatches of NBFIs.

Figure A2.38: Borrowing Mix of India's Infrastructure-Focused Nonbank Financial Institutions

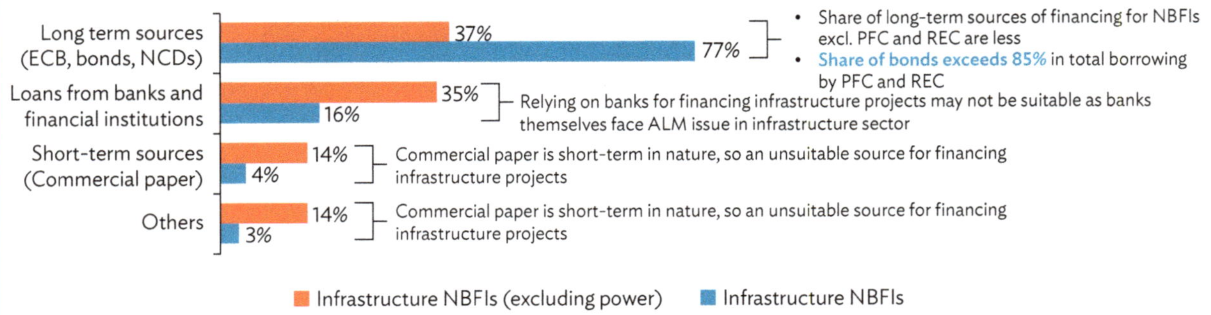

ALM = asset–liability mismatch, ECB = external commercial borrowing, NCD = nonconvertible debentures, NBFI = nonbank financial institution, PFC = Power Finance Corporation, REC = Rural Electrification Corporation.

Note: Excluding power means infrastructure NBFIs excluding PFC and REC.

Source: Reserve Bank of India; annual reports of infrastructure-focused NBFIs.

Table A2.45: Actions to Resolve Asset–Liability Mismatches of India's Nonbank Financial Institutions

#	Actions	Impact
1	Ensure enablers facilitate financing through bonds (e.g., credit-rating enhancement)	Enhanced credit ratings of borrowers and, subsequently, reduced coupon rates
2	Explore options for institutionalizing an active secondary market for loans	Enables focus on lending, rather than the rescue and recovery of distressed assets

Source: Study team analysis.

Rising gross nonperforming infrastructure loans. This happened for infrastructure-focused NBFIs because of stringent recognition norms for NPAs, PPP-related risks, the economic slowdown, and the weak credit-risk profile of borrowers (Figure A2.39). Table A2.46 outlines actions to resolve the rising NPAs of NBFIs.

Figure A2.39: Gross Nonperforming Assets of Infrastructure-Focused Nonbank Financial Institutions, FY2016–FY2020

(% of GNPA to total advances)

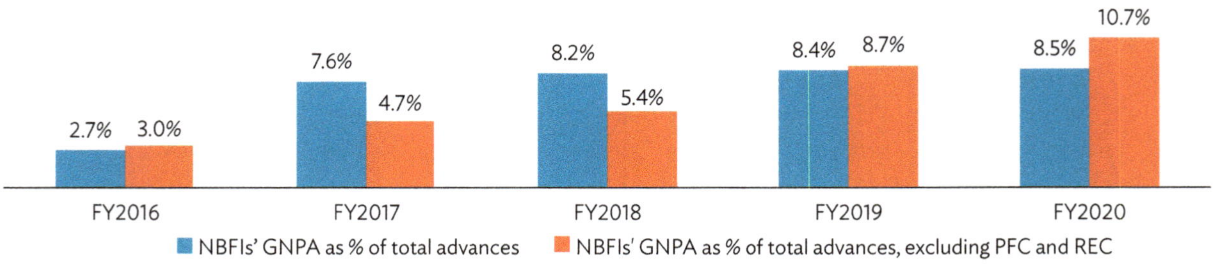

FY = fiscal year, GNPA = gross nonperforming assets, NBFI = nonbank financial institutions, PFC = Power Finance Corporation, REC = Rural Electrification Corporation.

Note: FY ends 31 March.

Source: Reserve Bank of India.

Table A2.46: Actions to Resolve Rising Nonperforming Assets of India's Nonbank Financial Institutions

#	Action	Impact
1	Set up credit guarantee funds for infrastructure projects	Reduced risk of outstanding loans becoming nonperforming. Might increase cost, but useful for addressing demand-risk concerns without going for annuity-based models
2	Stabilize Insolvency and Bankruptcy Code process	Case precedents on insolvency resolution and liquidation
3	Explore larger role of specialized institutions, such as asset reconstruction agencies and bad banks, to resolve distressed assets	Enables nonbank financial institutions to focus on lending rather than the rescue and recovery of distressed assets

Source: Study team analysis.

Insufficient underwriting capacity. Primary interactions with financing institutions indicated very few NBFIs have the skills to evaluate and finance infrastructure projects. In 2018, Infrastructure Leasing & Financial Services defaulted due to asset-liability mismatches. Figure A2.40 shows the market share of India's NBFIs.

Actions that India's NBFIs could take to improve their technical capability to underwrite infrastructure projects include capacity building programs with the assistance of multilateral and bilateral institutions.[30]

Figure A2.40: Market Share of India's Nonbank Financial Institutions

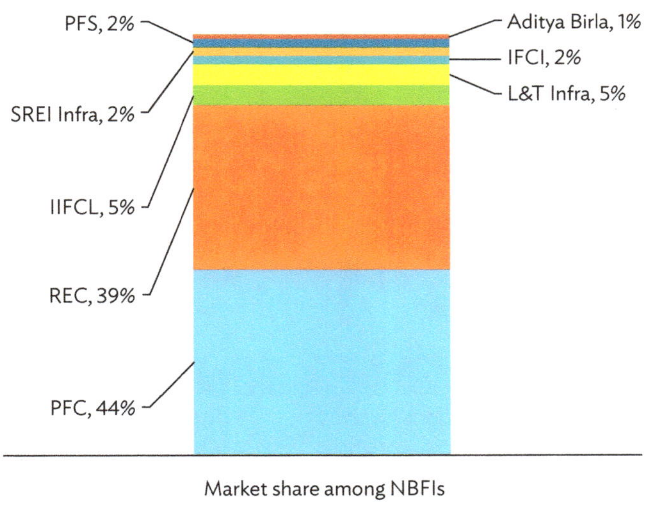

IFCI = Industrial Finance Corporation of India, IIFCL = India Infrastructure Finance Company Limited, L&T = Larsen & Toubro, NBFI = nonbank financial institution, PFC = Power Finance Corporation, PFS = Principal Financial Services, REC = Rural Electrification Corporation.

Source: Annual reports of the NBFIs; and secondary sources.

30 As suggested in the Asian Development Bank's 2014 technical assistance report titled *Promoting Capacity Building in Financial Institutions in Emerging Countries in South Asia.*

Lower-than-expected growth of infrastructure development funds. India's financial regulations stipulate that infrastructure development funds may only invest in operational projects with a track record of satisfactory performance of at least 1 year. Since 2014, the book size of these finds has increased 50-fold to ₹280 billion; this, however, is just 0.33% of the total exposure of banks to infrastructure (Figure A2.41). As India Infrastructure Finance Company Limited, a leading India infrastructure development fund, has put it, the "supply of commissioned infrastructure assets has been low and banks are reluctant to flip operational projects having lower credit risk, impacting the business volumes of IDFs (infrastructure development funds)." Table A2.47 outlines actions on the demand-side constraints on infrastructure development funds.

Figure A2.41: Asset Base Growth of India's Infrastructure Development Funds Against Return on Assets, FY2014–FY2019

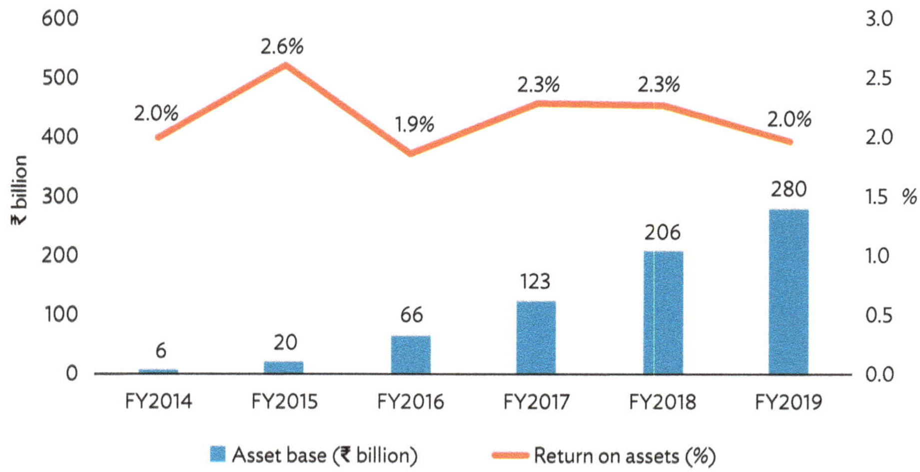

FY = fiscal year.

Note: FY ends 31 March.

Source: Annual reports of infrastructure development funds; and secondary sources.

Table A2.47: Actions to Address Demand-Side Constraints on India's Infrastructure Development Funds

#	Actions	Impact
1	Banks need to flip assets to other institutions, such as commercial banks, nonbank financial institutions, and insurance and pension funds	Addresses demand-side constraints impeding the deepening of infrastructure development funds
2.	Explore institutionalizing active secondary market for loans	Enables focus on lending, rather than the rescue and recovery of distressed assets

Source: Study team analysis.

Pension Funds

The two big hurdles affecting the capacity of pension funds to invest in transport infrastructure are a lack of high-quality investable bonds and pension coverage gaps.

Lack of high-quality investable bonds. Pension Fund Regulatory and Development Authority regulations require pension funds to make all bond investments in graded securities with a minimum AA rating from at least two credit rating agencies registered with the Securities and Exchange Board of India. This requirement limits the scope of pension funds to finance infrastructure, because less than 25% of infrastructure-related corporate issuances have a minimum AA rating (Figure A2.42). Table A2.48 outlines actions to improve the quality of investable bonds.

Figure A2.42: Long-Term Credit Ratings for Private Infrastructure Companies, FY2019

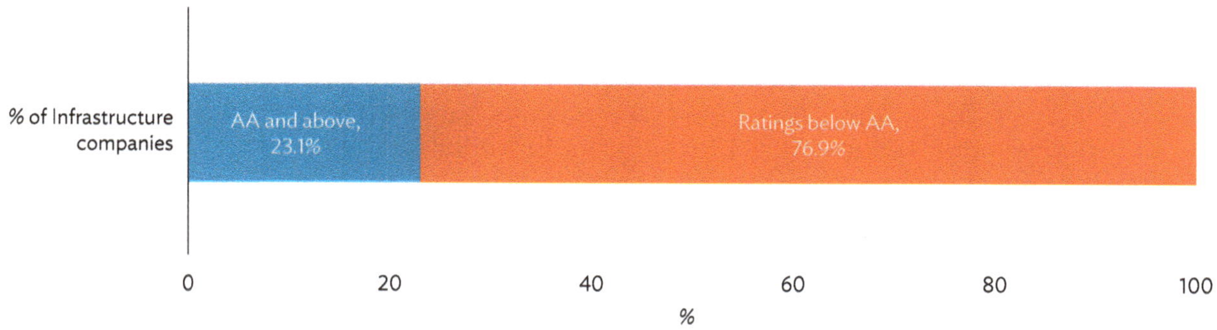

FY = fiscal year.

Note: FY ends 31 March.

Source: Annual reports of infrastructure development funds; and secondary sources.

Pension coverage gap. India's vast informal economy employs about 85% of the workforce, which has no formal pension coverage—a gap that needs filling. The low capital base for the country's pension funds means less funds for investing, such as in infrastructure. Pension plans only cover 7.4% of the working population (Figure A2.43). The global experience is that mandatory pensions encourage flows to capital markets. Pension sector reforms in Chile are an example of the salutary impact of mandatory contributions (Appendix 5). To increase pension coverage in India, awareness on pension and retirement planning needs to be raised, an action that would increase the penetration of pensions in the informal sector. The government could also consider mandatory participation in defined contribution plans, which would increase social security.

Table A2.48: Actions to Improve the Quality of Investable Bonds in India

#	Actions	Impact
1	Credit enhancement through guarantees and credit support, e.g., partial credit guarantees	Enhanced credit rating of bonds, leading to higher investor interest
2	Government guarantees for reducing regulatory, demand, and foreign exchange risks, payment obligations of government authorities, and early termination	Reduced financing risk profile of infrastructure projects

Source: Study team analysis.

Figure A2.43: Pension Coverage in India and Selected Countries
(% of working population)

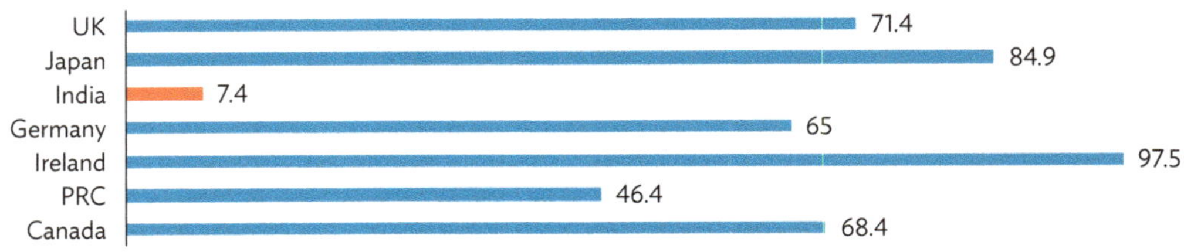

PRC = People's Republic of China, UK = United Kingdom.

Source: World Economic Forum. 2017. *Global Human Capital Report 2017*. Geneva. https://www.weforum.org/publications/the-global-human-capital-report-2017/.

External Commercial Borrowing

External commercial borrowing has helped India's infrastructure companies tap the external credit market. The government follows a well-designed policy for this type of borrowing by imposing restrictions on loan amounts, end-user restrictions, interest rate ceilings, and maturity periods. External commercial borrowing can be availed by the automatic and approval routes. Access to funds under the automatic route does not require the prior approval of the government or Reserve Bank of India. Borrowers going the approval route need the permission of both.

External commercial borrowing has grown substantially since 2015 for two reasons. The first is the attractive borrowing rates in overseas markets: the Reserve Bank of India sets a cap on the external commercial borrowing rate of London interbank offered rate (LIBOR) plus 450 basis points. So, if LIBOR is 2.0%, borrowing costs can be 2.0%–6.5%, much lower than domestic lending rates even with some hedging costs (4.0%–4.5%). The second is the liberalization of external commercial borrowing e.g., allowing external commercial borrowing to be used for working capital, general corporate purposes, or refinancing rupee loans, and allowing NBFIs to use this borrowing for on-lending for the purposes just mentioned. Many external commercial borrowing transactions have been done for infrastructure projects, particularly in power and ports. Adani Hazira Port Pvt. Limited, Vijayawada Tollway Pvt. Limited, and the NHAI are some of the borrowers that have raised external commercial borrowing for capital expenditure.

Total external commercial borrowing as of March 2020 was $51 billion, 1.5% of GDP, and corresponding outstanding loans to infrastructure was ₹12 billion, 24.3% of India's total external commercial borrowing. Investments in infrastructure through this channel grew from $4 billion in FY2015 to $12 billion in FY2020, accounting for 23% of total external commercial borrowing (Figure A2.44).

Because of the benefits of external commercial borrowing, the cost of these funds is usually cheaper from external sources if borrowed from countries with lower interest rates. The availability of a larger market can also help companies satisfy larger requirements from global players compared with domestically. Overall, external commercial borrowing provides access to international markets and gives good exposure to opportunities available globally. That said, the high hedging cost of foreign-denominated loans needs to be resolved to get the most out of external commercial borrowing. The high cost is because of volatile foreign exchange risk. The typical cost of rupee-dollar hedging was 6%–7% in 2019; this is higher than the euro–dollar hedging cost of 3%–4%.[31] Table A2.49 outlines an action to reduce hedging costs.

[31] Estimates of euro–dollar hedging costs based on LIBOR; rupee–dollar hedging costs based on Mumbai Interbank Forward Offer Rate.

Figure A2.44: External Commercial Borrowing in India, FY2015–FY2020
($ billion)

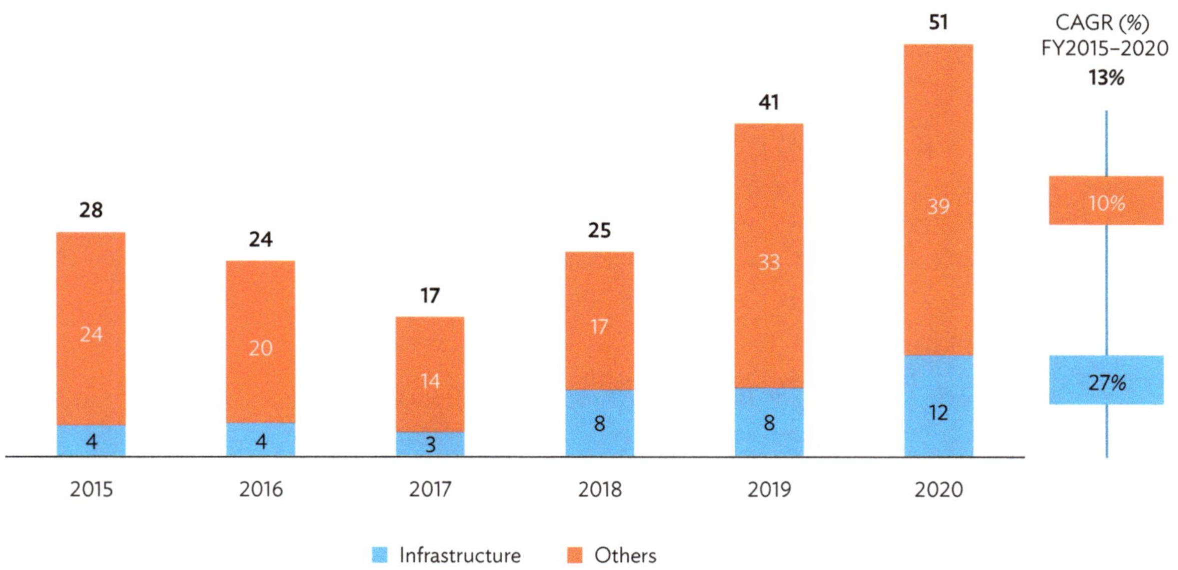

CAGR = compound annual growth rate, FY = fiscal year.

Note: FY ends 31 March.

Source: Reserve Bank of India.

Table A2.49: Action to Reduce India's Hedging Cost of Foreign Currency Loans

#	Action	Impact
1	Set up a hedging facility for transport infrastructure projects sponsored by government or a multilateral development bank, along with tolls and tariffs linked to inflation or an indicator that gradually passes through the foreign exchange risk[a]	• Lower hedging costs • Protects contractual obligations for long-term hedges • Natural forex hedge via inflation-linked tariffs

[a] As suggested in the 2017 World Bank blog on Foreign Exchange Risk: How a Liquidity Facility Could Help by Joaquim Levy. https://blogs.worldbank.org/voices/foreign-exchange-risk-how-liquidity-facility-could-help#:~:text=A%20liquidity%20facility%20in%20hard,reputation%20in%20fulfilling%20contractual%20obligations.

Source: Study team analysis.

Insurance Funds

Insurance funds in India have a large capital base, at about 19% of GDP. These funds, however, are constrained by not enough issues of investable bonds in infrastructure. Like pension funds, insurance funds face a lack of high-quality investable bonds and for the same reason—requiring a minimum AA credit rating.

Insurance Regulatory and Development Authority of India (IRDAI) regulations mandate that all insurer investments in the infrastructure sector be made in graded securities, with the grading not less than an AA rating by a reputed and independent rating agency. This requirement by the regulator constrains insurance funds from investing in infrastructure companies as less than 25% of infrastructure company corporate issuances are rated above AA. The actions that can be taken for insurance funds are the same as those for pension funds, as shown in Table A2.48.

Foreign Direct Investment

High currency hedging costs affect returns on foreign direct investment (FDI) in India. Here again, the cost of hedging based on the Mumbai Interbank Forward Offer Rate is higher than euro-dollar hedging.[32] The action to deal with high currency-hedging costs in FDI are the same as those for external commercial borrowing. A possible solution for reducing high hedging costs is through a facility similar to the International Bank for Reconstruction and Development's Catastrophe Deferred Drawdown Option. To tap the facility, countries must have an adequate macroeconomic policy framework and a satisfactory disaster risk management program in place or under preparation, which the International Bank for Reconstruction and Development monitors periodically. A forex liquidity facility would be similar to the Catastrophe Deferred Drawdown Option, and it could be easily adapted to be triggered by foreign exchange beyond a pre-agreed size.[33]

Debt Mutual Funds

The two big issues standing in the way of debt mutual funds investing more in infrastructure are the limited number of issues of investable bonds and limited liquidity in lower-rated bonds.

Limited issues of investable bonds. Securities and Exchange Board of India regulations require corporate bond funds to invest at least 80% of their assets in bonds rated AA+ and above in infrastructure, but infrastructure projects are generally rated BBB. As of July 2020, the long-term debt allocation (1 year plus) of debt mutual funds to corporate debt, including floating-rate bonds and non-convertible debentures, was about ₹39.7 billion—0.02% of GDP (Table A2.50).

Table A2.50: Long-Term Credit Ratings of Large Infrastructure Companies in India

Top Infrastructure Development Companies	Credit Rating (Long Term Debt)
L&T Infrastructure	CRISIL AAA- stable
Negarjuna Construction Company	India Rating A/Rating Watch Negative and ICRA A-
GMR Infrastructure	IVR BBB-/stable outlook
Gammon Infrastructure	Care D (issuer not cooperating)

CRISIL = Credit Rating Information Services of India Limited, GMR = Gandhi Mallikarjuna Rao, ICRA = Investment Information and Credit Rating Agency Of India, IVR = Invesco Mortgage Capital.

Source: Reports in the public domain from the rating agencies.

Limited liquidity in lower-rated bonds. Credit risk funds are a category of debt funds that invest at least 65% of their portfolio in lower than AA-rated securities. These funds, however, suffer from illiquidity since the liquidity risk is high because of redemption pressure. In early 2020, Franklin Templeton had to close six debt funds in India due to client redemptions and portfolio defaults. Illiquidity across portfolios led to large outflows of ₹192.4 billion in April 2020 in this credit risk category. Table A2.51 outlines actions to improve liquidity.

32 Estimates for euro-dollar hedging costs are based on LIBOR rates; rupee-dollar hedging costs are based on Mumbai Interbank Forward Offer Rate.

33 The World Bank used a foreign exchange liquidity facility to stimulate infrastructure bids with a $450 million guarantee to the Government of Argentina to support a renewable energy program, resulting in private investments of more than $2 billion.

Table A2.51: Actions to Improve Liquidity in Lower-Rated Indian Bonds for Mutual Debt Funds

#	Actions	Impact
1	Credit enhancement of bonds through guarantees and credit support; e.g., partial credit guarantee	Enhanced credit rating of bonds
2	Government guarantees to reduce regulatory, demand, and foreign exchange risks, payment obligations of government authorities, and early termination	Reduced financing risk profile of infrastructure projects
3	Allow banks to purchase bonds as part of the Liquidity Adjustment Facility	More liquidity in the market

Source: Study team analysis.

Equity Mutual Funds

Low returns are the key issue for equity mutual funds in infrastructure. Indeed, equity mutual funds investing in the infrastructure sector have not fared well in the recent past. NPAs and high sectoral beta in infrastructure have hampered returns (Table A2.52). Table A2.53 outlines actions to increase returns.

Table A2.52: Infrastructure Equity Mutual Fund Returns
(%)

Fund Name	3-Year Returns	5-Year Returns
L&T Infrastructure Fund	−7.59	5.37
Franklin Build India Fund	−3.76	4.36
SBI Infrastructure Fund	0.46	6.83
Nippon India Power & Infra Fund	−5.61	5.27

Note: Returns as of 16 September 2020.

Source: Value Research website. https://www.valueresearchonline.com/funds/selector/category/109/equity-sectoral-infrastructure/.

Table A2.53: Actions to Increase the Returns of Equity Mutual Funds Investing in Infrastructure in India

#	Actions	Impact
1	Project structures with credit enhancements	Enhanced credit rating of bonds resulting in better cash flows for project viability
2	Improve risk-sharing–based project structure with minimum guarantees	Reduced overall project risk of infrastructure projects

Source: Study team analysis.

Alternative Investment Funds (Category 1: Infrastructure Funds)

Compared with other alternative investment funds, these funds have struggled to raise commitments and need reviving. Securities Exchange Board of India data show the commitments of alternative infrastructure investment funds totaled ₹120 billion as of June 2020, down from March 2019 (Figure A2.45). One way of reviving this market segment is to encourage investment through tax benefits. Doing this could increase assets under management for alternative infrastructure investment funds, providing them with greater flexibility to finance large infrastructure projects.

Figure A2.45: Commitments Raised by India's Alternative Investment Funds, 2018–2020
(₹ billion)

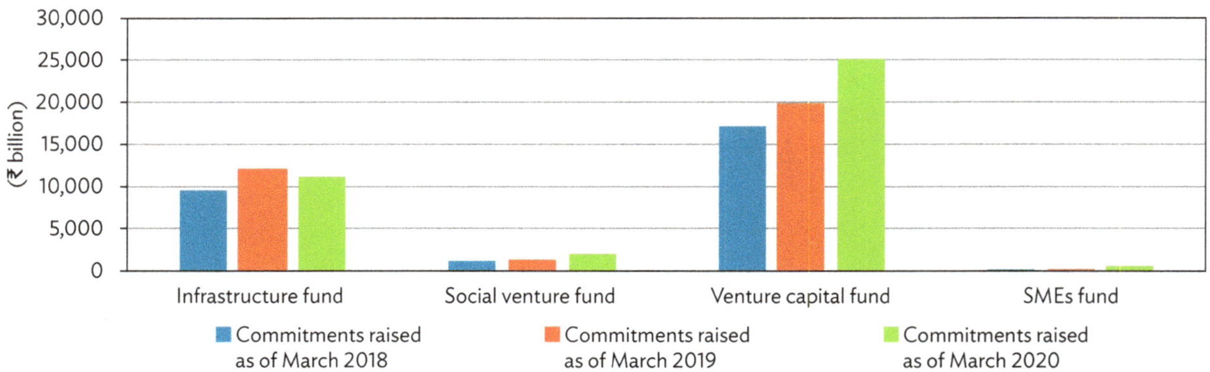

SMEs = small and medium-sized enterprises.

Source: Securities Exchange Board of India.

Alternative Investment Funds (Category 2: Private Equity Funds)

In port infrastructure, most private equity alternative investment funds have not managed to generate good exits because port traffic did not materialize due to overcapacity and policy changes that affected demand. This happened at Karaikal and Gangavaram ports. Similar to ports, asset churns have been difficult for road investments. Here, concessions using the hybrid annuity model concessions are generally not attractive for private equity investors. Table A2.54 outlines actions to improve the exits of private equity alternative investment funds.

Table A2.54: Action to Improve the Exits of Private Equity Alternative Investment Funds in India

#	Actions	Impact
1	Project structures with credit enhancements to mitigate default risk. Mitigating default risk allows for a project's senior debt to get a higher rating category than is possible from the project's credit fundamentals on a standalone basis	Better project returns and increased investor and lender interest
2	Concession agreement flexibility; this is needed for clauses addressing refinancing, termination payments, and demand risk	Improved project attractiveness for investors

Source: Study team analysis.

Debt Capital Market

A vibrant debt capital market is crucial to meet India's infrastructure financing needs. Developing the bond market requires multiple interventions. Table A2.55 identifies actions to invigorate the debt capital market.

Table A2.55: Key Issues and Actions to Invigorate India's Debt Capital Market

Issue/ Intervention area	Actions
The absence of a risk-free term structure of interest rates makes it difficult to price credit risk of instruments issued by the private sector and quasi-sovereign entities The Government of India issues bonds for different maturities even beyond 30 years. But most government securities' issuances and concomitant liquidity are concentrated in just a few maturity buckets	Increase issuances of long-term government securities
Liquidity of government securities	Promote retail participation in government securities to enhance liquidity
Liquidity and public listing of corporate bonds. Corporate bonds are predominantly privately placed due to high costs and stringent compliance associated with public listing of debt	Increase the listing of corporate bonds by rationalizing costs and documentation
Market making	Create a separate agency or institution to promote market making in corporate bonds along the lines of institutions established to promote government securities markets
Credit enhancement	Create an institutional mechanism or establish an organization to provide credit enhancement for lower-rated issues, especially for infrastructure and housing
Institutional investment restrictions	Best suited for making investment in corporate bonds given the long-term funding requirements for infrastructure, insurance, pension and provident funds Revisit the investment guidelines of institutional investors since the existing mandates of most of these institutions do not permit large investment in corporate bonds
Repurchases of corporate bonds	Banks should be allowed to use corporate bonds as collateral for repurchase operations

Source: Study team analysis.

The two key issues for India's debt capital market are (i) the lack of a benchmark yield curve for government securities, and (ii) inadequate liquidity and the low number of publicly listed corporate issuances.

Lack of benchmark yield curve. Issuances are concentrated in only a few maturity buckets, and about 80% of issuances are for maturities of below 15 years (Table A2.56). Because corporate bonds are priced for government securities, the low number of issuances beyond 15 years and the resultant illiquidity mean that it is hard to price them accurately. Table A2.57 outlines actions to smooth the yield curve and improve liquidity in government securities.

Table A2.56: Maturity Profile of Government of India Government Securities (as of June 2019)

Maturity	No. of Securities	Total Outstanding (INR trillion)	% Share Outstanding
0–5	32	1,650,679	29
5–10	22	1,700,495	30
10–15	14	1,084,612	19
15–20	6	397,696	7
20–25	6	389,014	7
25–30	4	319,000	6
30+	3	175,000	3

INR = Indian rupees.

Source: Securities and Exchange Board of India.

Table A2.57: Actions to Smooth the Yield Curve and Improve Liquidity in India Government Securities

#	Actions	Impact
1	Increase the issuance and trading of long-term government securities to deepen the bond market	Creates smooth benchmark yield curve for corporate bonds
2	Promote retail participation in government securities	Increased liquidity

Source: Study team analysis.

Inadequate liquidity and low number of publicly listed corporate issuances. India's corporate bond market is driven by institutional investors because corporate debt is nonstandardized, unlike shares—i.e., a company may have bonds of several different maturities and characteristics, and the prices of these bonds are negotiated offline, bilaterally, and reported and cleared on a delivery-versus-payment basis. This impedes liquidity. Table A2.58 shows trading volume and value in the corporate bond market.

About 90% of issuances are privately placed since public issues of debt securities are extremely time consuming. Typically, public issues of debt securities are completed in 3–6 months from the date of board resolutions authorizing the offer. Private placements of corporate debt can be completed within a month. Issuers also find the documentation and compliance requirements stringent for public issues. Table A2.59 outlines actions for improving liquidity and raising the number of publicly listed corporate issuances.

Table A2.58: India Corporate Bond Market Trading

Year/Month	No. of Trades	Traded Value (₹ million)
2017–18	23,886	459,934
2018–19[a]	54,574	954,637

[a] Trade value till 31 October 2018.

Source: Securities and Exchange Board of India.

Table A2.59: Actions for Improving Liquidity and Increasing Publicly Listed Corporate Issuances in India

#	Action	Impact
1	Reduce compliance and documentation requirements for public issue of debt securities	Higher trading in publicly listed debt
2	Create an electronic trading platform enabling multilateral negotiations to take place; i.e., an enhanced request-for-quote trading platform	Transparent and centralized trading with straight-through clearing and settlement

Source: Study team analysis.

Infrastructure Investment Trusts

Two key issues that India's infrastructure investments trusts face are legislation in the pipeline that will affect dividend returns and an illiquid secondary market for these investments.

Dividend returns. These are affected by a 2020 bill for a new finance act. In the earlier tax regime, dividends distributed by a domestic company were subject to a dividend distribution tax at an effective rate of 20.56% (including surcharge and cess). These dividends were generally tax exempt for resident and nonresident unitholders in India, although dividends may have been taxed in the home jurisdictions of nonresident unitholders. The dividend distributed by special purpose vehicles in which an InvIT holds the entire share, was exempt from the dividend distribution tax. The dividend received by business trusts from their special purpose vehicles was then distributed to the unitholders without any further tax being levied on it.

In current tax regime, the Finance Act, 2020 abolished the dividend distribution tax applicable to companies and shifted the incidence of taxation of dividend onto the shareholder or unitholder. Under the amended provisions, the dividend income of shareholders will be taxed at the applicable rate and special purpose vehicles are also required to withhold tax on this dividend income. InvITs, however, will continue to be exempt from tax on dividend income from special purpose vehicles. InvITs are required to withhold tax on dividend income received from special purpose vehicles. The Finance Act provides that dividends paid by the trust shall are exempt for unitholders provided special purpose vehicles paying dividends have not exercised the option to pay corporate tax under the 22% corporate tax regime.

Illiquid secondary market. Infrastructure investment trusts (InvIT) investors encounter problems selling units because of an illiquid secondary market for these investors, causing some units to trade below their sale price. One option to overcome this issue is to allow buyback options to sponsors at market-linked prices. This may help improve market liquidity and create unitholder value in the form of capital appreciation.

Public–Private Partnership Challenges: Concession Agreement Design, Dispute Resolution, and Risk-Sharing

PPP-related challenges from the design of concession agreements, dispute resolution, and risk-sharing emerged in interviews for this report with financing institutions, such as commercial banks and private project developers. These challenges need to be addressed to attract private financing in transport infrastructure projects. Sector-related PPP challenges indicated by stakeholders are as follows:

- **Road and road transport PPP projects**
  - **Termination of payment risks.** Here, debt is not covered during the life of a project (e.g., during refinancing, where the extended tenor of the loan facility is not acknowledged by the government for the applicability of termination payment).
  - **Project completion delays.** These happen because of delays in getting approvals and clearances, and in acquiring project land.
  - **Dispute resolution mechanism.** An effective one is needed.
  - **Conflicts of interest.** Independent engineers face conflicts of interest as project authorities provide salaries to independent engineers; 50% of these salaries provided by developers are also routed through project authorities.
  - **Problems in exiting investments.** Concessionaire liquidity face this issue because the exit clause states that a concessionaire can take exit from the project after 2 years from the start of commercial operations. But the concessionaire faces challenges in exiting if the start-date is not properly defined. Procedural delays can also occur when project authorities transfer O&M rights to secondary players.
  - **Improper detailed project reports.** During bidding, concessionaires know in advance that some additional work will be done in the future as the detailed project reports are not properly prepared and the actual demand of the project may not be as good. Because of this, concessionaires quote low, keeping in mind that money will be recovered during changes in the scope of work, which can lead to disputes and litigation.
  - **Aggressive bidding.** In a hybrid annuity model project, the bidding criteria is the present value of capital expenditure and first-year operating expenditure. Bidders with short-term horizons have capital expenditure and lower operating expenditure (i.e., lower than actual operating expenditure) to attract bigger government grants for capital expenditure. As grants increase, private financing through debt and equity is reduced and concessionaires' stakes in projects therefore decrease. After the concessionaire exits, the O&M entity faces bidding problems because actual O&M costs are high.
  - **Minimum revenue guarantee.** Not provided by the government.
  - **Project churn.** Selection process and contracting criteria allows developers with short-term horizons to be selected. As a result, projects get turned over within a span of 3 years, leading to operational inefficiency.
- **Ports and maritime development PPP projects**
  - Flexibility to cover material changes in market demand supply.
    - **Traffic demand variation.** Provision for change in concession period (within set limits) to adjust for lower or higher realization of traffic than estimated at the start of the concession (e.g., road model concession agreements).
    - Flexibility in minimum guarantee cargo or revenue based on government policies and international market conditions.
  - Grievance redressal and dispute resolution remains a concern.
    - Interventions have four stages of dispute resolution: amicable settlement, Dispute Review Board, arbitration, and litigation. These can take up a lot of time to reach a conclusion, resulting in the halt of operations in some cases.
    - Quick redressal mechanisms to reduce resolution time is needed, bearing in mind the role of Society for Affordable Redressal of Disputes for ports or the proposed adjudicate board.
  - Timely discharge of obligations by project authorities.
  - Clarity on entry and exit routes for investors.
    - **Change of ownership.** Article 11.2 of the model concession agreement (MCA) mandates at least a 51% equity holding for 3 years after the start of commercial operations and at least 26% for the rest of the concession period. This restricts the complete transfer of ownership and the entry of investors (buy-out companies).

        * **Specific clauses for financial investors.** The MCA should have a provision to ensure investors meet the original technical bidding criteria (e.g., a private equity firm can be mandated to hire an O&M contractor meeting the technical criteria).
        * **Clarity on refinancing means.** This is needed for asset recycling, bond raising, and other financing means (e.g., in a draft of the 2016 MCA, bond issuance was allowed under article 7.1b on concessionaire rights).
        * **Clarity on termination payments.** This is needed for ease in exiting investments. Debt due excludes refinanced debt unless done before the consent of project authorities.
        * **Concession period.** The maximum concession period is 30 years under Article 2.2 of the MCA. Having a longer period would make churning easier.
    - Need for an effective noncompeting facility clause.
        * The MCA has an optional competing facility clause whereby project authorities may not operationalize additional facilities within port limits until the completion of the 3-year exclusivity period or 70% capacity utilization for 2 consecutive years. However, the existing clause does not cover competition from nearby ports.
- **Railway and rail development PPP projects**
    - Indian Railways' control of the O&M of railway tracks potentially limits private sector participation in these activities.
    - Planning and project structuring is required to understand the need of different financing tools. A 10-year national rail master plan is being developed by Indian Railways, but it still needs to structure projects to be able to identify appropriate project financing tools.
- **Civil aviation and airport development PPP projects**
    - Design of contract and bidding documents.
        * The condition precedent to be fulfilled by the authority in the MCA does not include the appointment of an independent engineer.
        * Land acquisition delays.
        * For refinancing obligations, there is limited clarity on the conditions required to be met before refinancing to protect the interest of the authority in the MCA.
        * Clarity is needed on the entry and exit of investors. For change of ownership, the MCA mandates at least a 51% equity holding until the first-year completion of Commercial Operations Date and at least 26% for the rest of the concession period. This restricts the complete transfer of ownership and the entry of investors (buy-out companies).
    - Clarity is needed on tariff structure (flexible or fixed), indexation, and frequency of revisions to the regulatory framework for tariff setting. This can be done by providing a clear definition and the method for calculating each parameter with each sub-parameter (defined by airport category); this will eliminate interpretation issues for concessionaires and regulators.
    - Protection against traffic and foreign exchange risk.
    - Not enough airport sector experts for arbitration panels.
    - **Long bidding processes.** The bidding process from calling for expressions of interest to signing concession agreements takes 3–4 years. This effects project viability.
    - Limited effective dispute resolution mechanism. More airport sector experts are needed for arbitration panels and for tackling delays in dispute resolution.

Sector-specific model concession agreements should be periodically updated by conducting extensive deliberations, global benchmarking of clauses, and failure analyses—i.e., is analyses of PPP projects under dispute and assessments of specific issues that warrant modifications in model concession agreements.

Revenue Enhancement and Ways to Unlock Invested Capital of the Government and Project Authorities

To make a project more bankable and attractive to private investors, revenue generated from the externality effect of transport connectivity projects can be leveraged. The externality effect is the additional value created from newly constructed projects over and above their immediate benefits. Some of the key means of alternative financing are as follows:

Land Value Capture

Infrastructure development drives up land prices, creating the ideal situation to raise meaningful revenue. While value capture can be applied to a wide range of sectors, it is most appropriate for three project types: new land development; major capital projects, particularly in transportation; and infrastructure that supports basic services, such as water supply, wastewater treatment, and drainage.[34] Figure A2.46 shows the main methods to capture land value that the government could adopt. Japan and the People's Republic of China have successful models of LVC using various instruments. Box A2.6 gives some examples.

Figure A2.46: Land-Value Capture Methods in India

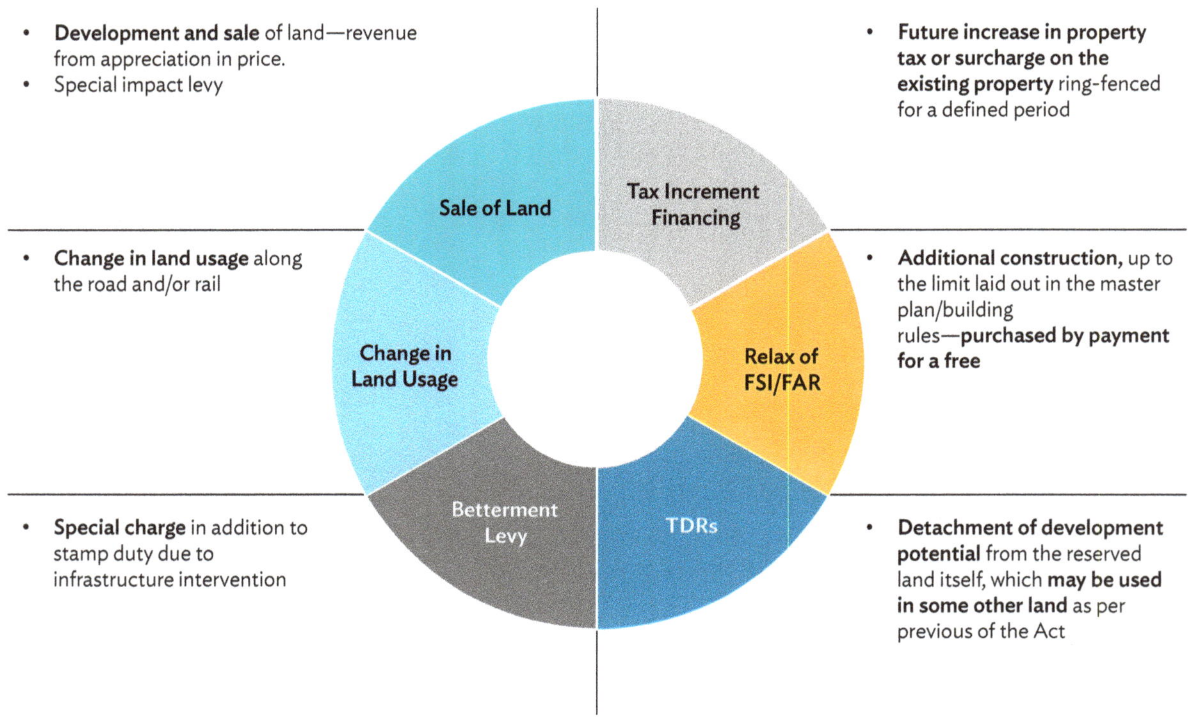

FAR = floor area ratio, FSI = floor space index, TDR = transfer of development rights.

Source: Reports in the public domain.

[34] ADB. 2017. *Meeting Asia's Infrastructure Needs.* Manila. https://www.adb.org/publications/asia-infrastructure-needs.

Box A2.6: Examples of Land-Value Capture in Japan and the People's Republic of China

Japan

The country's railways have typically captured the gains from rising land values. Tokyu Corporation, a major private railway operator running 105 kilometers of rail lines in the Greater Tokyo Area, combines real estate and railway development.

Tokyu carries out land readjustment projects along its rail lines in collaboration with the local government. It receives the land reserved for property development, internally allocating the capital gains from real estate development as railway finance. Landowners willingly contribute a portion of their land because they know its value will rise once the infrastructure is in place.

This type of real estate development accounted for 34% of Tokyu's net income for the fiscal years 2003–2012, against about 41% generated from transport fees.

People's Republic of China

Land capture in the People's Republic of China mostly involves land transfer fees—these are lump-sum payments by industrial developers for leasing land primarily through open bids for 40–70 years, with local government borrowing using land transfer fees as collateral.

Urban land is owned by the state with rural land collectively owned by villages. Local governments have the power to convert rural land to urban use or redesignate urban land use. Local governments can get large tracts of rural land and supply infrastructure, and then lease user rights to real estate developers. Farmers are often compensated on the basis of the land's agricultural production rather than its commercial market value, allowing local governments to earn premiums given the high bids paid by developers. Local governments can also acquire already improved urban land to consolidate and redesignate the land, and then strategically market it when demand is high.

Source: Asian Development Bank. 2017. *Meeting Asia's Infrastructure Needs*. Manila. https://www.adb.org/publications/asia-infrastructure-needs.

Revenue Enhancement Mechanisms

Revenue streams for India's infrastructure projects can be enhanced by exploring means other than user fees, such as advertisements, value-added services, and leasing certain project areas. The utilization of idle assets can be looked at as additional revenue generators. In roads and highways, the asset beyond the carriageway is usually idle. Ways to monetizing them as utility corridors can be evaluated. The Government of India rolled out the National Monetization Pipeline in FY2022 with a target of monetizing infrastructure assets worth approximately $75 billion across 13 line ministries and more than 20 asset classes.

The monetization for upcoming infrastructure assets should be planned during the project feasibility stage to improve the bankability of projects. Table A2.60 shows some of the innovative means that countries use to generate revenue from existing transport infrastructure.

The revenue generation mechanisms shown in Table A2.60 differ in their earning potential and ease of implementation. Figure A2.47 shows a phased approach for generating revenue from existing transport infrastructure.

Table A2.60: Revenue Generating Mechanisms from Transport Infrastructure

Countries	Mechanism
Australia	• Public toilets
Canada	• Roadside assistance
Germany	• Solar panels on highways
India	• Shops in subways • Association with restaurants • Bus branding
Malaysia	• Branding of toll plazas
Nigeria	• Branding of toll plazas
People's Republic of China	• Barrier gate advertisement
Singapore	• Public toilets
Switzerland	• Solar panels on highways
Türkiye	• Shops in pedestrian underpasses
Uganda	• Roundabout sponsorship
United Kingdom	• Roundabout sponsorship • Flyover advertisement • Underpass advertisement
United States	• Roadside assistance • Solar projects on highways

Source: Reports in the public domain.

Figure A2.47: Phased Approach to Generating Revenue for Transport Infrastructure Revenue

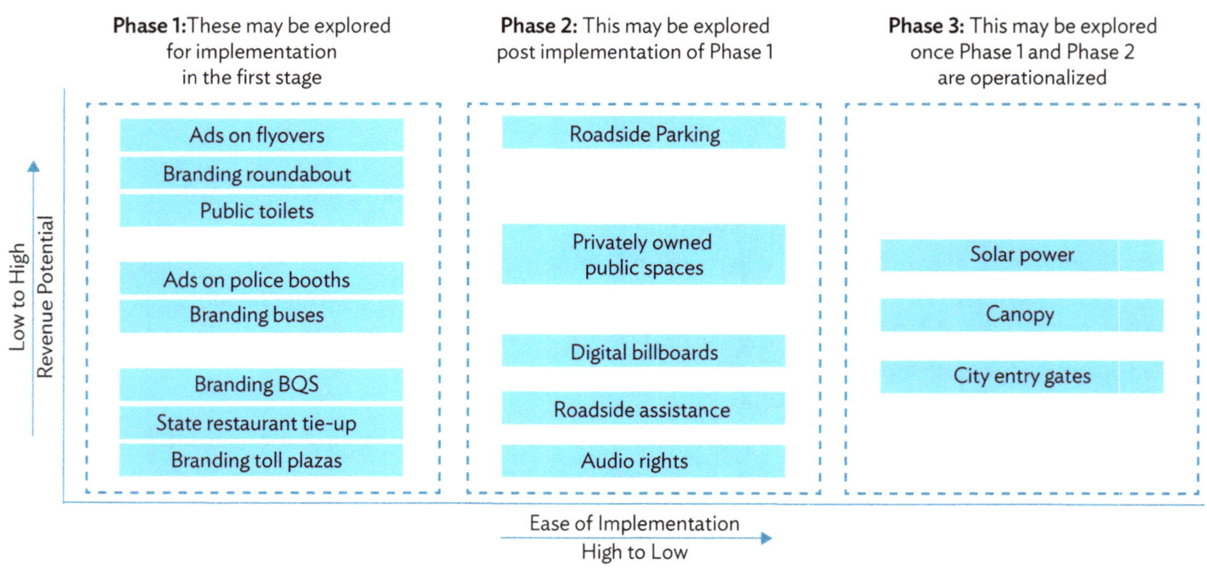

BQS = bus queue shelter.

Source: Reports in the public domain.

Asset Recycling

Asset recycling is an important funding tool used by governments to address funding gap issues and avoid increasing taxes or relying on public debt. For this funding tool, the government reviews public assets and identifies noncore and surplus assets that can be privatized. The proceeds are then reinvested in new infrastructure or for modernizing existing infrastructure.

India has a large base of road, port, airport, and other transport infrastructure assets. The National Highways Authority of India (NHAI) has already implemented this concept in toll–operate–transfer schemes, as shown in Box A2.7. For airports, 50-year contracts to operate six brownfield airports were bid out in 2018, and the Airport Authority of India plans to privatize more airports. Major ports are also exploring the transfer of their operational projects to private players. The government could roll out an asset monetization pipeline to instill confidence in investors. Doing this would provide clarity on the number, size, and type of assets that could be made available in the market.

Box A2.7: National Highways Authority of India's Toll–Operate–Transfer Scheme

The National Highways Authority of India (NHAI) identified and tendered nine highway assets as a single bundled project in the first phase of 2017's toll–operate–transfer (TOT) scheme covering 650 kilometers of highways in the states of Andhra Pradesh, Gujarat, and Odisha.

A 30-year concession was granted to operate the nine highways. As part of the concession agreement, upfront lease payments had to be made to the NHAI in exchange for operation and maintenance contracts based on specified key performance indicators. The payments were also used by the NHAI as capital for other infrastructure projects, primarily new highways.

The highest bid of $1.4 billion was received from Macquarie Group-Ashoka Buildco to manage first-phase highways, compared with the $900 million reserved bid price.

The NHAI has so far conducted four phases of TOT bidding with a fifth phase ongoing. Phase 2 and Phase 4 of implementation were canceled due to a lack of interest from private players.

National Highways Authority of India Toll–Operate–Transfer Bidding Phases

Phase	Road Length (km)	Amount Offered by Investors
Phase 1	650	$1.4 billion
Phase 2	586	Canceled
Phase 3	566	$0.7 billion
Phase 4	401	Canceled
Phase 5	160	Ongoing

NHAI is looking to raise $ 11.6 billion by offering 6,165 km of highways using TOT by 2024.

TOT = toll–operate–transfer.

Source: National Highways Authority of India.

Asset Securitization

Asset securitization raises money by upfront receipts estimated to be received in the future. The securitization proceeds can be invested for other under construction or conceptualized projects. It is an effective tool for governments to unlock their invested capital and reinvest in existing or new projects. This enables wider and long-term refinancing for existing infrastructure projects and frees up capital of current developers for reinvestment into new infrastructure projects.

InvITs are used in India and work like mutual funds. These trusts are designed to pool small sums of money from several investors to invest in assets that generate cash flow over time. Part of this cash flow is distributed as dividends payments to investors. These trusts are a good way to monetize revenue-generating infrastructure assets, the proceeds of which can be used by sponsor to either pay off interest payments in the initial period of low cash flows or to invest in new projects.[35]

Using InvITs for funding the construction of projects is being explored by private infrastructure companies in India. Some companies have already put their portfolio of operational projects into an InvIT, where cash flows from toll and annuity collections are remitted back to trust investors. IRB Infrastructure Limited and SREI Infrastructure Finance Limited (Bharat Road Network Limited) have floated their InvIT structure. No government agencies, either central or state, have done this. The NHAI is exploring the option of setting up an InvIT structure. Other project authorities who have a pool of stable revenue generating operational projects could also explore doing the same, and, once established, investors, including institutional investors and alternative investment funds, could be invited to participate in projects.

Using Development Finance Institutions Investment as a Multiplier for Crowding-In Private Capital

One method to make efficient use of public funding is leveraging multilateral development bank (MDB) funding to crowd in private capital in a project. Figure A2.48 shows how a contribution from MDBs to the tune of 20% of project cost can generate the remainder of further investment through various private financing tools. Participation of MDBs can boost investor interest in a project due to the high credibility of MDBs.

Meeting the challenges faced in implementing the financing tools discussed in this section will help address major barriers to financing infrastructure projects in India. In addition to financing these projects, the implementation of these infrastructure projects needs substantial PPP capacity and experience in implementation of projects.

[35] L&T Infrastructure Development Projects Limited setting up IndInfravit Trust is a good example of an Indian infrastructure investment trust. It has a strong and reputable investor base that includes the company itself with a 15.0% holding, Canada Pension Plan Investment Board (30.3%), Allianz Capital Partners (25%), and the Ontario Municipal Employees Retirement System (22.4%). The trust has acquired five L&T road projects and is in the process of acquiring further profitable infrastructure projects. *IndInfravit Annual Report. 2019–20.* https://indinfravit.com/annual-reports/

Figure A2.48: Leveraging MDB Funding to Crowd In Private Capital in a Project

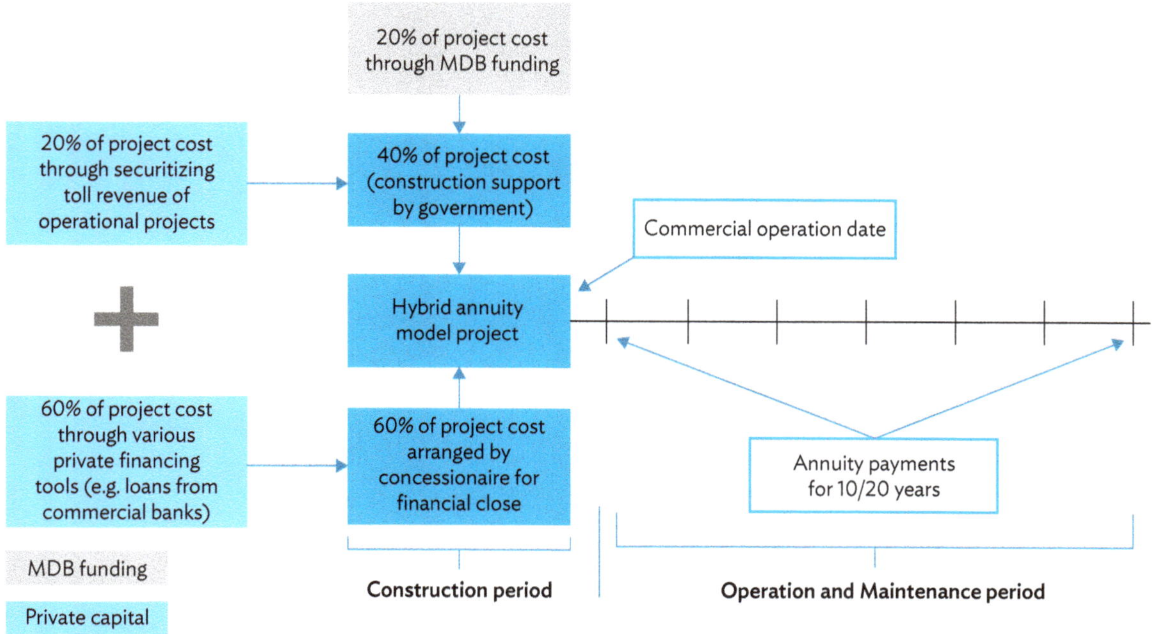

MDB = multilateral development bank.

Source: Study team analysis.

Public–Private Partnership Capacity Assessment

To understand the capacity and experience of India, and the areas that need to be improved to encourage private participation, this section contains a PPP capacity assessment using determinants under six defining areas to rate the country (as per Table A2.1).

Public–Private Partnership Law and Policy Support Capacity

Table A2.61: Ratings for PPP Law and Policy Support Capacity in India

#	Determinant	Rating
1	Is there a dedicated legal or policy instrument/guideline for PPPs?	3
2	What dispute resolution mechanisms are available for PPP agreements?	3

PPP = public–private partnership.

Source: Study team analysis.

Determinant 1: India has a well-developed decentralized PPP framework compared with other BIMSTEC countries, as the government has taken measures to enhance the PPP framework through sector-specific PPP models, such as the hybrid annuity and toll-operate-transfer models.

Determinant 2: Interviews with private developers in India for this report highlighted the need for effective dispute resolution mechanisms and ensuring the performance obligations of project authorities are adhered to. India has a sector-specific dispute resolution mechanism that uses various methods, such as amicable settlement, conciliation mediation, arbitration, and expert adjudication—and these are generally provided for in concession agreements. India has sector-specific arbitration panels, too. For example, the Society for Affordable Redressal of Disputes has units to cover, separately, roads and ports. The society consists of members from the private sector and government. The presence of technical experts as arbitrators further enhances the dispute resolution mechanism. Similar types of models could be adopted by other BIMSTEC countries.

NITI Aayog has set up two task forces to streamline dispute resolution in PPP contracts in India:

(i) Task Force on Policy Framework for Enforcement of Contracts—It has been constituted to review the implementation of the contracts under dispute and suggest remedial measures, etc.
(ii) Task Force on Conciliation Mechanism—It had formulated 'Guidelines for Resolution of Disputes between Government and Private Entities via Conciliation' as part of its recommendations. The prescribed mechanism entails a timebound conciliatory process enabling the parties to arrive at a mutually agreeable settlement with the aid of conciliators.

Private developers also have the option of international arbitration under the 1958 New York Convention on the Recognition and Enforcement of Foreign Arbitral Awards. The government applies the convention only to disputes arising from legal relationships, whether contractual or not, which are considered commercial under India's laws.

Public Sector Public–Private Partnership Capacity Support and Experience

Table A2.62: Ratings for Public Sector Public–Private Partnership Support Capacity and Experience in India

#	Determinant	Rating
3	If payment is likely to be made by the parent government, what is the credit rating of the parent government?	3
4	Is there a specialized government agency (or agencies) established for PPP purposes (e.g., PPP unit) and what are its roles?	3
5	Does the sponsoring agency have previous experience with PPPs?	3
6	Are different PPP concession models defined for the sector and are model concession agreements available?	3
7	Is there a streamlined approval process for PPP projects?	3

PPP = public–private partnership.

Source: Study team analysis.

Determinant 3: India's sovereign outlook by two of three global credit rating agencies has been revised to negative, while Moody's downgraded their rating to Baa3 from Baa2. Rising debt-to-GDP along with the rating downgrade makes private sector investments difficult for the Indian government.

Determinant 4: India has various agencies to enhance and streamline PPP project preparation processes and decision making. The government has issued guidance papers on this and has a PPP structuring tool kit. Table A2.63 lists three of these agencies and their role in improving the PPP framework.

Table A2.63: Agencies Promoting Public–Private Partnerships in India

Agency	Role
Department of Economic Affairs, PPP Cell, Infrastructure Division	This is responsible for policy-level PPP matters, including identifying projects, prefeasibility analysis, coordination with government agencies, procurement, model concession agreements, capacity building, and project operation and management.
India Infrastructure Project Development Fund	This is part of the Ministry of Finance's Department of Economic Affairs; it supports the development of PPP projects.
Public Private Partnership Appraisal Committee (PPPAC)	The Cabinet Committee on Economic Affairs, in 2005, approved the procedure for the approval of PPP projects through the PPPAC. The PPPAC is responsible for the appraisal of central government PPP projects.

PPP = public–private partnership.

Source: Study team analysis.

Determinant 5: Some 568 transport infrastructure PPP projects achieved financial closure from 1990–2020—a record that shows India has considerable experience in implementing these projects. Among them were projects in roads, airports, and ports. Of the 568 projects, the concession period of 10 was successfully completed, 530 are operational, and only 28 canceled or distressed.[36] PPPs for rail projects are a recent trend.

Determinant 6: Sector-specific model concession agreements exist for some transport sectors that have a framework for PPP agreements, which encourages private participation. For projects based on a standard model concession agreement, Public Private Partnership Appraisal Committee (PPPAC) approval is not required. For these projects, approval is only needed before financial bids are invited. Model concession agreements are available for roads, airports, and ports sectors, but not for rail.

Determinant 7: PPP projects are approved using PPPAC guidelines. The approval process includes in-principle approval from relevant transport agencies subject to clearing required project feasibility assessments. for the project. The following feasibility analyses are for projects to be approved for PPP implementation: technical, financial, and legal feasibility, environmental and social sustainability, value-for-money and fiscal affordability assessments, and a feasibility analysis for PPP structuring and risk allocation.

Public Sector Funding Assistance for Public–Private Partnerships

Determinant 8: Projects in the BIMSTEC master plan focus heavily on enhancing regional trade connectivity between member countries. Many of these projects may require support from the public sector from viability gap funding, government guarantees, or availability-based payments to attract private sector participation. Table A2.65 shows the PPP projects that received government support in India from 1990 to 2017.

[36] Canceled projects from which the private sector exited in one of the following ways: (i) selling or transferring its economic interest back to the government before fulfilling the contract terms (ii) removing all management and personnel from the project, or (iii) ceasing operations, service provision, or construction for 15% or more of the license or concession period following the revocation of the license or repudiation of the contract. Distressed projects where the government or the operator has requested contract termination are in international arbitration.

Table A2.64: Ratings for Public Sector Funding Assistance in Public–Private Partnerships in India

#	Determinant	Rating
8	Is government support for viability gap funding available for PPP projects?	3

PPP = public–private partnership.

Source: Study team analysis.

Table A2.65: Public–Private Partnership Projects in India Receiving Government Support, 1990–2017

Support	Number of Projects
Viability gap funding	245
Government guarantees	82
Availability-based payments	353

Source: Asian Development Bank. 2017. *Public–Private Partnership Monitor*. Manila. https://www.adb.org/publications/public-private-partnership-monitor.

The appraisal and approval of viability gap funding for projects is done by the PPPAC's Empowered Institution, which considers projects for approval up to ₹1 billion per project, subject to the budgetary ceiling indicated by the Ministry of Finance. The Empowered Institution also considers proposals that require funding support of over ₹1 billion and forwards these proposals to the Empowered Committee for approval. The committee considers projects for approval for viability gap funding from over ₹1 billion to ₹2 billion on recommendation from the Empowered Institution, also subject to the budgetary ceiling indicated by the Ministry of Finance. The committee also issues instructions on the eligibility of projects for viability gap funding support on requests from the Empowered Institution.

Land Acquisition and Environmental and Social Clearances

Determinant 9: The government supports land acquisitions for developing a project under the PPP framework by the public entity before the start of the bidding process. A key determinant of the PPPAC approving a PPP project is the amount of available land, which must not be less than 60% of the total land required for the project.[37]

Table A2.66: Ratings for Land Acquisition, and Environmental and Social Clearances in India

#	Determinant	Rating
9	Does the authority have experience in dealing with land acquisitions, environmental clearances, and rehabilitation and resettlement?	3
10	Does the authority have a dedicated team to streamline land acquisitions and environmental clearances and the experience to handle these areas?	3

Source: Study team analysis.

[37] Overall transport sector. Some sectors and authorities mandate 90% completion of land acquisition for PPPs.

Table A2.67: Land Acquisition Support by the Government in India

Land Acquisition Support	✓/×
Resettlement and compensation costs to residents	✓
Imposed limits on time frame to complete land acquisition	×
Dedicated agency to streamline land acquisition	×
Exemption from or reduction of land use fees	✓

Source: Asian Development Bank. 2017. *Public–Private Partnership Monitor.* Manila. https://www.adb.org/publications/public-private-partnership-monitor.

Determinant 10: Environmental impact assessments are mandatory for infrastructure projects under Ministry of Environment, Forest, and Climate Change requirements. The maximum time allowed to complete the various stages of obtaining an environmental approval is 210 days, excluding the time required to do an environmental impact assessment. Interviews conducted for this report found that approval delays are a major hindrance to private participation. Infrastructure projects also require a social impact assessment within 6 months from the project start date, as mandated by the Right to Fair Compensation and Transparency in Land Acquisition, Rehabilitation and Resettlement Act, 2013. For projects involving land acquisitions, project developers must get the consent of a majority of landowners. For PPP projects, consent is required from 70% of landowners, who are compensated under the National Resettlement and Rehabilitation Policy, 2007.

Market Capacity and Foreign Participation

Determinant 11: Interest in private participation in transport infrastructure has increased in India over the past decade. The country now has a well-established market of domestic and foreign private developers who have participated in infrastructure projects through PPP exits.

Determinant 12: Foreign participation is allowed in India with minimum constraints, i.e.,100% foreign ownership of transport infrastructure equity is allowed.

Table A2.68: Ratings for Market Capacity and Foreign Participation in India

#	Determinant	Rating
11	Is there sufficient market capacity and do private players have PPP experience?	3
12	Is foreign participation in PPP allowed?	3
13	Are there any restrictions on foreign investors' land use/ownership (i.e., do foreign investors have the same rights as locals?)	2
14	If payments are likely to be made from the authority's budget, is there any form of government guarantee available for these payments?	3
15	Is the exchange rate stable?	2
16	Is there a robust project finance market, which supplements the traditional corporate finance market?	2
17	Are debt instruments available for different project needs, such as senior, mezzanine, and subordinate debt, and take-out financing?	2

PPP = public–private partnership.

Source: Study team analysis.

Determinant 13: Property laws in India differ from state to state. But beyond that, when a person acquires or owns immovable property, the law gives that person the right to use, lease, sell, rent, transfer, or gift the land. The owner also has a right to mortgage an immovable property as a security for loans.[38] Landownership rights reside with state governments and there are some restrictions. But exemptions can be granted for infrastructure development projects.

Determinant 14: A major issue raised by foreign stakeholders in interviews for this report is the need for government credit guarantees for projects in the BIMSTEC master plan to secure revenue from these projects. These guarantees are provided in India, based on the results of project feasibility studies and negotiations between the foreign investor and the project authority (Table A2.69).

Table A2.69: Risks Covered by Government Credit Guarantees in India

Risk	✓/×
Currency inconvertibility and transfer risk	✓
Foreign exchange risk	✓
War and civil disturbance risk	✓
Breach of contract risk	✓
Regulatory risk	✓
Expropriation risk	✓
Government payment obligation guarantee	✓
Credit guarantees	✓
Minimum demand and revenue guarantee	✓

Asian Development Bank. *Public–Private Partnership Monitor*. Manila. https://www.adb.org/publications/public-private-partnership-monitor.

Determinant 15: As for exchange rate risks, India has low currency fluctuations and volatility.

Determinant 16: Most of India's transport infrastructure projects are financed by budgetary allocations and MDBs. Because India has a mature local capital market, most infrastructure PPP projects are financed domestically, often by state-owned banks. Each state has a separate credit rating assigned by credit rating agencies.

Determinant 17: India's various types of financing institutions, including various debt instruments and their access to transport infrastructure financing, were discussed in the earlier section on the country's transport infrastructure financing landscape (p. 127).

Life-Cycle Costs and Output Specifications

Determinants 18 and 19: India has vast experience carrying out transport infrastructure projects, so it can quantify construction and long-term operation costs, as well as output specifications.

[38] Government of India. Transfer of Property Act, 1882. Delhi.

Table A2.70: Ratings for Life-Cycle Cost and Output Specifications in India

#	Determinant	Rating
18	Can most of the costs, mainly related to construction and long-term operations, including maintenance, be quantified upfront with reasonable assumptions, and are historical data available?	3
19	Are objective output specifications readily available from a previous contract?	3

Source: Study team analysis.

Interventions for Investment Gaps in Transport Infrastructure

Implementing the BIMSTEC master plan list of projects will require a variety of financing tools. This section highlights the interventions that will be required to hone the financing tools available in India. India could adopt three key approaches for closing the investment gap in the transport infrastructure: (i) increase private investment in the sector by addressing the issues hindering the development of financing institutions, (ii) explore revenue enhancement avenues to increase government investable capital, improve project viability, and unlock capital investment in operational projects through asset securitization (e.g., InvITs and toll securitization) and asset recycling (e.g., toll-operate-transfer), and (iii) leverage MDB funding to crowd in private capital in projects.

Table A2.71 summarizes the key recommended interventions to augment the use of financing tools, banks and other financial institutions, and the capital market to reduce PPP-related risks in India.

Table A2.71: Summary of Recommended Finance Sector Interventions for India

Financial Institution/Tool	Issues	Actions
Commercial banks	Commercial banks encountering asset-liability mismatches due to the long-term nature of assets (loans) and short-term nature of deposits (liabilities)	Encourage secondary deals that allow banks to recycle their exposures, post-commercial operations date; flip assets to long term institutional investors or list of project bonds. (Pricing of debt should reflect this issue, i.e., price of bank debt and institutional debt or corporate bonds cannot be same; there should be a spread).
		Explore institutionalizing active secondary market for loans.
	Increasing nonperforming loans and stringent nonperforming asset recognition norms constraining credit allocation by banks for riskier infrastructure projects	Set up credit guarantee funds to reduce public-private partnership (PPP)-related risks, regulatory risk, demand risk, payment risk, and early termination.
		Introduce loan guarantee instruments for infrastructure projects (e.g., Multilateral Investment Guarantee Agency's Loan Guarantee and Asian Development Bank's Partial Credit Guarantee).
		Stabilize Insolvency and Bankruptcy Code process.
		Explore larger role for specialized institutions, such as asset reconstruction agencies and bad banks, to resolve stressed assets.
Nonbank financing institutions (NBFIs)	Infrastructure-focused NBFIs encountering asset-liability mismatches, as they are more reliant on short-term sources of financing	Ensure enablers can facilitate financing through bonds (e.g., credit rating enhancement).
		Explore institutionalizing a secondary market for loans.

continued on next page

Table A2.71 *continued*

Financial Institution/Tool	Issues	Actions
	Gross nonperforming loans have grown substantially for infrastructure-focused NBFIs	Set up of credit guarantee funds for reducing PPP-related risks, regulatory risk, demand risk, payment risk, and early termination.
		Stabilize Insolvency and Bankruptcy Code process.
		Explore larger role of specialized institutions, such as asset reconstruction agencies and bad banks, to resolve distressed assets.
	Very few NBFIs have the capability to underwrite under-construction transport infrastructure projects	Capacity-building program for NBFIs with the assistance of multilateral and bilateral institutions, as suggested in the Asian Development Bank's 2014 technical assistance report *Promoting Capacity Building in Financial Institutions in Emerging Countries in South Asia.*
	Growth of infrastructure development funds has been lower than anticipated due to the low supply of viable and good-quality operational projects	Banks need to flip assets to other institutions, such as banks, NBFIs, and insurance and pension funds.
		Explore institutionalizing a secondary market for loans.
Pension funds	Lack of high-quality investable bonds in infrastructure with minimum AA rating by at least two credit rating agencies registered with the Securities and Exchange Board of India	Credit enhancement of bonds through guarantees and credit support; e.g., partial credit guarantees.
		Government guarantees for reducing regulatory risk, demand risk, foreign exchange risk, payment risk, and early termination.
	Wide gap in pension coverage leading to lower capital base, resulting in lower available funds for infrastructure	Create awareness about pension and retirement planning.
		Mandatory participation in defined pension contribution plans.
External commercial borrowing	Hedging cost of foreign currency-denominated loans is high due to volatile currency risks	Create government or multilateral development bank-sponsored hedging facility, along with tolls and tariffs linked to inflation or any indicator that gradually passes through the forex risk
Insurance funds	Absence of high-quality investable bonds in infrastructure with minimum AA rating	Credit enhancement of bonds through guarantees and credit support, e.g., partial credit guarantees.
		Government guarantees for reducing regulatory risk, demand risk, foreign exchange risks, payment risk, and early termination.
Foreign direct investment (FDI)	High currency hedging costs affect FDI returns	Create government or multilateral development bank-sponsored hedging facility, along with tolls and tariffs linked to inflation or any indicator that gradually passes through the forex risk
Mutual funds (debt)	Limited issuance of investable infrastructure bonds and limited liquidity in lower-rated bonds for investing by debt mutual funds	Credit enhancement of bonds through various guarantees and credit support, e.g., partial credit guarantees.
		Government guarantees for reducing regulatory risk, demand risk, foreign exchange risk, payment risk, and early termination.
		Allow banks to purchase bonds as part of the Liquidity Adjustment Facility.

continued on next page

Table A2.71 *continued*

Financial Institution/Tool	Issues	Actions
Mutual funds (equity)	Low historical returns of equity mutual funds in the infrastructure sector	Enhanced project structures with credit enhancements.
		Improve risk-sharing-based project structures with minimum guarantees.
Infrastructure alternative investment funds	Infrastructure alternative investment funds commitments have stagnated compared with other alternative investment funds	Explore encouraging investment in infrastructure alternative investment funds through tax benefits.
Private equity alternative investment funds	Private equity alternative investment funds have had exit difficulties for infrastructure investors	Enhanced project structures with credit enhancements to mitigate default risk.
		Concession agreement flexibility, as there is a need for clauses addressing refinancing, termination payments, and demand risk.
Debt capital market	Absence of government benchmark yield curve or smooth yield curve and liquidity in government securities	Increase issuance and trading of long-term government securities to deepen bond market.
		Promote retail participation in government securities.
	Inadequate liquidity and low number of publicly listed corporate issuances	Reduce compliance and documentation requirement for public issues of debt securities.
		Create an electronic trading platform that enables multilateral negotiations to take place, i.e., an enhanced request-for-quote trading platform.
Infrastructure investment trusts	2020 bill for a new finance act would allow business trusts to withhold tax, affecting the dividend returns of investors	Abolish withholding tax for unitholders to avoid delayed reimbursement to help improve investor returns and make infrastructure investment trusts an attractive investment path.
	Infrastructure investment trusts face selling off units as there are no buyers in the secondary market and some units are trading below their sale price	Allow buybacks for sponsors at market price.
PPP challenges	Concession agreement design and dispute resolution concerns	De-risk projects in infrastructure sector by focusing on these four areas: Project preparation • Choose model (hybrid annuity model, toll–operate–transfer, etc.) appropriate to sector • Underwrite construction-period risks Bidding process reforms • Bring pre-appraised and partly pre-funded projects for bidding (possibly Infrastructure Development Bank) • Strengthen eligibility criteria, to ensure ability of bidder to invest equity Institutionalize renegotiation of PPP contracts. Ensure adherence to performance of authority's obligations • Limit appeal to one level • Create agency to guarantee authority's performance

Source: Study team analysis.

Myanmar

Transportation Infrastructure Financing Landscape

Sources of Transport Infrastructure Financing

The de facto government of Myanmar spends about 1.0%–1.5% of GDP a year on the transport sector (Figure A2.49). It has, however, a low private financing capability (estimated at below 0.1%). The Myanmar National Transport Master Plan 2014 requires infrastructure spending estimated at $20 billion up to 2030; this is about 3% of GDP a year.

Figure A2.49: Financing Sources and Annual Financing Needs for Transport in Myanmar (% of GDP)

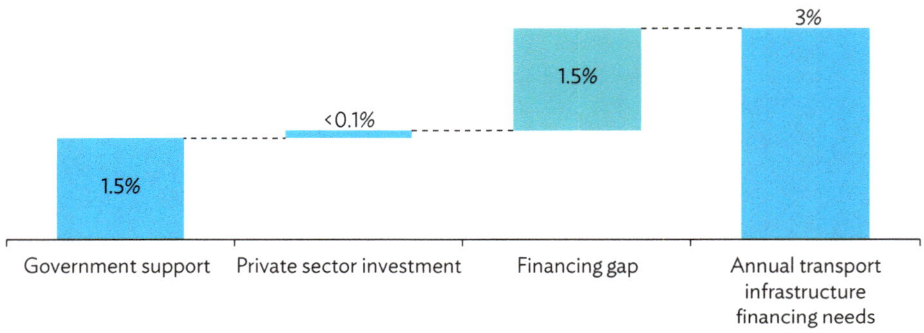

GDP = gross domestic product.

Source: De facto government of Myanmar. Myanmar National Transport Master Plan 2014; and World Bank Private Participation in Infrastructure database (accessed in 2020). https://ppi.worldbank.org/en/ppi.

PPPs in Myanmar have been used only for a few projects and they have been limited to port infrastructure. With no substantial private sector investment in infrastructure generally, Myanmar needs an additional 1.5% of GDP (Figure A2.49) to meet its annual transport infrastructure financing needs. The government recognized the importance of attracting private participation in infrastructure issuing a presidential notification in 2018 setting up the Myanmar Project Bank and a PPP center as part of its national development strategy.

Fiscal Support to Infrastructure Financing

The International Monetary Fund assesses Myanmar's external debt and debt distress risks as low.[39] Public debt, at about 40% of GDP, is considered sustainable (Figures A2.50 and A2.51). However, Myanmar's fiscal deficit in FY2020 (ended 30 September) is expected to widen to MK6.5 trillion, or 5.8% of GDP from 4.0% in FY2019. Because Myanmar does not have a sovereign debt rating from the global credit rating agencies, it depends on multilateral institutions or other governments for international borrowing support.

39 International Monetary Fund. 2020. Country Report. No. 20/88. Washington, DC. https://www.imf.org/external/pubs/ft/ar/2020/eng/downloads/imf-annual-report-2020.pdf.

Figure A2.50: Myanmar's Consolidated Debt, FY2014–FY2019
(% of GDP)

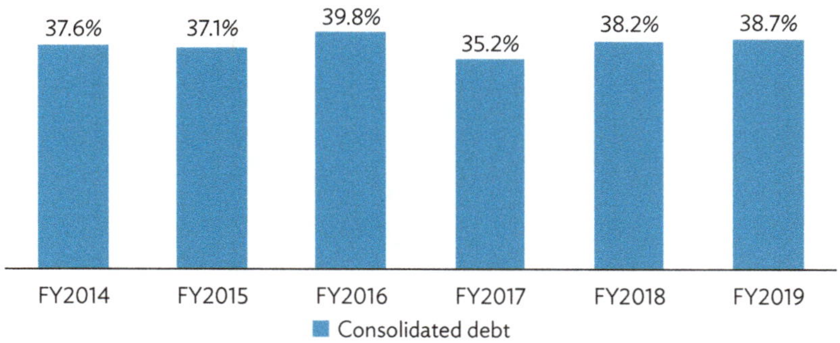

FY = fiscal year, GDP = gross domestic product.

Note: FY ends 31 March.

Source: Central Bank of Myanmar.

Figure A2.51: Government Fiscal Deficit in Myanmar, FY2016–FY2020
(% of GDP)

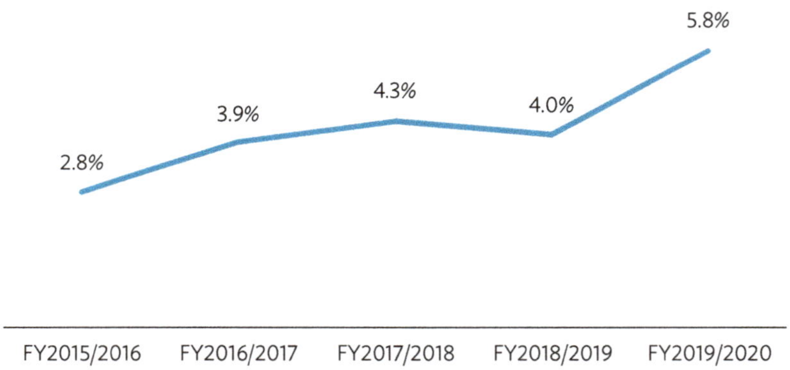

FY = fiscal year, GDP = gross domestic product.

Note: FY ends 31 March.

Source: Central Bank of Myanmar; and secondary sources.

Bridging the Financing Gap

Myanmar helped bridge its financing gap for transport infrastructure by increasing private investment after addressing the issues hindering the development and deepening the country's financing institutions and instruments, and exploring ways to enhance revenue and unlock government capital blocked in operational projects.

Myanmar's finance sector is underdeveloped. Financing comes mainly from FDI and commercial banks (Figure A2.52). FDI brings in most private financing for infrastructure, particularly from Hong Kong, China; Singapore; and Thailand.

Figure A2.52: Size and Contribution of Myanmar's Financial Institutions to Infrastructure

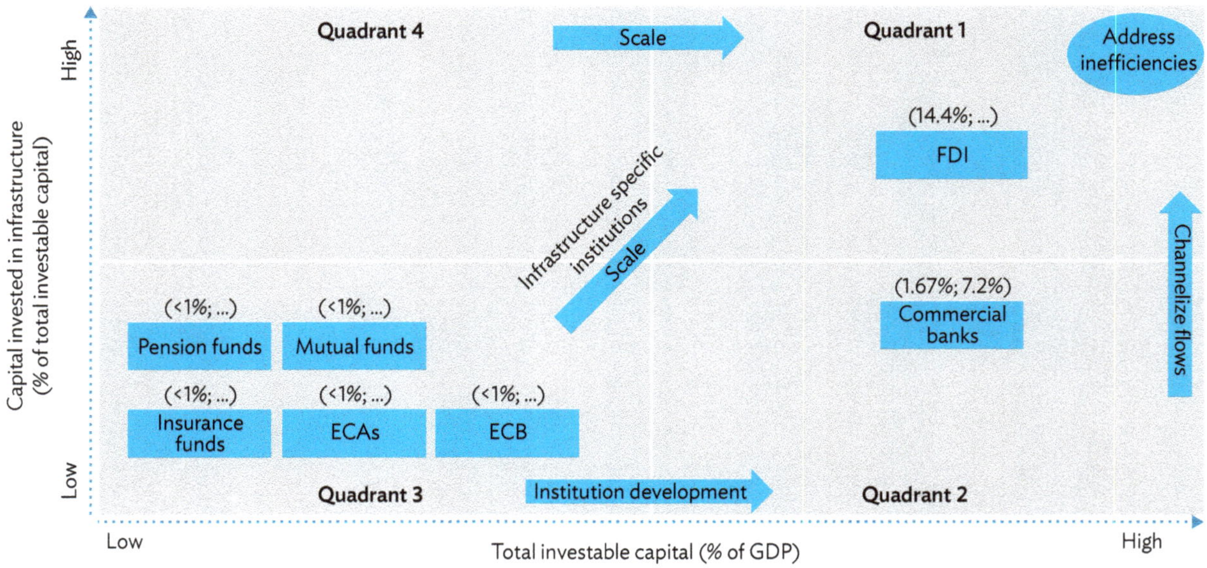

... = not available, ECA = export credit agency, ECB = external commercial borrowing, FDI = foreign direct investment, GDP = gross domestic product.

Note: Institutions where data is not available are placed based on a general understanding from primary and secondary research.

Sources: Central Bank of Myanmar; and secondary sources.

The country's commercial banks have limited capacity to finance infrastructure and are constrained by high nonperforming loans (NPLs), at about 20% of total loans as of July 2020. Because the institutions and tools to finance infrastructure are limited, Myanmar should focus on tackling the challenges facing its commercial banks and developing the capital market to attract other financing institutions to infrastructure financing, such as insurance and pension funds, which generally invest through the capital market.

Challenges of Developing Myanmar's Financing Institutions for Investing in Transport Infrastructure

Commercial Banks

Kanbawza Bank, Ayeyarwady Bank, and Co-operative Bank control about two-thirds of loans and deposits, and some 50% of bank branches.[40] These banks—called the Big Three—are expanding more rapidly than other local banks. The main state-owned banks are Myanmar Economic Bank, Myanmar Foreign Trade Bank, Myanmar Investment and Commercial Bank, and Myanmar Agricultural Development Bank. While distinct in their operational scope and policy mandates, these banks have common challenges. They have limited transparency and their financial reporting is irregular; their policy mandates seem outdated or unclear; and like privately owned competitors, state-owned banks require major investment in information technology and human capital.

[40] Milken Institute. 2017. *The Banking Sector in Myanmar: An Assessment of Recent Progress.* Thimpu. https://assets1c.milkeninstitute.org/assets/Publication/Viewpoint/PDF/083117-MyanmarBanking.pdf.

Overall, Myanmar's banking sector is underdeveloped compared with the banking sectors of other BIMSTEC countries. For instance, domestic credit to Myanmar's private sector grew from 6% of GDP in 2011 to 28% in 2019, a rate of growth that is much less than in other BIMSTEC countries.[41] Three key issues are impeding banking growth: low financial inclusion, restrictive interest rate policies, and a reliance on collateral-based lending.

Low financial inclusion. As of [add year survey was carried out], only 26% of Myanmar's adult population (ages 15 and above) had a bank account, far less than in other BIMSTEC countries.[42] In India, the rate is about 80%. In 2016, the volume of cash held outside the banking system was about 15% of GDP, compared with 30% of GDP in bank accounts, i.e., individuals and businesses kept about a third of the currency in circulation in cash, not in deposit accounts. A concerted push by Myanmar's commercial banks is needed to increase financial inclusion. Doing this would increase their capacity for lending.

Restrictive interest rate policies. This is hindering investment by commercial banks in riskier sectors, such as infrastructure. The Central Bank of Myanmar caps lending rates at +3% of its reference rate and a floor on deposit rates at –2% of the reference rate. These "nonmarket" rates raise the following challenges:

(i) Because infrastructure projects are considered higher risk during the construction than the operational phase, a cap on the cost of lending might not be able to cover construction-stage risks, especially time and cost overruns.
(ii) Both depositors and lenders may experience losses in real terms during periods of high inflation.
(iii) Interest rate controls limit the degree to which banks can compete based on the rates they offer.

Box A2.1 earlier has a case study from Kenya on the economic dangers of nonmarket interest rates that are of relevance to both Myanmar and Bangladesh. For Myanmar, the government could explore removing the lending-rate cap for construction-stage transport infrastructure, which is perceived as riskier than operations stage. This could increase lending for these projects.

Reliance on collateral-based lending. Lending in Myanmar generally followed strict collateral requirements. Until 2013, land was the only acceptable form of collateral. Since then, the Central Bank of Myanmar had expanded this to include gold, diamonds, machinery, some agricultural crops, fixed-deposit accounts, and government bonds. Banks, however, continue to demand land as the sole acceptable collateral. Furthermore, the banking sector demands high collateral amounts, often exceeding 200% of loan values; this is high by international standards.

Project lending is based on nonrecourse or limited-recourse financing that relies primarily on a project's cash flow for repayment, with the project's assets, rights, and interests held as secondary collateral. The collateral-based lending followed by Myanmar's commercial banks may not be suitable for infrastructure sector lending. Table A2.72 outlines actions that could facilitate greater lending by commercial banks for infrastructure.

41 Central Bank of Myanmar; Milken Institute. 2017. *The Banking Sector in Myanmar: An Assessment of Recent Progress*. Santa Monica, CA.
42 According to the 2017 survey in the Global Financial Inclusion Database.

Table A2.72: Actions to Increase Myanmar's Commercial Bank Lending to Infrastructure Projects

#	Actions	Impact
1	Central Bank of Myanmar could review its guidelines on the collateralization of loans to make practices hew close to international standards to avoid over collateralization	Increased project financing for infrastructure projects
2	Banks need to build capacity to be able to evaluate project financing lending risks	Increased infrastructure credit growth
3	Consider setting up a national infrastructure development bank. A regional development bank could be considered by the Bay of Bengal Initiative for Multi-Sectoral Technical and Economic Cooperation	Such a bank could cofinance infrastructure projects in conjunction with commercial bank financing and broaden the lending market

Source: Study team analysis.

Foreign Direct Investment

Myanmar's FDI inflows are focused on infrastructure. Myanmar receives funds mainly from the People's Republic of China; Singapore; Thailand; and Hong Kong, China. FDI-funded transport infrastructure projects include the new bridge over the Salween River and construction of Kyaukphyu port.

Several laws have been enacted to enable FDI, including the Investment Law, 2016, which established the Myanmar Investment Commission and governs all investment activity, and the Companies Law, 2017. To strengthen FDI, the government needs to make it easier to do business, resolve long-standing conflicts adding to investment complexity, and lower high currency hedging costs.

Ease of doing business. Myanmar ranks 165th out of 190 countries in the World Bank's 2020 Doing Business survey.[43] The World Bank acknowledges that Myanmar has introduced substantial improvements in five Doing Business areas—starting a business, dealing with construction permits, registering property, protecting minority investors, and enforcing contracts. Even so, the cost of doing business in Myanmar does not compare favorably with Indonesia, the Lao People's Democratic Republic, Thailand, and Viet Nam. The inadequate supply of continuous power is a major concern, as power shortages and scheduled blackouts occur regularly.

Long-standing conflicts adding to investment complexity. Although Myanmar has embarked on a major economic, social, and political transformation, domestic conflicts have weakened investor confidence—as evidenced by lower FDI inflows in recent years. Sanctions by the European Union and the United States have added to the uncertainty. Foreign companies, for their part, are increasingly focusing on environmental, social, and governance factors in evaluating whether to invest in Myanmar.

High currency hedging costs. Myanmar has an open economy, and its currency is prone to exchange rate volatility. Unlike advanced economies, Myanmar's financial markets do not have the breadth and depth of financial instruments required for hedging currency volatility, making currency hedging expensive. Myanmar can attract more FDI by undertaking structural reforms to reduce the hurdles to starting a business, securing reliable electricity, and

43 World Bank. 2020. *Doing Business 2020. Economy Profile Myanmar*. Washington, DC. https://www.doingbusiness.org/content/dam/doingBusiness/country/m/myanmar/MMR.pdf.

improving legal protection for investors. This would improve Doing Business rankings and increase the country's attractiveness for FDI (Table A2.73).

Table A2.73: Action Areas for Foreign Direct Investment—Myanmar

#	Actions	Impact
1	Myanmar can attract more FDI by undertaking structural reforms for reducing the hurdles to starting a business, securing reliable electricity, and improving legal protection for investors.	Improved Doing Business rankings and increased attractiveness for FDI

FDI = foreign direct investment.

Source: Study team analysis.

Debt Capital Market

Myanmar's nascent debt capital market requires a market infrastructure with intermediaries that can address supply-side issues and implement demand-side measures. Table A2.74 outlines actions for developing Myanmar's debt capital market.

Table A2.74: Actions to Develop Myanmar's Debt Capital Market

	Market Parameter	Current	Actions
Market infrastructure	Central counterparty/ clearing house	• Central counterparties absent • Counterparty roles undertaken by commercial banks	Establish a central clearing house/ counterparty. Develop a scripless clearing and settlement system (like the Clearing Corporation of India).
	Central security depository	• Myanmar has two central security depositories: Central Bank of Myanmar Financial Network System for government and central bank securities, and the Yangon Stock Exchange (YSX) for securities listed and traded on its markets	Government securities, some of which are still physical certificates and circulating until maturity, should be dematerialized for electronic trading and registration.
	Trading platform (stock exchange)	• YSX lists only equities due to regulatory restrictions	Trading should move from the interbank market to an organized over-the-counter market or to the YSX, which has a system and procedures for trading bonds.
Intermediaries	Primary dealers	• No primary dealers or market makers in the bond market	Introduce a primary dealer system to facilitate the auction of bills and, over the medium term, Treasury bonds.
	Credit rating agencies (CRAs)	• Myanmar not covered by international CRAs	The regulatory framework should be formulated for local credit rating agencies to establish partnerships with international CRAs.

continued on next page

Table A2.74 *continued*

	Market Parameter	Current	Actions
	Brokerage houses	• Only a handful of brokerage firms	The Securities and Exchange Commission of Myanmar should encourage more licensed and active brokerages.
Issuer	Government securities (maturity range and liquidity)	• Treasury bonds issued with tenors of 2, 3, and 5 years	Government needs to increase the tenor, quantum, and frequency of issuances to develop the market. For instance, in India the tenor of dated securities ranges from 5–40 years.
	Securities auction calendar	• Quarterly Ministry of Planning, Finance and Industry auction calendar	Publish an auction calendar on an at least half-yearly basis instead of quarterly and conduct auctions as per the preannounced auction calendar.
Investor	Commercial banks/primary dealers	• Central Bank of Myanmar (CBM) issues government securities as an agent of the government • Banks and nonbank financial institutions do not require specific licensing for participating in the interbank market or Treasury bond auctions conducted by CBM	Trading in government securities needs to be encouraged by developing an active trading book of banks. Regulations needed for establishing primary dealers.
	Pension/ insurance/ mutual funds	• Pension funds have established themselves as potential investors in the bond market, focused on government securities • Mutual funds not yet established in Myanmar	Establish mutual funds or unit trusts, or similar collective investment schemes, under securities or prudential legislation.
	Retail investors	• General or retail investors buy government securities (Treasury bonds) over the counter at Myanmar Economic Bank branches or through Myanmar Securities Exchange Centre using direct issuance	Because the retail share is low, CBM and Myanmar Securities Exchange Centre should conduct investor awareness campaigns for encouraging further retail investment in bond market.
	Foreign institutional and portfolio investors	• Not present. Foreign investors need to obtain approval for market access from the Directorate of Investments and Company Administration and regulations on this are expected shortly	Update legislation and rules for the bond and securities markets to include specific provisions for foreign investors.
External environment	Fiscal debt management	• Public Debt Management Law enacted in 2016 • Under the Comprehensive Medium-Term Fiscal Framework, the government remains committed to reducing CBM financing	The public debt threshold should establish domestic and foreign borrowing limits. The borrowing calendar should follow the borrowing framework. Fiscal policy should aim to phase out CBM financing by raising domestic revenue and increasing market-based financing of the deficit.
	Securities and exchange laws	• The law provides a framework for the financial markets • Helped establish the Securities and Exchange Commission of Myanmar, lists the licenses for businesses dealing in securities	Regulations needed for establishing primary dealers and mutual funds, and regulations covering foreign investors.

continued on next page

Table A2.74 *continued*

	Market Parameter	Current	Actions
	Treasury and cash management	• In fiscal year 2019, CBM financing accounted for 21% of domestic financing	Need for better coordination between the Treasury and CBM and more proactive planning on issuing treasury securities.
	Sovereign rating from international CRA	• Not rated	Myanmar should strive to get rated by an international CRA.

Source: Study team analysis.

Public–Private Partnership Capacity Assessment

Public–Private Partnership Law and Policy Support Capacity

Table A2.75: Ratings for Public–Private Partnership Law and Policy Support Capacity in Myanmar

#	Determinant	Rating
1	Is there a dedicated legal or policy instrument/guideline for PPPs?	1
2	What dispute resolution mechanisms are available for PPP agreements?	0

PPP = public–private partnership.

Source: Study team analysis.

Determinant 1: Myanmar does not have a PPP law or policy as such, but it has guidelines for implementing PPP projects. Most PPP projects that are currently being implemented have been initiated via unsolicited proposals from neighboring countries rather than local private participation. Myanmar's Public Private Partnership Centre, an agency under the Ministry of Planning, Finance and Industry, issued an order in 2020 setting out the tender processes for unsolicited project proposals.

Determinant 2: No clear guidelines on any dispute resolution mechanism exists for PPP agreements in Myanmar and details must be specified in the concession agreement

Public Sector Public–Private Partnership Support Capacity and Experience

Determinant 3: Myanmar does not have a sovereign debt rating by any of the international credit rating agencies.

Determinants 4 and 5: Myanmar has no regulations for selecting the financial structure and the duration of private partners engaged in PPP infrastructure projects. There are also no mechanisms to provide fiscal support to facilitate the participation of the private sector in infrastructure development. PPP guidelines do, however, have a provision on viability gap funding.

For roads, the Ministry of Construction has delegated a large share of its network to the private sector for maintenance and rehabilitation under the build–operate–transfer modality. Concessions are for brownfield projects, with a contractual term of 40 years, extendable to 55 years. Myanmar has 63 toll roads covering 5,545 km; these are managed by 28 private companies.

Table A2.76: Ratings for Public Sector Public–Private Partnership Support Capacity and Experience in Myanmar

#	Determinant	Rating
3	If payment is likely to be made by the parent government, what is the credit rating of the parent government?	0
4	Is there a specialized government agency (or agencies) established for PPP purposes (e.g., PPP unit) and what are its roles?	1
5	Is there a streamlined approval process for PPP projects?	1
6	Does the sponsoring agency have previous experience with PPPs?	1
7	Are different PPP concession models defined for the sector and are model concession agreements available?	1

PPP = public–private partnership.

Source: Study team analysis.

Determinant 6: The concessions agreements are very basic and do not adequately define key performance indicators. An ADB technical assistance project concluded in 2016 stated that all private operators, barring one or two, were underperforming. Most operators either ceased to maintain or upgrade assets or have either defaulted or come close to defaulting on their commercial and financial obligations. Many private operators have, however, expressed their willingness to restructure their contracts.[44]

Determinant 7: In addition, concession agreements are drafted for each project after discussions between the private player and the project authorities. There are no sector-specific model concession agreements for road, rail, airport, and port projects to provide a framework for PPP agreements to encourage private participation in transport infrastructure.

Public Sector Funding Assistance for Public–Private Partnerships

Determinant 8: Public sector financing for implementing PPP projects is very limited. The reason is that there is no financing authority to streamline or prioritize projects needing assistance from the public sector.

The government does not provide viability gap funding for PPP transport infrastructure projects, but it is trying to formulate a viability gap payment based on a predetermined level and conditions to make up for the limited profit (or losses) from user-fee income, which could help the private sector mobilize funds for project finance (Table A2.77).

Table A2.77: Ratings for Public Sector Funding Assistance in Public–Private Partnership in Myanmar

#	Determinant	Rating
8	Is government support for viability gap funding available for PPP projects?	1

PPP = public–private partnership.

Source: Study team analysis.

[44] ADB. 2016. *Strengthening Project Preparation Capacity in Asia and the Pacific.* Manila. https://www.adb.org/projects/49407-001/main.

Land Acquisition, and Environmental and Social Clearances

Determinants 9 and 10: Myanmar has no particular guidelines for environmental and social impact assessments for PPP projects. For land acquisitions, consultations should be held with affected residents and communities to raise awareness on these projects. Land acquisition procedures need to be clear to avoid exploitation or illegal confiscation, and these procedures need to guarantee the protection of livelihoods of local people. Environmental assessments are also needed for land acquisitions (Tables A2.78 and A2.79).

Table A2.78: Ratings for Land Acquisition, and Environmental and Social Clearances in Myanmar

#	Determinant	Rating
9	Does the authority have experience in dealing with land acquisitions, environmental clearances, and rehabilitation and resettlement?	0
10	Does the authority have a dedicated team to streamline land acquisitions and environmental clearances, and the experience to handle these areas?	0

Source: Study team analysis.

Table A2.79: Land Acquisition Support by the Government in Myanmar

Land Acquisition Support	✓/×
Resettlement and compensation costs to residents	✓
Imposed limits on time frame to complete land acquisition	×
Dedicated agency to streamline land acquisition	×
Exemption from or reduction of land use fees	×

Source: Asian Development Bank. 2017. Public–Private Partnership Monitor. Manila.

Market Capacity and Foreign Participation

Determinant 11: The capacity for private players to undertake transport infrastructure PPPs in Myanmar is negligible. Most of these projects are implemented by private developers with government-to-government credit lines from neighboring countries.

Determinants 12 and 13: Foreign participation is allowed and encouraged in Bhutan due to lack of indigenous private developers in the country. There are restrictions on landownership rights for foreign investors in Myanmar. However, exemptions have been granted for infrastructure projects in the country.

Determinant 14: The need for government credit guarantees to secure revenue for projects in the BIMSTEC master plan emerged as a major issue in interviews with private developers for this report. No risks are covered by government guarantees.[45]

Determinant 15: As for exchange rate risks, Myanmar has high currency fluctuations and volatility leading to higher hedging costs for long-term investments.

[45] ADB. 2017. *Public-Private Partnership Monitor.* Manila. https://www.adb.org/publications/public-private-partnership-monitor.

Table A2.80: Ratings for Market Capacity and Foreign Participation in Myanmar

#	Determinant	Rating
11	Is there sufficient market capacity and do private players have PPP experience?	0
12	Is foreign participation in PPP allowed?	3
13	Are there any restrictions on foreign investors' land use/ownership (i.e., do foreign investors have the same rights as locals?)	3
14	If payments are likely to be made from the authority's budget, is there any form of government guarantee available for these payments?	0
15	Is the exchange rate stable?	1
16	Is there a robust project finance market, which supplements the traditional corporate finance market?	0
17	Are debt instruments available for different project needs, such as senior, mezzanine, and subordinate debt, and take-out financing?	0

PPP = public–private partnership.

Source: Study team analysis.

Determinant 16: The capital market is underdeveloped and not able to finance infrastructure projects, which require long-term financing. Because of this, as noted earlier, transport infrastructure is financed predominantly through the government budget, multilateral and bilateral financial institutions, and government-to-government credit lines.

Determinant 17: Myanmar is in the early stages of financial reforms, which the government is treating as a priority. Myanmar's financial system is one of the world's least developed, and the country remains a cash-oriented economy. Public trust in the banking and financial industry has been affected by high inflation, bank runs, and insider lending. Local banks are playing their part in reform initiatives by seizing the opportunity to expand their branch networks and introduce new financial products. They are also entering into agreements with international credit card providers.[46] Microfinance is a main source of external financing for local micro, small, and medium-sized enterprises, as well being an available source of financing for personal and business funding.

Life-Cycle Cost and Output Specifications

Determinants 18 and 19: Myanmar does not have enough experience in transport infrastructure projects to quantify construction and long-term operation costs, as well as output specifications (Table A2.81).

Table A2.81: Ratings for Life-Cycle Cost and Output Specifications in Myanmar

#	Determinant	Rating
18	Can most of the costs, mainly related to construction and long-term operations, including maintenance, be quantified upfront with reasonable assumptions, and are historical data available?	0
19	Are objective output specifications readily available from a previous contract?	0

Source: Study team analysis.

[46] Central Bank of Myanmar. 2020. *Annual Report 2019–2020*. Yangon. https://www.cbm.gov.mm/sites/default/files/report/2021/Annual%20Report%202019-2020.pdf.

Possible Interventions

Myanmar can adopt the following key approaches to address the investment gap in the transport infrastructure sector: (i) increase private investment in the sector by addressing issues hindering development and deepening of financing institutions and; (ii) explore avenues for revenue enhancement (e.g., LVC, non-toll revenues such as advertisements, privately owned public spaces, etc.) to increase government investable capital, improve project viability, and unlock capital investment in existing operational projects through asset securitization (e.g., InVITs, toll securitization) and asset recycling (e.g., toll–operate–transfer models). Myanmar has large coastal areas and many commercial ports; those that are not strategic could be considered for asset recycling.

Table A2.82 summarizes the key recommended interventions to augment the use of financing tools, banks and other financial institutions, and the capital market to reduce PPP-related risks in Myanmar.

Table A2.82: Summary of Recommended Finance Sector Interventions for Myanmar

#	Finance Sector	Issues	Actions
1	Commercial banks	Low financing inclusion in the banking sector	Commercial banks need to undertake financial inclusion drive.
		Upper limits on the cost of lending hinders investment in risky sectors, such as infrastructure	For infrastructure projects, the government could explore options to remove the interest rate cap, and allow banks and other financial institutions to set lending rates based on the cost of funding, type of borrower, and project.
			Commercial banks should be given the flexibility to pricing loans to cover risk during the construction phase of transport infrastructure projects. Once they are operational, interest rates can be revised.
		Commercial banks primarily involved in collateral-based lending, demanding high collateral compared to international levels	The Central Bank of Myanmar should review its guidelines on the collateralization of loans and make rules based on international standards to avoid over-collateralization.
			Capacity of banks needs to be increased so that they can evaluate the risks for lending through project financing.
			The government could consider setting up an infrastructure bank or participate in such an institution, should one be set up, under the Bay of Bengal Initiative for Multi-Sectoral Technical and Economic Cooperation program.
2	Debt capital market	Nascent debt capital market	Develop debt market by, among other things, creating a central clearing house or counterparty and a scripless clearing and settlement system, establishing intermediaries (e.g., primary dealers, brokerage houses), addressing supply-side issues (e.g., Treasury bonds are limited to tenors of 2, 3, and 5 years), and implementing demand-side interventions (e.g., draw up regulations and legislation for the participation of foreign institutional and portfolio investors).

continued on next page

Table A2.82 *continued*

#	Finance Sector	Issues	Actions
3	Government borrowing	No sovereign rating by an international credit rating agency, which impedes the government's ability to secure financing from foreign capital markets	Secure a sovereign credit rating from an international credit rating agency.
4	Private sector participation	Public–private partnership (PPP) projects limited to ports projects; no PPPs so far in roads, railways, or airport sectors. Private investment in transport infrastructure largely absent	Improve and strengthen the enabling environment for PPPs by undertaking the following: **Robust project planning and preparation:** Project authorities or the PPP cells should work towards creating a pipeline of investable PPP projects. This would require inputs from transport master plans and subsequent assessment by project authorities to determine the projects that can be taken up on PPP mode. Necessary project preparation efforts such as developing detailed project reports, social and environment impact assessment, etc. should be undertaken and then projects put up for evaluation by prospective investors, including multilateral/bilateral financing institutions. **Develop suitable project structures:** Project authorities should build capacity to develop project structures and risk-sharing models; e.g., minimum revenue guarantees and annuity payments to cover demand risks, if required. Model concession agreements for PPP models should be prepared. **Increase the investor base:** Concession agreements should allow for asset recycling so that investors in operational assets also become eligible to participate. Explore revenue enhancement and asset securitization to unlock the invested capital in operational assets and increase cash inflows.

Source: Study team analysis.

Nepal

Transport Infrastructure Financing Landscape

Sources of Transport Infrastructure Financing

Nepal's finance sector mainly constitutes of banks and financial institutions with a 60% market share of commercial banks and 20% of other financial institutions. These banks prefer lending to priority sectors and meeting the working capital requirement of existing projects (considered low risk). Multilateral and bilateral sources account for 39% of Nepal's domestic government debt and 50% of government foreign debt, which mitigates fiscal risks.

Nepal's vision is to achieve middle-income status by 2030. The International Monetary Fund forecasts the economy growing by 6% year-on-year up to 2030. To achieve this, annual infrastructure investment of NRs360 billion—10% of GDP—will be needed over the next decade. Current public and private sources cover only 7% of GDP out of an annual investment need of 10% for infrastructure sector development (Figure A2.53). Annual capital public

Figure A2.53: Infrastructure Funding in Nepal
(% of GDP)

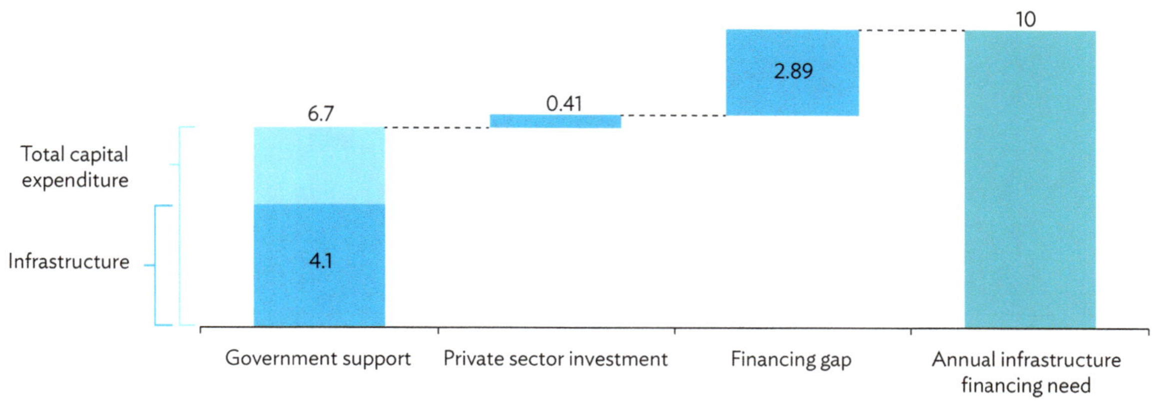

GDP = gross domestic product.

Sources: Nepal Rastra Bank. 2019. *Economic Survey 2019*. Kathmandu. https://mof.gov.np/uploads/document/file/Economic%20 Survey%202019_20201125024153.pdf; Global Infrastructure Hub website. https://www.gihub.org/; and World Bank data.

expenditure is 6.7% of GDP, out of which 2.6% is for transport infrastructure. Because of the increase in the tax waiver, total tax has been affected by the COVID-19 pandemic.

Because of Nepal's high annual investment needs and limited budgetary support from the government, the country depends on other financing instruments for infrastructure development. To augment this, foreign investment is also needed.

Nepal has a low public debt ratio compared with other South Asian countries. But its fiscal and current account deficits are relatively higher (Figures A2.54 and A2.55). The government aims to limit the fiscal deficit to 6% of GDP and government debt to 38% to constrain budget growth.

Figure A2.54: Nepal Central Government Fiscal Deficit, FY2017–FY2021
(% of GDP)

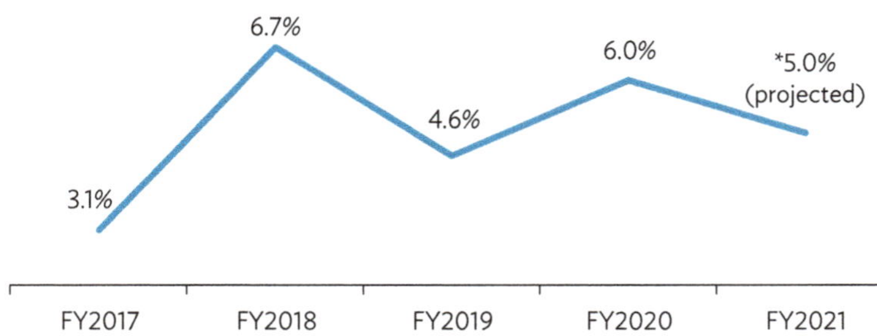

FY = fiscal year, GDP = gross domestic product.

Note: FY ends 15 July.

Source: Nepal Rastra Bank.

Figure A2.55: Nepal Government Debt
(% of GDP)

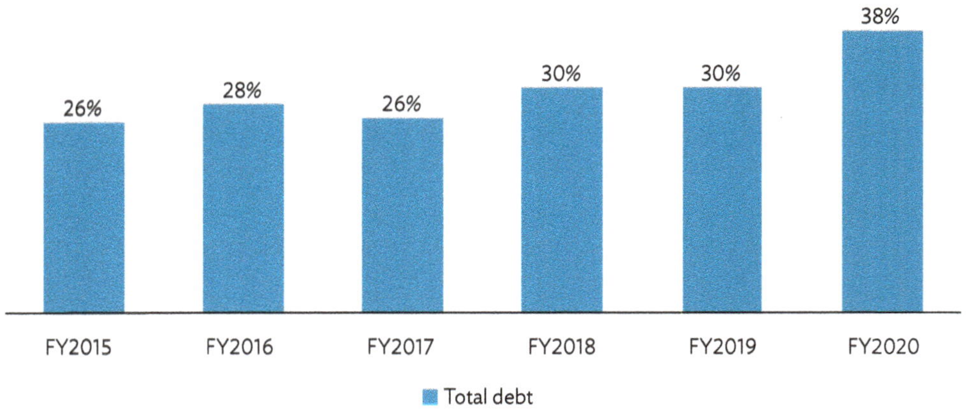

FY = fiscal year, GDP = gross domestic product.

Note: FY ends 15 July.

Source: Nepal Rastra Bank.

The COVID-19 pandemic put additional stress on government borrowing and the fiscal deficit target. Economic growth is forecast at 2.3% for FY2020 (ended 15 July). The government is targeting growth of 7.0% in FY2022. To promote growth, key sectors affected by the pandemic and specific rehabilitation programs have been prioritized This included revitalizing businesses in various sector (agriculture, industry, tourism, construction) affected by the pandemic.

Bridging the Financing Gap

Although the government has used innovative approaches to overcome its budget constraints, a significant financing gap needs to be bridged. For financing transport infrastructure, the following measures would help: (i) getting a sovereign credit rating so that funds can be sourced through foreign borrowing, (ii) developing and strengthening the capability for PPP projects to increase private sector participation, and (iii) exploring ways for strengthening banking and financial institutions (in addition to securing loans from multilateral and bilateral financial institutions). Figure A2.56 shows the contribution of Nepal's financial institutions to infrastructure development.

Despite the large market share of commercial banks, they only lend about 3% of their total investable capital to infrastructure projects. PPP projects have been tried in the past, but none were implemented. Because of this, commercial banks and other financial institutions are not experienced in this financing mode. Pension, insurance, mutual, and private equity funds need to be developed and encouraged to invest in infrastructure development.

Figure A2.56: Size and Contribution of Nepal's Financial Institutions to Infrastructure

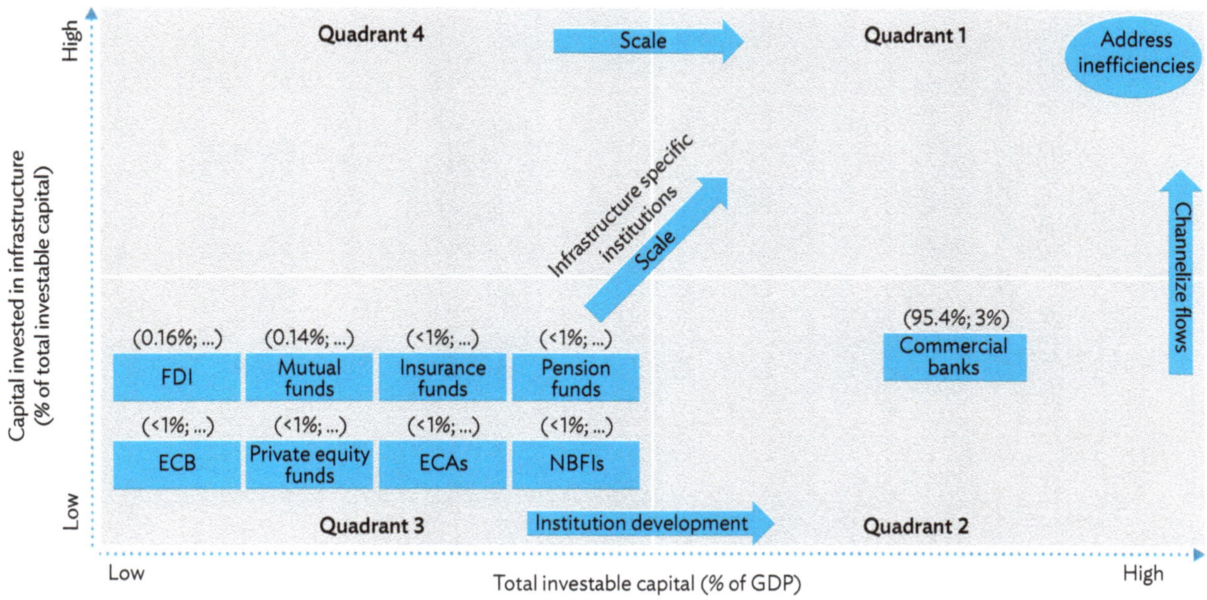

... = not available, ECA = export credit agency, ECB = external commercial borrowing, FDI = foreign direct investment, GDP = gross domestic product, NBFI = nonbank financial institution.

Notes:

1. Percentage figures provide a comparative measure and are based on the most recent available data as available.
2. Institutions where data is not available are placed based on general understanding from primary and secondary research.

Sources: Nepal Rastra Bank.

Challenges of Developing Nepal's Financing Institutions for Investing in Transport Infrastructure

The assessment of Nepal's financial institutions has been done in two parts. The first identifies the challenges faced by these institutions in providing capital to infrastructure projects, and suggests interventions to overcome them. This essentially covers the supply side of infrastructure financing. The second part identifies sector-related PPP challenges; this essentially covers the demand side of infrastructure financing.

Commercial Banks

Commercial banks dominate the finance sector, accounting for 64% of the sector's total assets.[47] However, the lending in transport infrastructure has been minimal, around 3%–4% over the past 5 years as shown in Figures A2.57 and A2.58. Figure A2.57 shows the exposure of commercial banks to transport infrastructure.

[47] Nepal Rastra Bank. 2018. *Financial Stability Report 2018–2019*. Kathmandu. https://www.nrb.org.np/contents/uploads/2020/07/FSR-2018-19-1.pdf.

Figure A2.57: Transport Infrastructure Exposure of Nepal's Commercial Banks
(% of total credit)

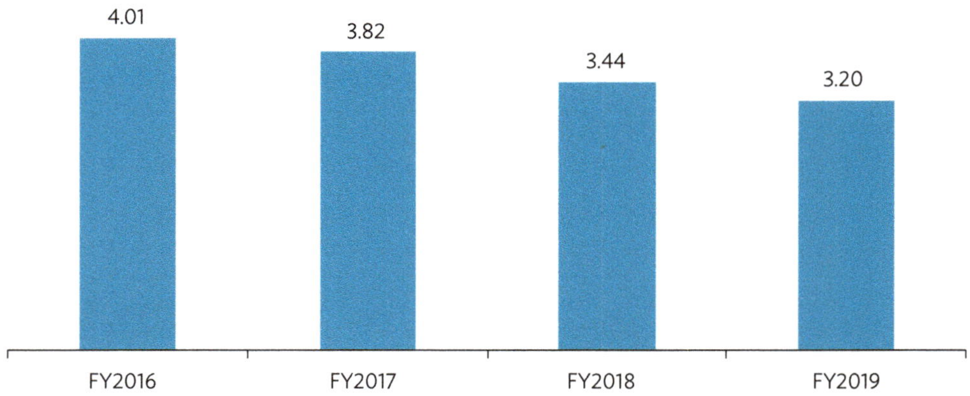

FY = fiscal year.

Notes: FY ends 15 July. Transport infrastructure includes heavy construction and transportation equipment, water transportation, Airjet, and railway and passenger vehicles.

Sources: Ministry of Finance; Nepal Rastra Bank; and study team analysis.

Figure A2.58: Credit Flow from Commercial Banks, FY2019

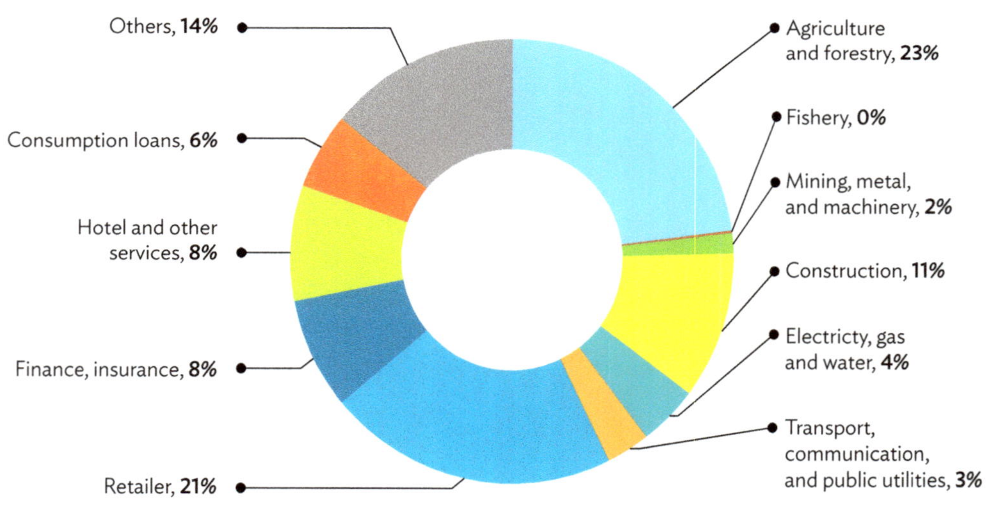

Sources: Ministry of Finance; Nepal Rastra Bank; and study team analysis.

Nepal's commercial banks face two key issues: an asset–liability mismatch in lending to infrastructure and project risk. On the former, the share of total deposits is 78%–80%, but the share of fixed deposits of a 5-year maximum tenure is less than 50% of total deposits (Figure A2.59). However, bank infrastructure lending is for an average tenure of 11 years. Table A2.83 outlines actions to address asset–liability mismatches.

Because of project risk and sector and borrower limits set by Nepal Rastra Bank, commercial banks prefer to lend to lower-risk projects, which constrains lending to infrastructure (Table A2.84). The central bank has set a 25% minimum level of total loan portfolios that must be lent to hydropower, tourism, and agriculture projects. Because of this, banks prefer lending to projects in these sectors. Further entity limits set by the central bank restrict banks to loans that can be offered to developers.

Figure A2.59: Share of Deposits by Type of Nepal's Commercial Banks, FY2019
(% of total deposits)

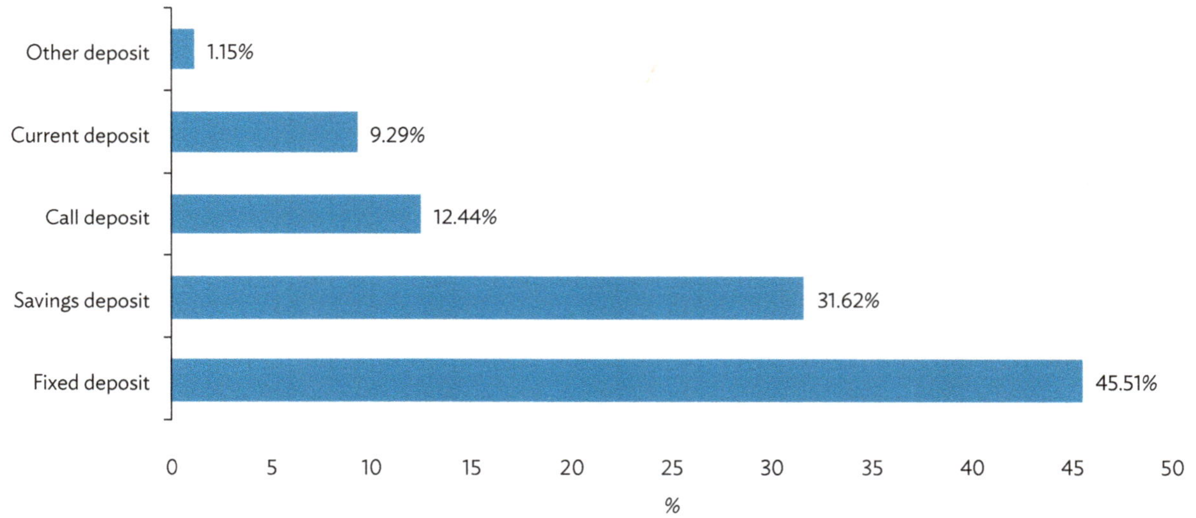

Sources: Ministry of Finance; and Nepal Rastra Bank.

Table A2.83: Actions to Tackle Asset–Liability Mismatches in Nepal's Commercial Banks

Actions	Impact
Develop a framework for rating the credit of construction entities, real estate developers, and projects. External credit rating agencies could be set up and developed to analyze business and financial risks. Companies in India could be used for benchmarking.	Provides lenders and sector participants with an independent opinion on the quality of the entity and/or project and thus prioritizes investments
Encourage secondary deals that allow banks to recycle their exposures post-commercial operations date. The examples include flip assets to long-term institutional investors; or listing of corporate bonds. Pricing of debt should reflect this (i.e., price of bank or institutional debt and corporate bonds cannot be same; there should be a spread).	Secondary investors will have more operational assets to invest in the development of bond market

Source: Study team analysis.

During construction, the financial viability of transport infrastructure projects largely depends on the cost of completion. Delays caused by late regulatory and legal approvals, and land acquisition, lead to cost overruns, which affect project returns. The lack of third-party credit rating agencies and limited technical skills are additional risks for commercial banks. Table A2.85 outlines actions to reduce the project risks that they face.

Table A2.84: Actions to Tackle Asset–Liability Mismatches in Nepal's Commercial Banks

Loan Type	Actions to Reduce Risks
Sector loan portfolio[a]	Less than 40% of total loan portfolio
Lending to hydropower and tourism sectors	At least 15% of total loans
Lending to single entity	Up to 25% of core capital

[a] 50% exempted for hydropower, power transmission, and cable car construction.

Source: Study team analysis.

Table A2.85: Actions to Reduce Project Risks Faced by Nepal's Commercial Banks

Actions	Impact
Nepal Rastra Bank has developed a credit rating mechanism for borrowers and projects based on type of business, financial performance, and other risks. The authorities should ensure the mechanism's monitoring framework is properly implemented so that debt pricing can be done accordingly	Reduced nonperforming loans and default risks boost investor confidence
Sector limits on infrastructure projects should be implemented and a framework for tax incentives and holidays needs to be developed	Attracts more investors and developers
Develop one-stop online platform for project-related approvals (legal and land)	Solves approval issues quickly and reduces clearance times

Source: Study team analysis.

Foreign Direct Investment

Nepal has double tax avoidance agreements with only 10 countries, which is a major enabler for FDI from these countries. FDI totaled NRs137.7 billion as of July 2016, 61% of which was from Australia, Ireland, Singapore, the United Kingdom, and the West Indies (Figure A2.60). No double tax avoidance agreements are in place with these countries, which are home to large institutional and individual investors. The Income Tax Department, in coordination with the Ministry of Finance and Nepal Rastra Bank, should enter into double tax avoidance agreements with these countries. Doing this would send a positive signal about Nepal as an investment destination.

FDI to Nepal as a percentage of GDP is much lower than other South Asian countries, although it has been growing (Figure A2.61). Moreover, actual FDI utilized is lower than the total FDI committed annually. FDI is also highly concentrated in communications, manufacturing, financial institutions, and utilities; FDI in transport infrastructure is negligible (Figure A2.62). Table A2.86 outlines actions to increase FDI.

Figure A2.60: Foreign Direct Investment in Nepal, FY2016
(NRs million)

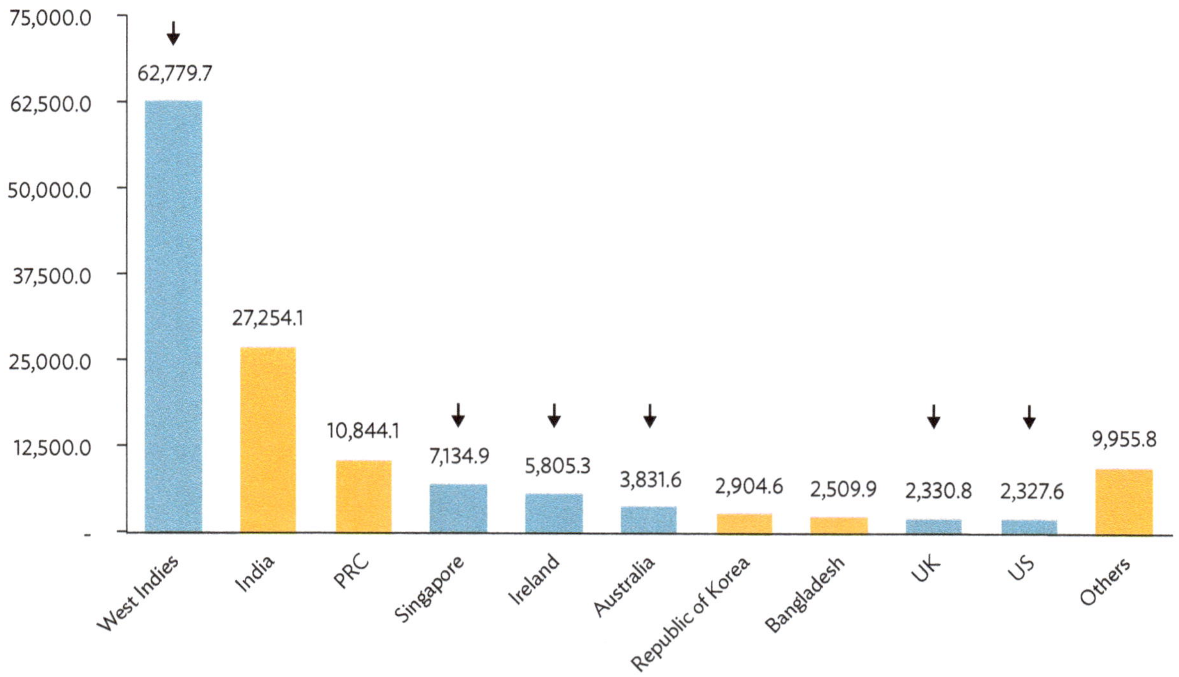

FY = fiscal year, NRs = Nepalese rupees, PRC = People's Republic of China, UK = United Kingdom, US = United States.

Notes: FY ends 15 July. The blue segments with arrows signify a lack of Double Taxation Avoidance Agreement (DTAA) between the specific country and Nepal.

Source: Study team analysis.

Figure A2.61: Foreign Direct Investment in Nepal and Selected Countries
(% of GDP)

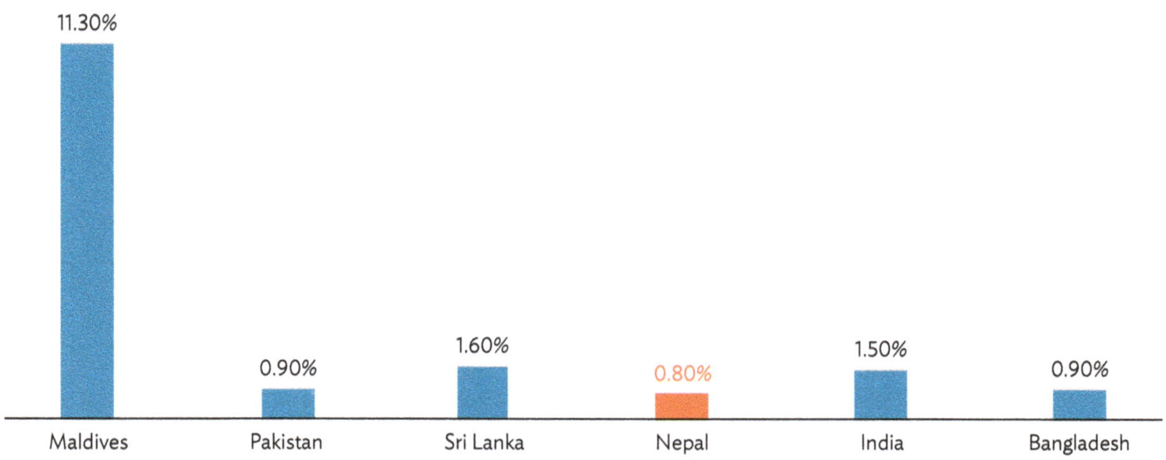

GDP = gross domestic product.

Source: Nepal Rastra Bank.

Figure A2.62: Foreign Direct Investment by Sector in Nepal

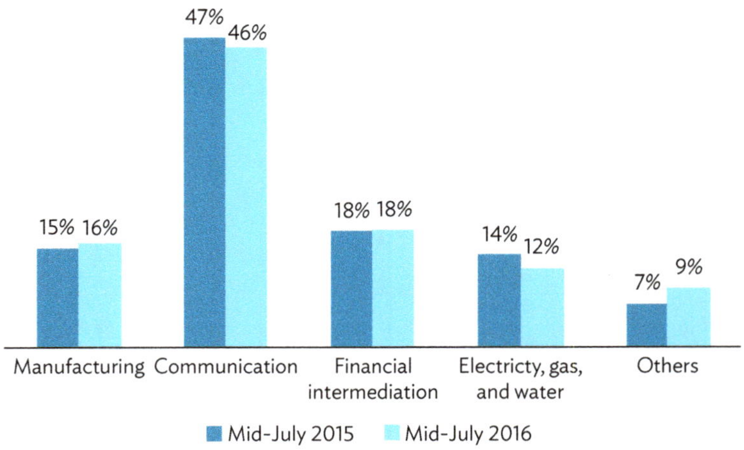

Source: Nepal Rastra Bank.

Table A2.86: Actions to Increase Foreign Direct Investment in Nepal

No.	Actions	Impact
1	Improve brand image in terms of ease of doing business, create awareness of investment opportunities, and improve policies for existing and potential investors	Boosted foreign investment
2	Digitize government procedures, including renewals, property rights, tax clearances, employment authorization, visa extensions. A framework is needed that can provide and implement services from one place	Easier processes for foreign investment
3	Ease processes for registering a company, arbitration settlement, land acquisition renewals, and repatriation of investments	Attracts foreign investor and increases foreign direct investment

Source: Study team analysis.

Insurance Funds

Insurance funds have been growing in recent years, although exposure to infrastructure remains limited. Developing this funding segment is constrained by a lack of expertise and skills for handling these instruments. The premium-to-GDP ratio of Nepal's insurance funds increased from 1.6% in FY2014 to 2.9% in FY2020. But as Figure A2.63 shows, insurance penetration in Nepal is much lower than the world average and other developed economies, although this has been growing (Figure A2.64). In Nepal, insurance companies prefer investing in government securities and other fixed-income instruments, such as fixed deposits, where the risk is lower and the yields higher. Insurance funds need to use research-based decision-making to diversify portfolios and have a rating mechanism to identify investment opportunities. A team could be set up in each insurance company to build the expertise to handle both. Doing this could reduce the risk of low returns and increase assured returns.

Figure A2.63: Insurance Penetration in Nepal and Selected Economies
(% of GDP)

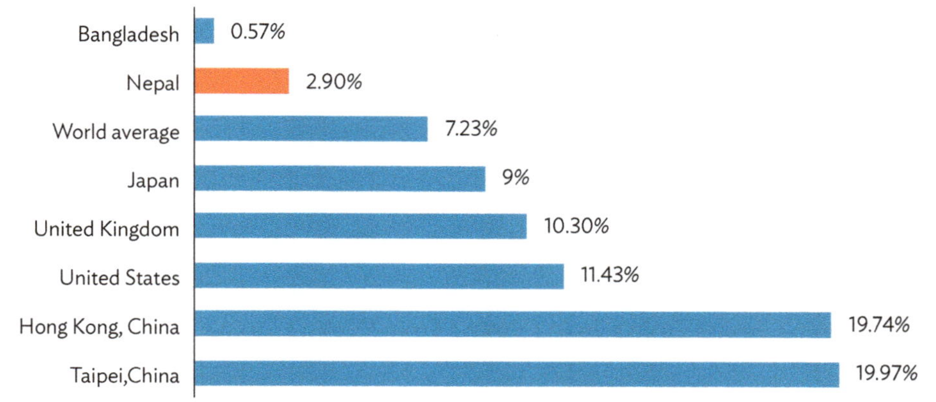

GDP = gross domestic product.

Source: Study team analysis; and secondary sources.

Figure A2.64: Insurance Penetration in Nepal
(% of GDP)

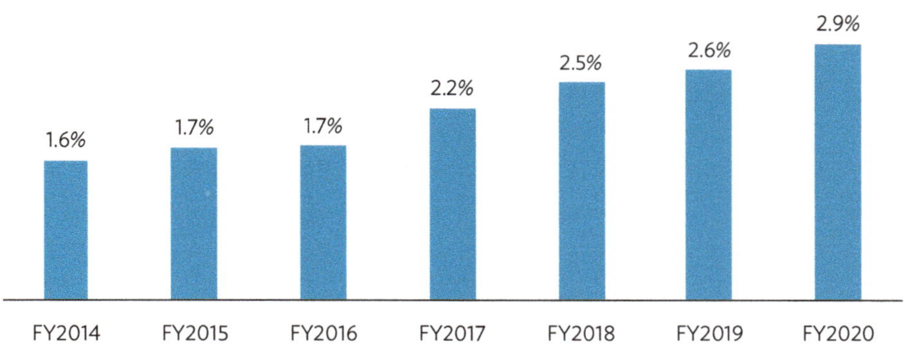

FY = fiscal year, GDP = gross domestic product.

Note: FY ends 15 July.

Source: Study team analysis and secondary sources.

Bond Market

Numerous issues constrain the development of Nepal's nascent bond market. It has no central depository system, no market information system or research companies, no domestic credit rating agencies or and no ratings from any global credit rating agencies.[48] Because government securities are still issued on paper, a scripless clearing and settlement system should be explored. Figure A2.65 shows outstanding amounts in domestic bonds, with the majority of investments in development bonds, as of FY2019. Table A2.87 outlines actions to develop a long-term debt market.

48 With one exception: the only market information system of any importance is found in the primary treasury bill market. Here, counterparts telephone each other to do a trade and settle in real time on behalf of other participants in the market.

Figure A2.65: Outstanding Domestic Bonds, FY2019

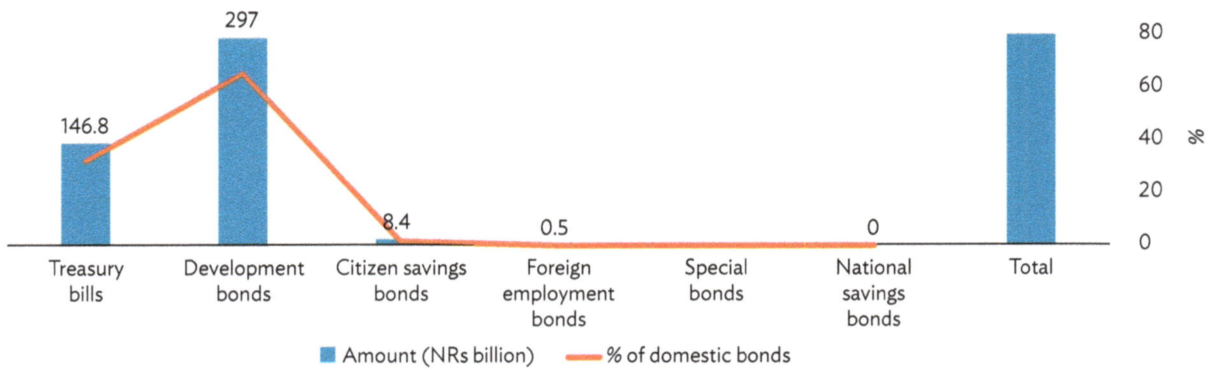

FY = fiscal year.

Source: PwC India. 2020. *A Roadmap for Strengthening Nepal's Bond Market.* India. https://www.pwc.in/assets/pdfs/consulting/financial-services/a-roadmap-for-strengthening-nepals-bond-market.pdf

Table A2.87: Actions to Develop a Long-Term Debt Market in Nepal

Actions	Impact
Nepal Rastra Bank could develop a negotiated dealing system as an electronic trading platform in the secondary bond market	Help enable seamless trading, ensuring market-based price discovery, and anonymous quoting and accepted prices
Improve and automate the central depository and clearing and settlement system, like Clearing Corporation of India	Help reduce the cost of trading
Nepal Rastra Bank could establish a comprehensive primary dealer framework for the bond market	Increase primary dealers in the market

Source: Study team analysis.

No specific guidelines exist for domestic entities to raise funds by issuing Nepalese rupee–denominated bonds (RDBs) in the overseas market. The lack of guidelines is a disincentive for investors and prevents wider participation in Nepal's bond market. Nepal Rastra Bank could develop guidelines to issue Nepalese RDBs that are in line with the RDB framework in India. This would open up new funding avenues. To promote new avenues of funding for Indian entities, the Reserve Bank of India, in 2014, issued guidelines for issuing Indian RDBs overseas as a part of its external commercial borrowing policy. The central bank set an all-in-cost ceiling for these bonds at 4.5% over the prevailing yield of government securities with corresponding maturities.

Nepal Infrastructure Bank

Nepal Infrastructure Bank Limited (NIFRA) services the financial needs of the infrastructure sector. It was set up under the Bank and Financial Institution Act as a national infrastructure development bank in 2018 with investments from the government, commercial banks, private companies, and individuals. The bank started operations in March 2019 with the ambitious goal of transforming the way infrastructure sector is financed in Nepal and fostering sustained economic growth. Because it is still early days for NIFRA, this report focuses on improvement areas that will help it become a nodal financial institution for infrastructure development.

In FY2021, NIFRA was in the process of raising $50 million from offshore bond issuances and NRs8 billion through initial public offerings. To increase its investment corpus, NIFRA is looking at raising funds from the Infrastructure Debt Fund. NIFRA, with the government, could plan to establish a NRs20 billion Infrastructure Debt Fund under specialized investment fund regulations. NIFRA could also consider raising at least NRs3 billion from domestic and international investors, to be invested in large infrastructure projects. NIFRA should also develop innovative financial instruments and services, such as an asset securitization platform, a PPP model, and supporting small infrastructure projects through an aggregation approach with various stakeholders, including the government, ministries overseeing power generation, and roads. Through these instruments, NIFRA can initiate discussions among stakeholders and provide support throughout the cycle of deal origination.

Challenges in PPP Projects

PPP projects in Nepal are not structured properly. Bureaucratic delays, policy uncertainty, limited transparency, insufficient institutional capacity, high transaction costs, and a lack of bankable projects, permits, and licenses, are just some of the challenges of infrastructure investments. And all these challenges delay the timely implementation of projects.

Banks do not have the skill set needed to analyze potential PPP projects. They have a limited understanding of the business and financial risks involved in infrastructure projects. From FY2009 to FY2019, PPPs that reached financial closure were overwhelmingly hydropower projects—22 of them, with a total investment of $2.1 billion. Over that period, only one road project ($350 million) and one water project reached financial closure.

In 2019, the government enacted the Public Private Partnership and Investment Act, which gave equal treatment to foreign and local investors. The act provided for the establishment of one-stop shops for approvals and clearances for project mobilization and implementation and PPP units. The purpose of these units is to clarify with investors any PPP procurement, tendering, finance, and allocation issues that may arise. But at the time of writing, neither a PPP unit nor an investment unit had been set up by Investment Board Nepal.

Currently Investment Board Nepal's Project Bank has a few PPP projects. These include the Kathmandu Valley Metro Project, the Kathmandu–Pokhara–Lumbini Railway, the Interstate and Intrastate Public Transportation Project in Sudurpaschim Province, the Integrated Agriculture Infrastructure Project, and the Bus Rapid Transit Project on the Kathmandu ring road. The board is tasked with taking these PPP projects from procurement to implementation stage. The COVID-19 pandemic will make the realization of these projects harder. Table A2.88 outlines actions to resolve PPP challenges.

Table A2.88: Actions to Resolve Public–Private Partnership Challenges in Nepal

Actions	Impact
Commercial banks to conduct staff learning exchange programs with other countries experienced in PPPs, and hold training and workshops, for developing the capability of PPP teams	Creates awareness of global PPP developments and enhances in-house capability
Commercial banks to enhance sector expertise, including law, finance, accounting, and infrastructure development	Better able to handle lending to risky projects

PPP = public–private partnerships.

Source: Study team analysis.

The following are additional steps that the government (refer to Box A2.8 which covers the key roles and responsibilities of Uganda's Public-Private Partnership Unit) needs to take to address key issues in PPP projects:

(i) Implement the Public Private Partnership and Investment Act, 2019 without delay. Investment Board Nepal and the government should work together to set up PPP units and the one-stop service.
(ii) Prepare the ground for private sector participation in infrastructure and other public sector projects by developing an appropriate legal, institutional, and contractual framework by defining the pricing policy of projects and allocating risk to private players.
(iii) Help government sectoral agencies to follow PPP rules and regulations. This will help quality control, policy formulation and coordination, technical assistance, and marketing.
(iv) Offer viability gap funding and set up a development fund for infrastructure projects for project development, land acquisitions and clearances, and statutory approvals.
(v) Establish robust governance structures and clear rules and regulations for allocating multiple project risks, including construction and interface risk among the government, Investment Board Nepal, and the private sector.
(vi) Conduct extensive stakeholder consultations and training on commercial, financial, legal, and negotiation aspects of PPPs and strengthen and develop the skills within institutions (commercial banks and infrastructure banks).
(vii) Conduct detailed technical, financial, legal, environmental, and social due diligence on both the sponsor and project.

Box A2.8: Uganda's Public–Private Partnership Unit

Uganda's Public–Private Partnership Unit has been in operation since 2015 and was created under an act passed in the same year. The unit's mandate is to collate and disseminate information on public–private partnership (PPP), including data on the contingent liabilities of the government in relation to a project.

The unit's roles and responsibilities are as follows:

- act as the center of project knowledge and performance;
- identify, develop, procure, and monitor projects;
- conduct preliminary economic cost–benefit analyses (to be done within 21 days of project approval by PPP unit);
- conduct feasibility studies;
- conduct studies and research on the practices and experience of PPPs internationally; and
- assist investors in the preparation and implementation of projects for implementation of the PPP program.

PPP investments from 1996 to 2017 totaled $1.9 billion. Advance projects include the Kampala–Jinja Expressway; the procurement process for this is underway.

Source: Reports in the public domain.

Public–Private Partnership Capacity Assessment

PPP Law and Policy Support Capacity

Table A2.89: Ratings for Public–Private Partnership Law and Policy Support Capacity in Nepal

#	Determinant	Rating
1	Is there a dedicated legal or policy instrument and/or guideline for PPPs?	3
2	What dispute resolution mechanisms are available for PPP agreements?	2

PPP = public–private partnership.

Source: Study team analysis.

Determinant 1: The Public Private Partnership Investment Act was passed in 2019. The act aims to contribute to economic prosperity through investments by domestic or foreign private companies in infrastructure construction and services. The act has provisions for managing PPP projects and for consolidating and, if necessary, amending legal provisions relating to these investments.

Determinant 2: The act has a dispute resolution mechanism. In the first instance, disputes are expected to be resolved amicably. If this is not possible, these are resolved under provisions of the Arbitration Act, 1999. If a foreign investor is involved in a PPP dispute, United Nations Commission on International Trade Law rules can be used.

Public Sector Public–Private Partnership Support Capacity and Experience

Determinant 3: Nepal does not have a sovereign debt rating by any of the international credit rating agencies.

Determinant 4: Nepal has a PPP unit. Its board of directors decide on whether to initiate the procurement process on the basis of the feasibility study conducted for the proposed project. It also provides policy coordination and guidelines for projects worth over NRs500 million or that require viability gap funding or grants from the government or revenue exemptions.

Table A2.90: Ratings for Public Sector Public–Private Partnership Support Capacity and Experience in Nepal

#	Determinant	Rating
3	If payment is likely to be made by the parent government, what is the credit rating of the parent government?	0
4	Is there a specialized government agency (or agencies) established for PPP purposes (e.g., PPP unit) and what are its roles?	3
5	Is there a streamlined approval process for PPP projects?	3
6	Does the sponsoring agency have previous experience with PPPs?	0
7	Are different PPP concession models defined for the sector and are model concession agreements available?	0

PPP = public–private partnership.

Source: Study team analysis.

Determinant 5: PPPs in Nepal are mostly government-to-government agreements in which the private player conducts a feasibility study to procure funding from multilateral sources. Under Nepal's PPP policies, the government is responsible for conducting the feasibility analysis for the project through the Public Private Partnership Agency. Table A2.91 shows the type of feasibility analyses required for PPPs in Nepal.

Table A2.91: Feasibility Analyses Required for Public–Private Partnership Projects in Nepal

Analysis Type	✓/×
Technical feasibility	✓
Financial feasibility	✓
Legal feasibility	×
Environmental and social sustainability	✓
Value-for-money assessment	×
Fiscal affordability assessment	×
PPP structuring and risk allocation	×
Initial market testing	×

PPP = public–private partnership.

Source: Asian Development Bank. 2017. *Public–Private Partnership Monitor*. Manila. https://www.adb.org/publications/public-private-partnership-monitor.

Determinant 6: Only one project has achieved financial closure in transport infrastructure sector since 1996 in Nepal.

Determinant 7: Nepal has no sector-specific model concession agreements—e.g., ports and roads for transport infrastructure—that can provide a framework for PPP agreements. Having this would encourage greater private participation.

Public Funding Assistance for Public–Private Partnerships

Determinant 8: The Public Private Partnership and Investment Act has a provision for viability gap funding. This funding is decided by the Ministry of Finance committee and based on the recommendation of the project's approving agency. Viability gap funding can be used for construction and operations, and for expanding important infrastructure projects that yield positive returns in the long-run but that are not immediately profitable.

Table A2.92: Ratings for Public Sector Funding Assistance in Public–Private Partnerships in Nepal

#	Determinant	Rating
8	Is government support for viability gap funding available for PPP projects?	3

PPP = public–private partnership.

Source: Study team analysis.

Land Acquisition and Environmental and Social Clearances

Determinants 9 and 10: The Geo Environmental and Social Unit oversees land acquisitions and environmental and social clearances. The unit studies and recommends geotechnical, environmental, and social issues pertaining to roads and bridge building and the compliance monitoring of projects (for which it gets World Bank assistance). This is done in close coordination with the Ministry of Environment and the Ministry of Forest and Soil Conservation. The unit does an initial environmental examination and then environmental and social impact assessments on road projects, including the impact on the neighborhood. This is followed by social and environment audits on these projects. The unit then advises Department of Roads on land acquisition, compensation, and resettlement for road projects.

Table A2.93: Ratings for Land Acquisition and Environmental and Social Clearances in Nepal

#	Determinant	Rating
9	Does the authority have experience in dealing with land acquisitions, environmental clearances, and rehabilitation and resettlement?	1
10	Does the authority have a dedicated team to streamline land acquisitions and environmental clearances, and the experience to handle these areas?	3

Source: Study team analysis.

Market Capacity and Foreign Participation

Determinant 11: Major impediments to private participation in infrastructure development projects are political and administrative instability, insufficient consistency in planning, and generally ineffective institutional support for project design and developing infrastructure PPPs.

Table A2.94: Ratings for Market Capacity and Foreign Participation in Nepal

#	Determinant	Rating
11	Is there sufficient market capacity and do private players have PPP experience?	0
12	Is foreign participation in PPP allowed?	3
13	Are there any restrictions on foreign investors' land use or ownership (i.e., do foreign investors have the same rights as locals?)	3
14	If payments are likely to be made from the authority's budget, is there any form of government guarantee available for these payments?	0
15	Is the exchange rate stable?	2
16	Is there a robust project finance market, which supplements the traditional corporate finance market?	1
17	Are debt instruments available for different project needs, such as senior, mezzanine, and subordinate debt, and take-out financing?	0

PPP = public–private partnership.

Source: Study team analysis.

Determinants 12 and 13: Foreign participation is allowed and encouraged in Nepal due to lack of indigenous private developers in the country. There are restrictions in landownership rights for foreign investors in Nepal. However, exemptions have been granted for infrastructure projects.

Determinant 14: The need for government credit guarantees to secure revenue for projects in the BIMSTEC master plan emerged as a major issue in interviews with foreign private developers for this report. Against this backdrop, Nepal needs sovereign credit guarantees for transport infrastructure projects, since the government covers none of the following: currency inconvertibility and transfer risks, foreign exchange risk, war and civil disturbance risk, breach-of-contract risk, regulatory risk, and expropriation risk. The government also does not provide credit guarantees or guarantees for minimum demand and revenue.

Determinant 15: As for exchange rate risks, Nepal has low currency fluctuations and volatility and its currency and strengthened steadily historically.

Determinant 16: Nepal's capital market does not have the capacity to handle PPP projects. The government should support the development of a credit-flow mechanism for the long-term financial sources required by the private sector to make investments in physical infrastructure and infrastructure services. The government is trying to develop new mechanisms for making long-term investments in physical infrastructure and infrastructure services by attracting foreign players.

Determinant 17: Despite considerable growth in Nepal's bank and nonbank finance sectors over the past decade, the country's legal framework and institutional setup is not conducive to the overall development of either the financial or private sectors, and reforms are urgently needed.

Life-Cycle Cost and Output Specifications

Determinants 18 and 19: Nepal has some experience in transport infrastructure projects so it can quantify construction and long-term operation costs, as well as output specifications (Table A2.95).

Table A2.95: Ratings for Life-Cycle Cost and Output Specifications in Nepal

#	Determinant	Rating
18	Can most of the costs, mainly related to construction and long-term operations, including maintenance, be quantified upfront with reasonable assumptions, and are historical data available?	2
19	Are objective output specifications readily available from a previous contract?	2

Source: Study team analysis.

Possible Interventions

Securing a sovereign credit rating is the top priority for increasing funds for transport infrastructure projects through foreign borrowing.

Nepal can also adopt the following key approaches to address the investment gap in the transport infrastructure sector: (i) increase private investment by addressing issues hindering development and deepening of financing institutions; (ii) explore avenues for revenue enhancement (e.g., LVC, non-toll revenues such as advertisements, privately owned public spaces, etc.) to increase government investable capital and improve project viability and unlock capital investment in existing operational projects through asset securitization (e.g., InviTs, toll securitization), and asset recycling (e.g., toll–operate–transfer models).

Brownfield toll roads could be pooled by the government for potential asset recycling—e.g., seven roads in Nepal are already collecting tolls and are potential candidates for this (Appendix 9). In the coming years, tolls will be levied on most of Nepal's roads.[49] Once they achieve stable revenue streams, they could be considered for asset recycling.

A summary of other key intervention areas are mentioned below:

Table A2.96: Summary of Recommended Finance Sector Interventions for Nepal

#	Finance Sector	Issues	Actions
1	Commercial banks	Asset–liability mismatch encountered by commercial banks in lending to infrastructure	Develop a framework for credit rating construction entities, real estate developers, and projects for external credit rating agencies to be able to analyze business and financial risks. For example, companies in India can be used for reference.
			Encourage secondary deals that allow banks to recycle their exposure, post-commercial operations date, and flip assets to long-term institutional investors or list corporate bonds (debt pricing should reflect this: i.e., price of bank debt and institutional debt or corporate bonds cannot be the same; there should be a spread).
		Because of project risks, sector and borrower limits set by Nepal Rastra Bank (NRB), commercial banks prefer lending to low-risk projects	NRB should develop a rating mechanism for borrowers and projects based on their business and financial performance and other associated risk. Authorities should ensure the rating mechanism is used properly so that pricing is accurate.
			Set sector limits for infrastructure projects. A framework for tax incentives and holidays should be developed.
			Develop a one-stop online solution for project approvals (legal and land).
			Commercial banks to conduct staff-learning exchange programs with other countries experienced in public–private partnerships (PPPs), and hold training and workshops for developing the capability of PPP teams.
			Commercial banks to enhance sectoral expertise including law, finance, accounting, development, and engineering.

continued on next page

[49] S. Mishtra. 2018. Toll Tax on Most Road Sections from Next Fiscal. *The Himalayan*. 18 January. https://thehimalayantimes.com/nepal/toll-tax-road-sections-next-fiscal.

Table A2.96 *continued*

#	Finance Sector	Issues	Actions
2	Foreign direct investment (FDI)	No dual tax avoidance arrangements with countries that are home to large institutional and individual investors	Inland Revenue Department in coordination with the Ministry of Finance should enter into dual tax avoidance arrangements with Australia, Ireland, Singapore, the United Kingdom, the United States, and West Indies, home to large investors.
		Low FDI as a percentage of gross domestic product and further lesser withdrawal of FDI investment. Although FDI has been growing in recent years, FDI in infrastructure is negligible	Improve brand image in terms of ease of doing business, create awareness of investment opportunities, and improve policies for existing and potential investors.
			Digitize procedures for property rights, tax clearance, employment authorization, visa extensions, among other areas. Design a framework to provide and implement these services from one place.
			Make company registration, arbitration settlements, renewals of land acquisition, and repatriation of investments easier.
3	Insurance funds	Limited expertise, technical and skill sets, research-based decision-making, and rating mechanisms for investment opportunities. Insurance funds have been growing in recent years, but little exposure to infrastructure	Set up teams within insurance companies and strengthen expertise in areas that are needed to be able to carry out PPPs
4	Bond market	No central market infrastructure or secondary market for fixed-income securities to support a bond market, resulting in underdeveloped bond market	NRB could develop a negotiated dealing system as an electronic trading platform in secondary bond market.
			Improve and automate the central depository and the clearing and settlement system, like Clearing Corporation of India.
			NRB could set up a comprehensive primary dealer framework for the bond market.
		No specific guidelines for domestic entities to raise funds by issuing Nepalese rupee-denominated bonds in the overseas market. Bond market also has inadequate guidelines for this	NRB could formulate guidelines to issue Nepalese rupee-denominated bonds. The guidelines could be in line with the Reserve Bank of India's framework on rupee-denominated bonds.
5	Challenges in PPP projects	Banks have limited capability to underwrite infrastructure projects and to handle other design issues in PPP projects	Implement Public Private Partnership and Investment Act, 2019 without delay. Investment Board Nepal and the government should work together to establish PPP units and the one-stop service. Government needs to prepare the ground for private sector participation by developing a legal, institutional, and contractual framework that defines the pricing policy of projects and allocates risk to private players.

continued on next page

Table A2.96 *continued*

#	Finance Sector	Issues	Actions
			The government should help sectoral agencies to follow PPP rules and regulations; this will help in quality control, policy formulation and coordination, technical assistance, and marketing. Use viability gap funding and create a project development fund to close funding gaps for infrastructure projects. Create robust governance structures and clear rules and regulations for allocating multiple risks, including construction and interface risks, among the government, Investment Board Nepal, and the private sector. Hold extensive stakeholder consultations and training on the commercial, financial, legal, and negotiation aspects of PPPs to develop and strengthen skills in commercial banks and infrastructure banks

Source: Study team analysis.

Sri Lanka

Transport Infrastructure Financing Landscape

Sources of Transport Infrastructure Financing

Sri Lanka's transport infrastructure financing needs are primarily financed through government budgetary support. Apart from this, project authorities also rely on internal and extra budgetary resources for funding projects. The authorities raise money through the sale of assets, such as bonds serviced by future cash flows. Sri Lanka is heavily reliant on international sovereign bonds, which comprise a sizable portion of maturing government debt. These sources of funding through government support contribute to around 4.1% of GDP annually. Government expenditure increases are restricted by constitutional limits on borrowings

Private sector investment in transport infrastructure is equivalent of just 0.1% of GDP; the annual investment requirement is 6.6% of GDP. As a lower-middle-income country, Sri Lanka's baseline financing need for the sector is 4.2%–7.1% of GDP. However, the climate change-adjusted need is 5.0%–8.2%, representing an average annual financing need of 6.6% of GDP.

Fiscal Support to Infrastructure

Sri Lanka's general government debt burden was an estimated 83% of GDP in FY2019 (i.e., before COVID-19) (Figure A2.66). Credit rating agencies forecast Sri Lanka's fiscal deficit rising to 8.0% of GDP in FY2020 (ended 31 March) from 6.8% in FY2019. Overall, high and rising debt servicing costs, lower revenue, and increased fiscal spending is expected to widen the budget deficit to 8%–9% of GDP in FY2021.

Figure A2.66: Government Debt in Sri Lanka, FY2015–FY2019
(% of GDP)

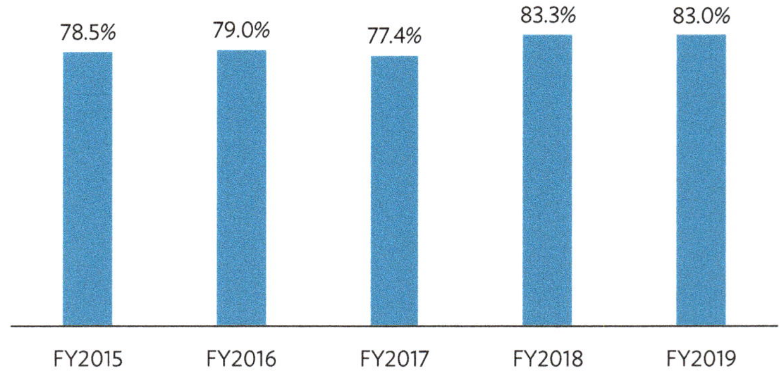

FY = fiscal year, GDP = gross domestic product.

Source: Study team analysis.

Fitch Ratings, in 2019, revised Sri Lanka's sovereign outlook to negative, and all three global credit rating agencies have downgraded their Sri Lanka ratings (Table A2.97). The country's rising ratio of debt-to-GDP, along with the ratings' downgrades, makes international borrowing difficult for the government.

Table A2.97: Sri Lanka's Sovereign Ratings and Outlook by Global Credit Rating Agencies

Agency	Rating	Outlook	Date
Fitch	Downgraded from B to B–	Negative	24 April 2020
Moody's	Downgraded from B2 to Caa1	Stable	28 September 2020
Standard and Poor's Global Ratings	Downgraded from B to B–	Stable	20 May 2020

Sources: Sovereign rating updates from Fitch Ratings, Moody's Investors Service, S&P Global Ratings.

With the scope for international borrowing reduced, Sri Lanka's transport infrastructure budget has little room to expand. Since 2019, the sector's allocation has been 7%–9% of total government spending, with capital expenditure accounting for 80%–90% of total transport budget allocations (Figures A2.67 and A2.68).

Figure A2.67: Sri Lanka Budget Allocation on Transport Infrastructure, FY2019–FY2021
(SLRs billion)

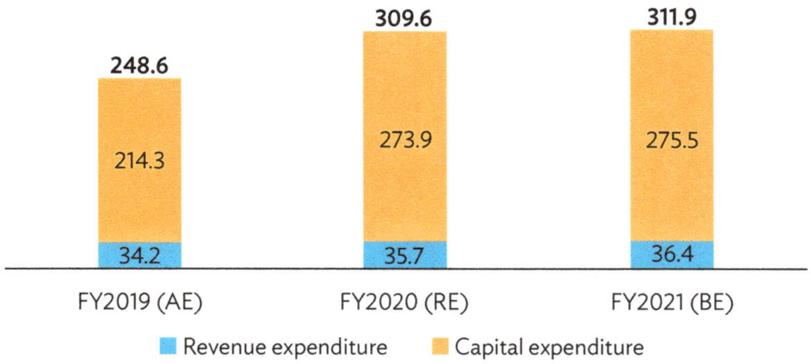

AE = actual expenditure, BE = budget estimate, FY = fiscal year, RE = revised estimate, SLRs = Sri Lanka rupees.

Note: FY ends 31 March.

Source: Ministry of Finance. Union Budget 2020.

Figure A2.68: Sri Lanka Budget Allocation on Transport Infrastructure, FY2019–2019
(SLRs billion)

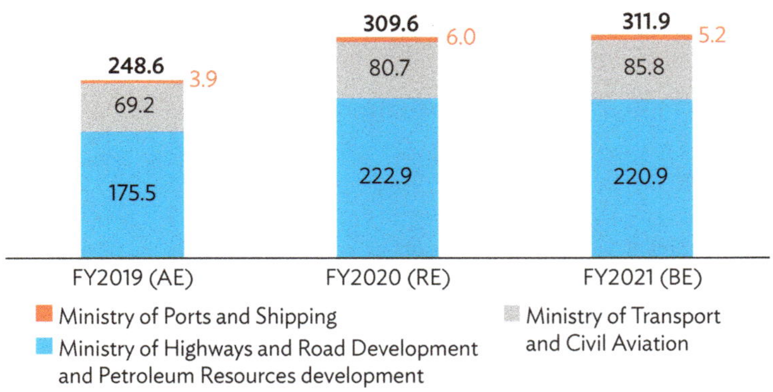

AE = actual expenditure, BE = budget estimate, FY = fiscal year, RE = revised estimate.

Note: FY ends 31 March.

Source: Ministry of Finance. Union Budget 2020.

Against the backdrop of a tight budget, COVID-19 has further aggravated the fiscal situation. The pandemic has especially hurt tourism, which, combined with weaker domestic demand, further hit Sri Lanka's public and external finances. The potential for an economic recovery in 2022 hinges on an early return of tourism and increasing domestic activity, which is highly uncertain—as is the course of the pandemic. Sri Lanka has to make about $4 billion dollars in debt service payments from 2020 to 2025, which, coupled with expectations of wide budget deficits over the coming years, will make government investment in infrastructure very difficult.

Bridging the Financing Gap

As fiscal support is unlikely to increase in the near term, Sri Lanka requires private sector support to augment government sources of financing. Figure A2.69 maps the country's financial institutions in Sri Lanka based on total investable capital (as a percentage of GDP) and their contribution to infrastructure financing (as a percentage of their capital base).

Figure A2.69: Sri Lanka's Financial Institution Mapping

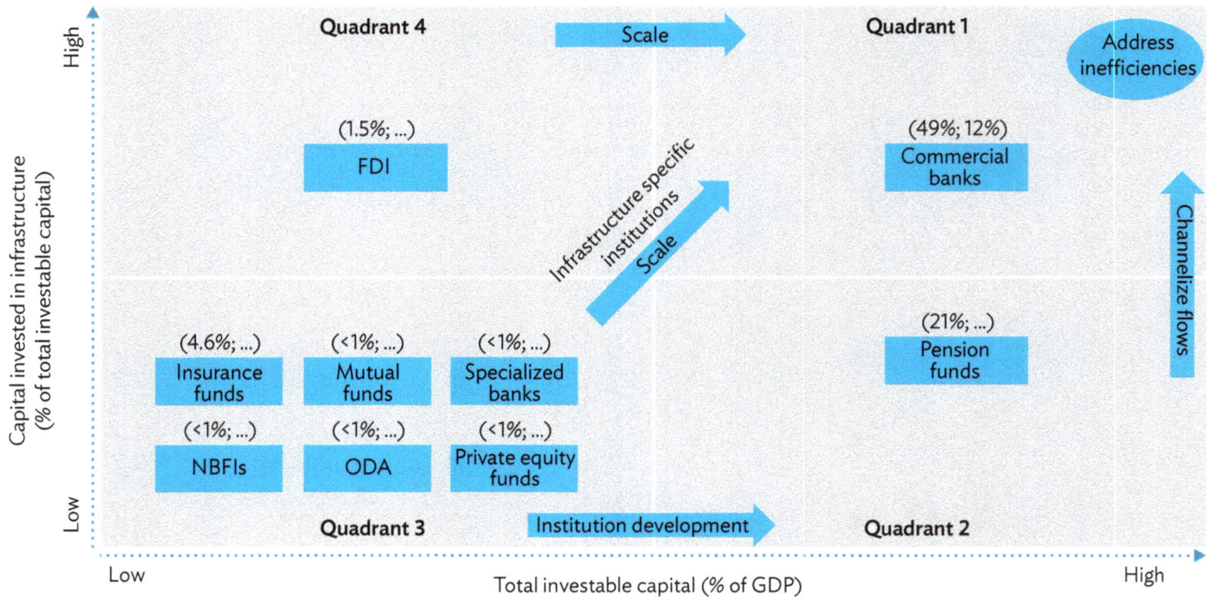

FDI = foreign direct investment, GDP = gross domestic product, NBFI = nonbank financial institution, ODA = official development assistance.

Notes:

1. Percentage figures provide a comparative measure and are based on the latest available data.
2. Institutions where data is not available are placed based on a general understanding from primary and secondary research.

Sources: Central Bank; and Insurance and Pension Regulators Security Commission.

Commercial banks dominate Sri Lanka's financial landscape but lend little to infrastructure because of a high base rate. Pension funds, dominated by the Employee Pension Fund and Employee Trust Fund, are conservative investors and are not much invested in infrastructure. FDI in Sri Lanka, however, has been focused on infrastructure, led by Hong Kong, China; India; and the People's Republic of China. Insurance, mutual, and pension funds need to be channeled into infrastructure through the capital market, but as the following sections explain, hurdles remain.

Challenges of Developing Sri Lanka's Financing Institutions for Investing in Transport Infrastructure

Commercial Banks

Commercial banks are among the largest financial institutions in Sri Lanka, with a total investable capital base at 49% of GDP. The sector has a credit exposure to infrastructure at around 12% of total investable capital. That could be increased if several regulatory issues are addressed to improve the performance of commercial banks in infrastructure financing, particularly restrictions on the cost of lending that limit profitability opportunities. In 2019, the Central Bank of Sri Lanka required banks to reduce interest rates on all Sri Lanka rupee–denominated loans and advances by at least 200 basis points. Banks are exempted if their interest rates are at or below 12.5%. Rates on certain products, while reduced, remain high (e.g., credit card annual percentage rates are capped at 28%), but leases and gold-backed loans are excluded.

Infrastructure projects are considered at higher risk during the construction phase than when they are up and running. Because of this, restrictions on the cost of lending might mean that risks are not covered, especially time and cost overruns. Ideally, the risk profile of infrastructure projects in the construction stage is much higher than in the operation stage. Banks may not be willing to take up the construction risk if lending rates are capped. To overcome this, the government could explore options for removing the interest rate cap.

Foreign Direct Investment

Sri Lanka has seen considerable FDI inflows in infrastructure, including $500 million in Colombo International Container Terminals.[50] To be able to attract more FDI in other sectors, such as manufacturing and services, given their long-term contributions to employment and the economy, Sri Lanka needs to create an enabling environment for attracting long-term FDI at scale. Two key issues that need resolving are (i) improving the ease of doing business and policy uncertainty and (ii) addressing high currency hedging costs due to currency volatility.

Ease of doing business and policy uncertainty. Sri Lanka ranks 99th out of 190 countries in the World Bank's 2020 Doing Business survey.[51] It ranks 85th on the indicator for starting a business, 138th on registering a property, and 164th on enforcing contracts. Policy uncertainty is high in Sri Lanka. Investors face fragmented policymaking, frequent policy changes, and slow policy implementation.[52] Political instability is a frequent cause of policy changes. Abrupt change in economic policy environments leads to high transaction costs for investors, making investment less attractive.

Landownership is a big FDI challenge. Foreign ownership is allowed in most sectors, but the landownership law prohibits foreigners from owning land, with some exceptions. Land is primarily state-owned (80%). Foreign ownership is governed by a disjointed institutional structure and a complex legal environment. Land administration is weak and cumbersome.

---

[50] Colombo International Container Terminals Limited is a joint venture company between China Merchants Port Holdings Company Limited, a listed blue chip company in the Hong Kong Stock Exchange, and the Sri Lanka Ports Authority. China Merchants Port Holdings holds 85% of the partnership while the balance 15% is held by Sri Lanka Ports Authority.

[51] World Bank. 2020. *Doing Business 2020*. Economy Profile Sri Lanka. https://www.doingbusiness.org/content/dam/doingBusiness/country/s/sri-lanka/LKA.pdf.

[52] Tatiana Nenova. 2020. Six Ways Sri Lanka Can Attract More Foreign Investments. 11 June. World Bank Blogs. https://blogs.worldbank.org/endpovertyinsouthasia/six-ways-sri-lanka-can-attract-more-foreign-investments.

High currency hedging costs. Repatriation norms are free of restrictions on converting, transferring, or repatriating funds, but the Sri Lanka rupee is volatile against the dollar, a result of a flexible exchange rate regime. Table A2.98 outlines actions to remedy the challenges just described.

Table A2.98: Actions to Attract Increase Foreign Direct Investment in Sri Lanka

#	Actions	Impact
1	Sri Lanka can attract FDI by working on low scoring Doing Business indicators	Creates an enabling business environment for foreign investors
2	Land reforms to improve access for foreign investors, and better governance and management of state land	Easier land access for foreign investors
3	Long-term strategies and policies for providing policy continuity and guiding paths	Increased investor confidence and less policy uncertainty

FDI = foreign direct investment.

Source: Study team analysis.

Debt Capital Markets

Sri Lanka's bond market consists of government securities (Treasury bills and bonds), corporate and bank bonds listed on the stock exchange, and unlisted corporate bonds. Sri Lanka has an active primary and secondary market in government securities and overseas issuances of sovereign debt. Sri Lanka's sovereign credit rating risk is a concern for capital markets as the government's fiscal stimulus has been criticized by credit rating agencies as being highly fluctuating and volatile. Sri Lanka has an active primary market for corporate bonds, but the secondary market is fairly inactive. Sri Lanka's capital market has yet to venture beyond traditional instruments, such as stocks and bonds, into derivatives and commodities. Introducing more sophisticated products would encourage the market's further development. The capital market faces three key challenges: an inefficient primary government securities bond market, limited demand for securities, and fragmented and undercapitalized intermediaries.

Inefficient primary government securities bond market. Current practices used in the primary issuance of government securities are characterized by limited coordination between the central bank's debt management function and the Ministry of Finance's fiscal operations. Most bond issuances have short- to medium-term maturities, resulting in lower liquidity at long maturities and higher refinancing risk. Canceled bids at primary auctions to lower the government's borrowing costs are frequent. To smoothen market expectations and create liquidity, these issues should be carefully planned and fully aligned with the government's fiscal operations and market demand. Table A2.99 outlines actions to tackle these challenges.

Table A2.99: Actions to Improve the Efficiency of Sri Lanka's Government Securities Bond Market

#	Actions	Impact
1	Auction calendars should be published, and benchmark issuances increased. Auctions should be held as announced.	Increased visibility on annual government issuances
2	Enhance capital base of primary dealers	Increased stability and resilience of primary dealer system
3	Create an electronic trading platform that facilitates multilateral negotiations (i.e., an enhanced request-for-quote trading platform)	Transparency and predictability in the market, and strengthened investor confidence

Source: Study team analysis.

Limited demand for securities. Institutional investors, such as insurance and mutual funds, do not have much of a presence in Sri Lanka's capital market; the largest participants are state-owned pension funds. Developing the mutual fund industry is hindered by the absence of a tax pass-through status and too few distribution channels. The insurance industry too needs to strengthen governance, streamline the industry's regulator, and provide greater investor protection. Alternative financial instruments need to be developed to broaden and deepen Sri Lanka's capital market. Table A2.99 outlines actions to increase demand for government securities.

Fragmented and undercapitalized intermediaries. Transaction costs on stock trades in Sri Lanka are high. New risk-based capital rules for intermediaries and the subsequent implementation of a recapitalization plan will be essential to restore market confidence in the industry and provide a foundation for brokers to conduct market making and short selling. A new training and certification framework is needed to accommodate new financial products and strengthen the financial literacy of retail investors through education. Table A2.100 outlines actions to strengthen the intermediaries.

Table A2.100: Action to Strength Sri Lanka's Intermediaries

#	Actions	Impact
1	Adopt a universal brokerage model where market intermediaries deal in all capital market products	Increased viability as having specialized brokers for different capital market products might not be economically viable
2	Expand the financial industry qualification framework to include multiple capital market instruments	Qualification framework will help accommodate new financial products and strengthen the financial literacy of retail investors through education
3	Develop and implement a comprehensive framework for risk-based minimum capital requirements for market intermediaries	Increased resilience of the intermediary industry

Source: Study team analysis.

Public–Private Partnership Capacity Assessment

Public–Private Partnership Law and Policy Support Capacity

Determinant 1: Sri Lanka does not have a specialized legal guideline for PPPs. The first formal PPP projects were implemented in Sri Lanka after the Bureau of Infrastructure Investment, under the Board of Investment, was set up in 1995 to facilitate infrastructure projects through private investment. PPP projects are implemented on the basis of guidelines issued in 1998 by the Ministry of Finance on government tender procedures for private sector build-operate-own, build-operate-transfer, and build-own-operate-transfer infrastructure projects, and the general public procurement manual and guidelines. Additions to the guidelines on unsolicited proposals were made in 2011 followed by addition of a Swiss challenge process to encourage private sector initiative without losing the benefits of tender processes in 2016.

Determinant 2: Sri Lanka's PPP dispute resolution mechanism includes litigation and local and international arbitration. Foreign laws can be chosen to govern PPP contracts.

Table A2.101: Ratings for Public–Private Partnership Law and Policy Support Capacity in Sri Lanka

#	Determinant	Rating
1	Is there a dedicated legal or policy instrument/guideline for PPPs?	2
2	What dispute resolution mechanisms are available for PPP agreements?	2

PPP = public–private partnership.

Source: Study team analysis.

Public Sector Public–Private Partnership Support Capacity and Experience

Determinant 3: Fitch Ratings, in 2020, revised Sri Lanka's sovereign outlook to negative, and all credit rating agencies have downgraded their Sri Lanka ratings. The country's rising ratio of debt-to-GDP, along with the ratings' downgrades, makes international borrowing difficult for the government.

Table A2.102: Ratings for Public Sector Public–Private Partnership Support Capacity and Experience in Sri Lanka

#	Determinant	Rating
3	If payment is likely to be made by the parent government, what is the credit rating of the parent government?	0
4	Is there a specialized government agency (or agencies) established for PPP purposes (e.g., PPP unit) and what are its roles?	2
5	Is there a streamlined approval process for PPP projects?	1
6	Does the sponsoring agency have previous experience with PPPs?	2
7	Are different PPP concession models defined for the sector and are model concession agreements available?	0

PPP = public–private partnership.

Source: Study team analysis.

Determinants 4 and 5: Sri Lanka has one appraisal stage for the preparation of PPP projects. The preparation of a financial and technical viability report on PPP projects, before the launch of a request for proposals, is mandatory. Approval by the Ministry of Finance or another ministry is required before a project can commence. Approval for a PPP project has to be obtained on the basis of the viability report; the relevant ministry, with the assistance of the Bureau of Infrastructure, has to submit the project to the Ministry of Finance for clearance, and a memorandum has to be submitted to the Cabinet for its approval. A common practice is to appoint independent and qualified advisors internationally to assist the government with project preparation.

Determinant 6: Sri Lanka has achieved financial closure for three transport infrastructure projects since 1996 leading to a lack of experience in PPP project structuring and implementation.

Determinant 7: Sri Lanka has no infrastructure sector-specific (e.g., road, rail, and port) model concession agreements.

Public Sector Funding Assistance for Public–Private Partnerships

Determinant 8: Projects may require support from the public sector in terms of viability gap funding, government guarantees, or availability-based payments to attract private sector participation. From 1990 to 2017, no PPP projects in Sri Lanka received government support in the form of viability gap funding, 25 received government guarantees, and 67 availability-based payments.

Table A2.103: Ratings for Public Sector Funding Assistance in Public–Private Partnerships in Sri Lanka

#	Determinant	Rating
8	Is government support for viability gap funding available for PPP projects?	0

PPP = public–private partnership.

Source: Study team analysis.

Land Acquisition and Environmental and Social Clearances

Determinant 9: The State Lands Ordinance regulates the grant and disposition of state land in Sri Lanka and the management and control of lands and foreshores. It also regulates the use of lakes and public streams. Under the ordinance, the President can make absolute or provisional grants of state land; sell, lease, or otherwise dispose of state land or enter into agreements for the same purposes; issue permits for the occupation of state land; issue licenses to take or obtain any substance or thing found on state land; and sell or lease the right to mine on state land.

Determinant 10: Under the Land (Restrictions on Alienation) Act, 2014 the Minister of Finance can, if certain provisions are met, exempt a foreign entity in engaged in banking, financial services, insurance, maritime, aviation, advanced technology, and infrastructure development project classified as strategic from the act.

Table A2.104: Ratings for Land Acquisition and Environmental and Social Clearances in Sri Lanka

#	Determinant	Rating
9	Does the authority have experience in dealing with land acquisitions, environmental clearances, and rehabilitation and resettlement?	1
10	Does the authority have a dedicated team to streamline land acquisitions and environmental clearances, and the experience to handle these areas?	0

Source: Study team analysis.

The National Environmental Act, 1980 makes environmental impact assessments mandatory. An assessment is a formal study used to assess the environmental impact of a proposed major development project. It identifies the natural resource constraints and other issues that could affect a project's viability. It also contains an environmental cost–benefit analysis if one has been done. An initial environmental examination report may also be required. This report assesses the significance of any impacts identified in the environmental impact assessment.

Table A2.105: Land Acquisition Support by the Government in Sri Lanka

Land Acquisition Support	✓/×
Resettlement and compensation costs to residents	✓
Imposed limits on time frame to complete land acquisition	×
Dedicated agency to streamline land acquisition	×
Exemption from or reduction of land use fees	×

Source: Asian Development Bank. 2017. *Public–Private Partnership Monitor.* Manila. https://www.adb.org/publications/public-private-partnership-monitor.

The National Involuntary Resettlement Policy, 2001 ensures that people affected by infrastructure projects are fairly and adequately compensated and relocated, and livelihoods protected; delays in project implementation and cost overruns are reduced. The policy also aims to make the transitions smooth for those being relocated and host communities alike. The 2008 Cabinet of Ministers approved the National Policy on Payment of Compensation, which established a uniform compensation system based on the Land Acquisition Act, the National Involuntary Resettlement Policy, and several other laws applicable to land acquisition and resettlement. The policy superseded ad hoc and special compensation packages used by government agencies, including the Road Development Authority.

Market Capacity and Foreign Participation

Determinant 11: Market capacity is limited because PPPs are at an early stage of development; there have been only two PPP port projects.

Determinant 12: The Foreign Exchange Act, 2017 provides that foreign individuals and entities can invest in all classes of shares of companies incorporated in Sri Lanka.

Determinant 13: The Land Act prohibits transfers of land titles to foreigners, foreign companies, and companies with 50% or more direct or indirect foreign shareholding. Exemptions can be granted, e.g., in case of infrastructure development projects that have been identified as strategic development projects, in terms of the provisions of the Strategic Development Projects Act of 2008.[53]

Determinant 14: Guidelines on PPPs are silent on the types of government support that can be provided in PPP contracts. Under the law, the state is required to pay resettlement and/or compensation costs to affected residents.[54]

Table A2.106: Ratings for Market Capacity and Foreign Participation in Sri Lanka

#	Determinant	Rating
11	Is there sufficient market capacity and do private players have PPP experience?	1
12	Is foreign participation in PPP allowed?	3
13	Are there any restrictions on foreign investors' land use and/or ownership (i.e., do foreign investors have the same rights as locals?)	2
14	If payments are likely to be made from the authority's budget, is there any form of government guarantee available for these payments?	1
15	Is the exchange rate stable?	0
16	Is there a robust project finance market, which supplements the traditional corporate finance market?	1
17	Are debt instruments available for different project needs, such as senior, mezzanine, and subordinate debt, and take-out financing?	0

PPP = public–private partnership.

Source: Study team analysis.

[53] Government of Sri Lanka. 2008. Strategic Development Projects Acts of 2008. Colombo.

[54] Government of Sri Lanka. 1978. Board of Investment Law No. 4 of 1978. Colombo.

Table A2.107 shows the risks covered by government guarantees in Sri Lanka. Government guarantees for currency inconvertibility and transfer risk, and foreign exchange and expropriation risks, can be provided through the agreement entered into by the developer with the Board of Investment, under section 17 of the Board of Investment Law, 1990.

Table A2.107: Risks Covered by Government Guarantees in Sri Lanka

Risk	
Currency inconvertibility and transfer risk	✓
Foreign exchange risk	✓
War and civil disturbance risk	✓
Breach of contract risk	✓
Regulatory risk	✓
Expropriation risk	✓
Government payment obligation guarantee	✓
Credit guarantees	✓
Minimum demand/revenue guarantee	✓

Source: Asian Development Bank. 2017. *Public–Private Partnership Monitor.* Manila. https://www.adb.org/publications/public-private-partnership-monitor.

Determinant 15: As for exchange rate risks, Sri Lanka has very high currency fluctuations and volatility leading to higher hedging costs for long-term investments.

Determinant 16: Most infrastructure projects in Sri Lanka are funded by loans obtained by the government, often bilateral loans or loans from multilateral agencies and, to a lesser extent, loans from local banks.[55] There have been either very few or no instances of infrastructure projects being funded by pension funds or from the capital market. State banks have been far more involved in financing of government infrastructure projects than the private banks.

Determinant 17: Usually, guarantees for debt repayment for infrastructure projects are given by the Treasury on behalf of the government, and this has been the most acceptable form of guarantee to all banks. Most private banks are wary of accepting guarantees from other government agencies, especially those that do not have revenue-generating capacity. But they are active lenders to profitable state-owned entities with assured cash flows and the ability to repay. Banks typically take mortgage rights on project assets when lending to infrastructure projects, but they evaluate a project's cash-generating capacity rather than the assets that can be mortgaged.

Payments by a government agency are usually paid into an account maintained at the lending bank. The lender does not usually take mortgage rights over the shares of the project company. While there is an appetite for PPPs by domestic investors, there are indications of significant liquidity constraints in the domestic market in terms of debt amounts and tenors available. One of the main reasons for the liquidity constraints has been the crowding-out effect of high levels of public borrowing. Commercial banks typically have limited capabilities to hedge their interest rate risk as Sri Lanka's swap markets are underdeveloped. Given the low amount of capital that many banks have in Sri Lanka, there is also the possibility that single borrower limits will prevent many domestic investors from raising the amounts of debt they would require for financing larger PPPs.[56]

---

55 Central Bank of Myanmar. 2020. *Annual Report 2019–2020.* Yangon. https://www.cbm.gov.mm/sites/default/files/report/2021/Annual%20Report%202019-2020.pdf.

56 ADB. 2016. *Sri Lanka Capital Market Assessment.* Manila. https://www.adb.org/projects/documents/sri-cmdp-capital-market-assessment-tacr.

Life-Cycle Cost and Output Specifications

Determinants 18 and 19: Sri Lanka has considerable experience in transport infrastructure projects to be able to quantify construction and long-term operation costs, as well as output specifications.

Table A2.108: Ratings for Life-Cycle Cost and Output Specifications in Sri Lanka

#	Determinant	Rating
18	Can most of the costs, mainly related to construction and long-term operations, including maintenance, be quantified upfront with reasonable assumptions, and are historical data available?	3
19	Are objective output specifications readily available from a previous contract?	3

Source: Study team analysis.

Possible Interventions

Sri Lanka should improve and strengthen the enabling environment for PPPs and explore ways to enhance revenue (e.g., LVC and non-toll revenue, such as advertisements, privately owned public spaces) to increase government investable capital, improve project viability, and unlock capital investment in operational projects through asset securitization (e.g., InvITs and toll securitization) and asset recycling (e.g., toll–operate–transfer).

The government is collecting tolls on 270 km of expressways classified as class E roads by the Road Development Authority. The government pools together these roads for asset recycling. Appendix 18 lists Sri Lanka's toll roads. The government could also identify non-strategically important ports—the country has many commercial ports—that could be bundled for asset recycling.

Table A2.109 summarizes the key recommended interventions to augment the use of financing tools, banks and other financial institutions, and the capital market to reduce PPP-related risks in Sri Lanka.

Table A2.109: Summary of Recommended Finance Sector Interventions for Sri Lanka

#	Finance Sector	Issues	Actions
1	Commercial banks	Restrictions on cost of lending, which limits profitability opportunities and so reduces investment in infrastructure	Ideally, the risk profile of construction-stage infrastructure projects is much higher than in the operation stage. Because banks may not be willing to take up the construction risk if lending rates are capped, the government could explore options for removing the interest rate cap for infrastructure projects.
2	Foreign direct investment	Need to improve ease of doing business and reduce policy uncertainty	Sri Lanka can attract investors by working on the parameters where its score is low in the World Bank's Doing Business survey, including property registration, getting credit, and enforcing contracts.
		High currency hedging costs due to currency volatility	Land reforms to improve governance and access to foreign investors.
			Long-term strategies and policies for providing policy continuity and guiding paths.

continued on next page

Table A2.109 *continued*

#	Finance Sector	Issues	Actions
3	Debt capital market	Inefficient primary government securities bond market	Auction calendars should be published, and benchmark issuances increased. Auctions should be held as announced.
			Enhanced capital base of primary dealers.
			Create an electronic trading platform that enables multilateral negotiations to take place, i.e., an enhanced request-for-quote trading platform.
		Limited demand for securities	Increase allocation of pension funds to corporate bonds.
			Promotion and awareness campaigns to increase retail participation in insurance and mutual funds (unit trusts).
		Fragmented and weak intermediate industry	Adopt a universal brokerage model where market intermediaries deal in all capital market products.
			Expand the financial industry qualification framework to include multiple capital market instruments.
			Develop and implement a comprehensive framework for risk-based minimum capital requirements for market intermediaries.

Source: Study team analysis.

Thailand

Transport Infrastructure Financing Landscape

Sources of Transport Infrastructure Financing

Thailand's transport infrastructure financing needs are primarily financed through internal and external budgetary sources and the investments of state-owned enterprises (SOEs). SOEs raise money mostly through the internal accrual of cash flows and sale of assets, such as bonds serviced by future cash flows. Insurance companies, and pension and mutual funds, are among the main subscribers for these bonds. These sources of financing through government support for transport infrastructure contribute to about 6.5% of GDP annually.

The government's flagship Eastern Economic Corridor comprises infrastructure projects worth about $21 billion. Thailand has planned PPP projects worth B1.1 trillion over 2020–2027 under the Master Plan on the Infrastructure and Social Development, which itself falls under the National Strategy, 2018–2037 (Figure A2.70). This indicates that a financing gap of 2.5% of GDP per year would need to be bridged compared with the existing investment of about 10% of GDP.

Fiscal Support to Infrastructure

Thailand's general government debt burden was 45.8% in FY2020. The Public Debt Management Office expects Thailand's ratio of public debt-to-GDP to rise to nearly 58% in FY2021 due to government spending to mitigate the impact of COVID-19 and lower revenue collection in FY2021 (ended 31 March 2021) (Figure A2.71).

In 2020, all three global credit rating agencies revised Thailand's sovereign outlook from positive to stable, citing sustained weakness in FDI inflows as the current sharp economic shock is likely to compound delays to policy making over the next several years (Table A2.110).

Figure A2.70: Thailand's Current Financing Sources and Annual Transport Infrastructure Financing Need
(% of GDP)

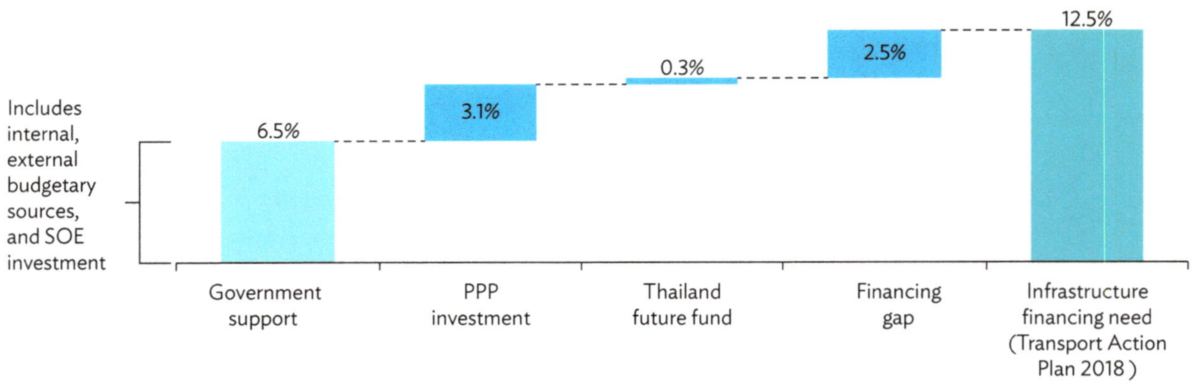

GDP = gross domestic product, PPP = public–private partnership, SOE = state-owned enterprise.

Source: Ministry of Transport calculations based on the Financing of Transport Action Plan, 2018.

Figure A2.71: Thailand Government Debt, FY2015–FY2020
(% of GDP)

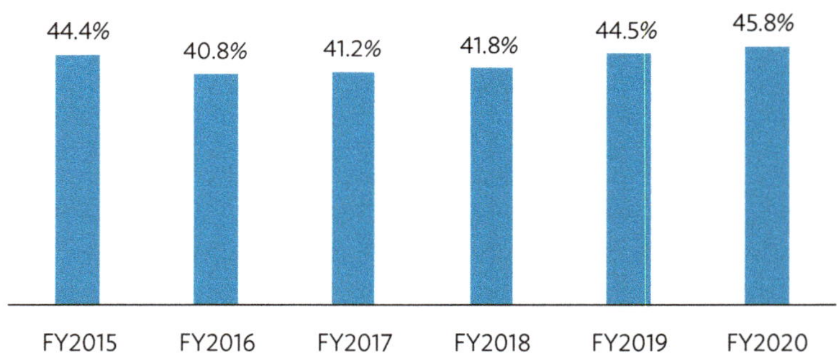

FY = fiscal year, GDP = gross domestic product.

Note: FY ends 31 December.

Source: Study team analysis; and secondary sources.

Table A2.110: Thailand's Sovereign Ratings and Outlook by Global Credit Rating Agencies

Agency	Rating	Outlook	Date
Fitch	BBB+ affirmed	Revised from Positive to Stable	17 March 2020
Moody's	Baa1 affirmed	Revised from Positive to Stable	21 April 2020
Standard and Poor's Global Ratings	BBB+ affirmed	Revised from Positive to Stable	14 April 2020

Sources: Sovereign rating updates from Fitch Ratings, Moody's Investors Service, and S&P Global Ratings.

Although the economic impact of COVID-19 has narrowed the scope for international borrowing, Thailand's transport sector SOEs have ample surpluses in their balance sheets to finance short-timeline projects. Since FY2018, the budget allocation for transport infrastructure has been 4%–5% of the total budget allocation, with capital expenditure accounting for about 90% of this allocation (Figure A2.72).

Figure A2.72: Budget Allocation for Transport Infrastructure in Thailand, FY2018 and FY2019

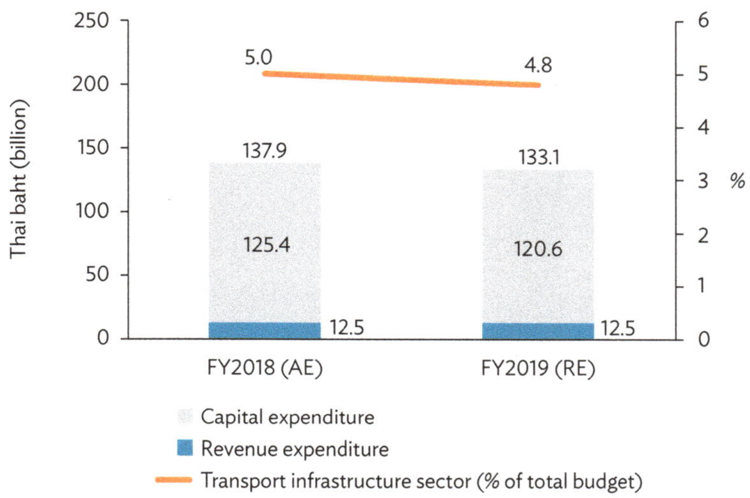

AE = actual expenditure, FY = fiscal year, RE = revised expenditure.

Source: Ministry of Thailand. Budget 2019.

In response to the economic distress caused by COVID-19, a B400 billion fiscal package was launched in March 2020, consisting of B150 billion in soft loans, debt payment extensions, and tax benefits, including reduced withholding taxes. The package also provided support for households, including reduced and delayed utility bills. While the government's response is focused on economic recovery through reforms and monetary policy, the focus now could shift to infrastructure due to its multiplier effect on creating jobs and lifting growth. And, as noted earlier, SOEs have the resources to finance key projects in the infrastructure pipeline.

Bridging the Financing Gap

Because the government's ability to support transport infrastructure projects is restricted by the Fiscal Sustainability Framework, which stipulates that the ratio of public debt-to-GDP must be under 60%, private sector support is needed to augment government sources of financing. Figure A2.73 shows financial institutions based on total investable capital (as a percentage of GDP) and their contribution to infrastructure financing (as a percentage of their capital base).

Thailand's commercial banks and insurance and mutual funds have a large total investable capital base. The commercial banking sector is mature, led by Bangkok Bank, Kasikornbank, and Krung Thai Bank. Thailand also has a well-developed bond market for channeling capital market funds for infrastructure development. Pension and insurance funds, as well as the Infrastructure Future Fund, (named Thailand Future Fund), are key private sources of infrastructure financing.

Figure A2.73: Thailand's Financial Institution Mapping

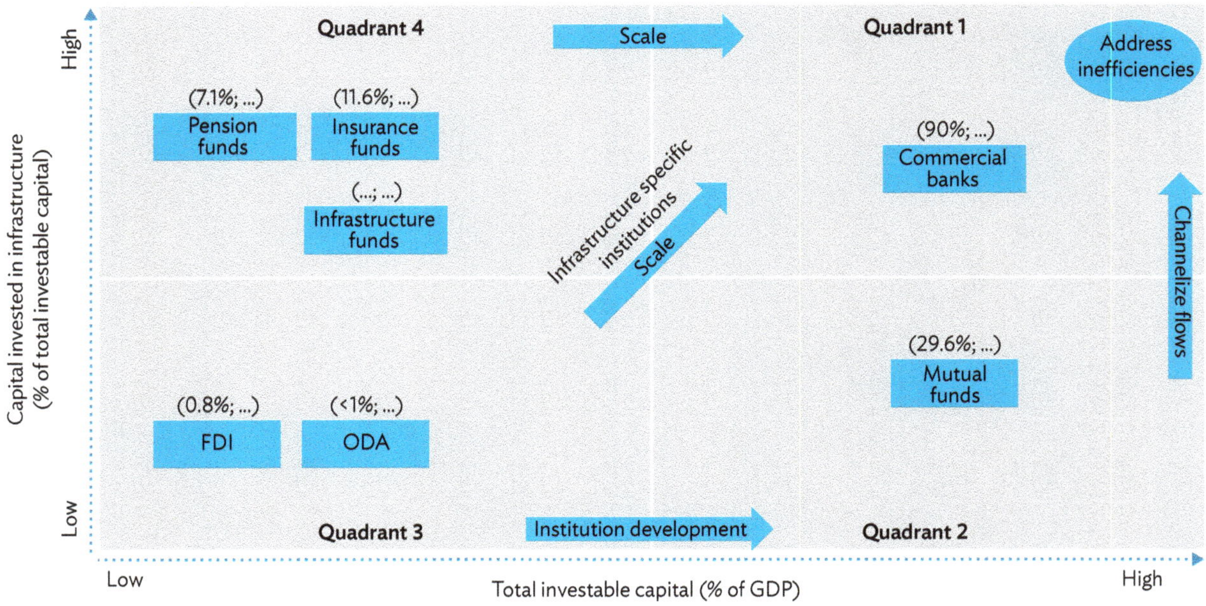

... = not available, FDI = foreign direct investment, GDP = gross domestic product, NBFI = nonbank financial institutions, ODA = official development assistance.

Notes:

1. Percentage figures provide a comparative measure and are based on latest available data.
2. Institutions for which data are not available are placed based on inputs from primary and secondary research.

Sources: Central Bank of Thailand; and secondary sources.

Challenges of Developing Thailand's Financing Institutions for Investing in Transport Infrastructure

Commercial Banks

Thailand's banking system is highly leveraged in terms of loans as a percentage of GDP (93% in 2019). This was the highest rate of leverage among BIMSTEC countries. Households are the biggest borrowers of Thai commercial banks: the ratio of household debt-to-GDP ratio was 79.1% in the third quarter of 2019, one of the highest among Association of Southeast Asian Nations countries. Commercial banks have limited capacity for financing infrastructure, which typically requires long-term financing, because of high locked-in capital in the household sector and the decreasing tenure of deposits.

Thailand's deposit rate has been decreasing in recent years, leading to shorter deposit tenures (Figure A2.74). The term deposit rate of a tenure of 2 years or more declined from 3.0% in 2014 to 1.8% in 2019. The share of term deposits of a tenure of 2 years or more as a share of total deposits declined to 2.0% in 2019. Because infrastructure projects have long gestation periods, financing through commercial loans is difficult. A bridge to bond financing transport infrastructure can be explored as Thailand's bond market develops to increase the exposure of commercial banks to the infrastructure sector.

Figure A2.74: Term Deposit Rate in Thailand, 2014–2019

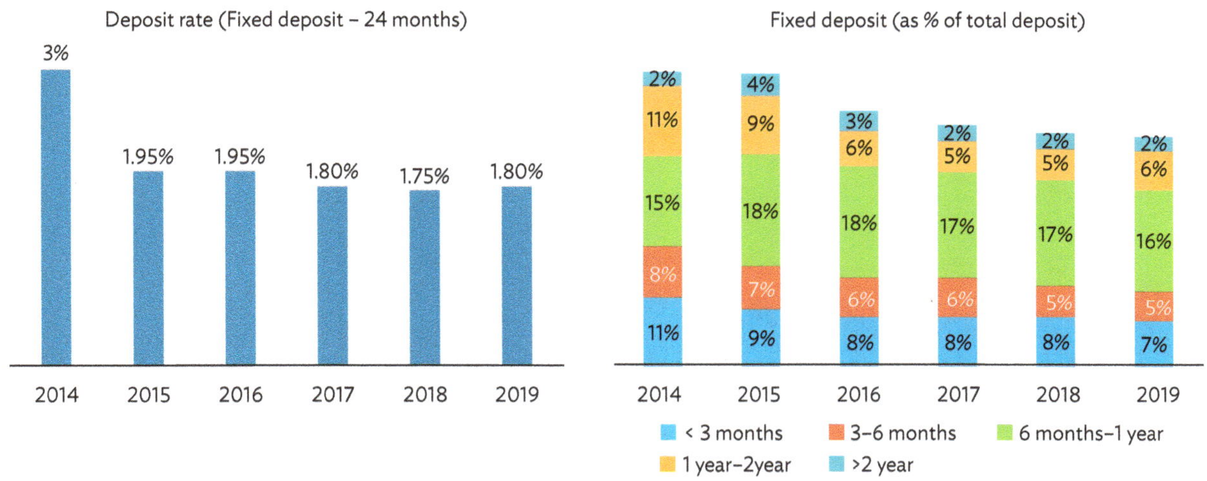

Notes:
1. A time deposit or term deposit is a deposit in a financial institution with a specific maturity date or a period to maturity, commonly referred to as its "term."
2. Current account and savings account deposit is the amount of money that gets deposited in the current and savings account of bank customers.

Sources: Bank of Thailand. 2019. *Financial Stability Report 2019*. Bangkok. https://www.bot.or.th/en/research-and-publications/reports/financial-stability-report.html.

Other key sources for infrastructure financing in Thailand are pension, insurance, and infrastructure funds (e.g., Thailand Future Fund). The country's developed capital market has helped channel flows from these institutional investors to infrastructure. The bond market is also well developed, and government and corporate debt securities are actively traded. Still, Thailand needs to balance further bond market development with maintaining fiscal stability. This will require increasing nonresident bond issues in the domestic market and encouraging onshore and offshore bond issuances.

Foreign Direct Investment

FDI in Thailand declined to $4.1 billion in 2019 from $10.4 billion in 2018. FDI in greenfield projects fell to $4.6 billion in 2019 from $7.1 billion in in 2018.[57] Thailand, in 2018, had a 2.6% share of the FDI to Southeast Asian countries ($155.8 billion). Combined, the FDI shares of Indonesia, Singapore, and Viet Nam was 84.4% of total FDI in the region. Manufacturing and financial services account for about 70% of FDI in Thailand. Two key issues need to be addressed to enable Thailand to increase FDI: double tax avoidance agreements, particularly with countries that are home to large institutions and individual investors, and high currency hedging costs.

Double tax avoidance agreements. Thailand has bilateral investment treaties with 42 economies, including Germany; Hong Kong, China; India; the People's Republic of China; and the United Kingdom—but not with Cayman Islands, Japan, or Singapore, sources of considerable FDI for Thailand. To attract more investors to infrastructure projects, treaties are needed with these and other economies that are important sources of FDI. Doing this would attract more institutional investors and high net worth individuals.

[57] The United Nations Conference on Trade and Development's World Investment Report 2020.

High currency hedging costs. Thailand's open economy means its currency is vulnerable to exchange rate volatility. Companies in Thailand can use hedging products, which are provided by authorized banks. But the cost is high—and borne by investors. Foreign exchange transaction costs have two components: an exchange fee, at 2.1% of the transaction amount, and a transfer fee of 4.5%. The key action point for Thailand would be engaging more hedging products provided by authorized banks. Doing this would improve Thailand's Doing Business ranking and make the country more attractive to foreign investors.

Public–Private Partnership Capacity Assessment

Public–Private Partnership Law and Policy Support Capacity

Determinant 1: The Public-Private Partnership Act, 2019 is the main policy instrument governing PPP projects in Thailand exceeding a value of B5 billion, as well as certain projects under B5 billion that meet prescribed criteria. The act has four foundational principles:

- **Facilitation.** The act aims to facilitate domestic investment by having PPP applicant-friendly procedures and incentives.
- **Alignment.** PPP projects must align with international standards and best practices.
- **Streamlined.** The act aims to simplify and shorten processes through increased flexibility and enhanced collaboration between the project stakeholders,
- **Transparency.** PPP projects under the act must be transparent and each step of PPP be thoroughly scrutinized.

Determinant 2: The dispute resolution mechanism has to be stated in PPP contracts. Arbitration is possible, provided the project owner can demonstrate the rationale and necessity for embarking on this process. In the past, most disputes have been resolved through negotiation rather than litigation. Court-annexed conciliation and mediation are also options. But processes in the Thai legal system can be lengthy; it usually takes more than 5 years to reach a court ruling.

Table A2.111: Ratings for Public–Private Partnership Law and Policy Support Capacity in Thailand

#	Determinant	Rating
1	Is there a dedicated legal or policy instrument/guideline for PPPs?	3
2	What dispute resolution mechanisms are available for PPP agreements?	3

PPP = public–private partnership.

Source: Study team analysis.

Public Sector Public–Private Partnership Support Capacity and Experience

Determinant 3: All three global credit rating agencies in 2020 revised Thailand's sovereign outlook from positive to stable, citing sustained weakness in FDI inflows as the current sharp economic shock is likely to compound delays to policy making over the next several years.

Determinants 4 and 5: Thailand established the State Enterprise Policy Office to provide policies and strategies related to PPPs, identify PPP projects aligned with strategies, and streamline PPP processes. However, the office has no authority to procure things for SOEs. SOEs have to do the procurement process by themselves under their own charter/act. There are two project appraisal stages, and 3–4 approvals need to be obtained to get the green light for project procurement. The approval of the Ministry of Finance or other ministry is also required before procurement can commence. Table A2.113 shows the required project feasibility analyses that need to be done for PPP projects.

Table A2.112: Ratings for Public Sector Public–Private Partnership Support Capacity and Experience in Thailand

#	Determinant	Rating
3	If payment is likely to be made by the parent government, what is the credit rating of the parent government?	3
4	Is there a specialized government agency (or agencies) established for PPP purposes (e.g., PPP unit) and what are its roles?	2
5	Is there a streamlined approval process for PPP projects?	3
6	Does the sponsoring agency have previous experience with PPPs?	3
7	Are different PPP concession models defined for the sector and are model concession agreements available?	0

PPP = public–private partnership.

Source: Study team analysis.

Table A2.113: Feasibility Analyses Required for Public–Private Partnership Projects in Thailand

Type of Analysis	✓/×
Technical feasibility	✓
Financial feasibility	✓
Legal feasibility	✓
Environmental and social sustainability	✓
Value for money assessment	✓
Fiscal affordability assessment	✓
PPP structuring and risk allocation	✓
Initial market testing	✓

PPP = public–private partnership.

Source: Asian Development Bank. 2017. *Public–Private Partnership Monitor*. Manila. https://www.adb.org/publications/public-private-partnership-monitor.

Determinant 6: Thailand has achieved financial closure for 30 transport infrastructure projects since 1996 which gives it considerable experience in PPP project structuring and implementation.

Determinant 7: Each PPP project is implemented by its own contracting agency or SOE, but for these projects, there are limited sector-specific (e.g., road, rail, ports) model concession agreements. This results in the lengthy process of drawing up project-specific concession agreements involving multiple approval processes between private stakeholders and contracting agencies—and because of this the private party sometimes loses interest.

Public Sector Funding Assistance for Public–Private Partnerships

Determinant 8: Projects may require support from the public sector in terms of viability gap funding, government guarantees, or availability-based payments to attract private sector participation. Table A2.115 shows the number of PPP projects that received government support in Thailand from 1990 to 2017.[58]

[58] Asian Development Bank. 2017. *Public–Private Partnership Monitor*. Manila. https://www.adb.org/publications/public-private-partnership-monitor.

Table A2.114: Ratings for Public Sector Funding Assistance in Public–Private Partnerships in Thailand

#	Determinant	Rating
8	Is government support for viability gap funding available for PPP projects?	3

PPP = public–private partnership.

Source: Study team analysis.

The Public–Private Partnership Act, 2019 does not explicitly address viability gap funding. It is up to the relevant government authority to determine how much capital to contribute to a PPP project based on the project's feasibility study and financial plan, and also the ability of the government to raise funds.

The government typically finances all or part of public transport projects, either through the budget or borrowing from multilateral institutions. Other contributions, such as equity, are also allowed under each project agency's establishment act.

Table A2.115: Government Support for Public–Private Partnership Projects in Thailand, 1990–2017

Support type	Number of Projects
Viability gap funding	4
Government guarantees	58
Availability and performance-based payments	117

Source: Asian Development Bank. 2017. *Public–Private Partnership Monitor*. Manila. https://www.adb.org/publications/public-private-partnership-monitor.

Land acquisition and Environmental and Social Clearances

Determinant 9: The key regulations governing land use rights and land acquisition are the Land Code Amendment Act, 2008, the Expropriation of Immovable Property Act, 1987, and Procurement of Immovable Property for Public Transportation Affair Act, 1997 (the latter for the use of immovable property without transferring of ownership).

The objectives of land use and the land boundaries of each project must be specified and issued in a royal decree. A compensation committee is then appointed to set the property value and amount. The right to develop the land is then transferred to the concessionaire for the duration of the concession period.

Table A2.116: Ratings for Land Acquisition and Environmental and Social Clearances in Thailand

#	Determinant	Rating
9	Does the authority have experience in dealing with land acquisitions, environmental clearances, and rehabilitation and resettlement?	2
10	Does the authority have a dedicated team to streamline land acquisitions and environmental clearances, and the experience to handle these areas?	0

Source: Study team analysis.

The Public–Private Partnership Act requires that PPP contracts have a provision for project assets, including the ownership and valuation of these assets. The draft standard PPP contract assumes that detailed arrangements on the ownership of land and project assets are decided between the parties.

Table A2.117: Government Support for Land Acquisition in Thailand

Land Acquisition Support	✓/×
Resettlement and compensation costs to residents	✓
Imposed limits on time frame to complete land acquisition	×
Dedicated agency to streamline land acquisition	×
Exemption from and reduction of land use fees	✓

Source: Asian Development Bank. *Public–Private Partnership Monitor*. Manila. https://www.adb.org/publications/public-private-partnership-monitor.

Determinant 10: The National Environmental Quality Act, 1992 is the law governing environmental matters in Thailand. The act defines the types of projects that require environmental impact assessments, environmental health impact assessments, and an initial environmental examination. Before commencing a project, investors should make sure they are familiar with the act's provisions or seek advice on this from the Environmental Impact Evaluation Bureau. In practice, an environmental impact assessment for most PPP projects is done by the host government agency before the issuance of a request for proposal. The environmental impact assessment also incorporates any social impact assessments that have been done for a project. The government is allowed to acquire land or immovable assets for public utilities or in the public interest under the Expropriation of Immovable Property Act. The cost of compensation and resettlement of local residents is managed by the government. Separate authorities need to be approached for land acquisitions and environmental and social clearances, which impedes the project implementation timelines in some cases.

Market Capacity and Foreign Participation

Determinant 11: Interest in private participation in transport infrastructure sector has increased in Thailand over the past decade. The country now has a well-established market of domestic and foreign private developers who have participated in infrastructure projects through PPP exits. Market capacity is sufficient and there are many private developers in Thailand with construction experience.

Determinants 12 and 13: Land ownership and usage laws is one of the key factors considered by the foreign shareholders in PPP transport infrastructure projects. However, Thailand's Land Law prevents foreigners and foreign-owned companies from owning land except in special circumstances and when authorized by the Board of Investment. Foreigners can either lease the land or enter into a joint venture with a local partner that provides land use rights. The typical lease term is 30 years with the possibility of renewing for an additional 30 years. Because there are difficulties in finding and preparing sites, many investors prefer joint ventures, with the local partner contributing the land and arranging clearances from local authorities for its use.[59]

[59] Government of Thailand. Foreign Business Act, 1999. Bangkok.

Foreign investors are allowed to import machinery and equipment. Taxes and duties can be waived, under certain conditions, by the Board of Investment on these imports.

Determinant 14: A major issue emerging from interviews for this report with private players is the need for government credit guarantees for projects in the BIMSTEC master plan to secure revenue from them. The Public–Private Partnership Act and the Standard Provisions Notification allow PPP contracts to include provisions on guarantees, but neither provide guidance or details on the nature of these provisions. The act states that if a PPP project requires a Ministry of Finance credit guarantee, and that this is approved in principle, the request for a credit guarantee goes to the Council of Ministers for approval; the council also sets the credit guarantee limit. Table A2.119 shows the risks covered by government guarantees.

Determinant 15: As for exchange rate risks, Thailand has very low currency fluctuations and volatility and has strengthened steadily, historically.

Determinant 16: Thailand has a mature local capital market compared with other members of BIMSTEC countries. Project financing is mostly done in the local currency. Foreign banks are willing to finance PPP projects in Thailand, but so far participation has only been in the power sector since the country's independent power producers, large and small, are considered well structured.

Table A2.118: Ratings for Market Capacity and Foreign Participation in Thailand

#	Determinant	Rating
11	Is there sufficient market capacity and do private players have PPP experience?	3
12	Is foreign participation in PPP allowed?	1
13	Are there any restrictions on foreign investors' land use/ownership (i.e., do foreign investors have the same rights as locals?)	1
14	If payments are likely to be made from the authority's budget, is there any form of government guarantee available for these payments?	1
15	Is the exchange rate stable?	3
16	Is there a robust project finance market which supplements the traditional corporate finance market?	3
17	Are debt instruments available for different project needs, such as senior, mezzanine, and subordinate debt, and take-out financing?	3

PPP = public–private partnership.

Source: Study team analysis.

Table A2.119: Risks Covered by Government Guarantees in Thailand

Risk	
Currency inconvertibility and transfer risk	✗
Foreign exchange risk	✗
War and civil disturbance risk	✗
Breach of contract risk	✗
Regulatory risk	✗
Expropriation risk	✗
Government payment obligation guarantee	✓
Credit guarantees	✗
Minimum demand and revenue guarantee	✗

Source: Asian Development Bank. 2017. Public–Private Partnership Monitor. Manila. https://www.adb.org/publications/public-private-partnership-monitor.

Determinant 17: Multilateral agencies and export credit agencies also play an important role in supporting project finance transactions in Thailand. Full or limited recourse is typically provided to sponsors as part of project finance packages, especially to support overruns.

Life-Cycle Cost and Output Specifications

Determinants 18 and 19: Thailand has considerable experience in transport infrastructure projects to be able to quantify construction and long-term operational costs, as well as output specifications.

Table A2.120: Ratings for Life-Cycle Cost and Output Specifications in Thailand

#	Determinant	Rating
18	Can most of the costs, mainly related to construction and long-term operations, including maintenance, be quantified upfront with reasonable assumptions, and are historical data available?	3
19	Are objective output specifications readily available from a previous contract?	3

Source: Study team analysis.

Possible Interventions

Thailand should look at improving and strengthening the enabling environment for PPPs and explore ways to enhance revenue (e.g., LVC; non-toll revenue, such as advertisements; and privately owned public spaces) to increase government investable capital, improve project viability, and unlock capital investment in existing operational projects through asset securitization (e.g., InvITs and toll securitization) and asset recycling (e.g., toll-operate-transfer). In the roads sector, the government could pool the 401 km of expressways and motorways collecting tolls for asset recycling (Appendix 18 lists the toll roads). Thailand has many ports and the nonstrategic ones could be considered for asset recycling.

Table A2.121 summarizes the key recommended interventions to augment the use of financing tools, banks and other financial institutions, and the capital market to reduce PPP-related risks in Thailand.

Table A2.121: Summary of Recommended Finance Sector Interventions for Thailand

#	Finance Sector	Issues	Actions
1	Commercial banks	The deposit tenure of commercial banks is decreasing, which may inhibit lending to infrastructure	Bridge to bond financing can be explored as bond market in Thailand is developed.
2	Foreign direct investment	More double tax avoidance agreements needed with countries that are home to large institutional and individual investors	Enter into bilateral investment treaties with Cayman Islands, Japan, and Singapore, among other countries.
		High currency hedging costs	Use more hedging products that are provided by authorized banks.

Source: Study team analysis.

Public–Private Partnership Capacity Summary

Table A2.122 ranks BIMSTEC countries on a scale of 0 to 3 based on the criteria detailed in the PPP capacity assessment framework in Table A2.1. The table gives a comparative picture of the areas that countries need to work on to improve their capacity to implement transport infrastructure projects through PPPs.

Table A2.122: Public–Private Partnership Capacity of BIMSTEC Countries

Area	Questions	Relevance	BAN	BHU	IND	MYA	NEP	SRI	THA
PPP law, policy support	Is there a dedicated legal or policy instrument or guideline for PPPs?	High	3	3	3	1	3	2	3
PPP law, policy support	What dispute resolution mechanisms are available for PPP agreements?	Medium	2	2	3	0	2	2	1
Public sector PPP capacity and experience	Are different PPP/concession models defined for the sector and sector specific model concession agreements available?	Medium	0	0	3	1	0	0	0
Public sector PPP capacity and experience	Is there a streamlined approval process established and followed by the authority for a project to be approved as a PPP?	Medium	3	3	3	1	3	1	3
Land acquisition and clearances	Does the authority have experience in dealing with land acquisition, environmental clearances, and rehabilitation and resettlement?	High	3	1	3	0	1	1	2
Land acquisition and clearances	Does the authority have a dedicated team to streamline land acquisitions and environmental clearances, and does it have experience handling these areas (in addition to counterparts from relevant departments)?	High	0	0	3	0	3	0	0
Public sector PPP capacity and experience	Is there a specialized government agency (or agencies) established for PPP purposes (e.g., PPP unit) and what are its roles?	Medium	3	3	3	1	3	2	2
Public sector PPP capacity and experience	Does the sponsoring agency have experience with PPPs?	High	2	0	3	1	0	0	3
Creditworthiness of the authority	If payment is likely to be made by the parent government, what is the credit rating of the parent government?	Medium	1	0	3	0	0	0	3

continued on next page

Table A2.122 *continued*

Area	Questions	Relevance	BAN	BHU	IND	MYA	NEP	SRI	THA
Creditworthiness of the authority	If payment is likely to be made from the authority's budget, is there any form of government guarantee available for the payments?	Medium	1	0	3	0	0	1	1
Public sector funding assistance for PPPs	Is government support for viability gap funding available in PPP projects?	High	2	3	3	1	3	0	3
Life-cycle cost	Can most of the costs, mainly related to construction and long-term operations, including maintenance, be quantified upfront with reasonable assumptions, and are historical data available?	High	3	0	3	0	2	3	3
Market capacity and interest	Is there sufficient market capacity and are there private parties with PPP experience?	High	1	0	3	0	0	1	3
Output specifications	Are objective output specifications readily available from a previous contract?	Medium	3	0	3	0	2	3	3
Foreign participation	Is foreign participation in PPPs allowed?	Country specific	3	3	3	3	3	3	1
Foreign participation	Is the exchange rate stable?	Country specific	3	1	2	1	2	0	3
Foreign participation	Are there restrictions on foreign investors' land use/ ownership rights (i.e., are they the same as for local investors)?	Country specific	3	3	2	3	3	2	1
Access to finance	Is there a robust project finance market, which supplements the traditional corporate finance market?	Medium	1	1	2	0	1	1	3
Access to finance	Is there a variety of debt instruments available for different project needs, such as senior, mezzanine, and subordinate debt, and take-out financing?	Medium	1	0	2	0	0	0	3

BAN = Bangladesh, BHU - Bhutan, BIMSTEC = Bay of Bengal Initiative for Multi-Sectoral Technical and Economic Cooperation, IND = India, MYA, Myanmar, NEP = Nepal, PPP = public–private partnership, SRI = Sri Lanka, THA = Thailand.

Sources: Government websites and interviews with government officials and other stakeholders.

COVID-19 Pandemic and Infrastructure Financing

COVID-19 severely affected the infrastructure sector in emerging, developing, and advanced economies. Infrastructure assets have experienced sharp reductions in revenue and under-construction projects have slowed on demand and supply shocks from lockdowns, the forced suspension of services, disruptions to global value chains, and deteriorating financial markets. Figure A2.75 highlights some of the lessons being learned for transport infrastructure from the COVID-19 pandemic and responses from countries globally.

Figure A2.75: COVID-19 Impact on Infrastructure Financing

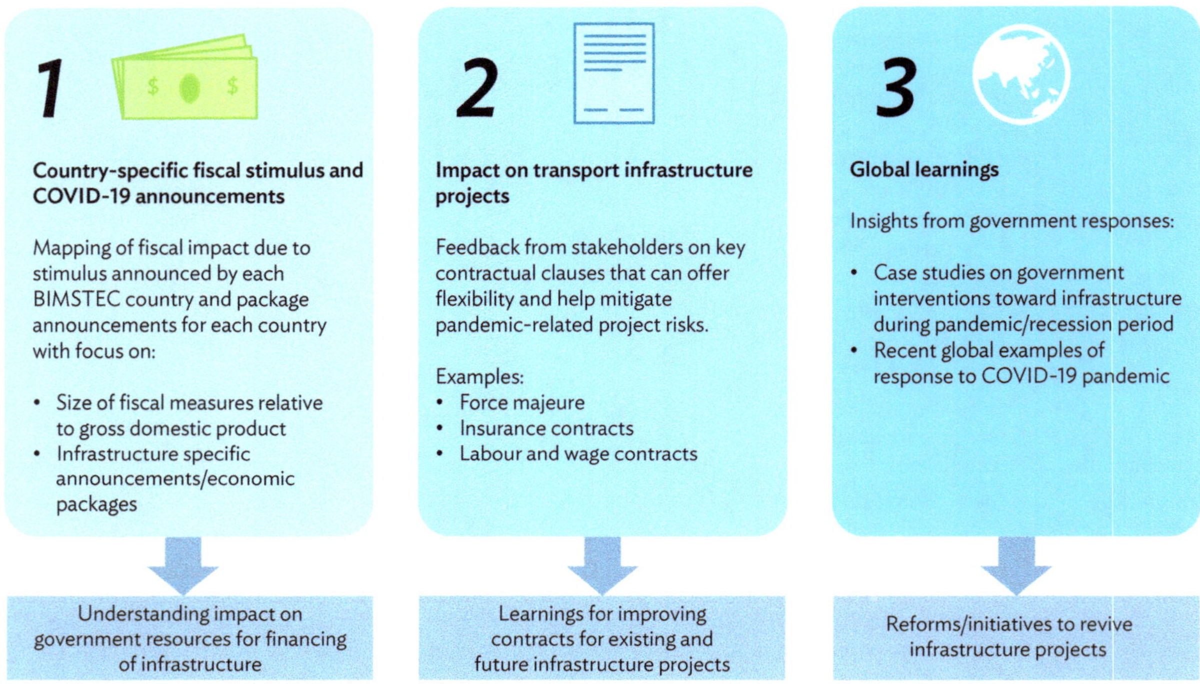

BIMSTEC = Bay of Bengal Initiative for Multi-Sectoral Technical and Economic Cooperation, COVID-19 = coronavirus disease.

Source: Study team analysis.

Country-Specific Fiscal Stimulus and COVID-19 Resilience Initiatives

The COVID-19 pandemic prevented work on multiple infrastructure projects, adversely affecting supply chains, plants, equipment and material, and workers across BIMSTEC countries. In Myanmar, the Request for Proposal deadline for the $1 billion Yangon Elevated Expressway was extended as bidders from Japan, the People's Republic of China, and the Republic of Korea requested an extension due to domestic COVID-19 outbreaks. Multiple projects in Bangladesh by construction companies from the People's Republic of China faced delays because of labor shortages. These projects included a railway from Chittagong to Cox's Bazar, a tunnel under the Karnaphuli River, and upgrading of the Dhaka Bypass Road. The government's priority projects—the Padma Multi-Purpose Bridge and Padma Bridge Rail Link Project—continued during the pandemic. But the pace of these projects slowed significantly due to the shortage of workers.

Across Asia, massive fiscal packages were launched to mitigate the impact of COVID-19 on businesses through tax incentives, grants, and debt restructuring. Government wage subsidy schemes are being used to strengthen social safety nets to cushion the impact of job losses. Central banks adopted monetary-easing measures to inject liquidity and stimulate the real economy through the finance sector.

BIMSTEC countries launched fiscal and nonfiscal stimulus packages, their sizes ranging from 0.1% of GDP to 10%. The Reserve Bank of India reduced the repo and reverse repo rates and announced liquidity measures totaling ₹3.7 trillion (1.8% of GDP) through long-term repo operations, a cut in the cash reserve ratio, and increasing the marginal standing facility to 3% of the statutory liquidity ratio. These measures indirectly provided support to the infrastructure finance market by injecting liquidity, reducing market volatility, and alleviating disruptions to the flow of credit. The Government of India launched numerous schemes that impacted the overall financing. Some of these schemes included:

(i) Platform for Infrastructure Debt Financing: Investment in debt platform of National Investment and Infrastructure Fund—₹6,000 equity
(ii) Support for Agriculture: ₹650 billion for subsidized fertilizers
(iii) Boost for Rural Employment: Additional outlay of ₹100 billion is being provided for PM Garib Kalyan Rozgar Yojana.
(iv) Boost for Project Exports: ₹30 billion boost for project exports through Indian Development and Economic Assistance Scheme
(v) Capital and Industrial Stimulus: ₹10.2 billion additional budget stimulus provided for capital and industrial expenditure on industrial infrastructure, green energy, etc.
(vi) Aatma Nirbhar Bharat Rozgar Yojana: To incentivize job creation during COVID-19 recovery
(vii) Emergency Credit Line Guarantee Scheme for micro, small, and medium-sized enterprises, businesses, MUDRA borrowers, and individuals
(viii) Production Linked Incentive: Worth ₹1.46 trillion to 10 champion sectors
(ix) Additional outlay for PM Awaas Yojana – Urban affordable housing plan ₹180 billion
(x) Support for Construction & Infrastructure: Relaxation of norms (Earnest Deposit Money & Performance Security) on Government Tenders
(xi) Income Tax Relief for Developers & Home Buyers: Differential between circle rate and agreement value in real estate income tax increased from 10% to 20% for a limited period

Bangladesh launched an economic stimulus package of Tk730 billion. Thailand's totaled B1.9 trillion, of which B400 billion is planned economic and social rehabilitation through projects aimed at creating jobs, strengthening communities, and building infrastructure. Sri Lanka, with its limited fiscal resources, launched, in March 2020, a cash transfer program totaling 0.1% of GDP for vulnerable groups. All these initiatives are meant to support waning demand caused by the pandemic.

The Government of Nepal announced, in July 2020, on a relief, recovery, and resilience strategy to help the country's economy emerge stronger from the COVID-19 crisis. The strategy will be critical for boosting the economy and enhancing trade facilitation. Measures include the Strategic Road Connectivity and Trade Improvement Project, which supports connectivity and trade with neighboring countries. In Bhutan, the government is fast-tracking the 12th Five-Year Plan that has infrastructure as a focus sector.

The pandemic has also caused significant supply-side disruptions. In the medium-to-long term, the private sector must play a key role in addressing these disruptions by contributing its knowledge, innovation, and efficiency to the delivery and operation of infrastructure, such as improving the efficiency of transportation links, logistics nodes, and supply chain networks.

As countries start to recover from the pandemic, PPP will become an important mode for leveraging private sector resources to develop infrastructure and create jobs. But this will by no means eliminate the public sector's role in funding and supporting these projects through, among other things, availability payments and minimum revenue guarantees.

Impact on Transport Infrastructure Projects

The international response to the rapid disruption to key infrastructure industries from the COVID-19 pandemic was ongoing at the time of writing. Table A2.123 summarizes the policy responses by BIMSTEC countries to the challenges faced by infrastructure projects during the pandemic.

Table A2.123: BIMSTEC Country Policy Responses to Infrastructure Challenges during COVID-19

Project Stage	Impact on Transport Infrastructure Projects from COVID-19	Policy/Response	BIMSTEC Country Examples
Planned projects	Limited private investment: COVID-19 resulted in demand uncertainty, impeding private sector investment in new projects.	Increase use of alternative sources of financing	Setting up a regional development fund: The Government of India allocated ₹200 billion to set up and capitalize a financial institution to act as a provider, enabler, and catalyst for infrastructure financing. A ₹5 trillion lending portfolio is to be created under the financial institution. Setting up a bad bank: In India, National Asset Reconstruction Company is ready to acquire stressed assets worth ₹828 billion involving 38 nonperforming assets in phases – 15 nonperforming assets accounts involving ₹503.4 billion by 31 March 2022 and the balance in the next fiscal year. This will indirectly create lending capacity for banks to increase lending to various sectors, including infrastructure.
	Limited fiscal space for government investment: Some BIMSTEC countries have limited fiscal room for infrastructure development because of high debt-to-GDP levels and lower revenue stemming from slower growth.	Increased private procurement of infrastructure and PPP projects	• Thailand plans PPP projects worth B1.09 trillion over 2020–2027 to revive its pandemic-hit economy. The 92-project plan includes 18 priority infrastructure projects worth B472 billion. • Bangladesh, under its 7th Five-Year Plan, needs to spend 6% of its GDP—nearly Tk1.3 trillion—on physical infrastructure and the service sector a year to achieve the development goals of Vision 2021 and Vision 2041. Of this, the share of PPP is estimated at 1.8% of GDP—$4.5 billion—a year, 30% of total investment in infrastructure and the service sector.

continued on next page

Table A2.123 *continued*

Project Stage	Impact on Transport Infrastructure Projects from COVID-19	Policy/Response	BIMSTEC Country Examples
Under-construction projects	Contractual disputes: COVID-19 led to many contractual defaults in the infrastructure sector, which, based on contract terms, could lead to termination, penalties, and other coercive actions against various parties.	Providing legal clarity on whether COVID-19 can lead to the invocation of force majeure clauses	In India, the Ministry of Finance clarified that the disruption of supply chains due to COVID-19 should be considered a natural calamity, suggesting that force majeure clauses could be invoked following due procedures, thereby offering contractual protection and relief to affected parties.
	Construction delays.	Time period extensions	Extension of time periods for contractor/ concessionaire by a period of 3–6 months, depending on site conditions in Bangladesh, India, and Thailand.
	Material cost increase and labor shortages.	Financial assistance and credit lines	• Vigilance action on raw material hoarding by traders in India. • Relax payment of security deposits. • The National Highways Authority of India providing timely and direct payments to contractors and special COVID-19 loans.
	Health risks for workers.	Standard operating procedures in accordance with government guidelines	In India's Eastern Dedicated Freight Corridor, protocols were set for staggered work at congested locations, checking and quarantining workers and supplies, inspecting and sanitizing work sites, and controlling access.
Operational projects	Cash flow disruptions due to reduced revenue (e.g., reduced tariffs, lower demand for airports and toll roads in the availability payment model	Lengthening concession agreements	• Airports of Thailand extended long-term commercial contracts awarded last year by King Power International Group and its subsidiaries by a year until 31 March 2032 in response to the COVID-19 crisis. • The National Highways Authority of India offered extensions of contract periods to private concessionaires affected by COVID-19 outbreaks and a nationwide lockdown.
		Adjusting guarantee payments	Airports of Thailand agreed to adjust minimum annual guarantee payment conditions due from Bangkok Suvarnabhumi Airport concessionaire until passenger traffic exceeds the forecasts made in the bid for 2021.

BIMSTEC = Bay of Bengal Initiative for Multi-Sectoral Technology and Economic Cooperation, COVID-19 = coronavirus disease, GDP = gross domestic product, PPP = public–private partnership.

Sources: News articles and reports available in public domain.

Global Learning Lessons for Infrastructure Projects

Infrastructure development has a huge multiplier effect by enhancing economic activity and generating jobs. This means the final impact it has on economic output is greater than the initial investment made. Infrastructure investment is therefore crucial for creating a positive legacy of economic growth that is more resilient, sustainable, and productive. Table A2.124 looks at measures taken globally by economies during the COVID-19 pandemic to revive their respective infrastructure sectors.

Table A2.124: COVID-19 Impact on Infrastructure Projects and Policy Responses

COVID-19 Impact	Policy/Response	Countries
Public finance projects: Delay in rollout and implementation/temporary suspension of pipeline	Prioritizing essential infrastructure and key recovery-phase projects	The People's Republic of China, Peru, Viet Nam
Public–private partnership projects (PPP): Construction delays due to supply chain interruptions and movement restrictions	Extending commercial operations date/temporary relief of key performance indicators	India, United Kingdom
	Providing liquidity lines, guarantee or credit enhancement funds to ensure liquidity access to companies	Germany, Spain
	Resuming activities, especially priority projects	Canada, Colombia, Malaysia, the People's Republic of China, Viet Nam
PPPs: Cash flow disruptions due to reduced revenue (e.g., reduced tariffs, lower demand, such as for airports and toll roads)	Lengthening concession periods	Colombia, Malaysia
PPPs: Cash disruptions due to availability payment model	Identifying essential services and projects, and continuing instruction payments	India
State owned-enterprises: Tariff reductions for utilities, reduced schedules for transportation	Subsidizing tariff reductions	Malaysia
	Transferring operating risks to government	United Kingdom
	Resuming activities, especially priority projects	Canada, Colombia, Malaysia, the People's Republic of China, Viet Nam
State-owned enterprises: Limited financial flexibility due to reduced access to financial markets (e.g., from sovereign downgrades)	Providing liquidity lines	

Sources: News articles and reports available in public domain.

Table A2.125 looks at how Europe and the United States used infrastructure investments to help deal with two past crises: the Great Depression and the Great Recession.

Table A2.125: Infrastructure Investment in Europe and the United States as a Response to Past Crises

Crisis	Infrastructure Investment Response
Great Depression 1929	**United States** New Deal: An array of projects and programs. These included 650,000 miles of road, 78,000 bridges, 125,000 civilian and military buildings, and 800 built or improved airports. The New Deal saw the creation of the Tennessee Valley Authority and the Bureau of Public Roads, which led to bridges and highways being built or improved. The Chickamauga Dam was built during the New Deal. At the center of the New Deal was the Reconstruction Finance Corporation, an independent agency within the federal government, that set up lending systems to channel private capital into publicly desirable investments. It innovated new systems of insurance to guarantee loans and enabled business to remain profitable during the Great Depression. Since lenders were risk averse, a key innovation was to have lenders contribute to an insurance pool, organized by the federal government.
Great Recession 2008–2009	**United States** Infrastructure spending was a key part of the 2009 American Recovery and Reinvestment Act. The legislation prioritized "shovel ready" infrastructure projects—those that could be completed within 3 years. Financing infrastructure-leveraged state resources through the Build America Bond program permitted state and local governments to issue tax credit bonds for any type of capital investment.
	Europe The European Union took actions to modernize its infrastructure with a focus on trans-European energy and broadband projects, mostly through frontloading existing budgets. Germany launched an €18 billion infrastructure program for education (childcare facilities, schools, universities), hospitals, transport, and information and communication technology. The Netherlands launched a €1.2 billion investment in health care, education, bridges, and ports, among other areas.

Sources: News articles and reports available in public domain.

The major lesson from the responses in Table A2.124 is that massive infrastructure investment is key to economic revival after a crisis. In response to the COVID-19 crisis, countries should consider financial innovation to initiate the recovery of financial systems, as was done during the New Deal's pooled insurance for lending and tax credit bonds for leveraging state and federal resources for infrastructure spending.

Multilateral development banks (MDBs) can play an important role through technical assistance and financial support for infrastructure projects (Table A2.126). For the BIMSTEC region, capacity building for PPPs, project preparation and financing support, and formulating and standardizing procurement documents, such as model concession agreements, can help reduce disruptions and resume infrastructure development in the region.

Table A2.126: Role of Multilateral Development Banks in BIMSTEC Transport Infrastructure

Country	PPP Law and Policy Support	Technical Assistance	Standardized Procurement Documents	Developing PPP Pipelines	Financing Support
Bangladesh	PPP law enacted in 2015	Assistance could be provided for strengthening the institutional capacity of Infrastructure Development Company and Bangladesh Infrastructure Finance Fund Limited to support PPP project implementation.	World Bank benchmarking of PPP procurement used, PPP model contracts standardized, and transaction documents developed.	Support for creating a pipeline of bankable PPP projects could be provided.	Support could be provided for deepening local currency markets to nearly all countries in the BIMSTEC. Further assistance for financing solutions, including project bonds, infrastructure funds, liquidity facilities, guarantees, blended finance platforms, and subnational financing models, could be provided. Support could be provided for developing financial structures and instruments to mobilize long-term investors; would involve developing financing solutions with potentially blended components provided by domestic and international financing institutions.
Bhutan	PPP policy and PPP unit created under the Ministry of Finance in 2016	Technical assistance for project preparation stages, such as prefeasibility studies needed.	Support could be provided for formulating standardized concession agreements, RFQs, RFPs.	Project pipeline development and pilot project implementation assistance could be provided.	
India	Assistance to evaluate the requirements of a PPP law could be provided, as could further support for project implementation	Assistance for institutional capacity building for the planned development fund BDF could be offered.	Model concession agreements have been created, with a few under revision. Assistance for setting up dispute resolution boards could be provided.	National Infrastructure Pipeline created. Assistance could be provided for generating the optimal private sector investment required for the pipeline.	
Myanmar	Assistance to evaluate the requirement of a PPP law could be provided, as could further support for implementation	Assistance could be provided for strengthening institutional capacity and setting up a PPP unit.	Support could be provided for formulating standardized concession agreements, RFQs, RFPs.	Project pipeline development and pilot project implementation assistance could be provided.	
Nepal	Public–Private Partnership and Investment Act, 2019	PPP unit in the Ministry of Physical Planning and Works including technical assistance.	Support could be provided for formulating standardized concession agreements, RFQs, RFPs.		

continued on next page

Table A2.126 *continued*

Country	PPP Law and Policy Support	Technical Assistance	Standardized Procurement Documents	Developing PPP Pipelines	Financing Support
Sri Lanka	Assistance to evaluate the requirement of a PPP law could be provided, as could further support for project implementation	Sri Lanka's Board of Investment manages PPPs and foreign investments. Support could be provided for a dedicated PPP division.	Guidelines in place on government tender procedure, model contracts, and bidding documents.	Project pipeline development and pilot project implementation assistance could be provided.	
Thailand	Public–Private Partnership Act, 2019	PPP committee (chaired by Prime Minister) and PPP unit State Enterprise Policy Office expected to provide technical assistance.	Standard contracts and guidelines for small PPP projects and PPP projects' database.	Public–Private Partnership Strategic Plan, 2017–2021 has a pipeline of projects.	

PPP = public–private partnership, RFP = request for proposal, RFQ = request for quotation.

Sources: News articles and reports available in the public domain.

APPENDIX 3

Comparative Assessment of Regional Institutions

The study team identified institutional gaps in the key regional institutions in the Bay of Bengal Initiative for Multi-Sectoral Regional Technical and Economic Cooperation (BIMSTEC) as compared to other regional institutions. Tables A3.1 to A3.4 make a comparative assessment using 4 parameters.

Parameter 1: Institutional Arrangements (Table A3.1).

Table A3.1: Institutional Arrangements

European Commission	Association of Southeast Asian Nations	Greater Mekong Subregion	South Asia Subregional Economic Cooperation	Bay of Bengal Multi-Sectoral Initiative for Technical and Economic Cooperation
• The Treaty on European Union lay down the responsibilities of EC governing and implementing bodies • Divided into departments that develop policies for specific areas. Each department is headed by commissioners from 27 EU countries • The College of Commissioners represents the apex of the EC and assumes collegial political responsibility for the work of the EC	• The Charter of the Association of Southeast Asian Nations (ASEAN) sets out the responsibilities of various bodies in the organization • Policy and strategy decision taken at ASEAN leaders' summit • ASEAN community councils comprise ASEAN political-security council, economic community council, socio-cultural community council • Each community council has under its purview relevant sectoral ministerial bodies	• Guided by general principles • Includes institutional arrangements at political and operational levels • A summit of leaders of GMS countries at the political level, a ministerial-level conference supported by a meeting of senior officials at the policy level, and sector forums and working groups at the project and operational levels • National inter-ministerial committee assisted by national secretariat coordinates GMS activities in each country	• No charter or binding agreement delineating responsibilities of various bodies under the SASEC • Secretary and joint secretary for policy-level decisions and working-level groups and forum for operational level interventions • Two special features: SAARC Secretariat maintains broad oversight over SASEC operations; much of the economic and cooperation between Bhutan and India, as well as between Nepal and India, has been supported under bilateral treaties since the late 1940s	• No charter or binding agreement delineating responsibilities of the various bodies under the BIMSTEC • Policy-making bodies: BIMSTEC summit comprising heads of states, ministerial meeting comprising foreign ministers, trade ministers • Operational bodies: Senior officials meeting comprising senior officials/ secretaries supported by working groups

continued on next page

Table A3.1 *continued*

European Commission	Association of Southeast Asian Nations	Greater Mekong Subregion	South Asia Subregional Economic Cooperation	Bay of Bengal Multi-Sectoral Initiative for Technical and Economic Cooperation
• Operational implementation is delegated to directors-general and heads of service, who lead the administrative structure of the EC • President and commissioners are chosen every 5 years through voting by European Parliament members • Highest-level meeting: College of Commissioners meets at least once a week	• Each sectoral ministerial body has senior officials and subsidiary bodies to undertake tasks • Highest-level meeting: ASEAN summit meets twice a year	• Represents in the region in providing broad strategic directions for future actions and culminates in a joint statement signed by the heads of government of member countries • Highest-level meeting: every 3 years	• Highest-level meeting: Not available	• No national inter-ministerial committee for coordinating activities in each country • Highest-level meeting: only four meetings since BIMSTEC was set up in 1997 (low compared to other regional institutions)

Sources: Websites of the regional institutions; and reports in the public domain.

Parameter 2: BIMSTEC's Approach and Principles while Executing Projects (Table A3.2).

Table A3.2: Approaches and Principles to Executing Projects

European Commission	Association of Southeast Asian Nations	Greater Mekong Subregion	South Asia Subregional Economic Cooperation	Bay of Bengal Multi-Sectoral Initiative for Technical and Economic Cooperation
• Formed for political and economic integration among EU member countries • Shapes EU's overall strategy, proposes new EU laws and policies independently, monitors implementation, manages EU budget, supports international development and aid • EU treaties are the primary law (binding agreement among EU member countries) • Regulations, directives, decisions, recommendations that comes from the principles and objectives of treaties is known as secondary law • Member countries must adopt measures to incorporate these laws into national laws • Adopted economic-corridor approach • Decision-maker: European Commission is steered by a group of 27 commissioners, known as the college. Together they take decisions on the commission's political and strategic direction	• Rule-based grouping • ASEAN is driven by policies and agreements • ASEAN members sign or ratify many agreements, many of which are binding. Example: ASEAN Charter, ASEAN Framework Agreement on the Facilitation of Inter-State Transport, ASEAN Framework Agreement on Multimodal Transport • Decision maker: ASEAN Summit (heads of state)	• GMS program was designed as a flexible "activity based" as opposed to a "rules based" form of cooperation, like ASEAN or forms of political and economic integration (e.g., EU). • As the program evolved, it started undertaking policy initiatives, such as the Cross-Border Transport Facilitation Agreement and the Intergovernmental Agreement on Power Interconnection and Trade. As a result, the GMS program's institutional structure became similar to, though to a lesser extent, overarching institutional structures, such as ASEAN and Asia-Pacific Economic Cooperation, which are driven by agreements and policies rather than projects. Thus, GMS program's institutional structure has evolved with increasing focus towards policy-oriented tasks • Adopted economic corridor approach • Decision maker: Key decisions are taken at ministerial meetings and GMS summit	• SASEC initiatives are country-driven, based on the full appreciation of the benefits that would accrue to projects implemented in a regional context • SASEC is institution-light, keeping the focus of programs at the level of working groups to steer project implementation, and with broad oversight by the SASEC nodal officials • SASEC follows less formal national and subregional institutional arrangements • Decision maker: SASEC nodal official meeting; consultation process agrees on agendas for coordination action	• No harmonized regulatory regime constricts trade and investment • Decision maker: Consultation process at ministerial meetings and BIMSTEC summit

EU = European Union.

Source: Study team analysis.

Parameter 3: BIMSTEC's Funding and Financing Instruments. Besides the financing sources mentioned above, a project can benefit from funding by commercial bank financing, bonds, and equity (provided by project shareholders or third parties such as pension funds) (Table A3.3).

Table A3.3: Funding and Financing Instruments

European Commission	Association of Southeast Asian Nations	Greater Mekong Subregion	South Asia Subregional Economic Cooperation	Bay of Bengal Multi-Sectoral Initiative for Technical and Economic Cooperation
• **Connecting Europe Facility** provides financial support (grants, loans) for strategic investment in transport, energy, and digital infrastructure (maximum cofinancing 50%) • **European Fund for Strategic Investment** supports investment in key sectors through financial guarantees • **Horizon 2020** provides funding for research and development projects with the aim of transferring great ideas from the lab to the market • **European Structural and Investment Funds** includes: – **Cohesion Fund** supports through (grants) projects reducing economic and social disparities and promoting sustainable development in 15 cohesion member states (maximum cofinancing 85%) – **European Regional Development Fund** aims to strengthen economic and social cohesion in the EU by correcting imbalances between its regions through (grants) (maximum cofinancing 85%) – EU influence over approvals, time frame, and specifications of projects becomes strong in EU funding	No regional fund	No regional fund	No regional fund	No regional fund
• **National, local government** provides grants, loans, and guarantees covering maximum 100% of project costs. No influence from European institutions on time frame or specifications, although EU agreements on interoperability exist	**National, local government** provides grants, loans, and guarantees covering maximum 100% of project costs	**National, local government** provides grants, loans, and guarantees covering maximum 100% of project costs	**National, local government** provides grants, loans, and guarantees covering maximum 100% of project costs	**National, local government** provides grants, loans, and guarantees covering maximum 100% of project costs

continued on next page

Table A3.3 *continued*

European Commission	Association of Southeast Asian Nations	Greater Mekong Subregion	South Asia Subregional Economic Cooperation	Bay of Bengal Multi-Sectoral Initiative for Technical and Economic Cooperation
LGTT/project bond initiative provides guarantee to enhance credit rating of borrowers; managed by EIB, European Commission	**Credit Guarantee and Investment Facility** provides credit enhancement for issuers with lower credit ratings to raise long-term funding both in their domestic market and across the region	Proposing to form regional guarantee facility	Facility not available	Facility not available
• **EIB,** the regional development bank, provides: – **Standard loans** for 80% of the budget, maximum cofinancing 75% – **Structured finance facility/special facility** for projects normally considered too risky for standard EIB loans and also often unattractive to the private sector so unlikely to be able to utilize the public–private partnership mode. Using structured finance facility/special facility makes a project more likely to be bankable to potential private sector partners; lending capped at €300 million per project (20% of the budget) – **Innovative instruments** (for 20% of the budget) - LGTT • EIB has influence over project specifications and management • **European Bank for Reconstruction and Development** provides loans at market rates	**ASEAN Infrastructure Fund** is a dedicated fund established by ASEAN member countries and ADB to address regional infrastructure needs by mobilizing regional savings, including foreign exchange reserves. Provides financing to sovereign or sovereign-guaranteed projects. Provides loan at the London interbank offered rates plus margin Regional financial institutions, including ADB and the World Bank, are active and provide concessional finance and grants Regional financial institutions, including AIIB, provide commercial loans	Regional financial institutions, including ADB and the World Bank, are active and providing concessional finance and grants Regional financial institutions, including AIIB, provide commercial loans	Regional financial institutions, including ADB and the World Bank, are active and providing concessional finance and grants Regional financial institutions, including AIIB, provide commercial loans	Regional financial institutions, including ADB and the World Bank, are active and providing concessional finance and grants Regional financial institutions, including AIIB, provide commercial loans

continued on next page

Table A3.3 *continued*

European Commission	Association of Southeast Asian Nations	Greater Mekong Subregion	South Asia Subregional Economic Cooperation	Bay of Bengal Multi-Sectoral Initiative for Technical and Economic Cooperation
• **Marguerite Fund** is actively supported by the European Commission, which contributed to the fund's seed capital, as part of the European Economic Recovery Plan. The Marguerite Fund is a pan-European equity fund that aims to act as a catalyst for infrastructure investments implementing key EU policies in the areas of climate change, energy security, and trans-European networks. The fund is also the first joint initiative of the EU's leading public financial institutions, including the EIB	Not available	Not available	Not available	Not available

EIB = European Investment Bank, LGTT = Loan Guarantee Instrument for Trans-European Networks Transport.

Sources: Websites of regional institutions; and reports in the public domain.

Parameter4: Private Sector Participation in Regional Projects across the global institutional bodies (Table A3.4).

Table A3.4: Private Sector Participation

European Commission	Association of Southeast Asian Nations	Greater Mekong Subregion	South Asia Subregional Economic Cooperation	Bay of Bengal Multi-Sectoral Initiative for Technical and Economic Cooperation
Many transport infrastructure projects implemented through PPPs (e.g., Perpignan–Figueiras Rail Concession, rail link between France and Spain)	Not available	A few corridor transport projects implemented through PPP mode (e.g., Phnom Penh–Sihanoukville Highway Corridor Project, Ha Noi–Lang Son Expressway Project)	A few corridor transport projects implemented through PPP mode	A few corridor transport projects implemented through PPP mode
European PPP Expertise Centre aims to increase the capacity of its members, all from the public sector, to engage in PPPs Members include the European Investment Bank, European Commission, and national and regional authorities responsible for PPPs	Not available	Not available	Not available	Not available

PPP = public–private partnership.

Sources: Websites of regional institutions; and reports in the public domain.

APPENDIX 4

Role of Regional Development Finance Institutions in Regional Integration

During conceptualization of the Bay of Bengal Initiative for Multi-Sectoral Technical and Economic Cooperation (BIMSTEC) Development Fund (BDF), governments can take on board lessons from other Development Finance Institutions (DFIs). This appendix presents general lessons that can be assessed in line with the mandate of the BDF.

General characteristics of development finance institutions:

(i) **Legally independent.** Development finance institutions (DFIs) are legally separate entities and are either wholly or partially government owned. A few have majority private ownership, e.g., Nepal Infrastructure Bank Limited.

(ii) **Financially sustainable.** DFIs should strive to be financially sustainable. Undertaking prudent risk assessments and selecting projects that can not only achieve development outcomes but also generate cash flows in the long run can help achieve this. Excessive financial dependency on governments undermines their essential features as banks and financial institutions, and puts them at risk of incurring undue government interference in their resource allocation and operations.

(iii) **Support public policy objectives.** DFIs are set up to fulfil certain development or strategic objectives. On the other hand, development banks are either for general development or they focus on specific sectors and segments, such as agriculture, housing, infrastructure, small and medium-sized enterprises, and start-ups.

(iv) **Receive government support.** Because DFIs are closely linked to the pursuit of public policy objectives, they receive government support in the form of equity contributions, budget appropriation, and guarantees.

(v) **Play an important role in providing long-term finance.** In addition, their liabilities are predominately long-term, which makes long-term finance feasible.

In terms of geographical reach, DFIs are classified into national, subnational, and multilateral (regional and global). The *NSE Development Financing Research Report* finds approximately 93% of DFIs are national and subnational and about 7% are multilateral. DFIs are often founded with two types of missions: general or specific. Most multilateral DFIs are for general purposes.

Two global DFIs and some 40 regional ones have been set up. The European Investment Bank is the oldest and biggest regional DFI (Table A4.1).

Table A4.1: Key Regional Development Finance Institutions

Institution	Asset Base ($ billion)	Priority Areas	Coverage
International Bank for Reconstruction and Development (World Bank's lending arm, established 1944)	297	Lends to governments of middle-income and creditworthy low-income countries	Global
International Development Association, member of the World Bank Group (established 1960)	199	Provides financing at highly concessional terms to governments of the poorest countries	Global
International Finance Corporation (established 1956)	96	Provides loans, equity, and advisory services to stimulate private investment in developing countries	Global
Multilateral Investment Guarantee Agency (established 1988)	–	Provides political risk insurance and credit enhancement to investors and lenders to facilitate foreign direct investment in emerging economies	Global
European Investment Bank (established 1958)	621	Cohesion, Climate, development, innovation and skills, infrastructure and small businesses	Europe (90% of operations)
Inter-American Development Bank (established 1959)	136	Agriculture, infrastructure and industrial development, education, health care, private sector development	Americas
African Development Bank (established 1964)	49	Agriculture, health, education, public utilities, transport, telecommunications, industry, and the private sector	Africa
Asian Development Bank (established 1966)	222	Provides loans, equity, and advisory services to stimulate private investment in developing countries	Asia and the Pacific
Islamic Development Bank (established 1974)	33	Agriculture, infrastructure and industrial development, education, health care, and private sector development	Africa, Americas, Asia
New Development Bank (established 2015)	12	Sustainable infrastructure (clean energy, transport infrastructure, irrigation, water resource management, urban development)	Brazil, India, the People's Republic of China, Russian Federation, South Africa
Asian Infrastructure Investment Bank (established 2016)	23	Provides loans, equity, and advisory services to stimulate private investment in developing countries	Asia and Oceania
European Bank for Reconstruction and Development (established 1990)	77	Various industries, including agriculture, infrastructure, and transport	Central and Eastern Europe, Central Asia

Source: Annual reports of the regional development finance institutions.

The main funding source of regional DFIs is borrowing from the capital market (Table A4.2).

Table A4.2: Sources of Funding for Key Regional Development Finance Institutions

Institution	Shareholders	Sources of Funding		
		Shareholder Funds (%)	Borrowing (bonds, commercial papers) (%)	Others (%)
European Investment Bank (rated AAA by Fitch Ratings and S&P Global Ratings)	28 European countries	13	80	7
New Development Bank (rated AA+ by Fitch and S&P)	BRICS. All members of the United Nations can be members of the bank; however, the share of BRICS nations can never be less than 55% of voting power	68	21 (issuing local currency denominated bonds to counter currency risks [CNY, ZAR, CHF])	11
European Bank for Reconstruction and Development (rated AAA by Fitch and S&P)	69 countries from five continents plus the European Union and the European Investment Bank	11	84	5
African Development Bank (rated AAA in international capital markets)	80 member countries comprising 54 regional member countries in Africa and 26 nonregional member countries from other regions	15	83	2
Islamic Development Bank	57 member countries. The basic condition for membership is that the prospective member country should be a member of the Organization of the Islamic Cooperation; Saudi Arabia has majority ownership, 23.5%	29	61	10

BRICS = Brazil, India, the People's Republic of China, Russian Federation, South Africa, CNY = Chinese Yuan, CHF = Swiss Franc, S&P = Standard and Poor's Global Ratings, ZAR = South African Rand.

Source: Annual reports of the regional development finance institutions.

Table A4.3 outlines the services offered by regional DFIs.

Table A4.3: Services Offered by Regional Development Finance Institutions

Institution	Knowledge and Capacity Building Support	Preparation and Implementation Support	Environmental, Climate, Social Impact Assessments	Advice on Procurement and Regulatory Issues	COVID-19 Response
EIB	European PPP Expertise Centre aims to increase the capacity of its members, all of which are from the public sector, to participate in PPPs. The Project Advisory Support Service Agreement provides support during all phases of the delivery of EU-funded projects. It also works closely with local teams and authorities to transfer knowledge to local staff.	Joint Assistance to Support Projects in European Regions improves the capacity of administrations and promoters by transferring knowledge on project preparation, environmental issues, and EU legislation. It speeds up the EU-approval processes by carrying out independent quality reviews preparing the groundwork for European Commission decisions.	Projects financed by the EIB must follow the bank's environment and social standards, as laid down in the EIB's Environmental & Social Handbook.	Procurement planning, in the form of feedback on technical issues identified in a review of project documents, such as tender documents, or draft terms of reference.	The EIB formed the Pan-European Guarantee Fund (with contributions by EU member countries) that provides guarantees to operations by the EIB and the European investment fund. Fund size up to $25 billion.
NDB	Not available.	The Project Preparation Fund is the NDB's multidonor fund to support the preparation of bankable projects by providing technical assistance.	NDB-financed projects must follow the bank's environment and social standards, as laid down in its Environment and Social Framework.	Procurement is usually done by member countries, unless otherwise permitted by NDB.	Up to $10 billion in crisis-related assistance and support for economic recovery.

continued on next page

Table A4.3 *continued*

Institution	Knowledge and Capacity Building Support	Preparation and Implementation Support	Environmental, Climate, Social Impact Assessments	Advice on Procurement and Regulatory Issues	COVID-19 Response
AfDB	African Legal Support Facility provides legal advice and technical assistance for negotiations of complex commercial transactions. Facility develops and proposes innovative tools for capacity building and knowledge management. African Development Fund is for low-income member countries. Fund provides concessional loans, grants, guarantees, and technical assistance for studies and capacity building. Middle-Income Country Fund is used for capacity building and strengthening of institutions in eligible regional member countries. Fund for African Private Sector Assistance provides grants for capacity building-support.	The Africa Investment Forum is an innovative marketplace dedicated to advancing projects to bankable stages, raising capital, and accelerating the financial closure of deals. The forum profiles bankable transformational projects, matching them with investors. Middle-Income Country Fund provides grants for the preparation of project engineering design, environmental impact assessment study, and analytical work, promoting PPPs by supporting legal and regulatory reform processes. Fund for African Private Sector Assistance provides grants for technical assistance.	Integrated Safeguards System consists of four components: (i) integrated safeguards policy statement—a declaration of commitment to environmental and social sustainability and to reducing risk of noncompliance, (ii) operational safeguards—policy statements that set out the operational requirements that bank-financed operations must comply with, (iii) Environmental and Social Assessment Procedures revised procedures—procedural and process guidance at each stage of the project cycle, and (iv) guidance on integrated environmental and social impact assessments.	AfDB has developed rules and procedures for procuring goods and services, and rules and procedures for recruiting consultants that govern bank-financed procurement. To assist borrowers, AfDB has, in collaboration with other multilateral development banks, developed standard bidding documents that should be used for contracts financed by the bank. AfDB is active in supporting the development and reform of public procurement systems in borrower countries.	AfDB created a coronavirus solidarity package to support short-term liquidity and working capital needs of businesses in AfDB's region of operation.

AfDB = African Development Bank, EU = European Union, COVID-19 = coronavirus disease, EIB = European Investment Bank, MIC = middle-income country, NDB = New Development Bank, PPP = public–private partnership.

Sources: Annual reports of the regional development finance institutions; reports in the public domain.

Commercial loans are a major instrument of regional DFIs (Table A4.4).

Table A4.4: Key Financing Instruments of Regional Development Finance Institutions

Institution	Loans	Equity	Guarantees	Blended Finance
European Investment Bank	Direct loans: Individual project loans from $25 million. Typically covers up to 50% of the total project cost for both public and private sector promoters (TENT-T -75%). Indirect loans: Loans made to local banks or other intermediaries which, in turn, offer financial support to the final recipient. Structured finance facility loans: These finance highly risky projects. Form: Commercial loans.	Equity financing primarily investing or coinvesting with funds focused on infrastructures, SMEs, and environment Investments represent 10% to 20% of fund size, with a maximum of 25%. Offers tenors that reflect the fund's life, normally 10–12 years, but the tenor can be 25 years or more. Fund manager driven (less bureaucracy). Venture debt (quasi equity).	Credit enhancement for project finance–subordinated financing, funded or unfunded guarantees, and contingent credit lines designed to enhance the credit quality/credit rating of the senior debt. SME guarantees.	Blended finance products coupled with additional financial instruments and grants from other donors.
New Development Bank	Major provider of sovereign loans with 80% share in overall investment portfolio. Nonsovereign loans comprise 19% share in overall investment portfolio. Six-month London interbank offered rate plus margin.	Equity investment is 1% of the overall investment portfolio	Not available.	Not available.
EBRD	Typically covers 35% of the total project cost financing for private sector projects, ranges from $5 million to $250 million. EBRD loans are based on current market rates and priced competitively. No concessional loans or grants. Form: Commercial loans.	Provides ordinary shares, preference shares, and subordinated loans, and participates in private equity funds that in turn invest in medium-sized companies. Equity finance is available from EBRD-supported private equity funds, donor-supported equity funds, and directly from the EBRD.	Provides guarantees and trade-related cash advances to promote foreign trade to, from, and within EBRD region.	EBRD manages donor funds in blending project loans.

continued on next page

Table A4.4 *continued*

Institution	Loans	Equity	Guarantees	Blended Finance
		EBRD's Equity Participation Fund mobilizes funds from global institutional investors to participate in EBRD's own direct equity investments.		
AfDB	Standard loans: Sovereign and nonsovereign. Maturity up to 20 years (15 for nonsovereign loans). Interest rate is base rate plus margin. Syndication of nonsovereign-guaranteed loans.	AfDB invests in equities either directly or indirectly through funds and other investment vehicles.	Partial credit guarantees cover a portion of scheduled repayments of private loans or bonds against all risks. Partial risk guarantees cover private lenders against the risk of the government or a government-owned agency failing to perform its obligations to a private project.	Not available.

AfDB = African Development Bank, ERBD = European Bank for Reconstruction and Development, SME = small and medium-sized enterprise, TEN-T = Trans-European Networks Transport.

Sources: Annual reports of regional development finance institutions; reports available in the public domain.

The European Investment Bank has been instrumental in financing cross-border projects—more than 100 of them since its inception—in the European Union. This has helped create seamless connectivity throughout Europe (Table A4.4).

Table A4.5: Regional Development Finance Institutions Cross-Border Projects

Institution	Type of Projects	Appraisal
EIB (timeline 4–5 months)	• Minimum project size: $25 million • For projects where the total cost is under €25 million, the EIB provides intermediated loans (credit lines) to local, regional, and national banks • Consistent with EIB priority objectives such as, in transport, TEN-T priority projects. Examples: – Eastern Africa Transport Corridor (EIB: €55 million) – Beira Litoral and Alta Shadow Toll Road, Portugal (EIB: €470 million) – Bolivia East-West Corridor (EIB: $84 million) – S7 Expressway (Gdansk Elblag) (EIB: $4.2 million)	Transport Lending Policy sets guidelines on project selection and lending. The following areas are evaluated while appraising a project: technical scope, implementation and operation capability of promoter, procurement, environmental impact, market and demand, investment cost and profitability.
NDB (6 months)	• Sustainable infrastructure projects • No cross-border projects financed yet in transportation sector • Other transportation projects. Example: Durban Container Terminal Berth Reconstruction Project (NDB: $200 million), Bihar Rural Roads Project (NDB: $350 million	As part of the assessment of a project, the bank's Credit and Investment Committee identifies different risk factors that can impact project performance, including nonfinancial risks, before the proposed transaction is recommended to the Board of Directors for approval.
AfDB	Regional Corridor projects. Example: Nacala Corridor (different sections) (AfDB: $421 million), Mtwara Corridor (AfDB: $335 million)	Not available.
European Bank for Reconstruction and Development	Example: M5 Toll Motorway, Hungary	Not available.

AfDB = African Development Bank, EIB = European Investment Bank, NDB = New Development Bank, TEN-T = Trans-European Networks Transport.

Sources: Annual reports of the regional development finance institutions; reports in the public domain.

APPENDIX 5

Case Studies

These are various case studies done through the course of the study and were decided to be collated into one section.

Chile Pension Reforms (1980–2000)

- The 1981 Capital Markets Act created a system of private pensions where mandatory contributions led to the creation of a new class of institutional investor, with funds suited for long-term domestic investment and a risk profile suitable for bond market investment.
- Deepened domestic capital markets allowed the government to extend debt maturity profiles and reduce its debts, foreign currency components, helping improve financial strength and resulting in Chile being rated investment grade since its first rating in 1993.

Figure A5.1: Chile Pension Sector and Bond Market, 1980–2000
(% of GDP)

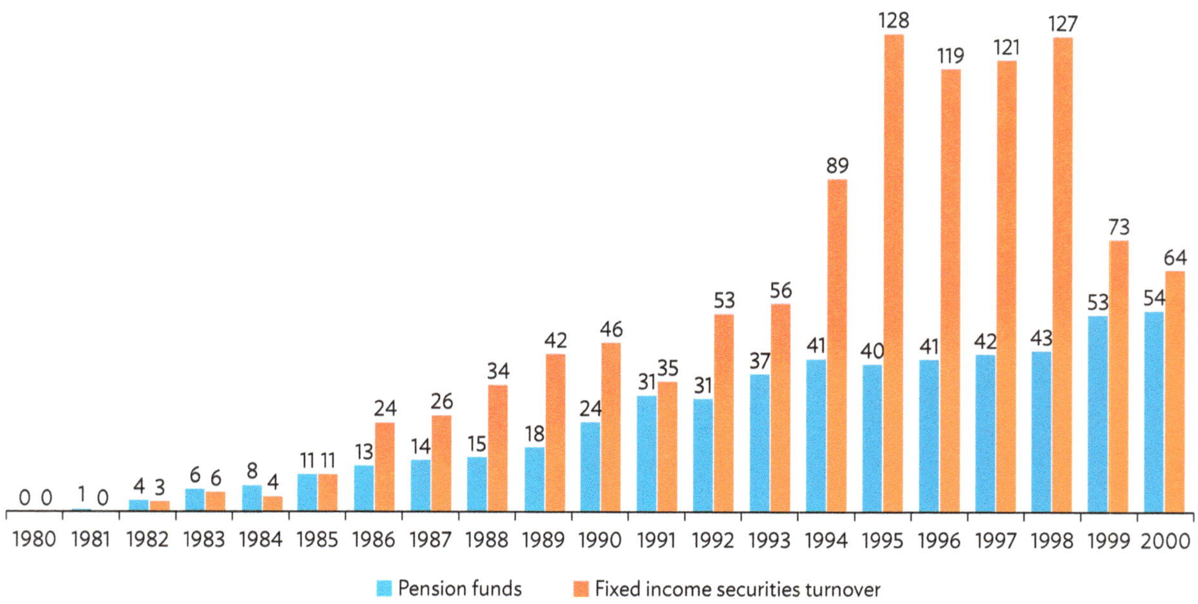

GDP = gross domestic product.

Source: Rodrigo Cifuentes, Jorge Desormeaux and Claudio Gonzalez. 2000. *Capital Markets in Chile: From Financial Repression to Financial Deepening*. Central Bank of Chile. Chile

Asian Infrastructure Finance Hub – Singapore

- Since 1978, the Singapore government has been reforming its finance sector, opening new financial markets, introducing full convertibility for various financial instruments, and enacting regulatory and fiscal incentives to attract foreign financial institutions to Singapore.
- Today, Singapore as a regional finance hub offers a full range of financial products and services, including currency trading, derivatives, loan syndication, mergers and acquisitions, insurance, wealth and asset management, and capital market activities.
- Singapore is strategically positioned at the heart of the region, and has a strong ecosystem of infrastructure development companies, financing and risk management institutions, consultancies, and law firms. More than 200 international asset management firms are located here and many of the world's leading names in insurance broking, captive management, and risk management are also present. These elements make Singapore well-placed to share its expertise with the region's stakeholders.
- Singapore has set up a new infrastructure office, Infrastructure Asia, to support the development of the region by bringing together local and international partners across the infrastructure value chain, including developers, institutional investors, multilateral agencies, and legal, accounting, and financial services providers.
- Infrastructure Asia is open for partnership with any foreign government or company looking to drive development in the infrastructure space or a Singapore-based firm looking to access Asian infrastructure opportunities. It offers to:

    (i) connect interested Asian governments with relevant domain experts (sub-segment champions) among developers, professional services, and technical and financing solutions to meet the specific needs of each project;
    (ii) bring parties with the requisite expertise to help partners bridge knowledge gaps and uplift capabilities in project development, financing, and implementation; and
    (iii) provide advisory services on project scoping and conceptual structuring to improve the viability and success of projects.

- Through Infrastructure Asia, Singapore is positioning itself as a broker for regional infrastructure investments, leveraging its experience as a global financial hub.

Source: Infrastructure Asia website. https://www.infrastructureasia.org/.

Connecting Europe Facility

The European Commission (EC) allocates funding for the Connecting Europe Facility (CEF) for a period of 5–6 years to work towards achieving Trans-European Network Transport (TEN-T) objectives.

TEN-T

Main objectives:

- Cohesion through accessibility and connectivity of all European Union (EU) regions
- Efficiency through removing bottlenecks, addressing missing links among different transport modes
- Sustainability by developing all transport modes that are economically efficient in the long term
- Increasing the benefits structured in two layers:
  - Comprehensive network aims to ensure the accessibility and connectivity of all EU regions
  - Core network, consisting of those parts of the network with the highest strategic importance for achieving the objectives of the TEN-T policy

Ring-fencing CEF

- Focuses on supporting cross-border projects, and addressing bottlenecks and missing links in core network
- CEF budget is ring-fenced as follows:

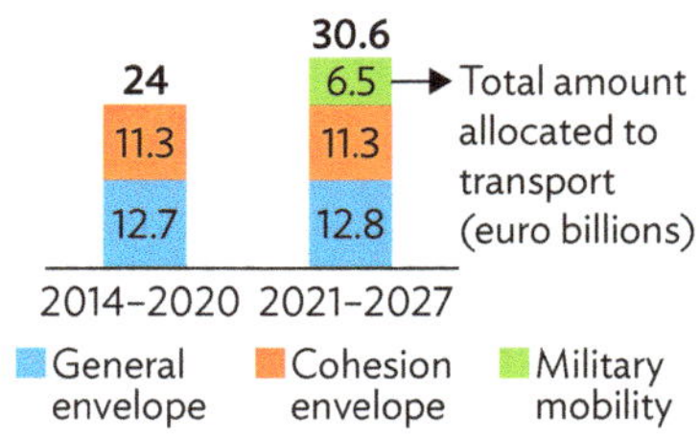

- General envelope: Available to all member states
- Cohesion envelope: Available to member states whose gross national income per capita is less than 90% of the EU average
- Military envelope: Enhances strategically important transport infrastructure projects and makes them suitable for military mobility

Managing CEF Grants

- CEF grants awarded through competitive calls for project proposals
- EC adopts multiannual work programs in transport sector for pre-identified projects of common interest
- For each call, EC assesses each proposal on the criteria of relevance, impact, and quality
- EC proposes the list of projects to be supported and the amount of funding to be allocated
- European Climate, Infrastructure and Environment Executing Agency responsible for managing allocated funds and supervising project implementation

CEF highlights:

- From 2014 to June 2019, 15 calls for proposals launched in transport
- €22.8 billion (93% of total CEF transport budget) has been allocated as of 2019

Source: European Commission website. https://commission.europa.eu/funding-tenders/find-funding/eu-funding-programmes/connecting-europe-facility_en.

ASEAN Charter

The ASEAN Charter, a binding intergovernmental agreement between the 10 countries of the Association of Southeast Asian Nations (ASEAN), sets out the responsibilities of various bodies in the organization, decision-making processes, and a dispute resolution mechanism.

ASEAN Summit (2 meetings per year)	Comprises heads of member states; provides policy guidance and makes stategic decisions
Coordinating Council (2 meetings per year)	Comprises foreign ministries; coordinates implementation of agreements and decisions of ASEAN Summit
Community Council (3) (2+ meetings per year)	Comprises national representatives for each council; ensures implementation of decisions of ASEAN Summit
Sectoral Ministerial Bodies	Implements agreements and decisions of ASEAN summit for their relevant sector
Committee of Permanent Representatives	Constitutes permanent representatives from member states; supports the work of community council, sectoral bodies
National Secretariats	Comprises national secretariats; act as focal points and coordinate the implementation of ASEAN decisions at national level

Source: ASEAN Charter. https://asean.org/wp-content/uploads/images/archive/publications/ASEAN-Charter.pdf.

Greater Mekong Subregion Cross-Border Trade Agreement, 2003

The Greater Mekong Subregion (GMS) Cross-Border Trade Agreement (CBTA) is a pioneering landmark accord, which consolidates, in a single legal instrument, all key nonphysical measures required for efficient cross-border land transport. The CBTA includes mechanisms that enable:

- facilitation of cross-border formalities: Single-window inspection, single-stop inspection, limits of number of documents required and reduction to the extent possible of, procedures and formalities required for cross-border traffic;
- cross-border transport of goods: Exemptions from routine customs physical inspections at borders, exemption of transit traffic from custom duties and taxes, and transportation of perishable goods get priority in clearance formalities;
- admittance of road vehicles: Vehicles (on designated open routes), drivers (with mutual recognition of driving licenses and visa facilitation), and goods (with regimes for dangerous and perishable goods) to cross national borders through the GMS road transport permit system; technical requirement of vehicles to satisfy agreed standards;
- infrastructure: Roads and bridges meet design standards, border crossing facilities, roads signs and signals; and
- institutional framework: Comprises of implementation bodies at national and regional levels and a regulatory body that monitors and assesses the functioning of the CBTA, including formulating proposals for amendment to the CBTA at the ministerial-level conference.

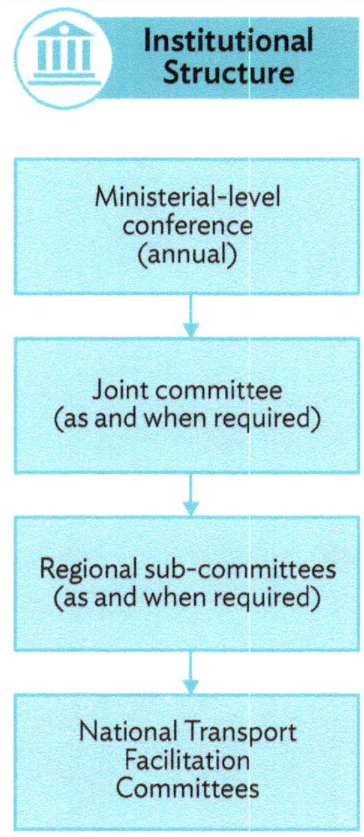

Source: GMS Cross Border Trade Agreement. https://www.adb.org/sites/default/files/publication/29294/gms-cbta-instruments-history.pdf.

Greater Mekong Subregion Northern Economic Corridor Project

The Greater Mekong Subregion Northern Economic Corridor Project connects Thailand and the People's Republic of China with a road link via the Lao People's Democratic Republic (Lao PDR). For the $97.7 million project, the Asian Development Bank provided $33.4 million in concessional ordinary capital resources lending.

Despite a significant stretch of the road traversing the Lao PDR, the People's Republic of China ($38.9 million) and Thailand ($44.4 million and additional repair costs of $11.3 million) shouldered two-thirds of the investment. The Lao PDR funded $3.2 million.

ADB's multifaceted role in the project included:

- helping mobilize financial resources;
- assisting in project design to ensure not only greater regional connectivity but also to include an isolated region of northern Lao PDR in the process of regional integration;
- assisting the Lao PDR, as the transit country, in negotiations on pricing policies, so that the new infrastructure would not place undue fiscal burden on the country's finances;
- working to ensure that the distribution of costs and benefits across the three countries was fair;
- providing the Lao PDR with concessional financing; and
- ensuring the project adopted a social and environmental management plan to include contracting arrangements that incentivized construction firms to mitigate social and environmental risks.

Source: Asian Development Bank. 2016. Infrastructure and Regional Cooperation. Annual Bank Conference on Development Economics. Tokyo. https://www.adb.org/sites/default/files/publication/156715/adbi-dp76.pdf.

N4 Toll Road

Region: South Africa and Mozambique, Africa

Description: Rehabilitation of the N4 Toll Road is one part of the Maputo Development Corridor Project. The corridor runs from the Johannesburg to Maputo.

Sector: Road

Financing Sources:

Equity: 20% from six shareholders contributing 10% of the equity, with the rest of the capital provided by the South African Infrastructure Fund and six other investors—Rand Merchant Bank, South African Mutual Life Assurance Society, Momentum Metropolitan Life Limited, Sanlam Asset Management (South Africa), Commonwealth Development Corporation (United Kingdom), and SCDM (Mozambique).

Debt: 80%. The debt investors include South Africa's four major banks and the Development Bank of Southern Africa. The governments of South Africa and Mozambique provided joint and severable guarantees of the project debt and, under certain conditions, guaranteed the equity.

Special purpose vehicle: Trans African Concessions (TRAC), a consortium of the Bouygues Group and two South African construction companies (Basil Read and Stocks & Stocks).

The previous road was free of charge. By assuming full traffic risk, TRAC faced demand and user payment risks in Mozambique. Traffic volumes in Mozambique were not as high as forecast and disadvantaged communities were unable and unwilling to pay high toll fees. To mitigate this risk, TRAC cross-subsidized the Mozambican part of the road with higher revenue from South African users. It also provided substantial discounts to local users and public transport services on both sides of the border. The road facilitated further private sector investment in Mozambique, which in turn raised traffic volumes.

Source: African Development Bank Website. https://esa.afdb.org/sites/default/files/TRANSGAMBIA%20ROAD%20CORRIDOR%20PROJECT-ESIA_ESMP%20Report%20%28002%29.pdf.

Bancassurance in India

Bancassurance is the provision of insurance (assurance) products by banks, most commonly through bank branches.

Major bancassurance challenges faced by banks in the insurance sector in India were:

- They had to develop core teams to handle insurance;
- They had to step into the role of risk manager for their clients;
- They had to promote personal insurance products aggressively to bank customers;
- They had to promote online selling of plain vanilla insurance policies; and
- Reward schemes and incentives had to be well defined for employees.

According to the Insurance Regulatory and Development Authority, private sector banks and insurance companies are the main drivers of bancassurance. Private insurance companies regard cooperative and regional rural banks as a cost-effective vehicle for insurers to tap into rural communities and fulfill their rural sector obligations.

Bancassurance gained momentum after the government issued a notification in August 2000 specifying that insurance could be undertaken by banks under of the Banking Regulation Act, 1949.

Insurance Penetration in India, FY2004–2014
(% of GDP)

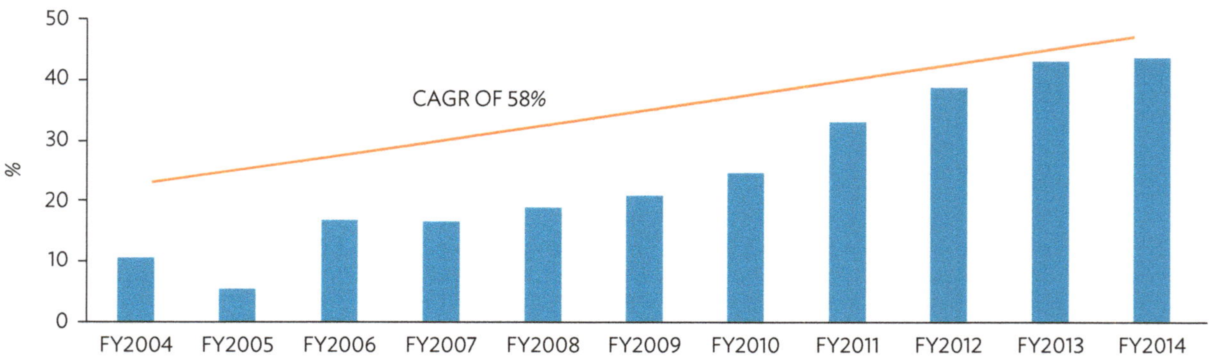

CAGR = compound annual growth rate, FY = fiscal year, GDP = gross domestic product.

Note: FY ends 31 March.

Source: Bhavna Sharma, Ruchika Bhateja. 2016. *Bancassurance in India: Promising Distribution Network of Insurance Industry, Pacific Business Review International.* 9 (3). http://www.pbr.co.in/2016/2016_month/September/10.pdf.

Key outcomes of implementing bancassurance in India include:

- Since 2002, public sector general insurers have tied up with leading public sector and private banks.
- Individual agent-oriented products evolved into bancassurance-friendly adaptations and aligned with the customer needs of banks.
- By 2005, the bancassurance channel was established as a mainstay in marketing and sales, and as a general growth path for insurers.
- Share of bancassurance premiums grew at a compound annual growth rate of 58.8% over 10 years in private life insurance, while the rate premium from other distribution channels (individual agents, banks, brokers, referrals) contributed only 31.6%. Bancassurance played well in India; its penetration (% of GDP) was 10.6% in fiscal year (FY) 2004, rising to 43.6% in FY2014.

Source: Bhavna Sharma, Ruchika Bhateja. 2016. *Bancassurance in India: Promising Distribution Network of Insurance Industry, Pacific Business Review International.* 9 (3).

Insurance in Egypt

Background

Although Egypt's insurance sector is well established, premiums total only about $2 billion as of 2019—small for a country with a population of 105.6 million in 2019. Insurance penetration is estimated at 1.2%, far below the global of average of 6.2%, and insurance density was just S$22.30 per person.

Inclusion is a problem, given a 25% poverty rate. In terms of financial inclusion, only 35% of the population has a bank account. The Egyptian Financial Supervisory Authority says, "Egypt faces major hurdles including a widespread absence of financial literacy and awareness regarding insurance products and their benefits."

Risks due to global uncertainties, domestic threats, falling tourism figures, and volatile economic growth could hit already weak consumer confidence and result in lower demand for nonessential products, like insurance.

Regulatory Reforms Promoting Bancassurance

In 2018, the central bank and the Egyptian Financial Supervisory Authority loosened regulations to allow banks to have bancassurance arrangements with up to four insurance companies: one general insurer, one general takaful operator, one life insurer, and one family takaful company.[a] Previously, a bank was allowed only to tie up with one general insurer and one life insurer.

In Egypt, similar to many African emerging markets, there has been a push to ensure that reinsurance activity is at least partly domestically domiciled. The government has been exploring the possibility of establishing a new national reinsurer since 2013. A new institution, if formed, would be domestically funded, with some government participation.

Insurance Law No. 10, 1981 does not distinguish between brokers and agents, referring to them as "intermediaries." The authorities have sought to formalize the market, starting with a law introduced in 2008 that recognizes this category of corporate broker and establishes minimum standards of training and limits for professional indemnity. While the regulator has tightened the framework on traditional distribution channels, it has begun to relax the administrative regime in other areas.

Outcomes

Key outcomes of Egypt's regulatory reforms for bancassurance include:

- Egypt significantly strengthened its insurance sector, growing its insurance density premium per capita from $8 in 1999 to $16 in 2017.
- The government is looking to increase the insurance sector's contribution to gross domestic product to 4.0% in 2022 from 1.2% in 2016.
- The draft National Strategy 2018–22 for nonbank financial services aims to double the value of insurance premiums to LE50 billion by 2022, and for investments made by insurance companies, the goal is to grow from LE86 billion in 2018 to LE150 billion in 2022.
- The above initiatives helped Egypt to be placed among the Goldman Sachs Group Inc.'s Next Eleven.[b]

[a] Takaful is a type of Islamic insurance wherein members contribute money into a pool system to guarantee each other. Takaful-branded insurance is based on sharia or Islamic religious law and covers health, life, and general insurance needs. Any claims made by participants are paid out of the takaful fund.

[b] The Next 11, also known as N-11, are the 11 countries that are poised to become the biggest economies in the world in the 21st century, after Brazil, Russia, India, and the People's Republic of China. The N-11 were selected by Goldman Sachs Group, Inc in a 2005 paper exploring the potential of Brazil, Russia, India, the People's Republic of China, and the N-11. The next 11 are Bangladesh, Egypt, Indonesia, Iran, Mexico, Nigeria, Pakistan, the Philippines, Türkiye, the Republic of Korea, and Viet Nam.

Source: Various secondary sources.

Eastern Africa Transport Corridor Financed by European Investment Bank

Project: Improvements of two separate road sections (58 kilometers) of the Northern Multimodal Corridor Road in central and southwest Uganda

Borrower: Republic of Uganda

Location: Kampala and Mbarara, Uganda

Project cost: €129 million

Financing structure: €55 million European Investment Bank (EIB) loan, €42 million European Commission grant, €32 million borrower's own funds

Subsidy: €16.5 million interest rate subsidy provided by the European Union–Africa Infrastructure Trust Fund for regional development

Value added:

- Long-term financing (20 years) benefiting regional transport infrastructure in East Africa
- Blending European Development Fund grant resources with an EIB loan enabling regional infrastructure development

Source: European Investment Bank Website. https://www.eib.org/en/projects/pipelines/all/20110361#:~:text=The%20project%20alleviates%20transport%20bottlenecks,elements%20which%20are%20key%20to.

Beiras Litoral and Alta Shadow Toll Road, Portugal, Financed by European Investment Bank

Portugal is a frontrunner in the use of public–private partnerships (PPPs) for infrastructure. One of the country's projects was a 167-kilometer motorway that links with Spanish road infrastructure. In 2005, the government launched bids for a PPP design–build–finance–operate project, where the recovery of costs would be handled by shadow tariffs based on vehicle distance usage.

The project cost was €1,135 million. No European Union funds were used, but the project was supported by a European Investment Bank loan.

Problems started at an early stage. The government did not specify standards of quality and service in the tendering process. This meant alterations to the specifications at later stages, affecting the bidding process, which caused delays and led to the tendering process being repeated. Final costs turned out to be three times the original estimates and shadow tolls had to be raised as a consequence.

Cost estimates from bidders were not assessed well because there were no public sector comparators. Because of this, it was not possible to assess whether the PPP was offering a better outcome than traditional public procurement.

The mishandling of precise specifications and requirements meant the government had to cover the delays and costs of conducting environmental impact assessments.

The increases in shadow tolls due to the larger-than-expected costs meant that the state budget from the highway agency was unable to cover the shadow toll payments. This prompted the government to introduce actual tolls. Luckily, usage of the highway has been high and toll-cost requirements have been sustainable.

To avoid a recurrence, the government created a specialized PPP unit to support the private developer in project implementation in effective land acquisition as well as environmental and social clearances with future PPPs.

Source: European Investment Bank Website. https://www.eib.org/en/projects/all/19971299.

Tanzania's Mtwara Corridor, Financed by African Development Bank

Links to a port on Mozambique's coastline need to be opened and access improved to the north of the country. Tanzania's road network serves as transit from land-locked Zambia and Malawi to the port of Mtwara. The discovery of oil, gas, and minerals has further stimulated the development of this corridor project.

African Development Bank (AfDB) supported the upgrading of two major road sections in Tanzania in line with the country strategy for transport infrastructure and also the regional development aims of Common Market for Eastern and Southern Africa, the East African Community, and the Southern African Development Community.

The 804-kilometer Mtwara road corridor connects Southern Tanzania and Zambia, with bank-supported road sections crossing Mozambique toward the Malawi Lake border, opening the way to Zambia. AfDB financed 558 kilometers of road upgrades and a one-stop border post between Tanzania and Mozambique in four phases of financing. The first two phases, in 2009 and 2012, involved the East–West link to Mtwara port. In 2016, AfDB financed the construction of a road connecting Tanzania and Mozambique, including a one-stop border post.

The outcomes included:

- regional trade increasing by 10% from 2009 to 2015;
- cumulated travel time on Namtumbo–Nagomano section decreasing from 10 to 6 hours;
- construction of a 7-meter-wide paved road;
- a 10% increase in tourism potential at the Selous Game Reserve and the Chief Songea historical site, Tanzania;
- the percentage of paved national roads increasing from 39% in 2009 to 45% in 2015; and
- the Human Development Index[a] increasing from 0.503 in 2009 to 0.611 in 2015.

[a] The Human Development Index (HDI) measures each country's social and economic development by focusing on the following four factors: mean years of schooling, expected years of schooling, life expectancy at birth, and gross national income (GNI) per capita

Source: African Development Bank (AfDB) Data portal. https://projectsportal.afdb.org/dataportal/VProject/show/P-Z1-D00-021.

APPENDIX 6

Evolution of the Secondary Market in Europe

The growth in borrowing requirements in Europe during the 1970s saw loan facilities traditionally provided on a bilateral basis increasingly replaced by larger credit lines from a pool of lenders, and then by loan facilities syndicated to the wider market. Up to the mid-1990s, participation in the secondary loan market in Europe was dominated by a small number of United States banks, predominantly investment banks, specialist debt traders, and vulture funds, with activity focused on the distressed market. However, from the mid-1990s onwards, institutional investors and other nonbank financial institutions increasingly looked to the secondary loan market to invest their money. Today's secondary loan market is utilized by a diverse and vast number of participants, including investment banks, commercial banks, hedge funds, pension funds, private equity funds, and specialist loan brokers, each looking to transact in par, near par, and/or distressed debt. In addition, government agencies, such as the Irish National Asset Management Agency, were set up to buy nonperforming debt as a result of the 2007–2009 financial crisis.

In order to address the issues of standardization of practices, a group of banks formed the Loan Market Association (LMA) in 1996. Loan volumes have since increased significantly and stood at €1,000 billion during 2018. LMA follows a rule-based approach. The time taken for settlement within the LMA is 10 to 20 days and the enforcement mechanism adopted by the LMA in penalizing defaulters has led to a highly disciplined market. Due diligence is mostly undertaken before execution of a trade, and the time taken in settlement is reportedly on account of documentation processes. Membership of the LMA currently stands at over 600, covering more than 50 nationalities, and consists of banks, nonbank lenders, borrowers, law firms, rating agencies, and service providers. The LMA has expanded its activities to include all aspects of the primary and secondary syndicated loan markets.

Source: Reserve Bank of India. 2019. *Report of the task force on the development of secondary market for corporate loans*. New Delhi.

APPENDIX 7

European Investment Bank Project Appraisal and Monitoring

The European Investment Bank (EIB) has increased its monitoring capacity over the years to cater to increasing public–private partnerships. The appraisal of risks requires the coordinated work of different parts of the bank's operational branches. That process includes analysis of the promoter's technical and market studies, in-house assessment of risk, and the capacity to perform detailed analysis of the technical merits of contracts.

The EIB monitors the projects it supports through all their stages—from contract signing to implementation and the operational phase—until the loan is paid back. In particular, the EIB monitors the servicing of loans, checks that funds are being used in line with objectives and projections, and keeps itself informed of developments involving the promoter and its partners. It also ensures that the projects it supports are carried out under the contract terms.

The strength of EIB's project appraisal and monitoring process plays an important role in providing confidence to other lenders to a project.

Source: W. van der Geest and J. Nunez-Ferrer. 2011. Appropriate Financial Instruments for Public–Private Partnership to Boost Cross-Border Infrastructural Development—EU Experience. *ADBI Working Paper.* No. 281. Tokyo: Asian Development Bank Institute. https://www.adb.org/sites/default/files/publication/156136/adbi-wp281.pdf.

APPENDIX 8
International Bank for Reconstruction and Development Catastrophe Deferred Drawdown Option

This is a contingent financing line that provides immediate liquidity following a disaster or a health emergency. Funds become available for disbursement after the drawdown trigger, typically an International Bank for Reconstruction and Development member country's declaration of a state of emergency and the conditions for tapping the facility being met.

On approval, a country must have an adequate macroeconomic policy framework and a satisfactory disaster risk management program in place or under preparation. This is monitored by International Bank for Reconstruction and Development.

A forex liquidity facility would be similar to the catastrophe deferred drawdown option. This is a well-tested product that insures countries against disasters, and it could be easily adapted to be triggered by foreign exchange shocks beyond a pre-agreed size.

Although the facilities are for catastrophe financing, the World Bank has recently used this facility leverage to stimulate infrastructure bids with a $450 million guarantee to Argentina's government to support a renewable energy program. This attracted private investments of more than $2 billion.

Source: World Bank, IBRD. 2020. *Annual Report 2020*. Washington, DC. https://openknowledge.worldbank.org/bitstream/handle/10986/34406/9781464816192.pdf.

APPENDIX 9
Asset Recycling in Developed Countries and India

Australia, Japan, and the United States are among developed countries that have successfully implemented asset recycling programs. In the United States in the mid-2000s, tolled expressways worth $1.8 billion were leased to private investors for $ 1.8 billion in Illinois and $3.8 billion in Indiana. In Australia, some 10 expressways were tolled in five states from 2014 to 2018. In this way, the federal government freed up A$52 billion from these transactions.

India is a success story for asset monetization since the toll–operate–transfer model was launched in 2018. The National Highways Authority of India has offered rights to operate and collect revenue from nine national highways (648 km) for 30 years under this scheme.

Under the toll–operate–transfer model, the concessionaire pays a one-time concession fee upfront to the asset owner and receives the right to toll a stretch of road until the concession period ends. During the concession period, the concessionaire is obliged to maintain and operate the road to prescribed standards.

From the above example of asset recycling in India, it can be concluded that low-cost funds from global investors can be availed in stable operating assets if the government plans the offerings well in terms of size of investment, quality of assets, and risk management.

India is exploring a similar model for other classes of infrastructure assets, such as ports, airports, power transmission and distribution, and railways. The monetization of assets in these sectors are being planned by transferring them to a trust, such as an infrastructure investment trusts or real estate investment trust, in which institutional investors (like pension funds) invest against a capital consideration that captures the value of future cash flows with or without transferring operational control. Six airports have been privatized using this model, and more are planned for privatization by 2025.

Source: *NHAI receives upfront consideration of Rs 5,011 crore towards TOT Bundle. 2020.* Press Information Bureau, Government of India.

APPENDIX 10

Financing by Brazilian Development Bank to Crowd-Out Private Investment

Pre-Reforms

Source of Funds	Mode of Operation	Effect on Economy
Funds from the National Treasury and Workers' Assistance Fund (FAT) and Civil Servant Asset Formation Program (PIS-PASEP) provided at below market rate, called TJLP (Taxa de Juros de Longo Prazo)	Lends at cost of borrowing + risk capital + cost of operations, which is lower than central bank benchmark rate	• Crowds out corporate lending • Subsidized rates pose unfair competition to banks; limited development of financial markets • Loans from Treasury weaken sovereign profile

Key Outputs

- Interest rates are more market aligned
- Investment gaps are plugged through funding of projects that cannot be financed by private sector or traditional banks (small and medium-sized enterprises or social sector projects)
- Complements the private and bank capital rather than replacing it

Key message: Financial institutions should not crowd-out private investment and should provide low-cost capital only to projects that cannot be financed by the private sector.

Source: Banco Nacional de Desenvolvimento Econômico e Social. http://www.bndes.gov.br/wps/portal/site/home.

APPENDIX 11

African Development Bank A and B Loan Structure

As part of its mission to mobilize capital for productive use in viable projects in Africa, the African Development Bank (AfDB) offers two loan syndication structures—the more common parallel cofinancing loan structure and the A and B loan structure. Under this structure, the AfDB acts as the lender of record by keeping part of the A loan and selling stakes in the B loan to investors who take full exposure to the underlying project credit risk in proportion to their stake.

B loan stakeholders benefit from the AfDB's preferred creditor status as a multilateral development bank. By introducing a B loan program, AfDB's prime objective is to attract private capital to Africa, drawn by a transaction with a lender of record and a cofinancer.

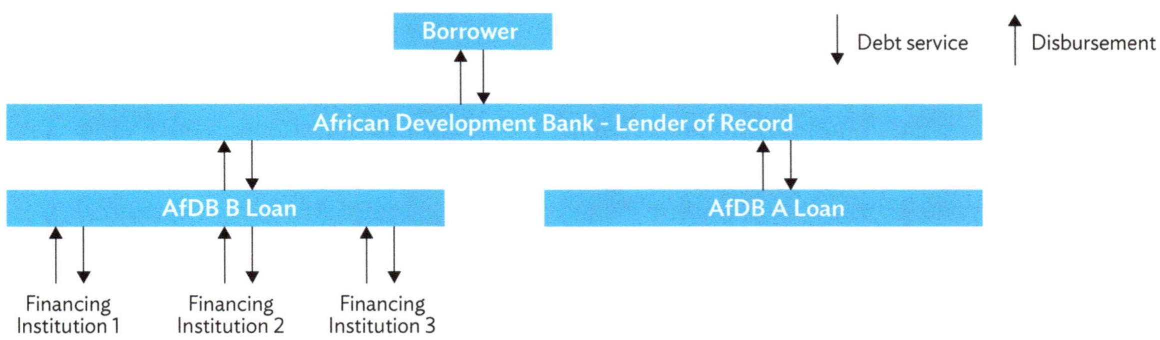

Source: African Development Bank website. https://www.afdb.org/en.

APPENDIX 12

European Investment Bank Structured Finance Facility

The Structured Finance Facility of the European Investment Bank (EIB) enables lending to projects with a higher risk profile and for more flexible financing solutions. Some of the key financing instruments for this facility have been showcased below:

Project Finance Loans with Direct Project Risk

- Represents about 20% of the EIB's overall Trans-European Transport Network (TEN-T) lending volume
- Project finance loan with the EIB taking direct project risk
- Provided on an equal footing basis with commercial banks already during construction period

Investment Funds/Marguerite Fund

- EIB invests equity in selected infrastructure funds with investment mandate covering the TEN-T to provide additional sources of equity finance for infrastructure projects and to enable it to extend its reach to eligible target projects beyond its traditional lending activities
- Overcomes shortage of equity in certain sectors or geographies
- Marguerite Fund: Infrastructure investment vehicle established in 2009 for long-term public and private institutional investors

Loan Guarantee Instrument for TEN-T

- Specialized instrument jointly developed by the EIB and the European Commission
- Provides contingent mezzanine debt, thereby protecting senior debt in projects exposed to traffic risk
- Improves capital structure and senior debt credit quality
- Lowers refinancing risk and potentially allows for funding cost reduction

Key message: The EIB involvement in a project by providing debt or equity increases confidence in that project among private investors and so attracts investments from that quarter.

Source: EIB.

APPENDIX 13

Association of Southeast Asian Nations Credit Guarantee and Investment Facility

The Credit Guarantee and Investment Facility (CGIF) of the Association of Southeast Asian Nations (ASEAN) helps companies in the ASEAN region to issue bonds by enhancing their credit ratings.

The CGIF provides guarantees in local currency-denominated bonds; the guarantees make it easier for corporations to issue local currency bonds with longer maturities. Having these guarantees in a project can attract private investment.

CGIF guarantees are irrevocable and unconditional commitments to pay bondholders on nonpayment by issuers throughout the tenor of the bonds. This commitment is backed by CGIF's equity capital, which has been fully paid-in by its contributors.

CGIF, in 2019, received an initial capital contribution of $700 million from ASEAN, the Asian Development Bank, Japan, the People's Republic of China, and the Republic of Korea. As of 20 August 2020, its capitalization was $1.1 trillion following a capital increase.

Figure A13.1: CGIF Cash Flow Diagram

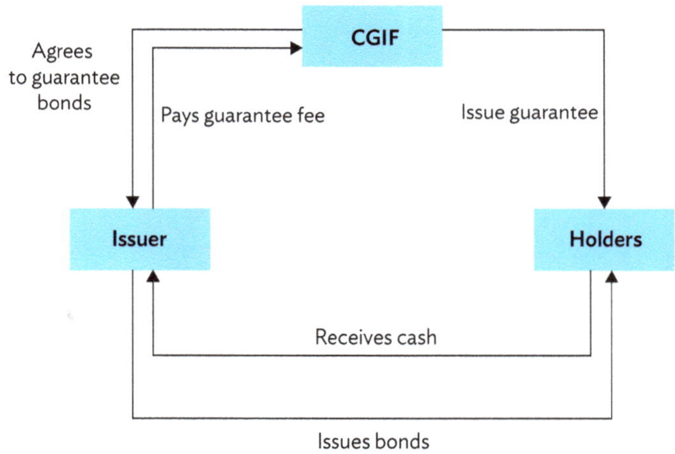

CGIF = Credit Guarantee and Investment Facility.

Source: ???

APPENDIX 14

Funds, Programs, Platforms of Development Finance Institutions for Project Preparation and Capacity Building Support

The key funds, programs, platforms of Development Finance Institutions (DFIs) is a specific terminology widely used by financial institutions in various demographics has been discussed below:

Funds:

- **Asian Development Bank:** Asia Pacific Project Preparation Facility provides financial assistance to developing member countries and their public sector agencies to support the financial, legal, and technical advisory services required to prepare and structure public–private partnership (PPP) transactions, and to enable reforms and capacity building that can be linked to potential or existing PPP transactions.
- **African Development Bank (AfDB):** Mortgage Investment Corporation Fund is used for capacity building and strengthening institutions in eligible Restricted Money Changers.
- **AfDB's African Private Sector Assistance Fund:** Administered by the bank, it provides grants for capacity-building support and technical assistance.
- **New Development Bank:** Project Preparation Fund is a multidonor fund designed to support the preparation of bankable projects by providing technical assistance.
- **New Partnership for Africa's Development:** Infrastructure Project Preparation Facility Special Fund was established to assist African countries, regional economic communities, specialized agencies, and related institutions by providing grant resources for: (i) preparing high-quality and viable regional/continental infrastructure projects with a view to requesting financing from public and private sources, (ii) developing a consensus and partnership for project implementation, and (iii) promoting infrastructure projects and programs that enhance regional integration and trade.

Forums and platforms:

- **AfDB:** Africa Investment Forum is an innovative marketplace dedicated to advancing projects to bankable stages, raising capital, and accelerating the financial closure of deals. The alternate investment funds profiles bankable transformational projects, matching them with investors.
- **SOURCE:** This is the multilateral platform for sustainable infrastructure led and funded by multilateral development banks supporting the development of projects to bridge infrastructure gaps and the digitalization agenda of governments.
- **G20:** Global Infrastructure Facility enables collective action among a wide range of partners, including donors, development finance institutions, governments, and the private sector, to leverage funding and expertise to build bankable pipelines of infrastructure projects that attract private financing.

Programs

- **AfDB:** African Legal Support Facility of African Development Bank provides legal advice and technical assistance in the negotiation of complex commercial transactions, and develops and proposes innovative tools for capacity building and knowledge management.
- **European PPP Expertise Centre:** Aims to increase capacity of its members, all of which are from the public sector, to enter into PPPs.
- **Project Advisory Support Service Agreement:** Under the European Investment Bank, provides hands-on support during all phases of European Union (EU) funded project delivery. At all times, works closely with local teams and authorities to ensure knowledge transfer to the local staff.
- **Joint Assistance to Support Projects in European Region:** Improves the capacity of administrations and promoters by transferring knowledge about project preparation, environmental issues, and EU legislation, and speeds up the EU approval process by carrying out an independent quality review which prepares the ground for the European Commission's decision.
- **Eastern Partnership Investment in Connectivity Facility:** Plans, prepares, and implements infrastructure projects on the Trans-European Network for Transport in Eastern Partnership countries.

Source: Regional institutions' data from their websites.

APPENDIX 15

Financing Tools Assessment Framework

The evaluation of financing strategies for transport infrastructure financing of different regions and countries requires an understanding of the various financing tools. To assess these tools, it is essential to have mapping of routes, instruments, and institutions that can finance infrastructure projects. Doing this helps identify the size and applicability of tools. For instance, capital market tools are nonexistent in Bhutan, making infrastructure financing through local bond markets difficult. Figure A15.1 shows a four-level order for mapping the financial tools in each country.

Figure A15.1: Institution Mapping

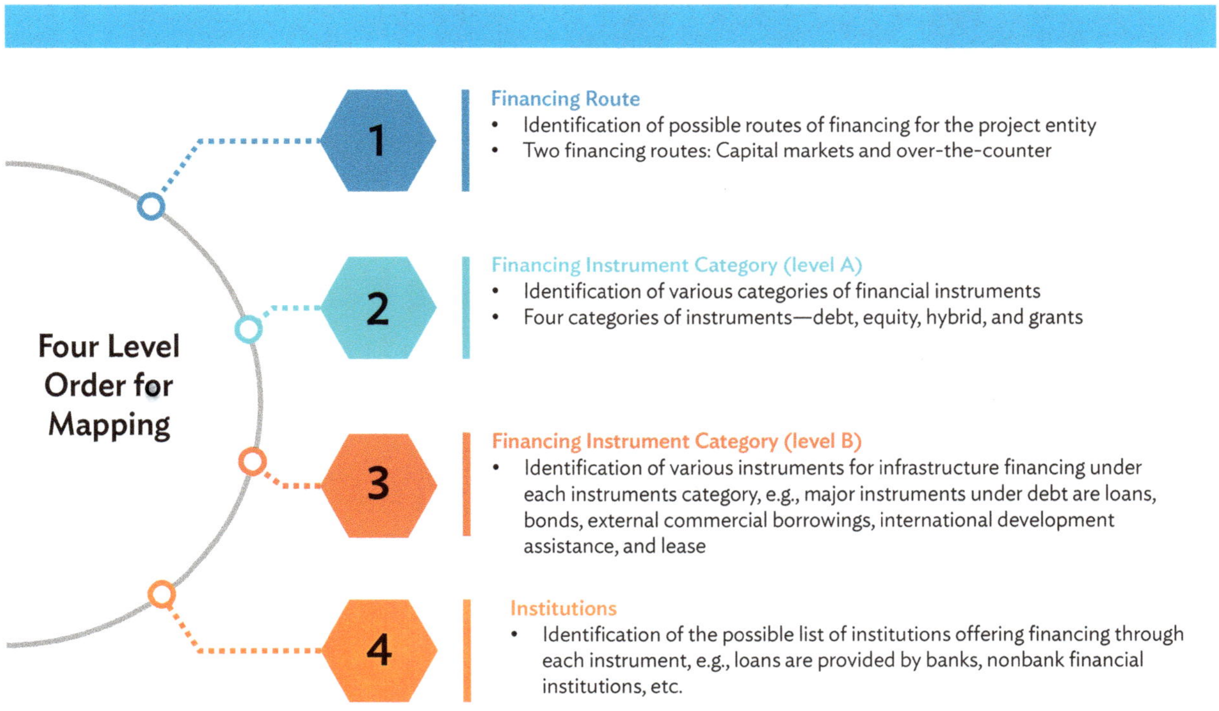

Source: Study team analysis.

Routes, instruments, and financing route: Broadly, infrastructure projects can access financing through two routes: over-the-counter (OTC) and the capital market.

Financing instrument category level A: The OTC financing route can be further classified into various financing instruments that are negotiated and dealt outside exchanges. These instruments are debt securities, equities, hybrid securities, and grants.

Financing instrument category level B: Various level 1 financing instruments can be classified further, e.g., debt securities can be classified into loans, bonds, external commercial borrowing, international development assistance, and leases.

Institutions: The financial institutions that provide these financial instruments are elaborated. Commercial banks, nonbanking financial institutions, and multilateral and regional development banks are the largest providers of loans via the OTC route.

Figure A15.2 gives a high-level view of the various institutions, instruments, and routes that exist in various locations.

Figure A15.2: Mapping of Routes, Instruments, and Institution Mapping

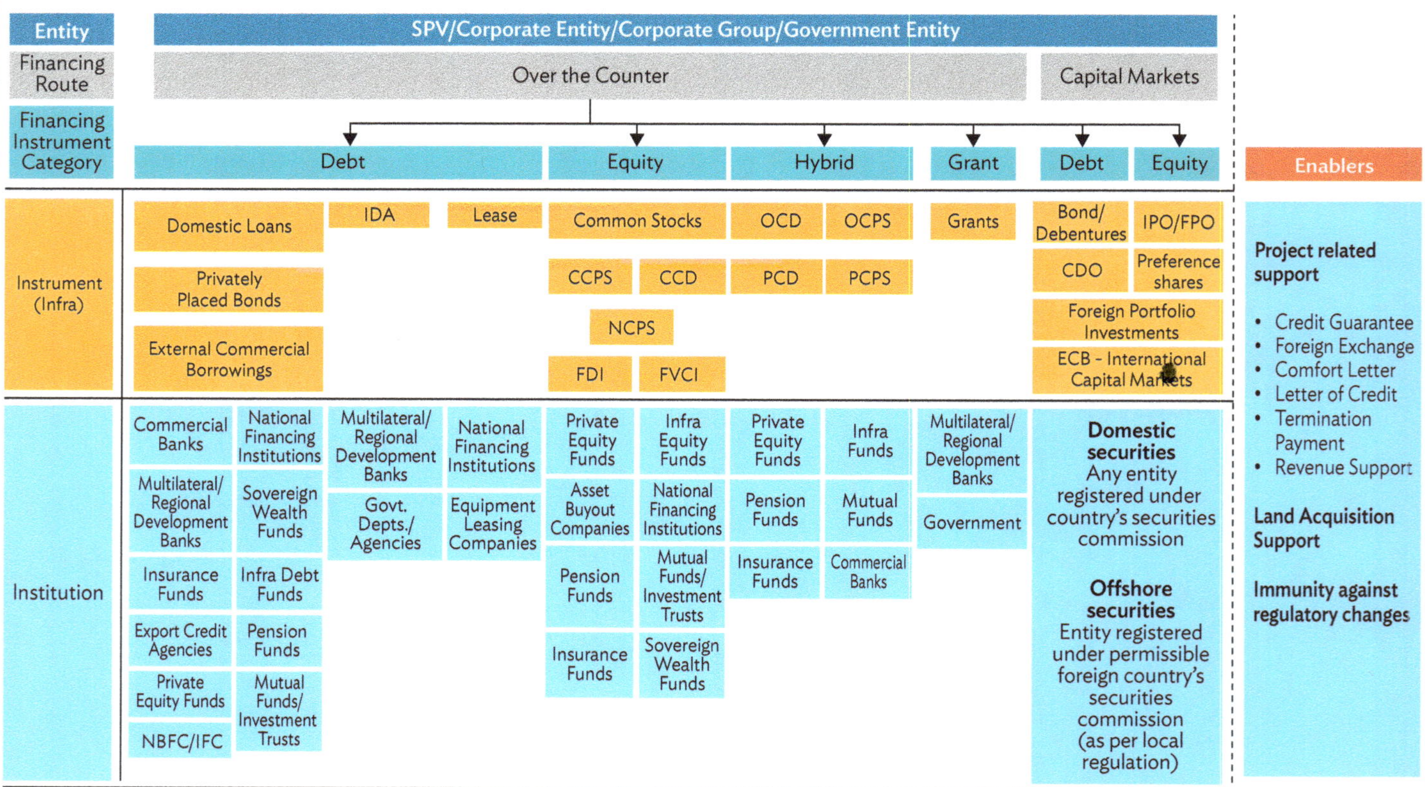

CCD = compulsory convertible debenture, CCPS = compulsorily convertible preference shares, CDO = collateralized debt obligation, ECB = external commercial borrowings, FDI = foreign direct investment, FPO = follow-on public offering, FVCI = foreign venture capital investor, IDA = International Development Association, IFC = International Finance Corporation, IPO = initial public offering, NBFC = nonbank financial company, NCPS = non-convertible preference shares, OCD = optionally convertible debentures, OCPS = optionally convertible performance shares, PCD = Participating Convertible Debentures, PCPS = participating convertible performance shares, SPV = special purpose vehicle.

Source: Study team analysis.

APPENDIX 16

Assessing the Affordability of Toll Rates

This appendix assesses the affordability of levying a toll rate on the Kolkata (India)–Benapole (Bangladesh)–Dhaka (Bangladesh)–Agartala (India) route.

The cost implication of levying a user charge of $0.06/kilometer (km)-vehicle along the Kolkata-Agartala route in Bangladesh for transporting tea would be to contribute about 1% to the overall transportation cost and about 0.1% to the annual cargo value.

Upgrading the Kolkata–Agartala route could result in an increase in average speed and benefit both industries and people. Figure A16.1 shows the benefits accrued to industries in terms of transportation cost savings and inventory cost savings. Transportation cost savings increase from zero to $0.10/km-vehicle and from zero to $0.13 million for annual inventory cost savings, as truck speed increase from 25 to 50 km/hour. There would be other benefits, including increased land values and reduced accidents. These benefits can be captured by levying user charges corresponding to the benefits accrued to stakeholders.

Figure A16.1: Transportation and Inventory Cost Savings

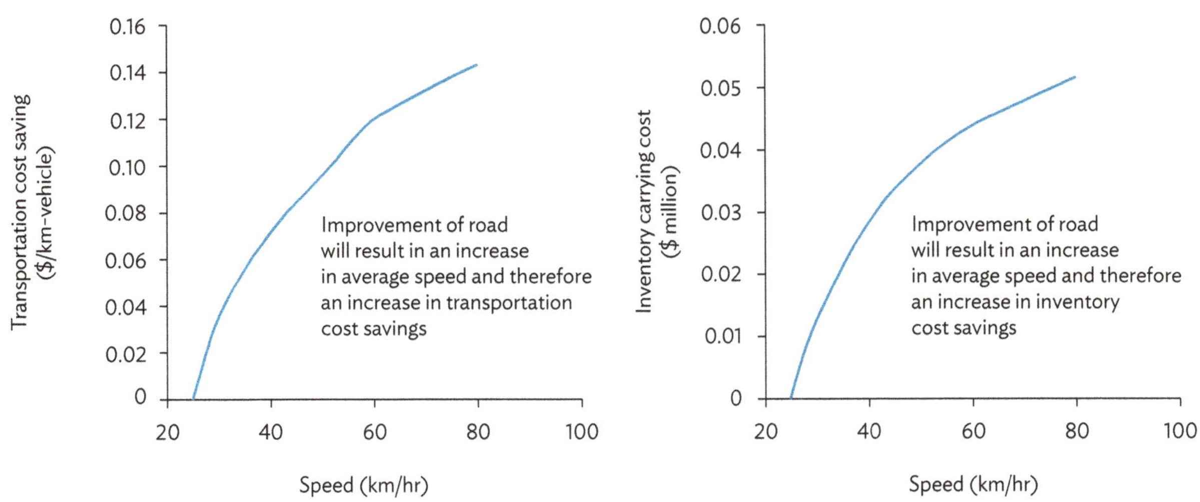

hr = hour, km = kilometer.

Source: Study team analysis.

APPENDIX 17

BIMSTEC Master Plan for Transport Connectivity Two-Lane Road Projects

#	Country	Project Description	Classification	Lane	Estimated Cost (2018 $ million)	Cost/ Capacity (km)	% Traffic Utilization
1	India	Jogighopa–Bilasipara	R2	2	200	2.7	72.7
2	India	Upgrading of Wangjing–Khudenthabi section in Manipur	R2	2	95	1.4	0.1
3	India	Two-laning from the Assam–Meghalaya border, Dudhanai to Dalu via Bagmara, NH 62	R2	2	412	2.1	24.9
4	India	Improvement of NH208 between Teliamura and Harina (158 km) in Tripura	R2	2	285	1.8	24.9
5	India	Two-laning of alternate route between Barak Valley (Silchar) to Guwahati via Harangajao–Turuk in Assam	N	2	452	1.8	40.0
6	India	Improvement of Manu–Simlung, NH 44 in Tripura	R2	2	170	1.5	62.3
7	India	Khowai–Agartala link road	R2	2	85	1.5	62.3
8	India	Improvement of NH 512 between km 82.4 and km 99.5, and between km 104.2 and km 106.6	R2	2	21	1.1	62.3
9	India	MaramPeren–Dimapur road in Manipur and Nagaland	R2	2	360	1.7	0.1
10	India	Hafflong–Tamelong via Lia Sang and Tavesam in Assam and Manipur	N	2	300	2.0	20.3
11	India	Ukhrul–Jessami, NH 202 in Manipur	R2	2	230	2.0	0.1
12	India	Development of the Siliguri–Mirik–Darjeeling link road	R2	2	150	1.7	47.1
13	India	Gelephu (Bhutan) to Samthaibari (near Hapachara in Assam)	R2	2	117	2.9	64.7
14	Nepal	Bardibas–Janakpur–Jaynagar Road and Dhalkebar–Janakpur–Bhittamond Roads	R1	2	65	0.9	19.0
15	Bhutan	Upgrading of the Gelephu–Trongsa National Highway (before 244 km, but shortened to 201 km), including four bridges	R2	2	82	0.6	11.9
16	Bhutan	Construction of the Gelephu–Panbang section of the SEWH	R2	2	57	0.7	13.4
17	Bhutan	Construction of the Lhamoizhingkha–Sarpang section of the SEWH (75 km, including about 14 bridges)	R2	2	52	0.7	11.9

continued on next page

Table *continued*

#	Country	Project Description	Classification	Lane	Estimated Cost (2018 $ million)	Cost/ Capacity (km)	% Traffic Utilization
18	Bhutan	Construction of the Nganglam–Dewathang section of the SEWH (75 km)	R2	2	48	0.6	37.1
19	Bhutan	Kharbandi–Pasakha–Gedu (55 km, including Singye Bridge)	R2	2	18	0.3	74.3
20	Myanmar	Construction of new Bago–Kyaikto road	R2	2	200	2.5	44.0
21	Myanmar	Yangon–Mandalay Expressway improvement project from Yangon to Payagyi (65 km)	N	2	105	1.6	24.0
22	Regional	Kolkata–Kalughat–Raxual, and Biratnagar–Sahibganj (Bangladesh) linkages	R2	2	2,000	2.2	43.1

BIMSTEC = Bay of Bengal Initiative for Multi-Sectoral Technical and Economic Cooperation, km = kilometer, N = national projects, NH = national highway, SEWH = South East-West Highway.

Sources: BIMSTEC Master Plan for Transport Connectivity; study team analysis.

APPENDIX 18

Major Toll Roads in BIMSTEC Countries

Name of Toll Road Managed by Government Authority	Road length	Country
Chaloem Maha Nakhon (First Stage Expressway System)	27.1 km	Thailand[a]
Chalong Rat (Kanchanapisek–Ramindra–At Narong Expressway)	28.1 km	Thailand
Burapha Withi (Bang Na–Chonburi Expressway)	55.0 km	Thailand
3rd Stage Expressway (Third Stage Expressway System, S1 section or At Narong–Bang Na Expressway)	4.1 km	Thailand
Kanchanapisek Expressway (Bang Phli–Suksawat Expressway or Southern Kanchanapisek Road)	34.0 km	Thailand
Motorway 7 (Bangkok–Chonburi–Pattaya Expressway)	125.9 km	Thailand
Motorway 9 (Eastern–Western Kanchanapisek Road)	131.0 km	Thailand
Hatikumrul-Bonpara highway	50.0 km	Bangladesh[b]
Chattogram Port Access Road	13.7 km	Bangladesh
Dhaka-Sylhet highway between Jagadishpur and Sherpur	74.0 km	Bangladesh
Southern Expressway	126.1 km	Sri Lanka
Outer circular highway	20.0 km	Sri Lanka
Colombo–Katunayake Expressway	25.8 km	Sri Lanka
Narayanghat–Hetauda road	...	Nepal[c]
Naubise–Muglin road	...	Nepal
Narayanghat–Butwal road	...	Nepal
Bhairahawa–Bhumahi road	...	Nepal
Kakadbhitta–Damak	...	Nepal[d]
Damak–Itahari	...	Nepal[d]
Biratnagar–Dharan	...	Nepal[d]
Koshi–Chaiharwa	...	Nepal[d]
Chaiharwa–Pathlaiya	...	Nepal[d]
Heautuda–Birgung	...	Nepal[d]
Birgung–Pathlaiya	...	Nepal[d]
Dhulikhel–Khurkot,	...	Nepal[d]
Khurkot–Sindhuli–Bardibas	...	Nepal[d]
Pachkhal–Melamchi	...	Nepal[d]

... = not available, Bay of Bengal Initiative for Multi-Sectoral Technical and Economic Cooperation.

Sources:. http://www.exat.co.th/index.php/th/service-eng/expressways-toll-rates.html; *Daily Star*. 2022. Dhaka–Mawa–Bhanga Expressway Toll Collection: Likely to Start from July. Updated 8 February. https://www.thedailystar.net/frontpage/news/dhaka-mawa-bhanga-expressway-toll-collection-likely-start-july-2040869; *The Himalayan*. 2017. Roads Board proposes Increasing Toll Rates. 22 August. https://thehimalayantimes.com/business/road-board-nepal-proposes-increasing-toll-rates.

APPENDIX 19

List of Regional Early and Planned Projects in the BIMSTEC Master Plan for Transport Connectivity

#	Countries involved	Project Description	Classification	Estimated Cost (2018 $ million)	Responsible Agency	Type of Asset Class
1	Bangladesh–Myanmar	Construction of direct road link between Bangladesh and Myanmar (Gundum [Bangladesh]/Taungbro-Bawlibazaar–Kyauktaw [Myanmar] (135 km)	R1	Not yet estimated	Roads and Highways Department	Roads and highways
2	Bangladesh–Myanmar	Four-laning of the Chattogram–Cox's Bazar–Teknaf Highway	R2	1,270	Ministry of Road Transport and Bridge/ Road transport and Roads and Highway Department	Roads and highways
3	India–Bangladesh	Two-laning from the Assam / Meghalaya border, Dudhanai to Dalu, via Bagmara, NH 62	R2	412	Public Works Department (PWD) Meghalaya	Roads and highways
4	India–Bangladesh	Improvement of NH 208 between Teliamura to Harina (158 km) in Tripura	R2	285	No update on public domain	Roads and highways
5	India–Bangladesh	Upgrading road between Kolkata and Bongaon near Petrapole on the India–Bangladesh border	R2	130	No update on public domain	Roads and highways
6	India–Bangladesh	Development of link roads between Srirampu–Dhubri and Phulbari to Tura with a new bridge across the Brahamputra River on NH 127B	R2	825	National Highway Infrastructure Development Corporation Limited (NHIDCL)	Roads and highways
7	India–Bangladesh	Improvement of Manu–Simlung, NH 44 in Tripura	R2	170	NHIDCL	Roads and highways
8	India–Bangladesh	Khowai–Agartala link road	R2	85	NHIDCL	Roads and highways
9	India–Bangladesh	Improvement of NH 512 between km 82.4 and km 99.5, and between km 104.2 and km 106.6	R2	21	PWD, West Bengal	Roads and highways

continued on next page

Table *continued*

#	Countries involved	Project Description	Classification	Estimated Cost (2018 $ million)	Responsible Agency	Type of Asset Class
10	India–Bangladesh	Upgrading of Paikan–Tura	R2	205	NHIDCL	Roads and highways
11	India–Bangladesh	Double tracking Bongaigaon–Kamakhya in Assam	R2	320	Northeast Frontier Railway Construction Organization	Railways
12	India–Bangladesh	Dhubri in Assam to Medhnipathar in Meghalaya with a double line rail cum road bridge over the Brahmaputra River at Dhubri (79 km)	R2	1,100	NHIDCL	Railways
13	India–Bangladesh	New Belonia–Feni line connecting with the India-Bangladesh border	R2	Not available	Northeast Frontier Railway Construction Organization	Railways
14	India–Bangladesh	Radhikapur–Birol rail link	R2	Not available	Ministry of External Affairs	Railways
15	India–Bangladesh	Development of National Waterway 2 on the Brahmaputra River from India-Bangladesh border at Dhubri to Sadiya (891 km)	R2	Not yet estimated	Inland Waterways Authority of India	Inland waterways
16	India–Bangladesh	Four-laning of the Rangpur to Burimari Highway (128 km)	R2	960	Roads and Highways Department	Roads and highways
17	India–Bangladesh	Construction of Sheikh Mujib Railway Bridge (parallel to the Jamuna bridge) with twin dual-gauge lines	R2	1,173	Bangladesh Bridge Authority	Railways
18	India–Bangladesh	Four-laning Daulatdia–Magura–Jhneidha–Jashore–Khulna (212 km)	R2	1,800	Ministry of Road Transport and Bridge (India) / Road transport and Highway Department (Bangladesh)	Roads and highways
19	India–Bangladesh	Four-laning of the Bhanga–Bhatiapara–Kalna–Lohagora–Narail–Jashore–Highway (135 km)	R2	1,100	Ministry of Road Transport and Bridge (India) / Road transport and Highway Department (Bangladesh)	Roads and highways

continued on next page

Table *continued*

#	Countries involved	Project Description	Classification	Estimated Cost (2018 $ million)	Responsible Agency	Type of Asset Class
20	India–Bangladesh	Construction of dual gauge railway between Bogura and Shahid M. Monsur Ali	R2	796	Bangladesh Railways funded by India's Indian Line of Credit-Export–Import	Railways
21	India–Bangladesh	Construction of dual-gauge, double rail line and conversion of existing rail line into dual gauge between Akhaura and Laksham	R2	784	Bangladesh Railways Construction-Max Group	Railways
22	India–Bangladesh	Conversion of existing meter gauge double line to dual gauge between Tongi and Bhairab	R2	751	Bangladesh Railways	Railways
23	India–Bangladesh	Upgrading Cumilla (Moynamati)–Brahmanbaria (Dharkar) 4-lane national highway (51 km)	R2	718		Roads and highways
24	India–Bangladesh	Four-laning Rangpur to Banglabandha (196 km)	R2	1,500	Roads and Highway Department	Roads and highways
25	India–Bangladesh	Construction of broad-gauge double-track line in section between Khulna and Darshana junction	R2	446		Railways
26	India–Bangladesh	Improvement of the Ashuganj River Port–Sarail-Dharkhar–Akhaura Land Port Road as a 4-lane national highway (50.6 km)	R2	430	Roads and Highway Department	Roads and highways
27	India–Bangladesh	Four-laning of the Sylhet to Tamabil Highway (65 km)	R2	400	Ministry of Road Transport and Bridge/ Road transport and Highway Department	Roads and highways
28	India–Bangladesh	Conversion of meter gauge double line to dual gauge between Bhairab Bazar and Akhaura, including rebuilding of the existing Bhairab and Titas bridges	R2	387		Railways
29	India–Bangladesh	Construction of broad gauge rail line between Chilahati and Chilahati border	R2	10	Bangladesh Railways	Railways

continued on next page

Table *continued*

#	Countries involved	Project Description	Classification	Estimated Cost (2018 $ million)	Responsible Agency	Type of Asset Class
30	India–Bhutan	Hapachara-Tulungia-Jogighopa-Gendera-Paikan Road	R2	228	NHIDCL	Roads and highways
31	India–Bhutan	Jogighopa-Bilasipara	R2	200	No update on public domain	Roads and highways
32	India–Bhutan	Gelephu (Bhutan) to Samthaibari (near Hapachara in Assam)	R2	117	PWD Assam	Roads and highways
33	India–Bhutan	Development of Gelephu Transport Hub	R2	Not yet specified	Conflicted between Road Safety and Transport Authority and Gelephu Thromde (municipal corporation)	Multimodal transport
34	India–Bhutan	Development of Nganglam Dry Port	R2	Not yet specified	Ministry of Economic Affairs Department of Trade Export Promotion Division	Trade facilitation
35	India–Bhutan	Development of Pasakha Dry Port	R2	30	Ministry of Economic Affairs Department of Trade Export Promotion Division	Trade facilitation
36	India–Bhutan	Construction of Allay Land Customs Station and access road (1.2 km) to Pasakha Industrial Estate	R2	17	Ministry of Economic Affairs Department of Trade Export Promotion Division	Trade facilitation
37	India–Bhutan	Upgrading of the Gelephu–Trongsa National Highway (before 244 km, but shortened to 201 km), including four bridges	R2	82	No update on public domain	Roads and highways
38	India–Bhutan	Construction of the Gelephu–Panbang section of the SEWH	R2	57	No update on public domain	Roads and highways

continued on next page

Table *continued*

#	Countries involved	Project Description	Classification	Estimated Cost (2018 $ million)	Responsible Agency	Type of Asset Class
39	India–Bhutan	Construction of the Lhamoizhingkha–Sarpang section of the SEWH (75 km, including about 14 bridges)	R2	52	No update on public domain	Roads and highways
40	India–Bhutan	Construction of the Nganglam–Dewathang section of the SEWH (75 km)	R2	48	No update on public domain	Roads and highways
41	India–Bhutan	Kharbandi–Pasakha–Gedu (55 km, including Singye Bridge)	R2	18	No update on public domain	Roads and highways
42	India–Bhutan	Development of Kokhrajhar (Assam)–Gelephu (Bhutan) (57 km), Pathsala (Assam)–Nanglam (Bhutan) (51 km), Rangiya (Assam) – Samdrupjongkhar (Bhutan) (48 km), Banarhat (West Bengal)–Samtse (Bhutan) (23 km), and Hasimara (West Bengal)–Phuentsholing (Bhutan) (18 km)	R1	To be estimated	Indian Railways (North-East Frontier Railway)	Railways
43	India–Myanmar	Upgrading of WangjingKhudenthabi section in Manipur	R2	95	No update on public domain	Roads and highways
44	India–Myanmar	Maram–Peren–Dimapur road in Manipur and Nagaland	R2	360	NHIDCL	Roads and highways
45	India–Myanmar	Four-laning of Imphal–Moirang, NH-150 in Manipur	R2	100	NHIDCL	Roads and highways
46	India–Myanmar	Ukhrul–Jessami, NH 202 in Manipur	R2	230	NHIDCL	Roads and highways
47	India–Myanmar	Provision of 69 new bridges along the Kalewa–Tamu Road	R2	54	Ministry of Construction	Roads and highways
48	India–Myanmar	Development of Tamu–Moreh border crossing	R1	Not yet estimated	Thai Chamber of Commerce, Ministry of Transport	Trade facilitation

continued on next page

Table *continued*

#	Countries involved	Project Description	Classification	Estimated Cost (2018 $ million)	Responsible Agency	Type of Asset Class
49	India–Myanmar	New lines linking Jiribam–Imphal (125 km) in Manipur, Imphal–Moreh (111 km) connecting with the India–Myanmar border, and a new line linking Moreh–Tamu–Kalay (128 km) onward to Mandalay	R1	3,062	Indian Railways (North-East Frontier Railway)	Railways
50	India–Nepal	Development of the Siliguri–Mirik–Darjeeling link road	R2	150	No update on public domain	Roads and highways
51	India–Nepal	Construction of Birgunj–Kathmandu Railway (115 km)	R2	2,500	Department of Railways Nepal	Railways
52	India–Nepal	Two-laning/ intermediate laning of Postal Highway (950–1,031 km), parallel and south of the East-West Highway (near the Indian border)	R2	500	Government. of Nepal	Roads and highways
53	India–Nepal	Upgrading of Narayanghat–Mungling–Kathmandu road (146 km) and studies on axle load control and road safety measures	R2	700	Department of Roads	Roads and highways
54	India–Nepal	Development of Kanchanpur inland container depot (ICD) in southwestern Nepal	R2	153	Nepal Intermodal Transport Development Board	Trade facilitation
55	India–Nepal	Nijgadh–Pathalaiya–Birgunj road upgrade	R2	200	No update on Public domain	Roads and highways
56	India–Nepal	Bardibas–Janakpur–Jaynagar Road and Dhalkebar–Janakpur–Bhittamond Roads	R1	65	No update on public domain	Roads and highways
57	India–Nepal	Widening of the Birgunj bypass to four lanes	R2	47	No update on public domain	Roads and highways
58	India–Nepal	Connection between the integrated check post (ICP) and the ICD bypass road at Birgunj	R2	12	No update on public domain	Roads and highways
59	India–Nepal	Nepal–India Transit Roads (e.g., Biratnagar, Birgunj, Bhairahawa, and Nepalgunj Roads connecting with Visakhapatnam, and Kolkata–Kanchanpuri (Bhimdatta) linkage	R1	Not yet estimated		Roads and highways

continued on next page

Table *continued*

#	Countries involved	Project Description	Classification	Estimated Cost (2018 $ million)	Responsible Agency	Type of Asset Class
60	India–Nepal	Kolkata–Kalughat–Raxual, and Biratnagar–Sahibganj (Bangladesh) linkages	R2	2,000	No update	Roads and highways
61	India–Nepal	Development of (i) Jaynagar–Janakpur–Bardibas (69 km, including 3 km in India and 66 km in Nepal), (ii) Jogbani–Biratnagar (19 km), (iii) Nepalganj–Nepalganj Road (12 km), (iv) Nautanwa–Bhairahawa (15 km), and (v) New Jalpaiguri–Kakarbitta (46 km).); and Basti and Kapilvastu (91 km)	R1	900	Indian Railways (North-East Frontier Railway)	Railways
62	Projects connecting multiple regions	Additional approach roads to ICPs/land ports (ICP Raxaul, Bihar approach road [7 km], ICP Bihar; Jogbani, Bihar approach road [1 km]; ICP Rupaidiha, Uttar Pradesh approach road [1.5 km]; ICP Sunaulli approach road [0.5 km], ICP Moreh approach road [3 km])	R2	To be specified	No update on public domain	Roads and highways
63	Projects connecting multiple regions	Development of ICPs, ongoing/planned (Dawki [Bangladesh border], Jaigaon [Bhutan border]; Banbasa, Bhithamore, Panitanki, Rupaidiha, and Sunauli [Nepal border], and Changrabandha, Fulbari, Ghojadanga, Hili, Kawrpuichhuah, Mahadipur, and Sutarkandi, Bangladesh border])	R2	Not fully specified	Land Port Authority of India	Trade facilitation
64	Projects connecting multiple regions	Development of rail siding logistics hubs within Raxaul, Jogbani, Petrapole, Hili, Nischintapur, and Sabroom land ports	R2	To be specified	Land Port Authority of India	Trade facilitation
65	Thailand–Myanmar	Improvement of the Bangkok–Kanchanaburi–Dawei road corridor by developing the section from Kanchanaburi to the Thailand/Myanmar border at Ban Phu Nam Ron	R2	1,300	Thailand Ministry of Transport, Department of Highways	Roads and highways

continued on next page

Table *continued*

#	Countries involved	Project Description	Classification	Estimated Cost (2018 $ million)	Responsible Agency	Type of Asset Class
66	Thailand–Myanmar	Construction of new Bago–Kyaikto road	R2	200	Department of Highways, Ministry of Construction	Roads and highways
67	Thailand–Myanmar	Gyaing (580 m), Kawkarait (796 m), and Zathapyin (480 m) bridges	R2	308	Ministry of Construction and Department of Bridges	Roads and highways
68	Thailand–Myanmar	Development of new Htee Kee (Myanmar) /Baan Phu Nam Ron (Thailand) border crossing road	R1	142	No info on public domain	Roads and highways
69	Thailand–Myanmar	Laem Chabang–Dawei Rail Link via Kanchanaburi	R1	5,100	Thai Chamber of Commerce Ministry of Transport, Ministry of Foreign Affairs (Myanmar)	Railways
70	Thailand–Myanmar	Development of new Htee Kee/Baan Phu Nam Ron border crossing	R1	142	Ministry of Construction and Neighbouring Countries Economic Development Cooperation, Thailand	Trade facilitation

NH = national highway, NHIDCL = National Highway Infrastructure Development Corporation Limited.

Source: BIMSTEC Master Plan for transport connectivity; study team analysis.

APPENDIX 20

National Early and Planned Projects in the BIMSTEC Master Plan for Transport Connectivity

#	Country	Project Description	Estimated Cost (2018 $ million)	Responsible Agency	Type of Asset Class
1	Bangladesh	Hazrat Shahjalal International Airport Expansion Project, Dhaka (Phase 2)	Not yet estimated	Civil Aviation Authority of Bangladesh	Airports
2	Bangladesh	Further development of Shah Amanat International Airport, Chattogram (construction of parallel taxiway)	Not yet estimated	Civil Aviation Authority of Bangladesh	Airports
3	Bangladesh	Development of Bangabandhu Sheikh Mujib International Airport to serve central Bangladesh	5,878	Civil Aviation Authority of Bangladesh	Airports
4	Bangladesh	Expansion of Osmani International Airport, Sylhet (Phase 1: passenger terminal building, cargo complex, fire station, control tower, maintenance building, apron, and taxiway)	289	Civil Aviation Authority of Bangladesh	Airports
5	Bangladesh	Bay multipurpose terminal on west coast of Chattogram, 6 kms from Chattogram port (one multipurpose and two container terminals)	2,100	Chittagong Port Authority	Ports
6	Bangladesh	Upgrading of Mongla Port (e.g., construction of container terminals including cargo handling equipment, tower, container delivery yard)	656	Mongla Port Authority	Ports
7	Bangladesh	Payra Port Development Project (first terminal, connecting road, bridge over the Andermanik River and related facilities)	474	Payra Port Authority	Ports

continued on next page

Table *continued*

#	Country	Project Description	Estimated Cost (2018 $ million)	Responsible Agency	Type of Asset Class
8	Bangladesh	Construction of Laldia multipurpose terminal at Chattogram, 4 km upstream of Karnaphuli River	353	Chittagong Port Authority	Ports
9	Bangladesh	Development of Matarbari Port in Cox's Bazar	320	Chittagong Port Authority	Ports
10	Bangladesh	Karnaphuli Container Terminal at Chattogram	200	Chittagong Port Authority	Ports
11	Bangladesh	Construction of double track high-speed railway from Dhaka to Chattogram via Cumilla and Laksham	3,734	Bangladesh Railways	Railways
12	Bangladesh	Construction of broad-gauge rail line from Bhanga junction (Faridpur) to Payra Port via Barishal	3,414	Bangladesh Railways	Railways
13	Bangladesh	Conversion of meter-gauge double line to dual gauge between Laksam and Chattogram	1,521	Bangladesh Railways	Railways
14	Bangladesh	Construction of second railway-cum-road bridge on Karnaphuli River at Kalurghat	241	Bangladesh Railways Funded by Economic Development Cooperation Fund (EDCF) (Tk7.9 billion) and Government of Bangladesh (Tk3.9 billion)	Railways
15	Bangladesh	Introduction of electric traction, including overhead catenary and substation, on the Narayanganj–Dhaka–Joydevpur rail section	67	No progress yet	Railways
16	Bangladesh	Construction of the Dhaka–Ashulia Elevated Expressway	2,098	Bangladesh Bridge Authority Contractors: China National Machinery Imp. & Exp. Corp.	Roads and highways
17	Bangladesh	Four-laning of the Dhaka (Katchpur)-Sylhet Highway (226 km, NH 2)	1,800	Roads and Highways Department	Roads and highways
18	Bangladesh	Four-laning Bhanga [Faridpur]-Barishal (130 km) and 4-laning Barishal–Patuakhali–Kuakata (106 km) with a link to Payra deep sea port	2,000	Ministry of Road Transport and Bridge/Road Transport and Highways Department	Roads and highways
19	Bangladesh	Construction of Bridge on Barguna–Pathorghata Road over the Bishkhali River	250	No update on public domain	Roads and highways

continued on next page

Table *continued*

#	Country	Project Description	Estimated Cost (2018 $ million)	Responsible Agency	Type of Asset Class
20	Bangladesh	Construction of Bridge along the Bhulta–Araihazar–Banchrampur–Nabinagar Road over the Meghna River	231	Bangladesh Bridge Authority	Roads and highways
21	Bangladesh	Construction of a Bridge along the Patuakhali–Amtoli–Barguna Road over the Payra River	200	Bangladesh Bridge Authority	Roads and highways
22	Bangladesh	Chattogram Port Access Road (13 km)	150	Ministry of Road Transport and Bridge/Road Transport and Highways Department	Roads and highways
23	Bangladesh	Four-laning of the Khulna–Mongla Highway (37 km)	300	Ministry of Road Transport and Bridge/Road Transport and Highways Department	Roads and highways
24	Bangladesh	Four-laning Paturia to Nabinagar, including Manikganj bypass	400	Ministry of Road Transport and Bridge/Road Transport and Highways Department	Roads and highways
25	Bhutan	Expansion of Gelephu Airport (feasibility and design studies, construction of new 3,000-meter runway and associated river diversion, Instrument Landing System (ILS) and runway lighting system, apron taxiway, terminal building, hangar, cargo building)	200	No information on public domain (Bhutan Civil Aviation Authority, Department of Air Transport)	Airports
26	Bhutan	Further expansion and development of Paro Airport (domestic terminal, runway resurfacing and widening)	5	No information on public domain (Bhutan Civil Aviation Authority, Department of Air Transport)	Airports
27	India	New Sriperumbudur Airport Development Project (Chennai), as part of Chennai–Bangalore Industrial Corridor Project	Not identified	Tamil Nadu Industrial Development Corporation	Airports
28	India	Development of Haldia Port	280	Kolkata Port Trust	Ports
29	India	Development of major port in Kanyakumari District, Tamil Nadu	3,059	V.O. Chidambaranar Port Trust	Ports

continued on next page

Table *continued*

#	Country	Project Description	Estimated Cost (2018 $ million)	Responsible Agency	Type of Asset Class
30	India	V.O. Chidambaranar Port Trust, Tuticorin (deepening harbor basin and approach channel, construction of breakwater/ bubble protection bund, strengthening of berths 1–6, widening of port entrance channel	800	VOCPT	Ports
31	India	Development of deep seaport at Tajpur (near Digha) along the coast of West Bengal	2,850	West Bengal Industrial Development Corporation Limited	Ports
32	India	Expansion of inner harbor at Paradip Port, 210 nautical miles south of Kolkata and 260 nautical miles north of Visakhapatnam	423	Paradip Port Trust	Ports
33	India	Expansion of outer harbor near the south breakwater at Paradip Port	2,450	Paradip Port Trust	Ports
34	India	Augmentation of capacity of Haldia Dock Complex, Kolkata Port Trust (new lock gate in existing dock/basin and modification of lock gate)	200	Kolkata Port Trust	Ports
35	India	Development of a new port at Sirkazh, Tamil Nadu	450	Not identified	Ports
36	India	Paikan–Dudhnoi–Guwahati	450	National Highway Infrastructure Development Corporation Limited (NHIDCL)	Roads and highways
37	India	Two-lane road bridge in Jogighopa across the Brahmaputra River	Cost not yet estimated	NHIDCL	Roads and highways
38	India	Guwahati and Jorabat Bypass	Not identified	NHIDCL	Roads and highways
39	India	Two-laning of alternate route between Barak Valley (Silchar) to Guwahati via Harangajao–Turuk in Assam	452	Public Works Department (PWD) Assam	Roads and highways
40	India	Hafflong-Tamelong via Lia Sang and Tavesam in Assam and Manipur	300	NHIDCL	Roads and highways
41	India	Elevated expressway to Chennai Port, along a new alignment	375	National Highway Authority India	Roads and highways

continued on next page

Table *continued*

#	Country	Project Description	Estimated Cost (2018 $ million)	Responsible Agency	Type of Asset Class
42	Myanmar	Development of Low-Cost Carrier (LCC) terminal at the new Hanthawaddy International Airport (77 km northeast of Yangon, near Bago),	Not yet estimated	Department of Civil Aviation, Ministry of Transport and Communication	Airports
43	Myanmar	Construction of new Hanthawaddy International Airport (77 km northeast of Yangon, near Bago), plus road and rail access, and ancillary facilities (e.g., aviation fuel supply; hotel, commercial, and administrative complexes)	1,812 (The estimated cost was previous data. This Cost will be updated)	Department of Civil Aviation, Ministry of Transport and Communication	Airports
44	Myanmar	Establishment of logistics hub and truck/trailer terminal in the Wartayar Industrial Zone (northwestern Yangon)	20	Myanmar Trade Promotion Organization Ministry of Commerce	Multimodal transport
45	Myanmar	Yangon–Dagon inland container depot (ICD)	16	No information on public domain	Multimodal transport
46	Myanmar	New port facilities at Dawei	3,050	No information on public domain (ITD resigned the deal in 2015)	Ports
47	Myanmar	Development of deep-sea port at Kyaukphyu	1,050	Rakhine State Government	Ports
48	Myanmar	Upgrading of Yangon–Pyay rail line (259 km)	120	Ministry of Transport and Communication	Railways
49	Myanmar	Yangon–Mandalay Expressway improvement project Mandalay portion (502 km, km 65 to 567)	Not yet estimated	No information on public domain (Department of Highways, Ministry of Construction)	Roads and highways
50	Myanmar	Yangon–Mandalay Expressway improvement project from Yangon to Payagyi (65 km)	105	No information on public domain	Roads and highways
51	Myanmar	Improvement of Thilawa–East Dagon Road (8.7 km, two lane)	42	No information on public domain	Roads and highways
52	Myanmar	Construction of Bago NH 1 bypass road	25	No information on public domain	Roads and highways
53	Nepal	Development of a second international airport on a greenfield site at Nijgadh, Bara, 135 km south of Kathmandu	650	Civil Aviation Authority of Nepal	Airports

continued on next page

Table *continued*

#	Country	Project Description	Estimated Cost (2018 $ million)	Responsible Agency	Type of Asset Class
54	Nepal	Expansion and upgrading of Gautam Buddha Airport, about 280 km west of Kathmandu	65	Civil Aviation Authority of Nepal	Airports
55	Nepal	Major development of Kathmandu Airport (Tribhuvan International Airport Capacity Enhancement Investment Program)	600	Civil Aviation Authority of Nepal	Airports
56	Sri Lanka	Development of Bandaranaike International Airport, Colombo, including a new passenger terminal with two piers (Package A) (handling an additional 9 million passengers per year) and construction of new apron and taxiways (Package B)	413	Civil Aviation Authority of Sri Lanka/Airport and Aviation Services (Sri Lanka)	Airports
57	Sri Lanka	Construction of West Terminal at Colombo	840	Sri Lanka Port Authority (SLPA)	Ports
58	Sri Lanka	Extension of East Terminal at Colombo	1,150	SLPA	Ports
59	Sri Lanka	Colombo Suburban Railway Development Project	1,134	Department of Railways	Railways
60	Sri Lanka	Kurunegala to Habarana new rail project (80 km)	980	Department of Railways	Railways
61	Sri Lanka	Colombo Elevated Expressway Program to connect the Outer Circular Highway with the center of the city (100% elevated)	950	No information on public domain (Road Development Authority)	Roads and highways
62	Sri Lanka	Ratmalana (Colombo) Airport to Southern Expressway (10 km)	600	No information on public domain (Road Development Authority)	Roads and highways
63	Sri Lanka	Eastern Expressway (Dambulla–Trincomalee, 90 km)	540	No information on public domain (Road Development Authority)	Roads and highways
64	Thailand	Development of Phase III at Laem Chabang	1,500	Port Authority of Thailand	Ports

NH = national highway.

Sources: BIMSTEC Master Plan for Transport Connectivity; study team analysis.

www.ingramcontent.com/pod-product-compliance
Lightning Source LLC
Chambersburg PA
CBHW041752220926
51847CB00014B/180
* 9 7 8 9 2 9 2 7 0 3 5 0 9 *